Business Cycles, Inflation, and Forecasting

NATIONAL BUREAU OF ECONOMIC RESEARCH

Geoffrey H. Moore

Business Cycles, Inflation, and Forecasting

Second Edition

National Bureau of
Economic Research
Studies in
Business Cycles No. 24

Published for the
NATIONAL BUREAU OF
ECONOMIC RESEARCH, INC.
by
BALLINGER PUBLISHING COMPANY
A Subsidiary of Harper & Row, Publishers, Inc.
Cambridge, Mass.
1983

International Standard Book Number: 0-88410-284-X (CL)
0-88410-285-8 (PB)

Library of Congress Catalog Card Number: 83-3829

Printed in the United States of America

Library of Congress Cataloging in Publication Data

Moore, Geoffrey Hoyt.
  Business cycles, inflation, and forecasting.

  (Studies in business cycles; no. 24)
  Includes bibliographies and index.
    1. Business cycles—Addresses, essays, lectures. 2. Inflation
(Finance)—Addresses, essays, lectures. 3. Economic indicators—
Addresses, essays, lectures. 4. Economic forecasting—Addresses,
essays, lectures. 5. National Bureau of Economic Research—
Addresses, essays, lectures. I. Title. II. Series.
  HB3711.M59   1983   338.5'42   83-3829
  ISBN 0-88410-284-X
  ISBN 0-88410-285-8 (pbk.)

Relation of the Directors to the Work and Publications of the National Bureau of Economic Research

1. The object of the National Bureau of Economic Research is to ascertain and to present to the public important economic facts and their interpretation in a scientific and impartial manner. The Board of Directors is charged with the responsibility of ensuring that the work of the National Bureau is carried on in strict conformity with this object.

2. The President of the National Bureau shall submit to the Board of Directors, or to its Executive Committee, for their formal adoption all specific proposals for research to be instituted.

3. No research report shall be published by the National Bureau until the President has sent each member of the Board a notice that a manuscript is recommended for publication and that in the President's opinion it is suitable for publication in accordance with the principles of the National Bureau. Such notification will include an abstract or summary of the manuscript's content and a response form for use by those Directors who desire a copy of the manuscript for review. Each manuscript shall contain a summary drawing attention to the nature and treatment of the problem studied, the character of the data and their utilization in the report, and the main conclusions reached.

4. For each manuscript so submitted, a special committee of the Directors (including Directors Emeriti) shall be appointed by majority agreement of the President and Vice Presidents (or by the Executive Committee in case of inability to decide on the part of the President and Vice Presidents), consisting of three Directors selected as nearly as may be one from each general division of the Board. The names of the special manuscript committee shall be stated to each Director when notice of the proposed publication is submitted to him. It shall be the duty of each member of the special manuscript committee to read the manuscript. If each member of the manuscript committee signifies his approval within thirty days of the transmittal of the manuscript, the report may be published. If at the end of that period any member of the manuscript committee withholds his approval, the President shall then notify each member of the Board, requesting approval or disapproval of publication, and thirty days additional shall be granted for this purpose. The manuscript shall then not be published unless at least a majority of the entire Board who shall have voted on the proposal within the time fixed for the receipt of votes shall have approved.

5. No manuscript may be published, though approved by each member of the special manuscript committee, until forty-five days have elapsed from the transmittal of the report in manuscript form. The interval is allowed for the receipt of any memorandum of dissent or reservation, together with a brief statement of his reasons, that any member may wish to express; and such memorandum of dissent or reservation shall be published with the manuscript if he so desires. Publication does not, however, imply that each member of the Board has read the manuscript, or that either members of the Board in general or the special committee have passed on its validity in every detail.

6. Publications of the National Bureau issued for informational purposes concerning the work of the Bureau and its staff, or issued to inform the public of activities of Bureau staff, and volumes issued as a result of various conferences involving the National Bureau shall contain a specific disclaimer noting that such publication has not passed through the normal review procedures required in this resolution. The Executive Committee of the Board is charged with review of all such publications from time to time to ensure that they do not take on the character of formal research reports of the National Bureau, requiring formal Board approval.

7. Unless otherwise determined by the Board or exempted by the terms of paragraph 6, a copy of this resolution shall be printed in each National Bureau publication.

(Resolution adopted October 25, 1926, as revised through September 30, 1974)

Contents

Part III   Forecasting

List of Tables

List of Figures

Preface to Second Edition

Those who have the fortitude to compare this book with the previous edition, published in 1980, will find:

- More up-to-date information on recent business cycles (Chapters 2, 3; Appendix Tables A-1 to A-6).

- A signaling system to identify the beginning and ending of recessions (Chapter 4).

- New findings on inflation (Chapters 15, 16, 18-20; Appendix Tables A-5, A-6).

- An update on leading indicators for the "big seven" countries (Chapter 6).

- A new leading index of employment and unemployment (Chapter 22).

- Three essays on current problems with our economic statistics (Chapters 18-20).

Some new material has been added in the form of postscripts to previously published chapters, drawing on current work at the Center for International Business Cycle Research. The assistance of Chantal Dubrin, Jean Maltz and other associates at the Center is gratefully acknowledged.

Several of the new chapters are the joint product of work with colleagues: Victor Zarnowitz, University of Chicago (Chapter 2 and 4);

John P. Cullity, Rutgers—The State University of New Jersey (Chapter 16); and Phillip Cagan, Columbia University (Chapter 20). I am doubly in their debt, first for the opportunity to work with them on the research, and now for their permission to use the results in my book.

Some of the essays reprinted here have not been up-dated. I can hardly claim that this was deliberate, nor will I admit to laziness, but I do want to suggest that the reader can take advantage of the deficiency. There is no better way to test the validity of an economic hypothesis or finding than to see whether it is confirmed by subsequent data. The title of Chapter 14, for example, says "Recession Slows Inflation." That was written in 1979. Has it continued to be true? Chapter 24, on the "Forty-Second Anniversary of the Leading Indicators" (which occurred in 1980), compares the performance of indicators between 1948 and 1975 with their performance prior to 1938. This kind of test of consistency can now be extended beyond 1975. From such an exercise students can learn not only what has happened in recent business cycles but also what is worth remembering. Again, the reader of Chapter 9, "Security Markets and Business Cycles," which was written before 1975, may be disappointed to find nothing about what happened to stock prices and interest rates since 1970. But what an opportunity to see whether they have continued to interact in the manner to which we became accustomed in the fifty years before then!

PART I

BUSINESS CYCLES

Chapter 1

What Is a Recession?

In the course of its studies of business cycles, the National Bureau of Economic Research has identified successive periods of business expansion and contraction in the United States and several other countries. Business cycle peak dates mark the end of a period of expansion and the beginning of a period of contraction; trough dates mark the end of a period of contraction and the beginning of a period of expansion. For the United States the chronology goes back to 1854 on a monthly and quarterly basis, and to 1834 on an annual basis (Table A-1). Between 1854 and 1981 (the last peak date) some thirty peaks and thirty troughs have been recognized. These dates identify thirty expansions and twenty-nine contractions. The thirteen contractions since 1920 are recorded in fuller detail in Table A-2.

This chronology of business cycles has come to be widely used in economic studies, in government reports, in business publications, and in the popular press. The contraction periods are commonly identified as "recessions." An explanation of the procedures used in establishing the dates may, therefore, help to explain what a recession is, at least in an operational sense. What causes recession is another matter and will not be considered here.

The peak and trough dates purport to identify business cycles defined as follows:

Business cycles are a type of fluctuation found in the aggregate economic activity of nations that organize their work mainly in business enterprises: a cycle consists of expansions occurring at about the same time in many

Reprinted, with more recent figures and references added, from *The American Statistician*, October 1967.

economic activities, followed by similarly general recessions, contractions, and revivals which merge into the expansion phase of the next cycle; this sequence of changes is recurrent but not periodic; in duration business cycles vary from more than one year to ten or twelve years; they are not divisible into shorter cycles of similar character with amplitudes approximately their own.[1]

This definition, formulated by Arthur F. Burns and Wesley C. Mitchell in 1946, is a modification of one published by the National Bureau in 1927. Hence it has been used, in substantially its present form, for more than fifty years. It imposes no fixed requirement upon the duration of business expansions or contractions, and even the limits on the period of a full cycle (expansion and contraction) are broad: more than a year to ten or twelve years. In practice, the shortest contraction recognized in the United States has been six months; the longest, sixty-five months. Since 1937, no contraction has exceeded a year and a half. Taking pre–World War II chronologies for England, France, and Germany into account, the full range for expansions has been from eight to one hundred six months, while contractions have lasted from six to eighty-one months. Thus, past experience suggests that contractions that fit the definition in other respects are likely to last at least six months.

Besides duration, the definition recognizes two other significant features of business cycles—amplitude and scope. Again, no precise numerical magnitudes are cited, and in practice no precise specifications with respect to amplitude or scope have been imposed.

The requirement as to amplitude is that expansions and contractions reflect an absolute rise and an absolute fall in "aggregate economic activity." A rise and fall in some limited measure of economic activity, such as manufacturing output or corporate profits, is not enough. Nor is a mere slowing down or cessation of growth in total activity enough to qualify as a contraction. Moreover, the requirement that cycles not be "divisible into shorter cycles with amplitudes approximating their own" means that if, for example, a long expansion is interrupted by a decline, the decline should be recognized as a contraction if, and only if, it is as large as the smallest contraction in the historical record.

The concept "aggregate economic activity" is not defined either. Reticence on this score is due to the fact that no single comprehensive measure of the nation's economic activity—whether in terms of output, income, expenditures, or employment—is available for a long historical period on a monthly or quarterly basis, comparable throughout in its economic coverage, and adequate throughout in its statistical foundation. The coverage and quality of economic data has improved markedly over the years. The vagueness of the specification simply recognizes the fact that one should use the best data available at any given time, taking careful account of possible biases due to changes in the quality of the information.

Even at the present time, reliance upon a single measure of total activity—say, gross national product in current dollars—might run into difficulty. First, there are uncertainties in the measurement of important sectors of GNP, especially in the preliminary figures. Then suppose that, because the general level of prices continued to rise for a while, GNP expressed in current dollars rose, while GNP corrected for price change declined, total employment fell, and unemployment rose. It might be generally conceded that a recession was under way, although the previously selected measure, GNP in current dollars, failed to show it because of inflation.

The definition describes business cycles as expansions in many economic activities followed by similarly general contractions, but does not say how many activities or what they are. In recent years statistical measures of the scope of expansions and contractions, known as diffusion indexes, have been constructed. But while these give some degree of precision to the concept, they are computed in many different ways and comprehend various measures of economic activity. No single index has been found to be clearly superior to every other.

What, then, is the procedure followed by the National Bureau in identifying a new business cycle peak or trough? Two aspects of the procedure can be distinguished. First, a decision must be reached as to whether a period of expansion has ended and a cyclical contraction has begun. Second, the date of the peak must be determined. Similar decisions are required when the problem is to determine whether a contraction has ended and an expansion has begun and when the date of a trough is to be fixed. The following discussion will be confined to the problem of peaks and the ensuing contraction.

The existence of a long and generally accepted historical chronology helps to make the task easier. An apparent contraction can be compared with earlier contractions recognized in the chronology and also with earlier episodes that had some of the earmarks of contractions but were not recognized as such. If its character measures up to the former group, it can be designated as a contraction. If, on the other hand, it appears to belong with the latter group, the problem is resolved accordingly.

Three principal kinds of historical comparison are made. First, the approximate duration of the contraction in aggregate activity that has occurred or seems likely to occur is compared with earlier contractions. Second, the relative depth of the decline in aggregate activity that has occurred or seems likely to occur is compared with the declines during earlier contractions. The specific measures include GNP in current and in constant dollars, industrial production, employment, unemployment, personal income, and other series. Table A–2 presents a few of these measures.

One procedure for making such comparisons is to assume a provisional business cycle peak date and compute the percentage change over the first three, four, five, and so on months following that date. Corresponding measures are computed for earlier contractions. This procedure can also be applied to earlier episodes that were not designated contractions. These comparisons show whether the size of the contraction to date is smaller or larger than the decline over the same interval on earlier occasions. Chapters 6 and 16 give examples.

Third, the same sort of historical comparison is carried out in terms of diffusion indexes to determine whether the current movement is as widely diffused among different economic activities or among different sectors or industries or regions as on the earlier occasions. Table A–2 shows, for example, how widespread the declines in employment have been during previous recessions.

Comparisons of the sort described are, of course, more tenuous when a contraction is in its early stages than when it is well under way. Sometimes the initial decline is so sharp and widespread that little doubt exists that the entire contraction will be comparable with earlier contractions. Or, the uncertainty may last for months without a decisive outcome. In this respect, for example, the mild contraction dated from April 1960 differed from the sharp contraction after August 1957. The period of hesitancy during 1962 also was difficult to evaluate at the time, although no contraction was designated, and this judgment seems vindicated by events.

Contemporary judgments on these matters need to be reinforced by an appraisal of (1) the causal factors underlying the recessionary developments and (2) the steps that the government has taken or may take that would offset or, perchance, reinforce recession. Developments elsewhere in the world—the occurrence of recessions abroad, world trade and capital movements, prices and interest rates in foreign countries—also have a bearing upon our own economic situation and our ability to react to developments at home. In short, mere statistical comparisons of the type described above, while essential, are not the only requirement for an informed judgment on the likelihood of a business cycle contraction.

If, as a result of these evaluations and comparisons, the conclusion is reached that a business cycle contraction comparable in its several dimensions with earlier contractions has begun, the problem of dating the peak is taken up. The objective here is to identify the month when aggregate economic activity reached its highest level and began to decline—that is, to determine when the general expansion culminated and a general contraction got under way. To do this we again examine various monthly and quarterly aggregates. These series have been classified in previous studies by the National Bureau as "roughly coincident indicators" on the ground that their peaks and troughs have usually roughly coincided with the selected business cycle peak and trough dates. This correspondence is, of course, no accident—the dates have been selected on the basis of many of these same indicators. But the peak months of the several indicators do not coincide precisely either with the selected dates or with each other. Hence a judgment and a choice must be made among competing dates on the basis of the evidence.

In practice we assemble seasonally adjusted data for such comprehensive series as the following:[2]

- GNP in current dollars (value of goods and services produced: two series, one based on expenditure, the other on income, the difference being the statistical discrepancy);

- GNP in constant dollars (current dollar GNP deflated by the implicit price index);

- Total business sales (dollar volume of manufacturers', wholesalers', and retailers' sales);

- Bank debits outside New York City (dollar volume of payments from demand deposit accounts);

- Index of industrial production (physical volume of mining, manufacturing, and utilities output);

- Unemployment rate (two series: one based on the number of insured unemployed, the other on reports by a sample of individuals on their employment status);

- Nonagricultural employment (two series: one based on reports by establishments covering the number of their employees, the other based on reports by individuals on their employment status);

- Manhours of nonfarm employment (number employed multiplied by the average number of hours worked per week); and

- Personal income (income of individuals from wages and salaries, interest, dividends, rent, and benefit payments).

Composite indexes constructed from these series are a helpful device for summarizing their movements. In addition, some of the major components of these series are also helpful, such as the final sales component of GNP, the retail sales component of total business sales, the commodity-industries component of nonagricultural employment, and the labor income component of personal income. These components throw light on the movements of the totals and sometimes are more decisive in their own movements. Various price indexes, particularly the producer price index, are useful in evaluating the movements of total sales as well as in judging the state of the market for goods and services.

We examine other related series for what they reveal about the significance of the movements in total activity. Both leading and lagging indicators can contribute to a judgment on whether a cyclical contraction has begun and, if so, when it started. Certain "leading indicators," such as new orders for durable goods, average workweek, housing starts, inventory change, stock prices, profits and profit margins, and the rates of change in money and credit typically will have entered upon declines earlier, and hence their movements will have become clearer, before the aggregates have declined appreciably. Certain "lagging indicators," such as total inventories, credit outstanding, and plant and equipment expenditures, are generally less erratic than many other series and help to confirm that a cyclical decline in the economy is under way and to indicate, within broad limits, when it started.

Diffusion indexes are useful not only to measure the extent to which a contraction has spread throughout the economy, but also to determine the approximate date when the balance turned from expansion to contraction. In the later stages of a business cycle expansion, the number of activities that are continuing to expand diminishes. At about the time that aggregate activity reaches its zenith, there is a rough balance between expanding and contracting forces. Thereafter, the contracting factors dominate. Diffusion indexes portray this changing balance in various ways depending upon their composition and method of construction.

All of these materials, then, aid in the formulation of a judgment as to the date of a business cycle peak. Sometimes they point quite clearly to a single month: sometimes the evidence is conflicting and presents a difficult choice. We have, however, felt that it was best to choose a single month in each case rather than to indicate a zone within which the peak probably lies or to specify alternative monthly dates. Users of the chronology should be aware, however, that a degree of uncertainty attaches to any particular date and that revisions of the underlying statistical materials may later suggest a different choice. Indeed, the National Bureau has from time to time reviewed the dates and revised some of them by a month or two or three. For many purposes, however, small errors or uncertainties in the dates are not of great consequence. One of the advantages of basing them on a wide variety of evidence is that it reduces the possibility of error and the need for subsequent revision.

For further analysis of the problem of identifying business cycle peaks and troughs, the reader may consult Chapters 2 and 5, and the following:

Arthur F. Burns and Wesley C. Mitchell. *Measuring Business Cycles.* New York: NBER, 1946, Chapter 4.

Geoffrey H. Moore, ed. *Business Cycle Indicators.* Princeton: NBER, 1961. Chapters 3, 5, 8, and Appendix A.

Lorman C. Trueblood. "The Dating of Postwar Business Cycles." *Proceedings of the Business and Economics Statistics Section of the American Statistical Association.* 1961.

G.W. Cloos. "How Good are the National Bureau's Reference Dates?" *Journal of Business,* January 1963.

G.W. Cloos. "More on Reference Dates and Leading Indicators." *Journal of Business,* July 1963.

Victor Zarnowitz. "On the Dating of Business Cycles." *Journal of Business,* January 1963.

Victor Zarnowitz. "Cloos on Reference Dates and Leading Indicators: A Comment." *Journal of Business,* October 1963.

Victor Zarnowitz and Geoffrey H. Moore. "The Recession and Recovery of 1973−1976." *Explorations in Economic Research* 4, no. 4 (Fall 1977).

Ilse Mintz. *Dating Postwar Business Cycles: Methods and their Application to Western Germany, 1950−67.* Occasional Paper 107. (New York: NBER, 1970).

Ilse Mintz. "Dating United States Growth Cycles." *Explorations in Economic Research* 1, no. 1 (Summer 1974).

Rendigs Fels and C. Elton Hinshaw. *Forecasting and Recognizing Business Cycle Turning Points* (New York: NBER, 1968).

Solomon Fabricant. "The Recession of 1969−70." In *The Business Cycle Today,* Victor Zarnowitz, ed. (New York: NBER, 1972).

Much of the current information relevant to the problem is provided in the United States Department of Commerce monthly report, *Business Conditions Digest.*

NOTES TO CHAPTER 1

1. Arthur F. Burns and Wesley C. Mitchell, *Measuring Business Cycles,* p. 3 (New York: NBER, 1946).

2. For a more recent list, see Chapter 2.

Chapter 2

The Timing and Severity of the 1980 Recession

Victor Zarnowitz* and Geoffrey H. Moore

In the sixty years of its existence, the National Bureau of Economic Research has been continuously engaged in studies of business cycles. Among the most widely used results of that program are the chronologies of periods of general economic expansion and contraction in the United States and several other countries. These are lists of annual, quarterly, and monthly dates that mark the peaks (signaling the start of recessions) and troughs (which signal the beginning of recoveries). For the United States, England, France, and Germany, these "reference chronologies" extend back more than 130 years.

The following is a brief report on the most recent NBER work in this area. On June 3, 1980, the Bureau's Committee on Business Cycle Dating issued a statement identifying January 1980 as the latest peak in the sequence of U.S. business cycles.[1] At the time no cyclical peak in real GNP had yet been recorded; indeed, that series had continued to increase to the first quarter of the year (1980:1). Thus the determination that the economy was already in a cyclical decline for some five months was by no means obvious and by historical standards relatively early.

The NBER judgment as to the date of the peak was strongly supported by a comprehensive analysis of contemporary economic conditions. Following a long period of very little growth in 1979, most of the important monthly indicators of macroeconomic activity de-

Reprinted from *NBER Reporter*, National Bureau of Economic Research (Spring 1981).

*NBER research associate and professor of economics and finance, University of Chicago.

clined early in 1980. The movements formed a sufficiently consistent pattern to denote a transition from a phase of slow growth to one of a cyclical contraction. Similar slowdown-and-recession sequences have been repeatedly observed in the past. In June, the fragmentary evidence for the second quarter of 1980 suggested that the economy was deteriorating much faster than in the first quarter.

About a month after the NBER dating decision, more complete, though still preliminary, figures for the second quarter became available. Eventually, it turned out that real GNP fell at a record annual rate of 9.9 percent in 1980: 2. Together with other evidence that had become available, this clearly confirmed the occurrence and documented the deepening of the recession.

Table 2-1 lists the dates of the most recent cyclical peaks in fifteen monthly and five quarterly series on output, employment, real sales, and some related processes. This set includes only comprehensive measures of economic performance that show directly whether business activity is rising or falling; hence, the series are classified as "roughly coincident" with the historical chronology of business cycle turning points. Indeed, most of these indicators have been used by the NBER in its past work on dating cycles. The table omits the "leading indicators" representing marginal employment adjustments, business and residential investment commitments (new orders and contracts, starts and permits, and so forth), money and credit flows, sensitive prices, and profits. Most of these early-warning cyclical indicators began declining in 1978 or the first half of 1979. Even so, the dispersion of the specific peak dates in Table 2-1 is rather wide.

The list of the downturns discloses scattered turns during 1979, but the principal cluster is in January-February 1980, with a large concentration of series on real income, real GNP, industrial production, and employment.

Short, random movements and measurement errors ("noise") obscure the evidence of any single time series. A group of indicators contains less noise and is therefore, on the whole, more reliable. There are statistical procedures to standardize different series so that they can be meaningfully combined, as applied in the monthly coincident index of the U.S. Department of Commerce, included in Table 2-1. This index followed an almost entirely flat course between March 1979 and January 1980 (see Table 2-2, footnote a) but declined sharply thereafter.

When other monthly indicators and the quarterly GNP series in real terms are added, the resulting broader composite indexes also peak in January 1980. This reflects largely the fact that, although housing construction and real manufacturing and trade sales weak-

Table 2-1. Chronology of Cyclical Peaks in Twenty Series on Aggregate Output, Employment, Real Income, Expenditures, and Sales, 1979-1980.

Date of Peak	Monthly Series	Quarterly Series (middle month of quarter)	Number of Series Reaching Peaks
March 1979	• Mfg. and trade sales, 1972$ Wages in goods industries, 1972$		2
June 1979	Number of unemployed (inverted)		1
July 1979	Unemployment rate (inverted) Insured unemployment rate (inverted)		2
September 1979	Retail sales, 1972$		1
January 1980	Index of coincident indicators[a] • Industrial production, total[b] Employment in goods industries Nonfarm employee hours Personal income, 1972$ • Personal income less transfer payments, 1972$		6
February 1980	Total civilian employment Nonfarm employment, household survey • Nonfarm employment, establishment survey	GNP, 1972$ Final sales, 1972$ Disposable income, 1972$ Goods output, 1972$ Personal consumption expenditures, 1972$	8
Number of series	15	5	20

Note: Series are listed according to the timing of their cyclical peaks as dated in the first column. For quarterly series, the turning points are identified by the middle month of the quarter. All monthly series are in physical units (aggregates or rates of employment and unemployment, indexes of production), except for five income or sales aggregates in constant (1972) dollars. All quarterly series are constant-dollar aggregates from the national income and product accounts.

[a] This BEA index (1967 = 100) is a weighted composite of the four monthly series marked • in this table. Its value was slightly higher in March 1979 (146.6)

Notes to Table 2-1. continued

than in January 1980 (146.1) but the latter date is more representative. The three-month averages centered on the two dates are 145.2 and 145.6, respectively.
b The March 1979 value (153.5) is slightly higher than the January 1980 value (152.7), but the latter is a better choice by the fact of the centered three-month averages (which are 152.4 and 152.6, respectively).

end early, the rest of the economy, mainly services and business fixed investment, held up relatively well during 1979. The personal saving rate fell to unusually low levels in this period of widely anticipated inflation and low real interest rates, a situation that helped prop up the economy temporarily despite the slow erosion of real after-tax income of a large part of the private sector.

Based on this evidence (consisting mainly of data through April 1980), the NBER committee concluded that January 1980 was the best choice for the business cycle peak date.[2] However, it warned that the selection was still tentative because of the risks of data revisions, particularly since the initial decline in the winter was rather hesitant; the decline in economic activity accelerated greatly in the spring quarter. In mid-March, credit restraints of unprecedented severity in peacetime were suddenly imposed by the Federal Reserve. The reaction to this unanticipated shock treatment turned out to be very strong. For example, total private borrowing (change in the debt of businesses and households) dropped 51 percent in 1980:2, from $353 billion to $171 billion (at seasonally adjusted annual rates). At the same time, growth rates of monetary aggregates fell sharply, partly into the negative range. Interest rates shot up to peaks of 14-20 percent in March and April, then fell abruptly to 7-12 percent in June and July.

The phase of rapid contraction was short-lived. The Federal Reserve moved in May to soften the credit controls and eliminated them completely on July 3. Private borrowing increased promptly and strongly in 1980:3. Reduced rates of increase in consumer prices and declines in interest rates helped improve consumer expectations and buying attitudes. Real retail sales and housing starts turned upward. The decline in the coincident index came to a halt in June–August, and the decline in real GNP in 1980:3. These events had been signaled by the leading index, which reached its lowest point in May.

The initial rise in that index has been as large as it usually is early in a business recovery—over 12 percent between May and November 1980, for example. Correspondingly, activity picked up strongly in many areas of the economy, although some, notably the automo-

Table 2–2. Selected Measures of Duration, Depth, and Diffusion of Business Cycle Contractions, 1948–1980.[a]

	Nov. 1948 Oct. 1949 (1)	July 1953 May 1954 (2)	Aug. 1957 Apr. 1958 (3)	Apr. 1960 Feb. 1961 (4)	Dec. 1960 Nov. 1970 (5)	Nov. 1973 Mar. 1975 (6)	Jan. 1980 July 1980[b] (7)
Duration (months)							
Business cycle	11	10	8	10	11	16	6
GNP, constant dollars	6	12	6	9	15	15	3
Coincident index	12	15	14	13	13	16	6
Industrial production	15	9	13	13	13	9	6
Nonfarm employment	13	16	14	10	8	6	5
Depth (%)[c]							
GNP, constant dollars	-1.4	-3.3	-3.2	-1.2	-1.1	-5.7	-2.6
Coincident index	-10.8	-9.2	-12.4	-6.8	-6.3	-13.9	-7.0
Industrial production	-10.1	-9.4	-13.5	-8.6	-6.8	-15.3	-8.5
Nonfarm employment	-5.2	-3.4	-4.3	-2.2	-1.6	-3.7	-1.4
Unemployment rate							
Maximum	7.9	6.1	7.5	7.1	6.1	9.1	7.6
Increase	+4.5	+3.6	+3.8	+2.3	+2.7	+4.2	+2.0
Diffusion (%)							
Nonfarm industries, maximum percent with declining employment	90	87	88	80	80	87	75
Date when maximum reached	Feb. 1949	Mar. 1954	Sept. 1957	Oct. 1960	May 1970	Feb. 1975	Apr. 1980

[a] From peak (first date) to trough (second date).

[b] Tentative: month of lowest value during 1980 of the composite index of four coincident indicators. This date may or may not prove to be the trough of the recession that began in January 1980.

[c] Percentage change from the peak month or quarter in the series to the trough month or quarter over the intervals shown above. For the unemployment rate, the maximum figure is the highest for any month associated with the contraction, and the increases are from the lowest month to the highest, in percentage points.

[d] Since 1960 (columns 4–7) based on changes in employment over six-month spans in 172 nonagricultural industries, centered on the fourth month of the span. Prior to 1960 (columns 1–3) based on cyclical changes in employment in thirty nonagricultural industries. For the latter index, the figures comparable to those in columns 4–6 are as follows: Apr. 1960–Feb. 1961: 82, Aug. 1960; Dec. 1960–Nov. 1970: 83, June 1970; Nov. 1973–Mar. 1975: 90, Jan. 1975. No overlap is available for the 1980 recession.

Source: U.S. Department of Commerce, U.S. Department of Labor, Board of Governors of the Federal Reserve System, National Bureau of Economic Research. For a similar table carrying the record back to 1920, see Appendix Table A–2.

bile industry, remained depressed. Thus industrial production gained 6.4 percent in July-November (a very vigorous annual rate of 20.5 percent).

Monetary growth accelerated greatly in the summer and fall of 1980. Fears that the new surge of money and credit creation would result in greater inflationary pressures, and that the Federal Reserve would once more precipitate a drastic retrenchment, fueled a second round of sharp interest rises within one year. Thus the prime rate rose above 20 percent (its previous high of late April) in the second half of December. At the concurrent inflation rates, the burden in real terms of these high costs of money was plain to see, and they soon became the focus of widespread expectations that the young recovery would falter.

The prospects for a sustained expansion are indeed uncertain. With the data available at the present time (early March 1981), July 1980 appears the most reasonable trough date. However, this date has not been reviewed or approved by the NBER Business Cycle Dating group, and it would be invalidated should another sufficiently large decline in aggregate economic activity develop in the near future.[3] Consequently, no reference date for the beginning of a new business expansion can as yet be identified with adequate confidence, and none has been determined by the NBER committee.

Nevertheless, it is interesting to ask how this last recession compares with the previous ones, a question that requires some preliminary cutoff date for the 1980 contraction. If the trough did in fact occur in July, real GNP will have declined for one quarter only in this recession, which is unusual—although the NBER, for good reasons, never agreed with the popular notion that a recession requires as a minimum two consecutive quarterly declines in real GNP. Thus some may query whether the 1980 decline did have the dimensions of a business cycle contraction.

Table 2-2 based on the assumption that the recession ended in July, removes such doubts. Although short, the 1980 decline in real GNP was larger than the declines in three of the six earlier post-World War II recessions. The total loss in the coincident index exceeded those that occurred during the recessions of 1960 and 1970. The comparisons for industrial production lead to a similar conclusion. Only in terms of the changes in employment and unemployment can the 1980 contraction be considered the mildest of the seven episodes since 1948. The trend toward milder declines in employment has been going on for many years, largely because of the growth in employment in the service industries, which as a rule are more recession-proof than the goods-producing industries.

According to the new estimates just released, real GNP increased at a 2.4 percent annual rate in the third quarter and at a 4.0 percent annual rate in the fourth quarter of 1980. The first of these figures falls short of, but the second exceeds, the long-term growth rate of U.S. aggregate output. Other indicators also suggest that July 1980 may mark the trough in the growth cycle, that is, the end of the below-trend phase that began in December 1978.[4] In particular, the rise in the coincident index after July 1980 was far greater than the long-term average growth rate for this series. Historically, the business cycle troughs and the growth cycle troughs have often coincided. On the assumption, albeit very tentative, that this will again prove to be the case, the latest low-growth phase would have lasted nineteen months (December 1978–July 1980), which is very close to the average for these periods after World War II (eighteen months). Hence, although the business cycle contraction was unusually short, the growth cycle contraction was of typical length.

In conclusion, the 1980 declines in the indicators of major economic activities were relatively short but widespread and deep enough to qualify as another business cycle contraction.

NOTES TO CHAPTER 2

1. Members include NBER Director Geoffrey H. Moore and the following NBER research associates: William Branson (Princeton), Martin Feldstein (Harvard), Benjamin Friedman (Harvard), Robert Gordon (Northwestern), Robert Hall, chairman (Stanford), and Victor Zarnowitz, Chicago.

2. The Committee did not fix a quarterly or annual peak date, but in our view the quarterly peak was the first quarter of 1980 and the annual peak was 1979.

3. That is, if, after a recovery of less than a year, economic activity should decline to a lower level than it reached in mid-1980, the July 1980 trough might not hold. The shortest business cycle expansion in the NBER chronology for the United States lasted ten months (3/1919–1/1920). Incidentally, this expansion was preceded by the shortest contraction, seven months (8/1918–3/1919). If July 1980 proves to be a trough, the 1981 recession will have lasted six months only. For the NBER chronologies of business cycles, see Appendix Table A-1.

4. Growth cycles are defined by the consensus of fluctuations in trend-adjusted data for the physical volume of aggregate economic activity. For a brief explanation of this concept and the chronology of U.S. growth cycles 1948–1978, see Chapter 4 and Appendix Table A-4. (Postscript: The NBER committee subsequently selected July 1980 as the business cycle trough and July 1981 as the peak. But the growth cycle contraction continued through 1980, 1981 and 1982. That is, the rapid-growth phase of the July 1980–July 1981 business cycle expansion proved too brief to be considered a growth cycle upswing.)

Chapter 3

Recession or Depression?

A good deal of talk is going around about whether the United States is, or soon will be, in a depression. That raises the question what is the difference between a depression and a recession, which is what most people have been calling the current decline.

My definitions:

A *recession* is a period of decline in total output, income, employment and trade, usually lasting six months to a year and marked by widespread contractions in many sectors of the economy.

A *depression* is a "Big Mac" recession. Fortunately, unlike many Big Macs, they are rare!

Some of us can still remember the Great Depression of the 1930s, but many cannot. Fortunately, we do have an extensive record of these periods, compiled and studied for many years by scholars at the National Bureau of Economic Research. The Bureau's chronology of business cycles in the U.S. starts in 1834, so the record of when each downswing in the cycle began and how long it lasted covers nearly 150 years. Between 1834 and 1980 there were thirty-four of these downswings and on average they lasted nineteen months. The longest, from 1873 to 1879, lasted sixty-five months. The second longest, from August 1929 to March 1933, lasted forty-three months, which is one reason why it became known as the Great Depression. The shortest was the six-month decline from January to July 1980. The NBER dates the current decline from July 1981, and the downswing, based on the latest published data, has lasted at least

Reprinted from *Across the Board*, the Conference Board Magazine (May 1982).

eight months. So far, then, it is clearly on the short side, but of course we may not have seen the end of it.

In deciding what movements in the economy qualify as a business cycle the NBER looks broadly at three dimensions of recessions: how long they last; how deep they get; and how wide are their effects among industries or other sectors of the economy. Table 3-1 brings together a sampling of measures of these dimensions for all the downswings since 1920, of which there were thirteen. The current episode is the fourteenth in the list.

To help in reading the table we have put the past recessions and depressions into four groups. In a class by itself is the Great Depression—longer, deeper, and more widely felt than any of the others. Next are two major depressions, 1920-1921 and 1937-1938. They did not last very long, but were very severe while they lasted, and nearly all industries reported declines in employment (last column). The remaining ten recessions fall into two groups, sharp and mild. Not every measure yields the same verdict on whether a recession is sharp or mild. The recession at the end of World War II (1945) shows an especially wide diversity, but the brevity of the decline, the low rate of unemployment, and the transitional nature of the period when industries were shifting back to peacetime production led to the decision to place it in the mild recession group. The 1980 recession is also in the mild group, even though the high in unemployment, 8 percent, was above that in some of the sharp recessions.

If the current recession were to have ended in March 1982, it would almost certainly belong in the mild recession category, which is where President Reagan said he would like to see it. If it did not end in March, the figures on the bottom line will get larger when we have more recent information. What we do know, from other information besides that in the table, is that when the current recession is compared with others since 1948 over the same period of time (the first seven or eight months), it is more like an average of the sharp recessions than the mild. That is to say, most measures of economic activity have declined more than they did in the first seven or eight months of the mild recessions, and about as much as they did in the sharp recessions. This is true also of the index of leading indicators, which gives some advance warning of things to come. It too has declined on a path similar to the average pattern for the sharp recessions (see Figure 6-5).

When we push this kind of comparison back to 1929, we find that what has happened during the first eight months of the current recession isn't even in the same economic ball park. For example, after

Table 3-1. A Capsule History of Recessions and Depressions, 1920-1982.

	How Long? (months)	How Deep?			Unemployment Rate		How Wide? (% of industries with employment decline)
		Real GNP (%)	Industrial Production (%)	Nonfarm Employment (%)	High (%)	Increase (%)	
The Great Depression (1933)	43	-33	-53	-32	25	+22	100
Two major depressions (1921, 1938)	16	-13	-32	-11	16	+10	97
Five sharp recessions (1924, 1949, 1954, 1958, 1975)	12	-3	-13	-4	7	+4	90
Five mild recessions (1927, 1945, 1961, 1970, 1980)	10	-2	-8	-2	6	+3	78
Current recession to date (see note)	8	-2	-9	-1	9	+2	76

Note: The first column is the period from the peak of the business cycle to the trough, as determined by the National Bureau of Economic Research. The next three columns show the percentage declines in output or employment from the high month or from the low to the high. For unemployment (columns 5 and 6) the highest monthly figure reached is shown as well as the increase from the low to the high. The last column is the percentage of industries that experienced a decline in employment over a six-month interval. The figure shown is the highest percentage reached during the depression or recession.

All the entries on lines 2, 3, and 4 are averages covering the respective depressions or recessions. Entries on line 5 are based on the latest published figures through March 1982. No forecasts are used.

Source: Center for International Business Cycle Research, Rutgers University.

eight months of the 1929 Depression—that is, from August 1929 to April 1930—nonfarm employment had dropped more than 5 percent, compared with about 1 percent in this recession. Translated to current employment levels that would have meant a loss of five million jobs instead of the current loss of about one million. One million is bad enough, but *five* million . . . ?

The statistics, of course, do not rule out the possibility of depression. They do show that some of the relevant evidence is consistent with a happier outcome.

(Postscript: Early in 1983 it seemed likely that the recession had reached bottom in December 1982. If this turns out to be the case, the 1981–82 recession, having lasted 17 months, with a drop of less than 3 percent in real GNP and a rise of about four percentage points in unemployment, would clearly belong in the sharp recession category.)

Chapter 4

Sequential Signals of Recession and Recovery

Victor Zarnowitz* and Geoffrey H. Moore

Early and confirming signals of business cycle peaks and troughs are produced sequentially on a current basis by a system of monitoring smoothed rates of change in the composite indexes of leading and co-incident indicators. Evidence is offered that the system would have identified each of the peaks and troughs of U.S. business cycles since 1949 without undue delays and false alarms. Countercyclical policies activated and deactivated by such signals would have desirable timing properties.

COUNTERCYCLICAL POLICY TRIGGERS: THE PROBLEM AND ITS SETTING

This chapter describes a sequential procedure for identifying the beginning and ending dates of business cycle recessions as promptly and accurately as practicable. Its origin lies in a study undertaken for

The research underlying this chapter was supported by a grant to the Center for International Business Cycle Research from the Economic Development Administration. The EDA bears no responsibility for the content. Earlier versions were presented at the annual meeting of the American Economic Association in Denver on September 5, 1980, and at the annual meeting of the Illinois Economic Association in Chicago on October 31, 1980. We are indebted to Steven McNees, John Myers, and David Woolford for helpful comments, and to Chantal Dubrin and J. Rao for efficient research assistance.

(*Journal of Business*, 1982, vol. 55, no. 1).
*University of Chicago and National Bureau of Economic Research.

the Economic Development Administration (EDA), U.S. Department of Commerce, which deals with the problem of designing and testing an efficient trigger formula for public works expenditures with the aid of a system of cyclical indicators. However, the proposed approach can be applied much more broadly to any temporary countercyclical policy program on the national level.

Federal policy programs of job creation through public works or public service employment have been repeatedly called *countercyclical* without in fact being so. Most such programs came into effect much too late to counter the cyclical *rises* in the national unemployment rate (which, of course, does not necessarily preclude their being appropriate for other reasons, e.g., because of relatively high *levels* of unemployment in the intended impact areas). In fact, public works programs were not enacted until nine to nineteen months after the cyclical decline in output had been reversed and that in employment nearly completed.[1] For the public service employment programs, the legislative and administrative lags have been considerably shorter, but not sufficiently so to produce significant countercyclical effects.[2] Moreover, no provision was made in any of the programs for effective cutoff dates related to signals of the progress of the recovery. In sum, the overall lags involved were such that the funds, instead of being spent to combat unemployment during recesssions, were actually spent when the expansion of the national economy was already well under way.

The tardiness of policies designed to stimulate employment not only reduces their intended stabilizing (antirecession) effects but also induces some unintended destabilizing effects. Government expenditures are likely to contribute more to excess demand and inflationary pressures during a business expansion than during a business contraction. Ill-timed fiscal and monetary policies can, of course, have similar effects.

The success of any discretionary countercyclical policy action depends critically on its timeliness; in addition, it must also have a sufficient degree of flexibility. However, the accuracy of economic forecasts tends to deteriorate as the forecast span lengthens and is generally not adequate for predictions looking as far ahead as a year or more. But shorter predictions of slowdowns and recessions, based on the actual record of cyclical indicators with early timing characteristics rather than on forecasts of such series, can be shown to provide useful first-alert signals which, when combined with confirmatory signals from measures of aggregate economic activity, are capable of producing a timely and reliable "triggering" mechanism.

The main problem with recent public works programs as well as other policies intended to be countercyclical lies in the long lags with which they are initiated and terminated. Most of the total delay is accounted for by the recognition, legislative, and administrative lags—which would be eliminated if the programs were effectively triggered at the onset and at the end of a recession.[3] As noted, the time between the allocation of funds and the employment of half the workers to be employed is approximately six to twelve months, which is not unduly long, given the duration of high unemployment created by recent recessions. The solution, then, lies primarily in making the policy action timely by tying it to certain prespecified indicator values which reliably signal the beginning and end of a recession. The required flexibility can be obtained by advance preparation of a backlog of useful projects to be mobilized progressively according to schedules related to a sequence of increasingly reliable signals.[4]

This study relates only to the problem of optimal *timing* of public employment policies in the context of cyclical movements in the U.S. economy as a whole. It is recognized that the effectiveness of the programs depends also on their size, financing, organization, and still other factors (such as any displacement and spillover effects), but these matters lie outside the scope of the present chapter.

The plan of the procedure consists in identifying certain signals from suitably smoothed rates of change in composite indexes of cyclical indicators, which normally occur in a predetermined sequence. The possibility of false alarms is reduced by using turning points first in the leading and then in the confirming indicators. Actions based upon the initial turning points should be of a limited and reversible nature, involving relatively small commitments of funds. When the initial points have been confirmed by the subsequent turning points, more definitive and substantial actions should be taken. The signals devised in this plan refer directly to business cycles as defined and dated by NBER, but they also make use of the concept of growth cycles, that is, alternating periods of above-average and below-average rates of growth in aggregate economic activity. Since a growth slowdown preceded each recent recession, signals of the former give some advance warning of business cycle peaks. At troughs, leads of this type are typically fewer and much shorter, but if the signals are somewhat late they are also less scattered and often easier to read.

In what follows, the rationale of the proposed strategy for using the cyclical indicators is outlined; the concept of the growth cycle and its relationship to the business cycle is explained; the procedures used and the results obtained thus far are presented and assessed; and some perspective is provided on the needs and the promise of further work.

CONCEPTS AND PROCEDURES

The proper objective of countercyclical policy programs is to reduce the number of cyclically unemployed at times of overall slowdowns and recessions. This might seem to indicate that the policies should be initiated (discontinued) when the national unemployment rate rises above (falls below) some specified "high" level for some sufficiently long time. Indeed, triggering formulas based on unemployment statistics have received much attention in recent programs of direct employment stimulation by fiscal means. But here, as elsewhere, policy targets should not be confused with policy indicators. While the behavior of total unemployment is strongly influenced by business cycles, it is very difficult to separate the cyclical component of unemployment from the other components—frictional, structural, and institutional. The use of high-unemployment trigger formulas will inevitably cause the programs to be badly mistimed, that is, to lag behind recessions and be active during expansions when unemployment may be relatively high for reasons other than cyclical declines or deficiencies in aggregate demand.

An analysis of a variety of labor market indicators shows that they are strongly affected by cyclical changes in the economy, but also that most of them are either too sluggish or too irregular in their timing to produce useful signals for our present purposes. However, one promising option is being explored in another study. This consists of combining several leading and trendless labor turnover series.[5]

The best of the options for a trigger formula, as currently considered, is a plan based on a comprehensive coverage of leading and confirming indicators of business expansions and contractions. There is ample evidence from a long series of studies that important and persistent timing sequences exist among series in each of the areas viewed as critical in business cycle theories. The following tabulation illustrates this in a general and selective way.[6]

Some of the main factors in business cycle theories:

Evidence from time series for the corresponding variables:

1. Interaction between investment and final demand, or between the investment and savings functions.

   Large cyclical movements in business investment commitments (order, contracts) lead total output and employment; smaller movements in investment expenditures coincide or lag.

2. Changes in the supply of money, bank credit, interest rates, and the burden of private debt.

Money and credit flows (rates of change) are highly sensitive, with typically early cyclical timing; market interest rates coincide or lag.

3. Changes in price/cost relations, in the diffusion, margins, and totals of profits, and in business expectations.

The profit variables all show large and unusually early cyclical movements, and so do stock price indexes. Unit labor costs contribute to this result by rising rapidly prior to and just after a business peak and falling prior to and just after a trough.

More specifically, series that represent early stages of production and investment processes (new orders for durable goods, housing starts, or permits) lead series that represent late stages (finished output, investment expenditures). Under uncertainty, less binding decisions are taken first. For example, hours of work are lengthened (shortened) before the work force is altered by new hirings (layoffs). Other timing sequences reflect important stock-flow relationships involving the demand for and supply of output of goods and services, as influenced by changes in business fixed capital and inventories, money and credit.

For well-supported theoretical reasons, a selected group of indicators representing a whole set of these relationships has much greater predictive value over time than any of the individual indicators.[7] This insight led to the construction of composite indexes of leading, coincident, and lagging indicators which indeed, as a rule, outperform the individual indicators. These indexes incorporate series that represent different economic processes but have similar cyclical timing. The best indicators from each economic-process group are selected by means of a detailed scoring procedure incorporating several major criteria (economic significance, statistical adequacy, consistency of timing and conformity to the cyclical movements of the economy at large, smoothness, and currency). For each timing category (say, the leading series), the chosen indicators are combined into an index with weights provided by their overall performance scores.[8]

Our procedure uses the data from the leading and coincident composite indexes published by the U.S. Department of Commerce in *Business Conditions Digest (BCD)* each month. Cyclical peaks in the leading index often occurred early in the low-growth phases and anticipated the beginning dates of recessions by variable but, on the average, rather long intervals, whereas the troughs in the index led the beginning dates of recoveries by quite short intervals. Reliable signals from the indexes proper, when we take into account the need for some smoothing and confirmation, would occasionally be too tardy for the purpose on hand. To obtain more timely and dependable indications, we found it advisable to use rates of change in the composite indexes with the aid of simple smoothing and decision rules.[9]

One such rule that turned out to be effective is that of taking the ratio of the current month's index to the average of the twelve preceding months and expressing the resulting percentage change at a compound annual rate.[10] This is a smoothed six-month rate, which involves the same loss of lead time as an ordinary six-month change (where the current month is compared with the single month's figure six months earlier). The two are affected in the same way by any special factors that pertain to the current month, but the ratio that uses the twelve-month centered moving average in the denominator is for this reason much less subject to erratic fluctuations than the ordinary rate of change over six-month moving periods.[11]

Each of the composite indexes published in *BCD* contains a "target trend" of 3.3 percent per year (0.272 percent per month). The purpose is to make the long-run trend in each index the same and equal to the trend rate of growth in the economy as a whole from 1948 to 1975, so that any differences in the behavior of the indexes are due to short-run factors.[12] Accordingly, the average value of the annualized rate-of-change series derived from the indexes over a long period is in each case approximately 3.3 percent. Thus, when the six-month smoothed rates of change described in the preceding paragraph are less than 3.3 percent, this means that the underlying index is rising at less than its long-term average rate. In the case of the leading index, this is an indication that a declining phase of the growth cycle is approaching; in the case of the coincident index, that it is probably under way. Likewise, when the annual rates of change come to exceed 3.3 percent, this means that an upswing in the growth cycle may be starting.

Growth cycles represent an important but not very familiar phenomenon which may require some additional explanation. They are movements in aggregate economic activity defined by the consensus of fluctuations in comprehensive indicators adjusted for their long-term trends. They are thus composed of specific cycles in the *deviations from trend* of time series representing output, income, trade, employment, and many other economic processes, and they differ from business cycles in that the latter are defined by the consensus of fluctuations in the *levels* of the same collection of comprehensive economic indicators (see Chapter 5).

A business cycle always involves at least one growth cycle, since in a contraction the short-term growth rate, being negative, is necessarily less than the long-term growth rate (which for an expanding economy is, of course, always positive—reflecting the growth of total resources and their productivity). A business cycle will involve more than one growth cycle on those occasions when its expansion contains one or more protracted low-growth phases (periods when the short-term growth rate, while remaining positive, falls below the trend rate for a year or so).[13] Consequently, there are some "extra" growth cycles in addition to those which stand in a one-to-one correspondence with business cycles. Since 1945 the U.S. economy has passed through seven recessions—the latest in the first half of 1980— and it has also witnessed three periods of below-average growth rate that did not encompass recessions.

Each of the seven expansions of the 1945–1979 period decelerated before peaking and ending in a contraction; in other words, each of the recessions was preceded by a phase of positive but below-normal economic growth. The lags of business cycle peaks behind the starting dates of the low-growth phases lengthened substantially over this period, from two to six months for the first four of the peaks, which occurred in 1948–1960, to eight to thirteen months for the last three, which have occurred since 1969. This development reflects several interrelated trends in an economy with an expanding government, intensified inflation, increasing role of services versus goods in national employment, and reduced rates of private investment and productivity.

Whereas the growth cycle peaks led the business cycle peaks, the growth cycle troughs (marking the transition from low- to high-growth phases) usually occurred at about the same time as the business cycle troughs. Occasionally, as in 1954, a growth cycle trough would follow a business cycle trough, that is, the recovery would start slowly, with the overall growth rate not getting up to the average level until some months later.

The NBER reference chronologies for growth cycles and business cycles, on which the above statements are based, are presented in the first two columns of Tables 4-1 and 4-2 for the peaks and troughs, respectively. These lists of dates have been established by a close examination of time series of levels and deviations from trend for a broad set of comprehensive indicators of real economic activity.[14] It should be noted that the expansions of recent business cycles varied

Table 4–1.   Three Signals of Recession: Timing at Business Cycle Peaks.

Growth Cycle Peak	Business Cycle Peak	First Signal (L < 3.3; C > 0)	Second Signal (L < 0; C < 3.3)	Third Signal (L < 0; C < 0)	Lead (–) or Lag (+), in Months, at Business Cycle Peaks		
					First Signal	Second Signal	Third Signal
7/48	11/48	N.A.	N.A.	N.A.	—	—	—
3/51	None	2/51	7/51	—	—	—	—
3/53	7/53	6/53	8/53	9/53	–1	+1	+2
2/57	8/57	12/55	1/57	8/57	–20	–7	0
2/60	4/60	8/59	5/60	8/60	–8	+1	+4
5/62	None	5/62	—	—	—	—	—
6/66	None	6/66	2/67	—	—	—	—
3/69	12/69	6/69	11/69	1/70	–6	–1	+1
3/73	11/73	7/73	12/73	2/74	–4	+1	+3
12/78	1/80	7/78	6/79	10/79	–18	–7	–3
Average	—	—	—	—	–10	–2	+1

Note: For full definitions of signals, see text. The following are regarded as false signals of a business cycle peak in constructing this table. First signal: a decline in the leading index rate below 3.3 percent in July 1977. Second signal: a decline in the coincident index rate below 3.3 percent in May–September 1956. October–November 1959, and April 1979. Third signal: a decline in the coincident index rate below zero in July 1956 and October–November 1959.

Table 4-2. Three Signals of Recovery: Timing at Business Cycle Troughs.

Growth Cycle Trough	Business Cycle Trough	First Signal ($L > 0$; $C < 0$)	Second Signal ($L > 3.3$; $C > 0$)	Third Signal ($L > 3.3$; $C > 3.3$)	Lead (−) or Lag (+), in Months, at Business Cycle Troughs		
					First Signal	Second Signal	Third Signal
10/49	10/49	8/49	1/50	3/50	−2	+3	+5
8/54	5/54	5/54	11/54	12/54	−0	+6	+7
4/58	4/58	5/58	9/58	11/58	+1	+5	+7
2/61	2/61	2/61	6/61	8/61	0	+4	+6
11/70	11/70	11/70	4/71	11/71	0	+5	+12
3/75	3/75	6/75	9/75	11/75	+3	+6	+8
7/80	7/80	9/80	12/80	2/81	+2	+5	+7
Average	—	—	—	—	+1	+5	+7

Note: For full definitions of signals, see text.

greatly in length but averaged about fifty months, that is, about 4.5 times the mean duration of the contractions. In contrast, the growth cycles that emerge after elimination of the secular upward trend are nearly symmetrical, with high- and low-growth phases averaging twenty and eighteen months. Such regularities are attractive to business-conditions analysts and increasingly recognized. Certainly, it is much easier to recognize a developing slowdown than to pinpoint the date of a future downturn, and this strong presumption is well supported by lessons from recent forecasts. Since most low-growth periods do end as recessions, the concept and measurement of growth cycles can help provide some advance warning of business cycle peaks. Even though a slowdown may not evolve into a recession, its recognition gives time for precautionary action. Similarly, it is more important to stop antirecession action when a rapid recovery is under way than when a recovery is proceeding slowly.

THE RESULTS: A SIGNALING SYSTEM AND ITS EX-POST RECORD

The cyclical movements in the leading index tend to occur earlier than those in the coincident index. Figure 4–1 shows, in a hypothetical diagram, the smoothed rates of growth in the two series, which for simplicity will be called the "leading index rate" (L) and the "coincident index rate" (C).[15] Among the earliest signs that an ongoing expansion may start to decelerate is a decline in the leading index rate. This development is more decisively indicated when a sustained decline of the growth rate in the leading index puts it below the average 3.3 percent line. A similar decline in the coincident index rate, which would normally occur later, confirms the onset of a general slowdown (low-growth phase) and suggests an increased possibility of a business cycle recession. If the leading index rate then falls below zero and the coincident index rate falls below 3.3 percent (not necessarily in this order), the probability of recession is heightened. Finally, if the coincident index rate follows the leading index rate by turning negative, chances are high indeed that the slowdown is being succeeded by an actual decline in overall economic activity, that is, a recession.

The expected sequence of signals at business cycle peaks, then, is when each of the following conditions is first observed:

- First signal ($P1$): The leading index rate falls below 3.3 percent, while the coincident index rate is positive ($L < 3.3$; $C > 0$).

Figure 4-1. Sequential Signals of Recession and Recovery: A Schematic Diagram.

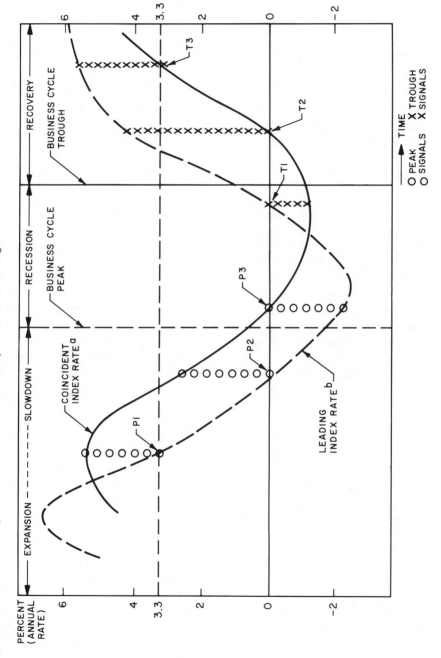

- Second signal ($P2$): The leading index rate becomes negative, and the coincident index rate falls below 3.3 percent ($L < 0$; $C < 3.3$).

- Third signal ($P3$): Both the leading index rate and the coincident rate become negative ($L < 0$; $C < 0$).

In Figure 4-1, the vertical links between the two curves remind us that these signals involve prespecified positions or changes in both index rates. The business cycle peak is expected to occur in the vicinity of $P3$, that is, no more than a few months earlier or later than that signal.

This system of signals would have identified each of the six business cycle peaks from 1953 to 1980 (we do not have sufficient data available to check the 1948 peak). The average lead at business cycle peaks was nearly ten months for the first signal, two months for the second signal. The third signal lagged the peak by an average of one month. As shown in Table 4-1, the variation of the individual leads or lags around these averages was considerable, with long advance warnings before the 1957 and 1980 peaks, very short leads and lags in 1953, and intermediate situations in the remaining cases. However, sizable leads prevailed for the first signal, and even the third signal involved no long lags. It is important, too, that the sequence of the signals was maintained in each of the episodes covered.

The first two signals also identified two of the three growth cycle slowdowns that did not become business cycle recessions (the first signal alone identified all three), but the third signal ruled out each of these instances. In addition, the system produced four "false warnings" that were not associated with either slowdowns or recessions, but none of these would have done real harm. Of these cases (listed in Table 4-1), two were single-month declines that related to the first or second signal only and were ruled out by the third. The other two were caused by the major steel strikes in 1956 and 1959 and would have been recognized as such at the time.[16]

At the latest business cycle peak, which on June 3, 1980 was identified by the NBER as January 1980, the timing of the signals was as follows: first signal, July 1978, a lead of eighteen months; second signal, June 1979, a lead of seven months; and third signal, October 1979, a lead of three months.

In this instance the third signal, where both the leading and coincident index six-month rates were negative for the first time, was interrupted in December 1979–January 1980, when the coincident rate turned positive for two months. In February 1980, it became negative again and remained negative through May. Hence the third signal either gave an advance warning three months before the January 1980 peak or a delayed warning one month after the peak.

In interpreting these results, one must allow for the fact that data are not available instantaneously. The indexes are published initially by the Commerce Department toward the end of the month following the month to which they refer. For example, the May indexes were released June 30. Hence, in terms of availability, the dates in Table 4-1 should be placed at least one month later.

At business cycle troughs, the signals we have selected are slightly different, occurring when each of the following conditions is first observed:

- First signal ($T1$): The leading index rate rises above zero, while the coincident index rate is negative ($L > 0$; $C < 0$). This means that the first signal of a trough must follow the third signal of a peak.

- Second signal ($T2$): The leading index rate rises above 3.3 percent, and the coincident index rate rises above zero ($L > 3.3$; $C > 0$).

- Third signal ($T3$): Both the leading index rate and the coincident index rate exceed 3.3 percent ($L > 3.3$; $C > 3.3$).

These signals identified the end of each of the seven business cycle recessions between 1949 and 1980, though with more of a lag than was true of the peak signals. The average timing of the three signals at the seven business cycle troughs is as follows: first signal, one month lag; second signal, five-month lag; and third signal, seven-month lag. The variation around these averages from one cycle to another is shown in Table 4-2. There were no false signals of recovery in any instance in which the preceding business cycle peak had already been identified by the three peak signals.

The lags of the signals at troughs are acceptable because at the beginning of recovery the level of activity is low (unemployment is at its cyclical peak levels), so that a program of public works expenditures may still be appropriate if it is tapering off and is discontinued after a brief period. While the third signal lags at business cycle troughs by seven months on average, most of the cyclical expansion is yet to come. In fact, in none of the seven instances would aggregate economic activity as measured by the coincident index have regained its previous peak level by the time the third signal was reached.[17]

Hence the seven-month lag means that recovery is well under way and not likely to be aborted but has not reached a point where capacity utilization has become a problem.

Figure 4-2 displays the behavior of the six-month smoothed rates of change in the leading index and in the coincident index relative to the business cycle peak and trough dates. The crossings of the 3.3 percent trend line and of the zero baseline—which underlie the signals of these dates as listed in Tables 4-1 and 4-2—are identified. This allows a visual assessment of the workings of the procedure.

One way to evaluate the set of signals here is to count the number of months during business recessions when the signals would have operated in the appropriate way—and likewise during business expansions. Table 4-3 does this for the third signal and shows that it operated in the correct direction nearly 85 percent of the time between 1949 and 1980. The signal of recession was "on" for about 8.5 years, compared with a total of about five years accounted for by the six recessions covered (since 1953). The record shows that these errors were heavily concentrated at the beginning of expansions and (to a lesser extent) at the beginning of recessions. The recession signal was always "off" before the economy recovered to its previous peak level (see text and note 17). In terms of public works expenditures, these are the most tolerable types of error. A brief delay in turning them off at the beginning of an expansion means that they will be concentrated during a part of the business cycle when economic activity is most depressed and inflationary pressures are apt to be receding.

This record is very different from the actual performance of public works expenditures in the past, where a major problem has been that they have been concentrated in periods of high activity rather than low. The set of signals described in this chapter should make possible a significant improvement on past performance in this respect.

Another kind of test is to see how the system works on similar data for other countries. The leading and coincident indexes currently compiled by the Center for International Business Cycle Research for six other countries provide the means for such a test. It is not, however, possible to compare the signals with business cycle peaks and troughs, because most countries do not have such chronologies. However, chronologies of growth cycles have been established by the Center. For an initial test we have selected one period, 1973-1976, when every country experienced not only a slowdown but also a recession. The results can be briefly summarized.

1. In each of the six countries (Canada, the United Kingdom, West Germany, France, Italy, and Japan), the three signals of peaks

Figure 4-2. Six-Month Smoothed Rates of Change in the Leading Index and in the Coincident Index. (*A, the leading index rate. B, the coincident index rate.*)

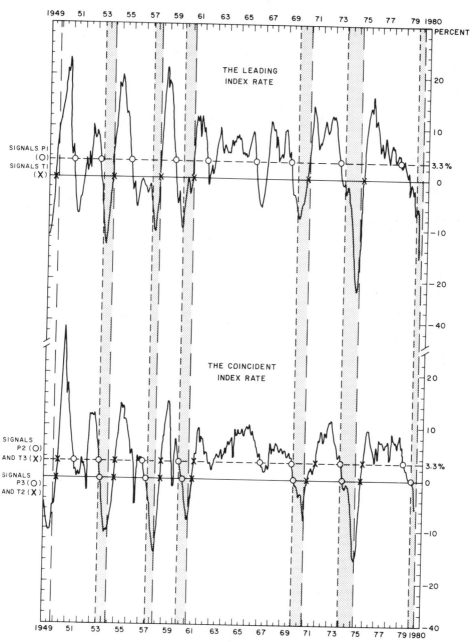

Table 4–3.   Countercyclical Record of the Third Signal.

A. Business Cycle Recessions

Business Cycle		Third Signal		Months of Recession				% of Total		
					Third Signal	Third Signal Incorrect		Third Signal	Third Signal Incorrect	
Peak (1)	Trough (2)	Peak (3)	Trough (4)	Total (5)	Correct (6)	at Beginning (7)	at End (8)	Correct (9)	at Beginning (10)	at End (11)
11/48	10/49	n.a.	n.a.	11	—	—	—	—	—	—
7/53	5/54	9/53	12/54	10	8	2	0	80	20	0
8/57	4/58	8/57	11/58	8	8	0	0	100	0	0
4/60	2/61	8/60	8/61	10	6	4	0	60	40	0
12/69	11/70	1/70	11/71	11	10	1	0	91	9	0
11/73	3/75	2/74	11/75	16	13	3	0	81	19	0
1/80	7/80	10/79	2/81	6	6	0	0	100	0	0
Total				61[a]	51	10	0	84	15	0

B. Business Cycle Expansions

Business Cycle		Third Signal		Months of Expansion				% of Total		
					Third Signal Correct	Third Signal Incorrect		Third Signal Correct	Third Signal Incorrect	
Trough (1)	Peak (2)	Trough (3)	Peak (4)	Total (5)	(6)	at Beginning (7)	at End (8)	(9)	at Beginning (10)	at End (11)
10/49	7/53	3/50	9/53	45	40	5	0	89	11	0
5/54	8/57	12/54	8/57	39	32	7	0	82	18	0
4/58	4/60	11/58	8/60	24	17	7	0	71	29	0
2/61	12/69	8/61	1/70	106	100	6	0	94	6	0
11/70	11/73	11/71	2/74	36	24	12	0	67	33	0
3/75	1/80	11/75	10/79	58	47	8	3	81	14	5
Total				308	260	45	3	84	15	1

C. Business Cycle Recessions and Expansions

	Cols. 5	Cols. 6	Cols. 7	Cols. 8	Cols. 9	Cols. 10	Cols. 11
Total	369	311	55	3	84	15	1

Note: Column 5 is the interval between the dates in columns 1 and 2. Column 6 is the interval between the dates in columns 3 and 2. Column 7 is the interval between the dates in columns 1 and 3. Column 8 is the interval (if any) from the date in column 4 to that in column 2. The false signals in 1956 and 1959 listed in the note to Table 4-1, which were associated with strikes, are ignored in this table.

[a] Exluding 1948–1949.

occurred in the expected sequence during 1973-1974, and the three signals of troughs did likewise during 1975-1976.

2. At the growth cycle peak in each country, the lag of the first signal, averaged across the six countries, was two months, while the second and third signals lagged by an average of five and six months, respectively. At the growth cycle trough, the average lags for the six countries were zero, six, and eight months, respectively.

3. The system produced no false signals in any country during 1973-1976, but in Japan the third signal of a trough was subject to unusual delay. In this set of indexes, the "target-trend" growth rate for each country is equal to the rate of growth in its real GNP during 1966-1976. For Japan, this is 7.8 percent per year. The coincident index rate did not reach that level until 1979 and then only briefly, even though a growth cycle trough was recognized in March 1975. Growth in Japan has, of course, slowed since the 1973 oil crisis. The growth cycle chronology allows for this change in trend, but the criterion used in the third signal does not. This points to one of the potential problems with the target-trend aspect of the signal system, although Japan was the only country where it had a significant effect.

In general, the results of this test on data for other countries correspond well with those for the United States. At peaks the lags are longer than those shown for the United States in Table 4-1, but this is because growth cycle peaks (used in six countries) precede business cycle peaks. At troughs, where growth cycle and business cycle turns usually coincide, the lags for the six countries are nearly the same as those for the United States. As additional experience is gained, for example, in applying the system on a current basis, we shall be in a better position to appraise its virtues and limitations.

MODIFYING THE SYSTEM FOR USE
WITH CURRENT DATA

An important limitation of the foregoing tests is that they use historical, not current, data. The index series are based on the best information available at the present time, that is, on figures which, for all but a few of the most recent months, have undergone several revisions. In actual practice, business analysts and forecasters cannot work with these data since they cannot afford the long delays entailed in waiting for the revisions to be completed. Realistically, the choice they have is restricted to using either the preliminary data, which involve the least delay but also are the least accurate, or the first revised data, which add another month to the lag of the indexes behind the events but improve the quality of the information.[18]

Table 4-4 compares the monthly values of the leading index rate and the coincident index rate as they appeared in preliminary data and in first revised data. These series begin in October 1976 because consistent information of this type is not available for the earlier years.[19]

The leading index rate based on preliminary data (L_p) dipped below the 3.3 percent level intermittently for a total of eight months between February 1977 and August 1978. These declines were generally short and shallow, but, under the strict application of the rules stated above, each of these months is associated with a false signal, identified in the table by the symbol ($P1$) (see columns 1 and 3). Only in November 1978 did the series L_p begin signaling the recession consistently, by falling and staying below 3.3 percent (and soon thereafter below 0 percent). Accordingly, it is in that month that a true signal of the peak, denoted as $P1$, is shown in the table for the first time (the first appearance of a true signal is marked with an asterisk). The $P1$ signal was reported in each of the five following months.

The coincident index rate based on preliminary data (C_p) declined below 3.3 percent in May 1979 and remained below that level until after the 1980 recession, thus yielding (together with the leading index rate) a true second signal of the peak, $P2$ (see columns 2 and 3). However, C_p slipped intermittently below zero in four months between August 1979 and January 1980, producing false third signals of the peak ($P3$). The true third signal, $P3$, is first dated March 1980; it stayed on for six months, through August 1980.

When first revised data are used for the leading index rate (L_r) and the coincident index rate (C_r), the frequency of false signals is drastically reduced. The series L_r shows four months of false first signals ($P1$) between January 1977 and August 1978 (columns 5, 7). This compares with eight such months in the preliminary series L_p (see columns 3 and 7). According to the series C_r, the true second signal $P2*$ occurred for the first time in April 1979 and stayed on for six consecutive months (columns 6, 7). When one allows for the longer information lag due to the revision, this timing is effectively the same as that of the preliminary series C_p (see columns 3 and 7). There are no false signals of the $P2$ type in either C_r or C_p. Further, the use of C_r would result in fewer and less confusing false signals of the $P3$ type than use of C_p would. Finally, the revised data gave the third true signal of the peak, $P3$, for the first time in February 1980 and

Table 4-4. Sequential Signals of Recession and Recovery, Two Variants, Applied to Preliminary and Revised Data, 1976–1981.

Year and Month	Preliminary Data[a]				First Revised Data[b]			
	Leading Index Rate (L_p) (1)	Coincident Index Rate (C_p) (2)	Signals of Business Cycle Turns		Leading Index Rate (L_r) (5)	Coincident Index Rate (C_r) (6)	Signals of Business Cycle Turns	
			Level Signals[c] (3)	Band Signals[c] (4)			Level Signals[c] (7)	Band Signals[c] (8)
1976								
October	4.1	2.7	—	—	4.5	2.8	—	—
November	5.5	4.0	—	—	6.1	4.2	—	—
December	8.2	5.2	—	—	7.3	5.7	—	—
1977								
January	3.6	4.0	—	—	3.1	3.4	(P1)	—
February	3.1	4.3	(P1)	—	3.7	4.9	—	—
March	5.6	7.3	—	—	6.4	7.9	—	—
April	6.5	8.4	—	—	6.5	7.6	—	—
May	5.3	8.2	—	—	5.0	8.2	—	—
June	3.1	8.1	(P1)	—	3.8	7.3	—	—
July	2.9	7.2	(P1)	—	3.8	7.0	—	—
August	4.7	5.8	—	—	5.5	5.5	—	—
September	5.4	6.3	—	—	6.0	6.0	—	—
October	6.4	6.3	—	—	7.3	6.4	—	—
November	5.8	6.8	—	—	6.3	5.8	—	—
December	6.9	6.4	—	—	7.0	7.1	—	—
1978								
January	2.4	5.5	(P1)	—	3.6	3.7	—	—
February	2.7	4.3	(P1)	—	4.0	3.7	(P1)	—
March	3.0	6.1	(P1)	—	3.2	6.3	—	—
April	3.7	8.3	—	—	5.2	8.6	—	—
May	4.2	7.9	—	—	4.2	7.5	—	—
June	4.2	7.3	—	—	4.8	7.3	—	—
July	2.5	7.7	(P1)	—	2.0	7.0	(P1)	P1*
August	2.9	6.2	(P1)	—	2.9	7.0	(P1)	P1
September	4.0	5.7	—	—	4.3	6.1	—	P1
October	4.5	6.7	—	P1*	3.7	7.2	P1*	P1
November	1.9	8.0	P1*		2.4	7.8	P1	P1

	value	value	signal	signal	value	value	signal	signal
1979								
January	-.7	6.8	P1	P1	2.9	6.0	P1	P1
February	.1	5.2	P1	P1	1.0	4.8	P1	P1
March	-.3	4.7	P1	P1	1.6	6.1	P1	P1
April	-5.0	3.3	P1	P1	-2.6	2.0	P2*	P2*
May	-1.8	.9	P2*	P2*	-2.0	3.0	P2	P2
June	-2.2	1.4	P2	P2	-3.2	2.0	P2	P2
July	-3.6	1.3	P2	P2	-3.7	1.3	P2	P2
August	-3.5	-.9	(P3)	P2	-2.3	.4	P2	P2
September	-.7	-.1	(P3)	P2	-2.1	.3	(P3)	P2
October	-3.5	.5	—	P2	-4.0	-.4	(P3)	P2
November	-5.8	-.2	(P3)	P2	-5.4	-.5	(P3)	P2
December	-4.8	.2	—	P2	-6.3	-.2	—	P2
1980								
January	-6.7	-.9	(P3)	P2	-6.5	.8	—	P2
February	-6.1	.1	—	P2	-6.0	-.4	P3*	P2
March	-9.8	-2.2	P3*	P3*	-8.4	-2.5	P3	P3*
April	-15.3	-5.5	P3	P3	-15.0	-5.6	P3	P3
May	-17.3	7.9	P3	P3	-17.0	-8.5	P3	P3
June	-11.3	-10.7	P3	P3	-13.4	-10.1	P3	P3
July	-4.2	-11.4	P3	P3	-6.8	-9.3	P3	P3
August	-2.2	-8.0	P3	P3	-2.5	-8.5	P3	P3
September	3.0	-7.2	T1*	T1*	4.7	-5.0	T1*	T1*
October	7.1	-2.4	T1	T1	6.9	-1.9	T1	T1
November	9.5	.2	T2*	T2*	9.5	-.1	T1	T1
December	7.7	1.5	T2	T2	7.1	1.7	T2*	T2*
1981								
January	6.0	3.0	T2	T2	7.4	2.6	T2	T2
February	6.2	2.3	T2	T2	4.8	3.5	T3*	T2
March	7.4	3.9	T3*	T2	8.7	4.7	T3	T3*
April	8.6	4.7	T3*	T3*	7.7	3.5	—	T3
May	2.7	3.3	(P1)[d]	T3	—	—	—	—

a Based on the first published BCD figures (with a publication lag of one month).

b Based on the second published BCD figures (with a publication lag of two months).

c The symbols are those used in the text, e.g., P1 denotes the first signal for peaks, T2 the second signal for troughs, etc. The false signals are in parentheses, e.g., (P1) or (T2), the true signals are not. The first time a true signal appears it is marked by an asterisk, e.g., P1* or T2*. For the explanation of the systems of level signals and band signals, see text.

d The level of L_p in May 1981 (2.7 percent) represents a first peak signal (P1) which may or may not prove to be a false signal. Subsequent data as of September 1981 show a P1 signal in June 1981 and a P2 signal in August 1981, but no P3 signal.

repeated it in each of the six ensuing months. This is again equivalent to the timing of the corresponding signal in the preliminary data (March-August 1980). The NBER designated January 1980 as the business cycle peak on June 3, 1980.[20]

The trough of the 1980 recession occurred in July 1980, according to a recent finding by the NBER (July 8, 1981). Our first, second, and third trough signals are dated September and November 1980 and March 1981, respectively, according to the preliminary data, and September and December 1980 and February 1981 according to the revised data. The lags involved, two to nine months, are similar to those observed in recent recoveries (see Table 4-2 and text).

Let us sum up the results obtained at this point: The simple device of using the first revised instead of the preliminary indexes turns out to be rather effective in dealing with the problem of false signals (as exemplified by the data relating to the January 1980 peak). But another approach appears to work better still. It consists in redefining the signaling system by using bands of ± 1.0 percent around the critical levels of 3.3 percent and 0 percent. This would approximately allow for the dispersion of the values of the random components of the composite indexes.[21]

Figure 4-3 shows how the "band approach" would work by means of a schematic diagram analogous to Figure 4-1 (which applies to the level approach used up to this point). Here the first signal of the peak, assuming the coincident index rate is above zero, occurs when the leading index rate declines across the band 3.3 percent ± 1.0 percent. If, after that happened, the leading rate rose again but stayed within the band (at points like A in Figure 4-3, for example), the signal would not be invalidated; for the signal to be revealed as false, the leading index rate would have to rise above the band (e.g., to point B). The second peak signal occurs when the leading rate falls below the band 0 percent ± 1.0 percent, and the coincident rate falls below the band 3.3 percent ± 1.0 percent. The third peak signal is given when the coincident rate falls below the band 0 percent ± 1.0 percent, while the leading rate remains below zero. The criterion defining false signals is everywhere the same: Backing up *into* the band does not invalidate the previous signal; reverse crossing *through* the band does.

The expected sequence of signals at business cycle peaks, then, is when each of the following signals is first observed:

- First signal ($P1$): The leading index rate falls below 2.3 percent; the coincident index rate will usually be higher than 2.3 percent, but we require only that it be nonnegative ($L < 2.3$; $C \geqslant 0$).

Figure 4-3. Sequential Signals of Recession and Recovery: The Band Approach.

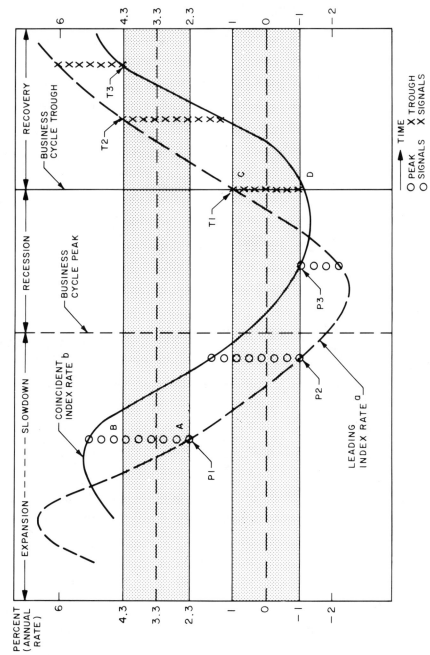

- Second signal ($P2$): The leading index rate falls below-1.0 percent and the coincident rate falls below 2.3 percent ($L < -1.0$; $C < 2.3$).

- Third signal ($P3$): The coincident index rate falls below -1.0 percent, while the leading index rate is still negative ($L < 0$; $C < -1.0$).

At business cycle troughs, the first signal occurs when the leading index rate rises across the band 0 percent ± 1.0 percent while the coincident rate remains below that band. If, thereafter, the leading rate falls back within the band (say, to point C), the signal continues to apply; if it falls below the band (say, to point D), the signal is taken to be false. The second trough signal is given when the leading rate rises across the band 3.3 percent ± 1.0 percent and the coincident rate rises across the band 0 percent ± 1.0 percent. The third signal occurs when both rates rise above the band 3.3 percent ± 1.0 percent. Again, the criterion for distinguishing false from true signals remains as defined above.

To sum up, the expected sequence of signals at business cycle troughs is given by the first occurrence of the following:

- First signal ($T1$): The leading index rate rises above 1.0 percent while the coincident index rate is less than 1.0 percent ($L > 1.0$; $C < 1.0$). A $T1$ must follow a $P3$.

- Second signal ($T2$): The leading index rate rises above 4.3 percent and the coincident index rate rises above 1.0 percent ($L > 4.3$; $C > 1.0$).

- Third signal ($T3$): Both the leading index rate and the coincident index rate rise above 4.3 percent ($L > 4.3$; $C > 4.3$).

To be reasonably successful, the band approach requires that (1) the proportions of observations that fall into the two bands be small for both index rates, L and C; and (2) the reverse crossings through the bands be very infrequent for both series. Unless the first condition applies, either L or C or both may meander within the bands, with the effect of delaying and perhaps obscuring the signals. Unless the second condition applies, false signals will present a problem.

Fortunately, the evidence suggests that the two requirements are likely to be met by the data. As shown in Table 4-5, less than 7 percent of the observations for the leading index rate fell in the band 3.3 percent ± 1.0 percent and about 6 percent fell in the band 0 percent ± 1.0 percent. For the coincident index rate, the corresponding

Table 4-5. Frequency Distributions of Monthly Observations on Six-Month Smoothed Rates of Change in the Leading Index and in the Coincident Index, 1948-1981.

	Frequency of Observations							
	Leading Index Rate (L)				*Coincident Index Rate (C)*			
Class Interval (% Points)	*N* *(1)*		*%* *(2)*		*N* *(3)*		*%* *(4)*	
4.4 and over	199		51.4		195		50.4	
3.4-4.3	13		3.4		24		6.2	
2.4-3.3	13	26	3.4	6.7	24	48	6.2	12.4
1.1-2.3	16		4.1		29		7.5	
.1-1.0	9		2.3		14		3.6	
-1.0-0.0	14	23	3.6	5.9	19	33	4.9	8.5
-1.1 and under	123		31.8		82		21.2	
Total	387		100.0		387		100.0	

Note: The measures in this table refer to the series plotted in Figure 4-2A (for *L*) and Figure 4-2B (for *C*). The series are based on the composite indexes published in U.S. Department of Commerce, Bureau of Economic Analysis, *Business Conditions Digest* (BDC) 1979.

percentages are somewhat larger but still moderate: a little over 12 percent and 8 percent, respectively. Thus, the *L* series was outside of the two bands 87 percent of the time, and the *C* series was outside of the same bands 79 percent of the time.

Returning to Table 4-4, let us inspect columns 4 and 8, which register the signals produced by the band approach for the preliminary and first revised data, respectively. There are no false signals at all in either set; that is, no reverse crossings of the bands occurred during this period of more than four years. This is a major advantage of using the band signals rather than level signals (cf. column 4 with 3, and column 8 with 7). There is no significant advantage to applying the band approach to the first revised data rather than the preliminary data (cf. columns 4 and 8).

The timing of the band signals is in most cases identical with the timing of the corresponding level signals, as shown in Table 4-6. Hence this method, like the use of revised data, would cause no additional delay in the signals associated with the last recession and recovery. We conclude that the proposed procedure offers a promising way of dealing with the difficult and important problem of false signals on a current basis.

It is somewhat surprising that the band signals do not show more of a lag relative to the level signals, since the two approaches differ in a way that would seem to suggest the presence of such lags (cf. Fig-

Table 4–6. Timing of the Signals of Peaks and Troughs, Two Variants, Preliminary and First Revised Data, 1976–1981.

| | Preliminary Data | | | | First Revised Data | | | |
| | Level Signals | | Band Signals | | Level Signals | | Band Signals | |
Type of Signal	Date (1)	Lead (−) or Lag (+) (2)	Date (3)	Lead (−) or Lag (+) (4)	Date (5)	Lead (−) or Lag (+) (6)	Date (7)	Lead (−) or Lag (+) (8)
Business Cycle Peak Signals								
P1*	Nov. 1978	−14	Nov. 1978	−14	July 1978	−18	Nov. 1978	−14
P2*	May 1979	−8	May 1979	−8	April 1979	−9	April 1979	−9
P3*	March 1980	+2	March 1980	+2	Feb. 1980	+1	March 1980	+2
Business Cycle Trough Signals								
T1*	Sept. 1980	+2	Sept. 1980	+2	Sept. 1980	+2	Sept. 1980	+2
T2*	Nov. 1980	+4	Dec. 1980	+5	Dec. 1980	+5	Dec. 1980	+5
T3*	March 1981	+8	April 1981	+9	Feb. 1981	+7	March 1981	+8

Note: All leads and lags are in months. For the peak signals, they are measured from the NBER reference date for the business cycle peak: January 1980. For the trough signals, they are measured from the NBER reference date of July 1980 (see text and note 20). On the symbols for the types of peak and trough signals and the underlying data, see Table 4–4.

ures 4–1 and 4–2). As a last test available to us, we have therefore applied the band approach to the historical data extending back to 1948. The results are presented in Tables 4–7 and 4–8, which may be compared with Tables 4–1 and 4–2, respectively. The mean timing of the three band signals at business cycle peaks is –8, –3, and +3 months, a slight overall delay relative to the corresponding measures for the level signals (–10, –2, and +1). At troughs, the average leads or lags of the two sets of signals are virtually identical.

It should also be noted that sequences of all three peak signals appear in Table 4–7 only in connection with business cycle recessions, not growth cycle slowdowns. The latter are associated either with first and second signals (as in 1951) or with the first signal only (as in 1962 and 1966). The absence of the $P3$ signal in each of these instances also rules out any trough signals in the years 1952, 1963, and 1967. In all these respects, there is a basic similarity between the band signals of Tables 4–7 and 4–8 and the level signals of Tables 4–1 and 4–2. The main difference is the absence of false signals, which constitutes a substantial advantage of the band approach.

THE TIMING OF THE SIGNALS AND INFLATION

Ideally, countercyclical policies should be timed so as to also have some stabilizing effects on prices in general. If the price level increased in business expansions and decreased in business contractions, the two aims of policy, far from being in any way inconsistent, would actually be complementary. In the 1940s and earlier, the comprehensive price indexes did tend to fluctuate with the business cycle. In the recent era of persistent inflation, the general level of prices of goods and services no longer shows any comparable degree of downward flexibility. Thus, as shown in Figure 4–4, the six-month smoothed rate of change in the consumer price index (to be called, for simplicity, the CPI rate) became negative in 1949–1950 and 1954–1955, during and immediately after the first two business cycle contractions of the post–World War II period; but it stayed positive during each of the five recessions that occurred in the following quarter-century.

However, despite the upward trend in inflation since the mid-1960s, the CPI rate continued to show a cyclical pattern. The only significant declines in this (and other) measures of inflation occurred during recessions or, increasingly, in the early recovery phases (Figure 4–4). Inflation decelerated sharply on most of these occasions,

Table 4-7.   Three Signals of Recession: Timing at Business Cycle Peaks—The Band Approach, 1948–1980.

Growth Cycle Peak	Business Cycle Peak	First Signal (L < 2.3; C > 0)	Second Signal (L < -1.0; C < 2.3)	Third Signal (L < 0; C < -1.0)	Lead (−) or Lag (+), in Months, at Business Cycle Peaks		
					First Signal	Second Signal	Third Signal
7/48	11/48	N.A.	N.A.	N.A.	—	—	—
3/51	None	3/51	7/51	—	—	—	—
3/53	7/53	6/53	8/53	9/53	−1	+1	+2
2/57	8/57	1/56	7/56	9/57	−19	−13	+1
2/60	4/60	9/59	6/60	9/60	−7	+2	+5
5/62	None	5/62	—	—	—	—	—
6/66	None	6/66			—	—	—
3/69	12/69	6/69	11/69	4/70	−6	−1	+4
3/73	11/73	8/73	1/74	3/74	−3	+2	+4
12/78	1/80	11/78	5/79	3/80	−14	−8	+2
Average	—	—	—	—	−8	−3	+3

Note: For full definitions of the signals, see text. Revised data are used prior to October 1976, preliminary data since then.

Table 4-8. Three Signals of Recovery: Timing at Business Cycle Troughs—the Band Approach, 1949-1981.

Growth Cycle Trough	Business Cycle Trough	First Signal (L > 1.0; C < 1.0)	Second Signal (L > 4.3; C > 1.0)	Third Signal (L > 4.3; C > 4.3)	Lead (−) or Lag (+), in Months, at Business Cycle Peaks		
					First Signal	Second Signal	Third Signal
10/49	10/49	8/49	1/50	3/50	−2	+3	+5
8/54	5/54	5/54	11/54	12/54	0	+6	+7
4/58	4/58	6/58	10/58	11/58	+2	+6	+7
2/61	2/61	3/61	6/61	8/61	+1	+4	+6
11/70	11/70	11/70	5/71	12/71	0	+6	+13
3/75	3/75	6/75	9/75	11/75	+3	+6	+8
7/80	7/80	9/80	12/80	4/81	+2	+5	+9
Average	—	—	—	—	+1	+5	+8

Note: For full definitions of the signals, see text. Revised data are used prior to October 1976, preliminary data since then.

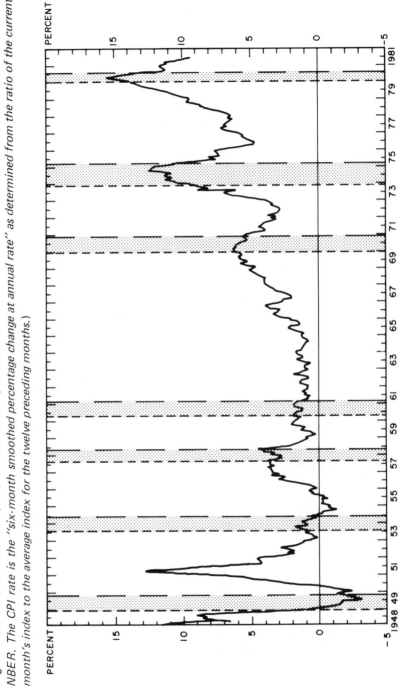

Figure 4-4. Rate of Inflation (CPI) and Business Cycles. (*Dotted areas are business cycle recessions as determined by the NBER. The CPI rate is the "six-month smoothed percentage change at annual rate" as determined from the ratio of the current month's index to the average index for the twelve preceding months.*)

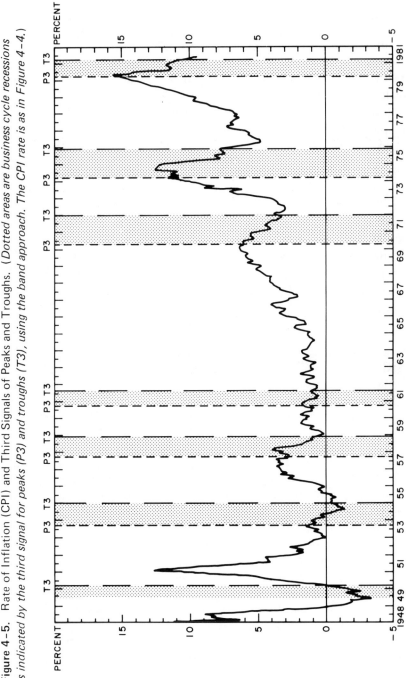

Figure 4-5. Rate of Inflation (CPI) and Third Signals of Peaks and Troughs. *(Dotted areas are business cycle recessions as indicated by the third signal for peaks (P3) and troughs (T3), using the band approach. The CPI rate is as in Figure 4-4.)*

as in 1958–1959, 1970–1972, 1974–1976, and 1980–1981; unfortunately, the accelerations during the expansions in 1968–1969, 1972–1974, nd 1976–1979 were larger yet.[22] This suggests that, in order not to aggravate inflation, countercyclical policies ought to be strictly confined to periods of business cycle contraction and early recovery when the upward pressures on the price level typically abate. They should not be initiated before the expansion tapers off and should be discontinued well before the next expansion heats up.

Our system of sequential signals is consistent with these precepts. If countercyclical policies were not significantly activated until the third peak signal, $P3$, and were fully deactivated by the third trough signal, $T3$, the relation to the inflation rate would be as shown in Figure 4–5. Each of the time intervals between $P3$ and $T3$ (indicated by the broken vertical lines bounding the dotted areas) corresponded closely to a phase of decline in the CPI rate. In the first two cycles, the off ($T3$) signals more or less coincided with the local inflation troughs as represented by the minima of the CPI rate; since 1958, they have preceded the low points of inflation by several months on each occasion. Hence the use of the signaling system would produce counterinflationary as well as countercyclical timing of discretionary economic policies.

AN UPDATE OF THE SEQUENTIAL SIGNALING SYSTEM

The recent record of the signals, using the "band approach" described above, is displayed in Figure 4–6. At the 1981 peak the first signal came in June 1981, the second in August, and the third in October. The business cycle peak, as designated later by the National Bureau, was July 1981. Hence the first signal led the peak by one month, the second lagged by one month, and the third lagged by three months. The first signal did not give as early a warning as on most past occasions, and all three signals were more tightly concentrated than usual.

The first subsequent signal of a trough came in July 1982, when the growth rate for the leading index reached 1.9 percent, after having been negative during the preceding twelve months. In August the growth rate dipped to 0.7 percent, but since this was still within the −1.0 to +1.0 percent band, the signal was not reversed. In September the growth rate rose to 3.9 percent, and it climbed higher in October, November, and December, the latest month as of this writing. Meanwhile, the coincident index growth rate remained negative, so the second trough signal had not arrived by December. As of the end of

Figure 4-6.   Recession and Recovery: Sequential Signals.

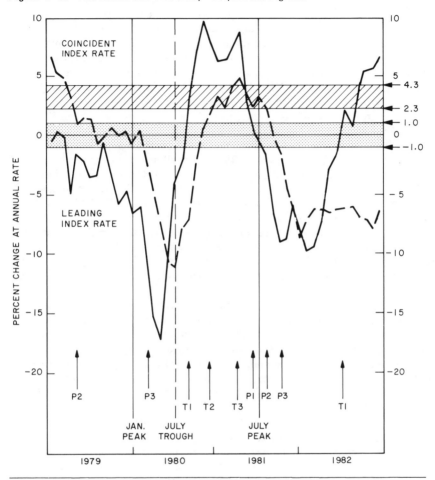

1982, therefore, confirmation that a recovery was underway, as provided by the second and third signals, was still lacking.

NOTES TO CHAPTER 4

1. Thus the Accelerated Public Works Program was enacted in September 1962, that is, nineteen months after the end of the 1960–1961 business cycle contraction as dated by the NBER. For the Public Works Impact Program (August 1971), the lag behind the trough of the 1969–1970 recession was nine months. The enactment of the Local Public Works Program in July 1976 followed by sixteen months the NBER reference date for the end of the 1973–1975 contraction.

2. The Public Employment Program was created by the Emergency Employment Act in July 1971, eight months into the recovery from the 1969–1970 recession. The Comprehensive Employment and Training Act (Title VI) was enacted in December 1974—thirteen months after the business cycle peak, but three months before the trough as dated by NBER. It is estimated that about six months elapsed between the allocation of funds and the employment of half the number of workers (half the direct jobs to be created) under these programs. The lags with which the policies take effect are, on the average, longer for public works, where the half-life is of the order of one year. (See Vernez and Vaughan 1978: 48–59).

3. While it is true that some public works (new large projects) have long implementation lags, others (renovations and small new projects) take much less time to complete. Public employment service programs have relatively short outside lags, with the best results showing 60 percent to 70 percent of the peak number of jobs filled in six months, as shown for EEA in 1971–1972 and CETA VI in 1974–1975 by Vernez and Vaughan (1978: 56).

4. Note the following passage from an early, authoritative document: "Within limits, expenditures for public works can be timed to serve the interests of stability, but only if a reservoir of engineering studies and blueprints for specific projects has been prepared well in advance of need" (Council of Economic Advisers 1954: 123).

5. The composite index of "marginal employment adjustments" compiled by the Bureau of Economic Analysis (BEA) of the U.S. Department of Commerce includes the average workweek, accession rate, and layoff rate (all in manufacturing) and the average initial claims on state unemployment insurance. Two of these series (the workweek and the layoff rate) are components of the BEA index of twelve leading indicators used in the procedure described in the text below. For a modified version of the employment adjustment index, see Chapter 22, below.

6. This is of necessity but a starkly condensed list which groups together several types of explanations, e.g., (1) includes accelerator-multiplier models, hypotheses stressing autonomous investment, disturbances, lags, innovations, etc.; (2) covers both the older theories that assign a central role to fluctuations in bank credit and interest rates and the current monetarist theories; and (3) refers to the roles of cost-price imbalances, volatility of prospective rates of return, and expectational errors. Nor is this tabulation in any sense exhaustive. For an overview of business cycle literature with references, see Zarnowitz 1972: 1–38. For a bibliography of indicator studies, see Zarnowitz 1972 and Chapter 21, below.

7. Careful observation led to an acceptable working definition of business cycles as a recurrent but not periodic sequence of cumulative expansions and contractions that spread unevenly over the myriad of processes and participants that constitute a market economy yet are sufficiently synchronized to show up as fluctuations in the overall aggregates of real income, output, employment, and trade. The historical movements display certain well-established and important (but far from immutable) regularities along with many unique features of the individual processes and cycles. There are plausible hypotheses that are not nec-

essarily mutually exclusive, but there is no unified theory that has succeeded in explaining all that seems essential about business cycles. Thus, prediction cannot reliably depend on any single presumptive chain of cause and effect. The composition of factors that influence the course of the economy can and does vary from one business cycle to another, so some indicators may work better in one environment, others in a different environment. To increase the chances of getting true signals, it is therefore advisable to construct indexes from data of historically tested usefulness, with diversified economic coverage. It is also important and helpful that, in such indexes, much of the independent measurement error and other noise in the included series are smoothed out.

8. The series are also subjected to a standardization procedure designed to put them on an equal basis and to prevent the more volatile series from dominating the index. Further, trend adjustments are used, as noted later in this chapter. For detail on the construction, record, and predictive value of the composite indexes of cyclical indicators, see Zarnowitz and Boschan 1975a, b; U.S. Department of Commerce, Bureau of Economic Analysis 1977; Vaccara and Zarnowitz 1978: 41-50, 1979; and Chapters 24 and 25 below.

9. Another technique with a good claim to be considered is the use of trend-adjusted indexes, again after smoothing. But trend estimation is often difficult and uncertain, especially near the end of a series, and this is precisely where attention must be focused in a signaling system.

10. This is done by raising the ratio to the 12/6.5 power (the average of the twelve preceding months is located 6.5 months before the current month).

11. In fact, the smoothed six-month change at annual rate was found to compare favorably with a simple twelve-month change, the popular "same month year ago" comparisons. The latter series, while slightly smoother, lagged behind the former by one or two months at nearly every turn.

12. Specifically, the trends are made equal to the average of the long-term trends in the four components of the index of roughly coincident indicators (number of employees on nonagricultural payrolls; index of industrial production; personal income less transfer payments in constant dollars; manufacturing and trade sales in constant dollars). For each of these monthly series, a loglinear trend is computed by converting the percentage change from the centered initial cycle average (1949-1954) to the centered terminal cycle average (1970-1975) into a monthly rate by the compound interest formula. (For further details, see U.S. Department of Commerce, Bureau of Economic Analysis 1977: 74-76, 1979: 157.) The target trend will be reestimated each time a new trough-to-trough cycle is completed in the four coincident indicators. Frequent updating of the target trend rate is not practicable, but this should not cause any serious errors because the change in the secular trend of the economy is gradual and small in the short run.

13. Theoretically, business cycle contractions could likewise be interrupted by high-growth phases, but there are no instances of this sort in recent history, and none would be expected in times when all recessions are relatively short. In the seven completed business cycles of the post-World War II period (1945-1980), the contractions ranged in length from six to sixteen months and averaged ten months.

14. The series represent aggregate output, employment and unemployment, income, and sales; all are in constant dollars or physical units or quantity index numbers. The trends are estimated by interpolation between segments determined with the aid of ratios to long (seventy-five-month or twenty-five-quarter) centered moving averages; they are estimated so as to cut through and contain no significant elements of the short cyclical movements in the series. Various composite and diffusion indexes based on the same set of indicators are used as well. (For further detail and applications, see Zarnowitz and Boschan 1977: 34-38; Zarnowitz and Moore 1977.)

15. The rates of growth actually used in this chapter are smoothed six-month changes in annualized form, as described in the text. Of course, these indexes, like any others built from real economic indicators, contain much "noise," short erratic movements, which are entirely disregarded in Figure 4-1.

16. The coincident index rate was below 3.3 percent for five months in 1956 and was negative in one month. In 1959, it was below 3.3 percent (and negative) for two months.

17. The following tabulation compares the lags of the third signal with those involved in the recovery of the coincident index to its previous peak level (in the 1980-81 recovery the index did not regain its peak level):

Business Cycle Trough	Lag of Third Signal (months)	Lag of Recovery in the Coincident Index (months)
Oct. 1949	5	8
May 1954	7	12
April 1958	7	13
Feb. 1961	6	9
Nov. 1970	12	13
March 1975	8	24
Average	8	13

18. The main reason for the large revisions in the preliminary index is that it is constructed from only ten of the twelve components. The figures for the two components (net business formation and net change in inventories on hand and on order in 1972 dollars) are not yet available. These figures are added to the index one month later in the first revision (however, lately the figures for the net business formation have lagged two months). The preliminary coincident index is based on three of the four components (the figures for manufacturing and trade sales in 1972 dollars are added one month later in the first revision).

19. The content and method of constructing the composite indexes of cyclical indicators were altered in several aspects by the compiling agency in 1976. (See U.S. Department of Commerce, Bureau of Economic Analysis 1977, for more information.)

20. See Zarnowitz and Moore 1981.

21. The standard deviation of the irregular component of the leading index rate is 0.91 percent; the corresponding statistic for the coincident index rate is 1.00 percent.

22. During much of the 1973–1974 recession (through September 1974), the CPI rate continued on an upward course, largely reflecting the earlier "supply shocks" of sharp rises in prices of imported oil and other materials. Such a long and large increase in the inflation rate during a period of business contraction was then, and still is, unique in U.S. business cycle history.

REFERENCES

Council of Economic Advisers. *Annual Report*. Washington, D.C.: Government Printing Office, 1954.

Moore, Geoffrey H. "The Forty-second Anniversary of the Leading Indicators." In William Fellner (ed.), *Contemporary Economic Problems 1979*. Washington, D.C.: American Enterprise Institute, 1979. (Reprinted below, Chapter 24.)

_____ . "A New Leading Index of Employment and Unemployment." *Monthly Labor Review* 104 (June 1981): 44–47. (Reprinted below, Chapter 22.)

U.S. Department of Commerce, Bureau of Economic Analysis. *Handbook of Cyclical Indicators: A Supplement to Business Conditions Digest*. Washington, D.C.: Government Printing Office, 1977.

_____ . *Business Conditions Digest* 19 (March 1979): iii–iv.

Vaccara, Beatrice N., and Zarnowitz, Victor. "How good are the leading indicators?" *1977 Proceedings of the Business and Economic Statistics Section*. Washington, D.C.: American Statistical Association, Pt. 1, pp. 41–50, 1978.

_____ . Forecasting with the Index of Leading Indicators. Cambridge, Mass.: NBER Working Paper 244 (May 1979).

Vernez, Georges, and Vaughan, Roger. *Assessment of the Countercyclical Public Works and Public Service Employment Programs*. R-2214-EDA. Rand Corporation, Santa Monica, Calif., 1978.

Zarnowitz, Victor. "The Business Cycle Today: An Introduction." In Victor Zarnowitz (ed.), *The Business Cycle Today*. New York: NBER, 1972.

Zarnowitz, Victor, and Charlotte Boschan. "Cyclical Indicators: An Evaluation and New Leading Indexes." *Business Conditions Digest* (May 1975): v–xxii.

_____ . "New Composite Indexes of Coincident and Lagging Indicators." *Business Conditions Digest* (November 1975): v–xxiv.

_____ . "Cyclical Indicators." In *Interaction in Economic Research, 57th Annual Report*, New York: NBER, September 1977, pp. 34–38.

Zarnowitz, Victor, and Geoffrey H. Moore. "The Recession and Recovery of 1973–1976." *Explorations in Economic Research* 4 (Fall 1977): 471–557.

_____ . "The Timing and Severity of the Recession of 1980. *NBER Reporter* (Spring 1981): 19–21. (Reprinted above, Chapter 2).

Chapter 5

Growth Cycles: A New-Old Concept

In terms of the "growth cycle," the longest expansion in economic activity since World War II ran from March 1975 to December 1978, a period of forty-five months. The next longest expansion, 1954–1957, lasted only thirty months. The average for the eight expansions between 1949 and 1973 was twenty months, about the same length as the average contraction.

The growth cycle is a relatively new concept of the business cycle. It is also a very old idea. The growth cycle is a fluctuation around the long-run trend—a trend-adjusted business cycle, if you like. In these days of great public sensitivity to economic slowdowns, the growth cycle is a concept whose time has come. Perhaps one should say that it is ready to be born again. The concept is useful in analyzing the experience of countries with very rapid growth rates, like West Germany and Japan before the 1970s, as well as those with slower growth rates, like the United States and the United Kingdom. The rapidly growing countries were not immune to fluctuations in their growth rates that were very similar to those experienced by the slower growing countries.

The growth cycle concept is also useful because of two major differences between it and the ordinary business cycle. Growth cycle downturns occur sooner than business cycle downturns, so one can identify them earlier. They also occur more frequently. Between 1948 and 1973 there were six business cycle downturns but nine growth cycle downturns. December 1978, if that date proves to be correct, marked the tenth downturn. Because of their greater fre-

Reprinted from *The Morgan Guaranty Survey*, August 1979.

quency there are more cases to generalize from, and one can distinguish between the six slowdowns that became recessions and the
three that did not (see Appendix Table A-4).

A company's or an industry's statistics can be analyzed in relation
to these slowdowns—for example, their duration or severity. Take
gasoline consumption. A slowdown or recession in the economy
might mean fewer trucks and commuters on the road, a falloff in
vacation travel, and more interest in car pooling or other ways of
reducing unnecessary trips. Sales of new cars and the accompanying
increase in mileage traveled might be smaller, and some customers
would shift to the less expensive models with greater fuel economy.
The figures on gasoline, indeed, show effects of this sort. The increase in gas consumed on highways has been smaller during the nine
economic slowdowns since 1948 than during the adjacent expansions. The average rate during the expansions was 6 percent per year,
compared with 4 percent during the slowdowns. During the slowdowns that became recessions, the growth rate in gas consumption
was only 3 percent.

Studies at the National Bureau of Economic Research, which are
being continued and expanded at the Center for International Business Cycle Research at Rutgers University, have established some
significant findings about growth cycles. Here are three samples:

1. Leading indicators have a better record of forecasting growth
cycles than of forecasting business cycles. The reason is that these
indicators—which include such factors as housing starts, profit margins, stock prices, and orders for goods—are sensitive to slowdowns
of any kind, whether of the recessionary variety or not. To para-
phrase Paul Samuelson's memorable statement about the stock
market, when the leading indicators were forecasting nine out of
the past six recessions, they also were forecasting nine out of the past
nine slowdowns.

Figure 5-1 demonstrates this proposition. Every one of the nine
growth cycles is reflected in a swing in the growth rate of the leading
index. The three slowdowns that did not turn into recessions (1951–
1952, 1962–1964, 1966–1967) were marked by smaller dips in the
leading index than those that did. Every time the growth rate of the
leading index (measured over the preceding six months, as explained
in the figure) fell below its long-term rate (3.3 percent per year), a
peak in the growth cycle was at hand. This happened for several
months in the summer of 1978 for the first time in this expansion
and again beginning in November. Hence, the slowdown in the economy that became evident in the spring of 1979 was registered in the
leading index several months beforehand.

Figure 5-1. Rate of Change in U.S. Leading Index During Preceding Six Months.

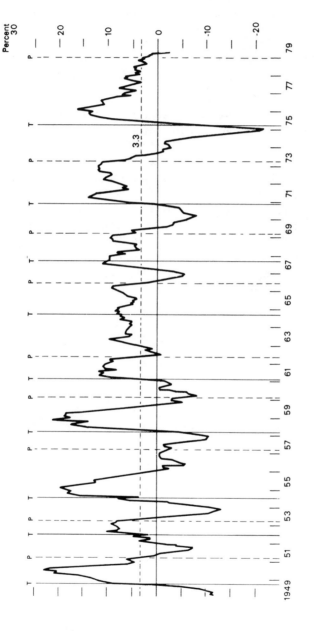

Note: Vertical lines mark the peaks (P) and troughs (T) in the growth cycle (National Bureau of Economic Research). The December 1978 peak is tentative. The rate of change in the leading index (U.S. Department of Commerce) is equal to the current month's index divided by the average of the twelve preceding months, expressed at an annual rate. The horizontal broken line is the long-term growth rate in the index, 3.3 percent, 1948–1978.

2. Leading, coincident, and lagging indicators behave in much the same way in relation to growth cycles in other industrial countries as they do in the United States. This means that the same indicators that display leading properties in the United States also display them abroad. Interestingly, too, the ratio of coincident to lagging indicators, which is basically a measure of imbalance in the economy, is a leading indicator of growth cycles in all the countries for which it is available.

3. Growth cycles are closely related to the rate of inflation. Indeed, every major decline in the inflation rate since 1948 has been associated with a growth slowdown. That is, no improvement in inflation has been achieved without a slowdown—often accompanied, unfortunately, by some rise in unemployment. That is true in the United States, Canada, the United Kingdom, West Germany, France, Italy, and Japan (see Chapters 6 and 14). Such a tie between economic activity and price pressures has been with us for a long time. Recently I discovered that the close connection had been documented in an analysis, published in 1926, of business cycles in relation to trends in wholesale prices that covered U.S. history from 1790 to 1925 (see Chapter 15). Our Founding Fathers faced much the same problem that we do.

Chapter 6

An Introduction to International Economic Indicators

For many years a system of leading, coincident, and lagging economic indicators, first developed in the 1930s by the National Bureau of Economic Research, has been widely used in the United States to appraise the state of the business cycle. Since 1961 the current monthly figures for these indicators have been published by the U.S. Department of Commerce in *Business Conditions Digest.* Similar systems have been developed by government or private agencies in Canada, Japan, the United Kingdom, and more recently in many other countries. Because of differences in content or methodology, however, these independent efforts do not provide comparable materials. In 1973 the NBER Bureau began to develop an international economic indicator system (IEI) that would provide comparable data, organized and analyzed in a comparable manner, for a number of industrial countries. The Center for International Business Cycle Research at Rutgers University in New Jersey has continued this work since 1979. The research has demonstrated that such a system can be helpful in tracking an international recovery or recession, in revealing factors that are holding back recovery or leading to recession, in anticipating changes in foreign trade flows, and in providing early warning of new inflationary trends. The Organization for Economic Cooperation and Development (OECD) and statistical agencies in Canada, the United Kingdom, West Germany, France, Italy, Japan, and the United States have cooperated with the NBER and with the Rutgers Center in compiling and analyzing the current data for this

Reprinted from *International Economic Indicators: A Sourcebook*, by Geoffrey H. and Melita H. Moore, Greenwood Press, forthcoming.

system of indicators. The practical results of this research program are now available for use.

In this chapter the functions of the indicator system are explained and the evidence summarized concerning its strength and weaknesses, and it is demonstrated how the system can be used to forecast business cycles, exports and imports, and inflation rates.

FUNCTIONS OF THE IEI SYSTEM

The first NBER study of business cycle indicators, conducted in 1937 by Wesley C. Mitchell and Arthur F. Burns, had as its immediate objective the use of indicators to signal a cyclical revival—that is, the ending of a recession, specifically the ending of the severe recession in the United States that began in spring 1937. When the work was taken up again after World War II, the objective was broadened to include signals of a cyclical downturn, and NBER studies completed in 1950, 1960, and 1966 as well as a Commerce Department study in 1975 focused on both the beginning and the end of recessions. An international system designed along similar lines should signal both peaks and troughs in each of the countries covered as well as in several countries taken together. In short, an important function of the IEI system is to detect a worldwide recession or recovery promptly. The importance of this function is underlined by the fact that international recessions—those in which many countries participate more or less simultaneously—have been more serious than localized recessions. One need only point to 1973–1975 and 1980–1982 to find examples of recessions that were both serious and international.

A second, and closely related, function of the indicator system is to measure the scope, severity, and unusual features of an international recession or recovery while it is in progress. For example, during the 1975–1976 recovery in the United States it became common practice, in reports devoted to the economic outlook, to compare the current recovery with previous recovery periods in this country. Similar comparisons were made during the 1980 recession. News magazines, business journals, annual reports of corporations, government reports, and newspapers used this device as a method of appraisal. But few of the publications made such comparisons for other countries, despite their relevance from a world point of view or their value in the diagnosis of specific problems pertaining to other countries. One of the reasons is that the necessary information is not readily accessible. An international economic indicator system should enable comparisons of this type to be made routinely and kept up to date.

A third function is to help appraise prospects for foreign trade. The leading indicators are sensitive measures of the general state of demand. Although many other factors affect the volume of exports and imports, demand is surely fundamental. A trade deficit can come about because of sluggish demand for exports from a country's trading partners while its own demand for imports is growing. Since the leading indicators include such demand-related factors as new orders, inventory change, hiring rates, and profitability, one can expect that they would relate to the demand not only for domestic goods but also for foreign products. Leading indicators for an importing country, therefore, should tell us something about how much it is likely to import, or how much its trading partners are likely to export to it. The international indicator system should therefore help us anticipate changes in the flow of trade to the countries for which leading indicators are available as well as changes in the trade balances among these countries.

Fourth, a system of international indicators can provide early warning signals of an acceleration or deceleration in the rate of inflation. Inflation is in part a demand phenomenon, and, as noted before, many of the indicators are demand oriented. Inflation is also an international phenomenon. All countries experience it, and waves of inflation often occur at about the same time in many countries. An appropriate set of international indicators should show how the price system responds to and feeds back upon the rest of the economy, including, of course, those variables that are under some degree of policy control, such as the money supply, the flow of credit, or the fiscal deficit.

LEADS AND LAGS IN RECOVERY AND RECESSION

The international economic indicator system consists of groups of leading, coincident, and lagging indicators covering a wide variety of economic processes that have been found to be important in business cycles. The leading indicators are for the most part measures of anticipations or new commitments. They have a "look-ahead" quality and are highly sensitive to changes in the economic climate as perceived in the marketplace. The coincident indicators are comprehensive measures of economic performance: real GNP, industrial production, employment, unemployment, income, and trade. They are the measures to which everyone looks to determine whether a nation is prosperous or depressed. The lagging indicators are more sluggish in their reactions to the economic climate, but they serve a useful purpose by smoothing out and confirming changes in trend that are first reflected in the leading and coincident indicators. Moreover, their very sluggishness can be an asset in cyclical analysis, because when they do begin to move, or when they move rapidly, they may show that excesses or imbalances in the economy are developing or subsiding. Hence the lagging indicators can (and often do) provide the earliest warnings of all, as when rapid increases in costs of production outstrip price increases and threaten profit margins, thus inhibiting new commitments to invest, which are among the leading indicators.

A conspectus of the U.S. indicators arranged according to the type of economic process they represent and the cyclical timing they exhibit is in Table 6-1. The compilation for other industrial countries is designed to represent substantially the same processes arranged in a similar manner. The degree of success in accomplishing this varies from one country to another, as shown in Table 6-2.

The attempt to duplicate the U.S. system abroad does not mean that all countries are thought to be alike or that other indicators could not be found that would serve equally well or better. Duplicating the U.S. system is not an ultimate goal but merely a practicable interim target. The U.S. indicator system has the advantage of being familiar to many users, and both its empirical properties and the ecohomic logic on which it was based have been thoroughly investigated by many scholars over a long period.[1] This logic seems applicable to many countries where free enterprise prevails. Orders placed for machinery that is made to order are likely to lead machinery production in any market-oriented economy and are likely also to lead the production of the goods the machinery helps to produce. Similarly, in any enterprise economy, changes in the relations between prices and costs influence incentives to expand future output and to make capital investments. In countries where there are markets for common stock, stock prices can be expected to be especially sensitive to changes in profit prospects as well as to changes in interest rates, and hence to anticipate the effects of these changes on output, investment, and employment.

The selection of the U.S. indicator list as a target also advances the objective of providing sets of indicators as comparable as possible across countries. Unless some attention is paid to this, comparisons of cyclical movements in different countries are likely to become hopelessly confused. To cite one example, the index of leading indicators published by the British Central Statistical Office includes a series on interest rates treated invertedly—that is, a rise in rates is counted as a depressing factor, and vice versa. This is not an unreasonable position to take, but in the U.S. classification interest rates are treated on a positive basis and are included among the lagging indicators (see Table 6-1). It is recognized that at times a rapid rise in such indicators can be interpreted as an adverse development. A straightforward comparison of the U.S. and U.K. leading indexes as published in each country would run afoul of this difference in procedure.

Nevertheless, it is obvious that the system should not be held in a straitjacket, and that adaptations to the way business is done in each country and to the particular statistical data available should be made as more experience with the system accumulates and additional research is conducted. Perhaps two systems will evolve, one in which international comparability is strictly maintained, and one in which each country's own data and cyclical response mechanisms are used to best advantage—always avoiding, as far as possible, arbitrary differences in methodology.

The acid test of the plan to assemble comparable sets of indicators for each country according to the U.S. system lies in whether such data behave in the way U.S. experience has led one to expect. To perform this test long-run trends were fitted to each indicator, including those for the United States, cyclical turning points in the deviations from trend were identified, a chronology of growth-cycle turns for each country was set up to represent the peaks and troughs in aggregate economic activity (after allowance for trend), and the leads and lags of each trend-adjusted indicator were measured with respect to these growth-cycle turns. The trend-adjustment procedure, although subject to difficulties of its own, was essential to the identification of cyclical movements in countries that had experienced almost continuous rapid growth through the period from 1948 to 1973. Computer programs, carefully monitored to rule out dubious results, helped to enhance the objectivity of the data processing. A summary of the findings on cyclical timing based on composite indexes constructed from each group of indicators, is given in Table 6-3.

The leading indexes constructed from indicators corresponding to those classified as leading on the basis of U.S. data, lead as a rule in each of the other countries except France. The coincident indexes, of course, show virtually no lead or lag, because they and their components are used to determine the growth-cycle chronologies themselves. The lagging indexes lag. Significantly, because the grouping of the indicators is based on U.S. experience only and not on experi-

Table 6-1.   Cross-classification of U.S. Indicators by Economic Process and Cyclical Timing.

Economic Process	Cyclical Timing		
	Leading	Roughly Coincident	Lagging
Employment and unemployment	Average workweek, manufacturing. New unemployment insurance claims, inverted	Nonfarm employment. Unemployment, inverted	Long-duration unemployment, inverted
Production, income, consumption, and trade	New orders, consumer goods and materials[a]	Gross national product[a] Industrial production Personal income[a] Manufacturing and trade sales[a]	
Fixed capital investment	Formation of business enterprises Contracts and orders, plant and equipment[a] Building permits, housing		Investment expenditures, plant and equipment[a]
Inventories and inventory investment	Change in business inventories[a]		Business inventories[a]
Prices, costs, and profits	Industrial materials price index Stock price index Profits[a] Ratio, price to unit labor cost, nonfarm		Change in output per manhour, manufacturing, inverted
Money and credit	Change, consumer installment debt[a]		Commercial and industrial loans outstanding[a] Bank interest rates, business loans

Notes to Table 6-1

[a] In constant prices.

Sources: The list and classification is substantially the same as that prepared in 1966 and published in Geoffrey H. Moore and Julius Shiskin, *Indicators of Business Expansions and Contractions* (New York: NBER, 1967). The chief modification is that those series marked with [a] are converted to constant prices. The timing classification for each series is the same as shown in *Business Conditions Digest* for all turns (see Table 1, column1, in any recent issue), except as follows: Unemployment is unclassified (U) at all turns in BCD because it leads and lags at peaks and lags at troughs, but here it is classified roughly coincident, as in the 1966 list. Four series that here are in constant prices are shown in BCD only in current prices: change in consumer installment debt, investment expenditures for plant and equipment, commercial and industrial loans outstanding, and change in output per man-hour, manufacturing, inverted, which is the constant price equivalent of labor cost per unit of output. The constant price series are assigned the same classification as the current price series.

Table 6–2.   A Classification and List of International Economic Indicators.

United States	Canada	France
Leading		
1.0 Average workweek, manufacturing	1.0 Average workweek, manufacturing	1.0 Average workweek, manufacturing
2.0 New unemployment claims[a]	2.0 New unemployment claims[a]	2.0 New unemployment claims[a]
3.0 New orders, consumer goods[b]	3.1 New orders, durable goods[b]	3.1 Change in unfilled orders[c]
4.0 Formation of business enterprises	n.a.	n.a.
5.0 Contracts and orders, plant and equipment[b]	5.1 New orders, equipment[b]	
	5.2 Nonresidential building permits[b]	
6.0 Building permits, housing	6.0 Residential building permits	n.a.
7.0 Change in business inventories[b]	7.0 Change in business inventories[b]	6.0 Residential building permits
8.0 Industrial materials prices	8.0 Industrial materials prices	7.0 Change in stocks[b]
9.0 Stock price index	9.0 Stock price index	8.0 Raw materials prices
10.0 Profits[b]	10.0 Profits[b]	9.0 Stock price index
11.0 Ratio, price to labor cost	11.0 Ratio, price to labor cost	n.a.
12.0 Change in consumer debt[b]	12.0 Change in consumer debt[b]	11.0 Ratio, price to labor cost
		n.a.
Coincident		
13.0 Nonfarm employment	13.0 Nonfarm employment	13.0 Nonfarm employment
14.0 Unemployment rate[a]	14.0 Unemployment rate[a]	14.1 Registered unemployed, number[a]
15.0 Gross national product[b]	15.0 Gross national expenditures[b]	15.0 Gross domestic production[b]
16.0 Industrial production	16.0 Industrial production	16.0 Industrial production
17.0 Personal income[b]	17.0 Personal income[b]	n.a.
18.0 Manufacturing and trade sales[b]	18.1 Retail trade[b]	18.1 Retail sales[b]
Lagging		
19.0 Long-duration unemployment[a]	19.0 Long-duration unemployment[a]	19.0 Long-duration unemployment[a]
20.0 Plant and equipment investment[b]	20.0 Plant and equipment investment[b]	20.0 Plant and equipment investment[b]
21.0 Business inventories[b]	21.0 Business inventories[b]	21.0 Business inventories[b]
22.0 Productivity change, nonfarm[a]	22.1 Productivity change, manufacturing[a]	22.0 Productivity change, nonfarm[a]
23.0 Business loans outstanding[b]	23.0 Business loans outstanding[b]	23.0 Business loans outstanding[b]
24.0 Interest rates, business loans	24.0 Interest rates, business loans	24.0 Interest rates, business loans

United States	United Kingdom	West Germany
Leading	**Leading**	**Leading**
1.0 Average workweek, manufacturing	1.0 Average workweek, manufacturing	1.1 Short-hour workers[a]
2.0 New unemployment claims[a]	n.a.	2.0 Unemployment applicants[a]
3.0 New orders, consumer goods[b]	n.a.	n.a.
4.0 Formation of business enterprises	4.1 New companies registered	4.1 Insolvent enterprises[a]
	4.2 Business failures	
5.0 Contracts and orders, plant and equipment[b]	5.1 New orders, engineering industry[b]	5.1 New orders, investment goods[b]
	5.2 New orders, construction[b]	
6.0 Building permits, housing	6.0 Housing starts	6.1 Residential construction orders[b]
7.0 Change in business inventories[b]	7.0 Change in stocks[b]	7.0 Inventory change[b]
8.0 Industrial materials prices	8.0 Basic materials prices	8.0 Basic material prices[d]
9.0 Stock price index	9.0 Stock price index	9.0 Stock price index
10.0 Profits[b]	10.0 Profits[b]	10.1 Income from enterprise[b]
11.0 Ratio, price to labor cost	11.0 Ratio, price to labor cost	11.0 Ratio, price to labor cost
12.0 Change in consumer debt[b]	12.0 Increase in hire purchase debt[b]	12.0 Change in consumer debt[b]
Coincident	**Coincident**	**Coincident**
13.0 Nonfarm employment	13.0 Employment, industry	13.1 Employment, mining and manufacturing
14.0 Unemployment rate[a]	14.0 Registered unemployed, number[a]	14.0 Registered unemployment rate[a]
15.0 Gross national product[b]	15.0 Gross domestic product[b]	15.0 Gross national product[b]
16.0 Industrial production	16.0 Industrial production	16.0 Industrial production
17.0 Personal income[b]	17.0 Personal income[b]	17.0 Disposable income[b]
18.0 Manufacturing and trade sales[b]	18.1 Retail sales[b]	18.1 Manufacturing sales[b]
		18.2 Retail trade[b]
Lagging	**Lagging**	**Lagging**
19.0 Long-duration unemployment[a]	19.0 Long-duration unemployment[a]	n.a.
20.0 Plant and equipment investment[b]	20.0 Plant and equipment expenditure[b]	20.0 Plant and equipment expenditure[b]
21.0 Business inventories[b]	21.0 Business inventories[b]	21.0 Business inventories[b]
22.0 Productivity change, nonfarm[a]	22.0 Productivity change, industry[a]	22.1 Productivity change, industry[a]
23.0 Business loans outstanding[b]	23.1 Industrial and agricultural loans outstanding[b]	23.1 Bank loans outstanding[b]
24.0 Interest rates, business loans	24.0 Interest rates, business loans	24.1 Interest rates, large loans

(Table 6–2. continued overleaf)

Table 6-2. continued

United States	Italy	Japan
Leading	**Leading**	**Leading**
1.0 Average workweek, manufacturing[a]	1.1 Monthly hours, industry	1.1 Overtime worked, manufacturing
2.0 New unemployment claims[a]	n.a.	n.a.
3.0 New orders, consumer goods[b]	3.1 Change in unfilled orders[c]	n.a.
4.0 Formation of business enterprises	4.1 Declared bankruptcies[a]	4.1 Business failures[a]
5.0 Contracts and orders, plant and equipment[b]	n.a.	5.0 New orders, machinery and construction[b]
6.0 Building permits, housing	6.0 Residential building permits	6.1 Dwelling units started
7.0 Change in business inventories[b]	n.a.	7.0 Change in inventories[b]
8.0 Industrial materials prices	n.a.	8.0 Raw materials prices
9.0 Stock price index	9.0 Stock price index	9.0 Stock price index
10.0 Profits[b]	n.a.	10.0 Profits[b]
11.0 Ratio, price to labor cost	11.0 Ratio, price to labor cost	11.0 Ratio, price to labor cost
12.0 Change in consumer debt[b]	n.a.	12.1 Change in consumer and housing debt[b]
Coincident	**Coincident**	**Coincident**
13.0 Nonfarm employment	13.0 Nonfarm employment	13.0 Nonfarm employment, regular workers
14.0 Unemployment rate[a]	14.0 Unemployment rate[a]	14.0 Unemployment rate[a]
15.0 Gross national product[b]	15.0 Gross domestic product[b]	15.0 Gross national expenditures[b]
16.0 Industrial production	16.0 Industrial production	16.0 Industrial production
17.0 Personal income[b]	n.a.	17.1 Wage and salary income[b]
18.0 Manufacturing and trade sales[b]	18.1 Retail sales[b]	18.1 Retail sales[b]
Lagging	**Lagging**	**Lagging**
19.0 Long-duration unemployment[a]	n.a.	n.a.
20.0 Plant and equipment investment[b]	20.1 Plant and equipment expenditures[b]	20.0 Plant and equipment expenditure[b]
21.0 Business inventories[b]	21.0 Business inventories[b]	21.0 Business inventories[b]
22.0 Productivity change, nonfarm[a]	n.a.	22.1 Productivity change, industry[a]
23.0 Business loans outstanding[b]	n.a.	23.1 Total loans outstanding[b]
24.0 Interest rates, business loans	24.0 Interest rates, business loans	24.1 Interest rates, business loans

Notes to Table 6-2

[a] Treated invertedly in the composite indexes.

[b] In constant prices.

[c] Change in net balance of survey responses.

[d] Not included in leading index for West Germany.

Note: Series numbers are based on the U.S. list. The digits after the decimal indicate whether the series is substantially the same as the U.S. series (0), or only roughly equivalent (1 or 2).

Source: Center for International Business Cycle Research, Rutgers University.

Table 6-3.   Cyclical Timing of Economic Indicators during Growth Cycles, Seven Countries.

| | United States 1948– 1981 | Canada 1948– 1981 | United Kingdom 1952– 1981 | West Germany 1950– 1981 | France 1951– 1981 | Italy 1956– 1977 | Japan 1953– 1975 | Averages: | |
								Six Countries Except U.S.	Seven Countries
At growth-cycle peaks									
Lagging index, inverted	-15	-13	-24	-12	-12	-14	-14	-15	-15
Leading index	-2	-2	-10	-7	0	-9	-4	-5	-5
Coincident index	+1	0	0	0	+2	0	-1	0	0
Lagging index	+5	+5	+7	+2	+2	+2	+8	+5	+5
At growth-cycle troughs									
Lagging index, inverted	-11	-16	-19	-18	-16	-7	-14	-15	-14
Leading index	-2	-4	-9	-2	0	-6	-5	-4	-4
Coincident index	0	0	0	0	0	+3	0	0	0
Lagging index	+6	+4	+8	+4	+5	+10	+8	+6	+6

Source: Center for International Business Cycle Research, Rutgers University.

ence in the country itself, the sequence of turns among the leading, coincident, and lagging groups in each country corresponds roughly to the sequence in the United States. The detailed results show that this sequence has been repeated at virtually every turn in each country. Moreover, this consistency includes the tendency for the turns in the lagging indexes to precede opposite turns in the leading indexes, corresponding to the economic logic noted previously (compare the top line with the second line in each panel of the table). The sequences do not appear to differ systematically from one country to another; hence it is appropriate to average them (see the last two columns of the table). The average sequence is set forth schematically in Figure 6-1. Since the growth-cycle chronologies and the recorded leads and lags are based on trend-adjusted data, the rising and falling phases are roughly symmetrical, as are the intervals into which they are subdivided by the turns in the indexes.

Nevertheless, it is true that there are wide variations in the lengths of lead or lag from one cycle to another or from one indicator to another. The system is neither simple nor mechanical. But the historical record is available to help guide current interpretations, and it appears to support the basic hypothesis underlying the scheme, namely, that the U.S. indicator system is broadly applicable overseas.

The composite indexes referred to in Table 6-3 have been computed using a method employed for some years by the U.S. Depart-

Figure 6-1. Average Sequence of Cyclical Turns in Three Composite Indexes during Growth Cycles, Seven Countries.

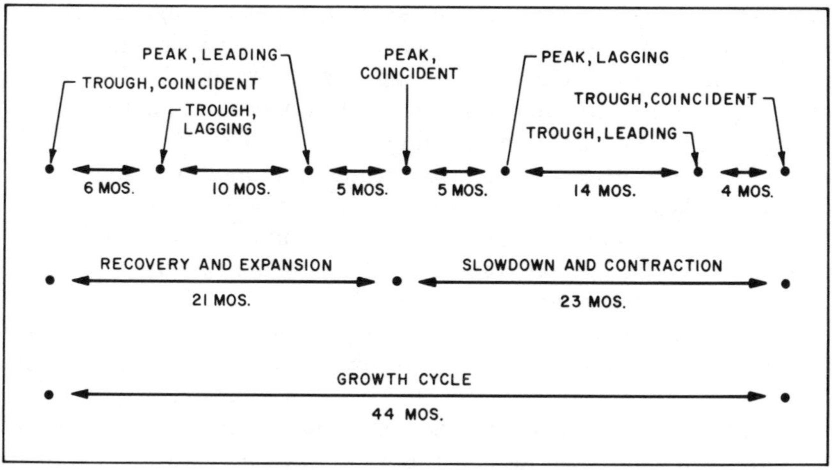

Source: Table 6-3.

ment of Commerce. The indexes are constructed so that their trend rate of growth during 1966–1976 is equal to that of real GNP for the country concerned during the same period. The procedure corrects for the rather haphazard long-run trends that are likely to result from combinations of indicators that, despite efforts to obtain comparability, are not precisely the same in the several countries. In addition to the indexes with trend equal to the trend in GNP, indexes are available with the long-run trend eliminated. These depict the growth cycles discussed previously. The trend rates of growth in the individual indicators are of interest in themselves for the purposes of analyzing each country's long-run rate of growth.[2] Finally, short-run rates of growth in the indexes have been compiled, based on changes over successive intervals of six months or twelve months. These rates also depict the growth cycles, but they do not depend upon any trend-fitting procedure and hence avoid the uncertainty that is inevitably attached to bringing such trends up to date.

Although the procedure ensures that the long-run trend in the indexes will be approximately the same as the trend in real GNP, the fluctuations in the indexes are larger than those in GNP, partly because most of the components are more sensitive than GNP, partly because most of them are monthly rather than quarterly. Another reason is that the average month-to-month change (without regard to sign) in each country's industrial production index is used as a standard by which to adjust the month-to-month change in the index, and industrial production usually undergoes wider swings than GNP. The indexes thus provide measures of economic performance based not on a single indicator but on a group of significant indicators that are relatively homogeneous with respect to cyclical timing. As a consequence of both the cyclical homogeneity and the variety of economic data included, the indexes are relatively free of the month-to-month irregularities that beset most economic time series.

Figure 6–2 compares the leading and coincident indexes for the United States and for six other countries combined (Canada, United Kingdom, West Germany, France, Italy, and Japan) during 1972–1982. In the combined index each country's index is weighted by the country's GNP in 1970 (expressed in U.S. dollars). Figure 6–3 shows the growth rates for the same indexes.[3] Both charts demonstrate the capacity of the leading indexes to keep a few months ahead of the broad measures of economic performance contained in the coincident indexes.

Another illustration of the kind of sequence that can be expected by monitoring the leading and the coincident indicators, covering a longer historical period, may be found in Figure 6–4. Here the

Figure 6-2. Leading and Coincident Indexes, United States and Six Other Countries, 1972–1982.

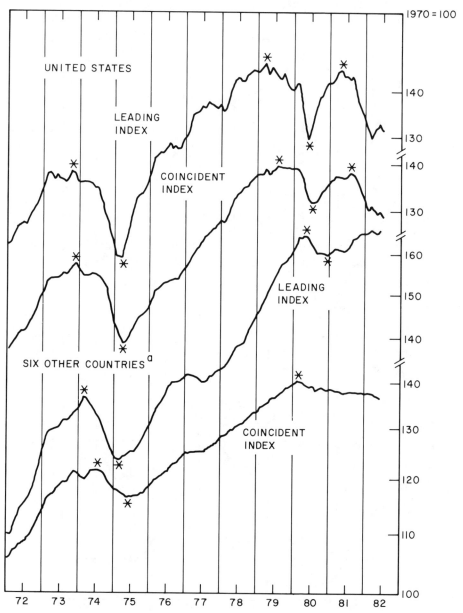

* Specific cycle peak or trough.

a Canada, United Kingdom, West Germany, France, Italy, Japan.

Source: Center for International Business Cycle Research, Rutgers University.

Figure 6-3. Growth Rates in Leading and Coincident Indexes, United States and Six Other Countries, 1972–1982 (*Twelve-Month Smoothed Percentage Change*).

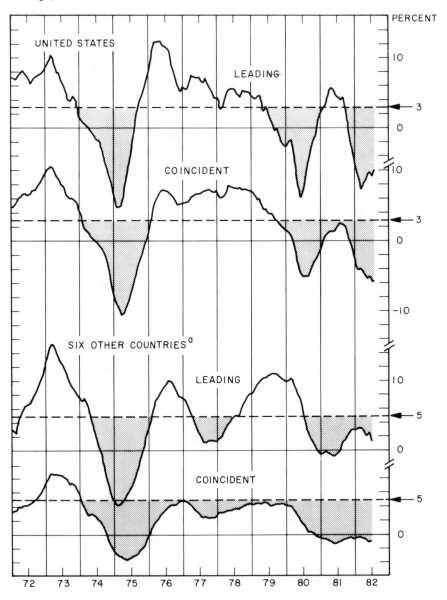

Note: Arrows indicate rate of change, 1966–1976, in the indexes and in real GNP.
[a] Canada, United Kingdom, West Germany, France, Italy, Japan.
Source: Center for International Business Cycle Research, Rutgers University.

Figure 6-4. Growth Rates in Leading Index and in Industrial Production, Western Europe, 1956–1982 (*Twelve-month smoothed percentage change*).

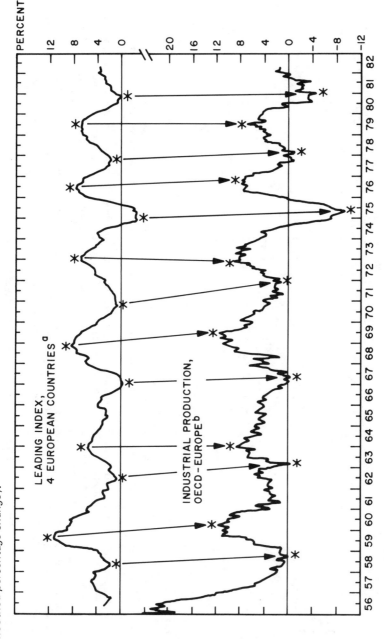

LEADING INDEX, 4 EUROPEAN COUNTRIES [a]

INDUSTRIAL PRODUCTION, OECD-EUROPE [b]

[a] United Kingdom, West Germany, France, Italy.

[b] Includes in addition to the above four countries: Austria, Belgium, Finland, Greece, Ireland, Luxembourg, The Netherlands, Norway, Portugal, Spain, Sweden, and Switzerland.

Sources: Leading Index, Center for International Business Cycle Research; Industrial Production Index, Organization for Economic Cooperation and Development.

Table 6-4. Leading Indexes and Industrial Production, Seven Countries (*Leads and Lags at Turning Points in Rates of Change*).

	Period Covered	Number of			Total	Average Lead (−) or Lag (+), in Months
		Leads	Coincidence	Lags		
United States	1958–1979	10	2	0	12	−3
Canada	1958–1979	6	3	2	11	−1
United Kingdom	1957–1979	5	3	3	11	−4
West Germany	1959–1979	8	—	2	10	−4
France	1959–1979	7	1	5	13	−3
Italy	1958–1979	9	1	1	11	−4
Japan	1958–1979	10	2	1	13	−2
Total, seven countries		55	12	14	81	−3
Composite indexes: Western Europe[a]	1956–1979	9	1	1	11	−4
Six countries[b] excluding United States	1972–1979	4	0	0	4	−2

Note: The rates of change in both the leading and industrial production indexes are percentage changes over twelve months, smoothed, as explained in the text.

[a] The leading index, compiled by the Center, includes the United Kingdom, West Germany, France and Italy, weighted by their real GNP, in U.S. dollars, in 1970. The industrial production index, compiled by OECD, includes the above four countries plus Austria, Belgium, Luxembourg, Finland, Greece, Ireland, The Netherlands, Norway, Portugal, Spain, Sweden, and Switzerland, weighted by gross domestic product originating in industry.

[b] Canada, United Kingdom, West Germany, France, Italy, Japan. In the leading index, compiled by the Center, the countries are weighted by their real GNP, in U.S. dollars, in 1970. In the industrial production index, compiled by the U.S. Department of Commerce, the countries are weighted by gross domestic product originating in industry, in U.S. dollars, in 1975.

Source: Center for International Business Cycle Research, Rutgers University.

growth rates in the composite leading index for four European countries are compared with the industrial production index for OECD Europe. Industrial production is one of the most widely used economic indicators around the world, and it is one of the components of our coincident indexes. Many countries do not have quarterly estimates of gross national product but do have monthly figures on industrial production. Covering manufacturing and mining and often including utilities and construction activity, the index pertains to a sector of the economy that is highly sensitive to business cycles.

For all these reasons it is important to watch the industrial production index, and to contemplate where it is going next. Here is where the leading indexes can be helpful. The comparison in Figure 6-4 reveals that the swings in the growth of industrial production in Europe correspond to those in our leading index with considerable fidelity. Detailed study shows this to be true also of the data for each country. Furthermore, the turns in the leading index growth rates usually precede those in industrial production and are easier to recognize because the leading indexes are smoother and less influenced by erratic movements. As Table 6-4 shows, leads outnumber lags by nearly four to one. The average lead time for all seven countries covered by the table is three months.

The economic basis for this relationship is that the components of the leading index represent actions of an anticipatory nature that are especially sensitive to changes in cost and profit prospects and the state of demand. New orders for equipment, contracts placed for construction work, and housing starts are obvious examples. The length of the average workweek is one of the first adjustments made when manufacturers detect a shift in demand and reduce or increase overtime work or the number of part-time employees. By combining a dozen or so of such measures into a single index, the idiosyncrasies of any single one of them are muted, and the result is a leading index possessing the properties described. These properties do not make it an infallible instrument for appraising the outlook in any country. But when a businessman judges the future of his company, he does not regard the current state of his orderbooks as an infallible guide either. That does not stop him from wanting to know what state they are in. It is the same with the leading indexes. They reflect actions that are likely to affect production a few months hence, and consequently are useful guides to the state of the market.

RECESSION-RECOVERY PATTERNS

Once an historical chronology of business cycles or growth cycles has been established and a collection of indicators assembled, it becomes possible to compare the current behavior of the indicators with their patterns of change during the corresponding stages of previous cycles. Although no two business cycles are exactly alike, there are family resemblances, and they can be employed systematically to evaluate the current situation and glimpse what lies ahead.

Methods of making such comparisons have been employed for many years in the United States. The Commerce Department's *Business Conditions Digest* regularly carries charts of this type, and the Rutgers Center for International Business Cycle Research issues periodic reports utilizing the technique.[4] The comparisons help one to anticipate what is typical business cycle performance and to observe whether current performance is in line with it or not. Although every business cycle has its own surprises, partly because of policy actions taken, many developments are not surprising, having occurred many times before. Hence a look at what has happened during the later stages of past business cycles is also a look ahead.

An example of how this works in practice is provided by Figure 6-5. The behavior of the U.S. leading and coincident indexes during the recession that started from the business cycle peak of July 1981 is compared with their average pattern during the seven preceding recessions. These seven can be divided into two groups: four recessions that were relatively sharp (1949, 1954, 1958, 1975) and three that were mild (1961, 1969, 1980). Such a chart gives one a quick grasp of how mild or severe a current recession is, how it compares in duration, whether the usual signs of recovery are developing, and so on.

IMPLICATIONS FOR FOREIGN TRADE

The effect upon the economy of one country of a slowdown in economic growth in other countries is likely to be most visible in that country's exports. The volume of exports depends upon the trend of economic activity in the country to which the exports go. Ordinarily this is measured by gross national product or industrial production, both of which are among the coincident indicators. Since the leading indicators, as we have seen, usually anticipate the movement of the coincident by several months, the leading indexes for the trading partners may also anticipate the movements in exports to them. A number of tests of this hypothesis have been made, using the leading indexes to forecast the rate of change in the volume of trade to and from particular countries or groups of countries, and for trade as a whole as well as for various commodity groupings. The results of this research show that a substantial proportion of the year-to-year

Figure 6-5. Patterns of Current and Previous Recessions.

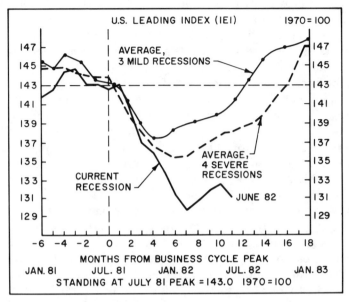

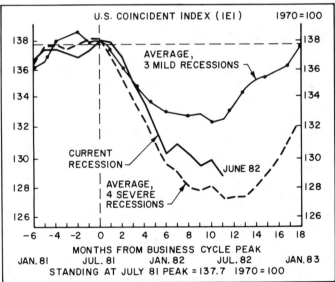

Note: The vertical line at zero represents business cycle *peak dates*. The current and previous business cycles are aligned so that their peaks fall on this line. The horizontal line represents the *level* of the data at business cycle peaks. The historical data are converted to indexes with their business-cycle peak levels equal to the current business cycle peak level.

changes in trade flows can usually be accounted for in this manner. Figure 6-6 displays the results of one such test, where the percentage rates of growth in U.S. exports to all countries, after allowance for changes in prices, are compared with the prior changes in an export-weighted leading index for the six countries outside the United States. Despite the fact that exports are affected by many other factors not explicitly taken account of in this simple model, the method tracks the major swings fairly well.

The same method can be employed to forecast the exports of any country, developed or developing, that trades with the industrial countries for which we have leading indexes. We have already obtained similar results for the exports of the United Kingdom, West Germany, Japan, and for a major group of developing countries. Naturally this method by itself has serious limitations, since it ignores other factors that influence the quantities of goods exported. Changes in exchange rates, tariffs and other barriers or incentives to trade, supply conditions, and pricing policies are taken into account only insofar as they affect the leading indicators for the importing countries. Yet, in view of the importance of trade flows and trade balances in the economic relations among nations, even a modest contribution to our economic intelligence in appraising trade prospects is worthwhile.

IMPLICATIONS FOR INFLATION

Growth cycles are closely associated with the rate of inflation. Indeed, as far as U.S. experience is concerned, declines in the rate of inflation have been associated with virtually every slowdown or contraction in real economic growth and have not occurred at other times. Both parts of this proposition are important. Declines in the rate of inflation have not been as rare as is commonly believed, but they have occurred only at times of slower economic growth, never at times of rapid growth. The proposition appears to be true in other countries as well as in the United States.

The international indicator system is helpful in examining the evidence, and so is the concept of the growth cycle described earlier. This distinguishes periods of rapid growth from periods of slow growth by reference to a long-run trend. Trend-adjusted data rise as long as the short-run rate of growth exceeds the long-run rate. They decline as long as the short-run rate is less than the long-run rate. The peaks and troughs in trend-adjusted data, therefore, delineate periods of rapid and slow growth relative to the trend rate.

Figure 6-6. U.S. Exports and an Export-Oriented Leading Index.

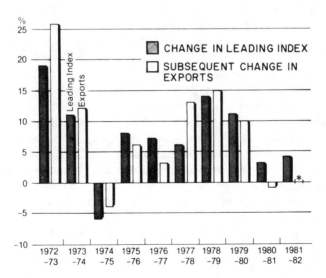

* Not available.

Note: For 1972–1973, the change in the leading index is based on the ratio of the December 1972 index to the average index during the preceding twelve months. The change in exports is based on totals for 1972 and 1973. Similar calculations are made for other years.

For the United States, a chronology of growth cycles based on trend-adjusted data for the physical volume of aggregate economic activity is used in Figure 6-7 as a backdrop against which to examine the movements in the rate of change in two price indexes. The index of industrial materials prices—that is, prices of metals, textiles, rubber, and the like—shows an especially close relation to the growth cycle. Downswings in the rate of change in these prices occurred in every period of slow growth or recession, and upswings occurred in every period of rapid growth. Often, as in 1956 and 1959, the downswings began before the onset of the slow-growth periods. This price index is one of the leading indicators in Table 6-1; here it leads not only the growth cycle but also the rate of change in the consumer price index (CPI), the bottom line in Figure 6-7. The CPI, which of course includes the prices of services as well as commodities, responds to the growth cycle as well, but often with a lag of a year or more. The lags have been so long, especially in recent years, that sometimes the rate of inflation in the CPI has risen almost throughout the period of slow growth or recession, giving the erroneous impression that slow growth had no influence on inflation.

Watching both price indexes together, and bearing in mind their differences in sensitivity and tendency to lag, enables one to see that growth cycles have pervasive influences upon the price structure. The change one sees in the consumer price index (as, for example, the decline in its rate of increase from autumn 1974 to spring 1976) is a lagged response to or reflection of similar developments in commodity markets that react far more promptly to changes in demand pressures or supply conditions.

Corresponding data and growth cycle chronologies for the six other countries covered in the international indicator system suggest that similar relations are to be found in these countries. Conditions that produce rates of economic growth greatly in excess of long-run trend are conducive to an acceleration of inflation, while conditions that make for slow growth or recession are conducive to a reduced rate of inflation or even to deflation. When ordering is brisk and order backlogs accumulate, sellers have opportunities and incentives to raise prices, and buyers are less averse to paying them. Costs of production tend to creep up, labor turnover increases, control over efficiency and waste tends to decline. New commitments for investment are made in an optimistic environment, building up demand for limited supplies of skilled labor and construction equipment. Credit to build inventories is more readily available and is in greater demand, even if higher interest rates must be paid for it, thereby raising costs. Labor unions see better opportunities to obtain favorable con-

Figure 6–7. Rates of Change in Leading Index and in Two Price Indexes during Growth Cycles, United States, 1955–1982 (*Twelve-Month Smoothed Percentage Change*).

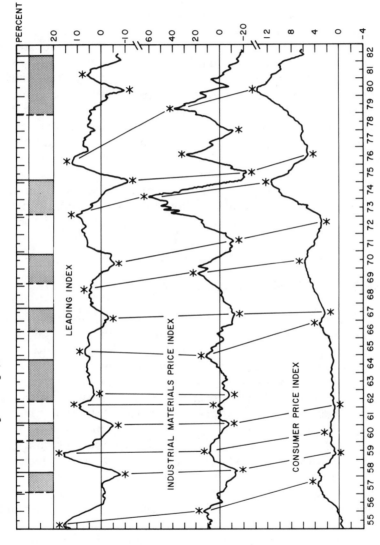

Note: Shaded areas represent slowdowns in economic growth as determined from trend-adjusted measures of aggregate output, income, sales, and employment. Lines connect corresponding peaks and troughs in the rates of change in the three indexes.

Sources: Leading Index, Center for International Business Cycle Research, Rutgers University. Industrial Materials Price Index: 1948–1961, Department of Commerce, Bureau of Economic Analysis; 1962 on, Journal of Commerce. Consumer Price Index, U.S. Department of Labor, Bureau of Labor Statistics.

tract settlements, and their members are more willing to strike to get them. All these conditions apply to more and more firms and industries and produce upward pressure on more and more prices. Indeed, one of the principal factors underlying a rising rate of inflation in the general price level is not just that some prices rise in big jumps but that more prices rise at more frequent intervals.

During periods of slow growth or actual decline in aggregate economic activity, the opposite conditions prevail. Firms and industries cut back their output, reduce or eliminate overtime, shave costs, give bigger discounts off list prices, reduce inventories, repay bank debt, and postpone new investment projects or stretch out existing ones. Quit rates decline, indicating that workers feel they must hang on to their jobs, and labor demands for pay raises become more conservative. Interest rates drop. As price increases become less widespread and less frequent, and as more price cutting takes place, the rate of inflation declines.

Since many of the processes sketched here are represented among the leading and lagging indicators, they can also be employed to monitor inflation, evaluate its twists and turns, and judge its prospects. We hope, therefore, that this potential use for the indicators presented will not be overlooked.

FURTHER RESEARCH AND DEVELOPMENT

A continuing research and development program is essential if the system of international economic indicators described is to be used effectively and improved. As already noted, the Rutgers Center for International Business Cycle Research is conducting such a program. Coverage of the indicator system has already been extended to many additional countries, including Sweden, the Netherlands, Belgium, Switzerland, Australia, South Korea, and Taiwan. Attention is being given to speedier access to data, new types of graphic displays, and other analytical tools. Methods of trend-adjusting current data are being tested, as well as methods of defining early warning signals of recession and recovery. Detecting an international recession promptly and measuring its scope and severity, appraising trade prospects, and getting early warning signals of new inflationary trends are matters of vast consequence to the peoples of the world. If the contents of this book contributes to these tasks, it will have served its end.

NOTES TO CHAPTER 6

1. For a list of NBER publications that explain the behavior of and relationships among particular indicators, see Chapter 21.

2. The method of trend-fitting is described in Charlotte Boschan and Walter Ebanks, "The Phase-Average Trend: A New Way of Measuring Economic Growth," In *Proceedings of the Business and Economics Statistics Section,* American Statistical Association, 1978.

3. The growth rates are calculated by taking the ratio of the current month's index to the average index for the twelve months ending six months ago. This method produces a rate of growth (or decline) that is similar to but smoother than, the percentage change in the index from the same month a year ago. The twelve-month average smooths away erratic factors, such as a strike or unusual weather, that may have affected the year-ago figure. The method does not, of course, smooth out any erratic influences affecting the current month. An alternative method is to take the ratio of the current months's index to the average of the twelve immediately preceding months, and express the result at an annual rate. This gives a more up-to-date estimate of the growth rate than the one shown in Figure 6-3, but also is more affected by erratic movements in the current month.

4. *Recession-Recovery Watch* has been a bimonthly publication of the Center since 1979.

Chapter 7

Presenting Employment and Unemployment Statistics in a Business Cycle Context

SUMMARY

"Last year was a good one for the United States. We reached all of our major economic goals for 1977. Four million new jobs were created—an all-time record—and the number of unemployed dropped by more than a million. Unemployment right now is the lowest it has been since 1974, and not since World War II has such a high percentage of American people been employed."[1] These are the words of President Carter, in his first State of the Union message, delivered January 20, 1978. For balance, clarity, and succinctness the statement cannot be faulted. It is a fitting text for some suggestions aimed at improving the presentation of employment and unemployment statistics.

I shall first summarize my recommendations and then explain and elaborate the arguments for each of them.

1. The Bureau of Labor Statistics should publish and emphasize in its press releases and articles the percentage of the working age population that is employed, the percentage unemployed, the percentage in the armed forces, and the percentage not in the labor force. These figures, which add to 100 percent, should be shown not only for the total working age population, but also for each major age, sex, and racial group and for various geographic areas.

Reprinted from Background Paper No. 22, National Commission on Employment and Unemployment Statistics, August 1978. The original title of the background paper was "Improving the Presentation of Employment and Unemployment Statistics."

2. The Bureau of Labor Statistics should publish a monthly chart-book of employment and unemployment statistics and a companion yearbook that would facilitate interpretation of current information. It might be called *Employment Conditions Digest* (*ECD*).

3. The Bureau of Labor Statistics should present and analyze leading, coincident, and lagging labor market indicators, including an analysis of the economic rationale underlying their behavior and a historical record. These should be included in *ECD*.

4. To aid in appraising the state of the economy, the Bureau of Labor Statistics should publish comparisons of current changes in employment and unemployment with corresponding changes during earlier periods of recession or recovery, as the case may be. These also should be included in *ECD*.

5. The Bureau of Labor Statistics should develop a number of readily available statistical series that are needed to facilitate analysis of the employment situation and should also develop a monthly statistical report on the number and kind of job vacancies that are available.

6. A continuing audit of employment statistics, conducted by an authoritative agency or group such as the National Research Council, should be established to follow up the recommendations of the present commission and to advise on the needs for new data and on problems concerning existing data as they emerge in the years ahead.

EMPLOYMENT AND UNEMPLOYMENT RATES

As President Carter's State of the Union message illustrates, employment and unemployment do not change at the same pace. During 1977 an unprecedented number of new jobs were created—four million—but unemployment was reduced by only one million, not an unprecedented decline at all.[2] The percentage of the population with jobs reached a peacetime high, but unemployment receded only to the level of 1974, when the economy was still in recession. Thus the employment and unemployment figures can point to different conclusions about the state of the economy.

The most widely used figure pertaining to the unemployment situation—which interestingly enough the President did not mention—is the unemployment rate. This is the percentage of the labor force that is unemployed. The figure for December 1977 was 6.4 percent, after seasonal adjustment. Since the labor force is the sum total of the employed and the unemployed, the employment rate, on this base, is simply the complement of the unemployment rate—93.6 percent in December, seasonally adjusted. No new information is added by this employment rate—its movements are always exactly equal and opposite to those of the unemployment rate.

The unemployment rate is unquestionably a useful statistic. Over a long period of time, as the population grows, the number employed and unemployed grow with it more or less, so that in comparing unemployment with some earlier period one needs to take this growth into account. The question is whether using the labor force as the base is the best way to do it. Can another way be found that would preserve some of the information about employment that is lost when the labor force is used as the base?

The answer carries with it some important advantages. An appropriate base is the population of working age. This obviously is the most direct way to take account of the growth in population. Ignoring those under sixteen years of age is reasonable, since in many instances these children are below the legal working age. Perhaps some upper age limit should be used also, but that is a far more controversial matter, since people can be found working at almost any age. For example, in December 1977, 1.2 million persons seventy years and over were employed, or about 8 percent of the population of that age; 40,000 were unemployed. One cannot, therefore, omit this age group (which is the top age group reported in the statistics) without omitting some of the employed and some of the unemployed. One might also omit the armed forces—that is, include only the civilian population in the base. However, since for some purposes it is desirable to consider those in the armed forces as employed, and in any case a marked change in their number, as in wartime, will affect civilian employment and unemployment, it seems best to include them in the population base and to calculate the percentage that each group—employed, unemployed, armed forces, and not in the labor force—constitutes of the total. All these percentages would then be on the same base and hence comparable with one another, and they can be combined or compared as one wishes.

This simple shift in the base—from labor force to total working age population—has a number of important effects. Probably the most important is that it allows the employment and unemployment percentages to move independently of one another. Most of the time they will move in opposite directions, the percentage employed rising and the percentage unemployed falling, or vice versa, but sometimes the percentage employed will rise and the percentage unemployed will rise also, which forces one to consider the question whether things are getting better or getting worse on grounds other than arithmetic.

Consider, for example, Table 7—1, which compares the situation in March 1978, the thirty-sixth month of the recovery that began in March 1975, with the situation in the corresponding months of the five preceding recoveries that lasted as long as thirty-six months. A number of interesting points emerge: (1) the percentage employed was higher in March 1978 than in the corresponding month of any of the previous recoveries; (2) the percentage in the armed forces was smaller than in any previous recovery; (3) the percentage unemployed was higher than in any previous recovery (having increased rather steadily from one recovery period to the next); and (4) the percentage outside the labor force was smaller than in any previous recovery.

Considering unemployment alone, the current recovery has been the least auspicious of the five. In fact, the unemployment figures suggest that recoveries have become steadily weaker ever since 1949. The employment figures do not show any such trend. According to them, the current recovery is the best ever by a full percentage point, which at present population levels means about 1.5 million people. That is, if the current recovery had merely equaled rather than exceeded the previous record, a million and a half fewer people would have been employed than actually were employed in March 1978. This is surely important information, and it would be completely obscured if one looked solely at the unemployment rates or at their obverse, employment rates calculated as a percentage of the labor force.

The steady reduction in the percentage of the population engaged in the armed forces raises the question what effect this reduction has had upon employment and unemployment. The figures do not answer this question, of course, but they do show that if the armed forces are counted together with the civilian employed, the March 1978 employment percentage is still the highest.

Finally, the current low percentage of the working age population not in the labor force suggests that many of those previously outside the labor force have now entered it, which implies that this group constitutes a kind of reserve labor force. While many of those not in the labor force are unable to work for various reasons (family responsibilities, school attendance, or illness), others report that they both want and intend to seek work in the near future or would do so if the job market improves. The fact that the proportion of the working age population not in the labor force has become smaller means that shifts do take place and that this group includes many potential employees. The reduction in this secondary labor reserve has, therefore, offset in some respects the rise in the unemployed, the primary labor reserve. Some of those who previously reported that they were

Table 7–1. Distribution of the Working Age Population in the Thirty-sixth Month of Five Recovery Periods.

Thirty-sixth Month of Recovery	Percentage Distribution of the Population Sixteen and Older					Number of Persons Sixteen and Older
	Civilian Employed	Armed Forces	Unem- ployed	Not in Labor Force	Total	
March 1978	58.2	1.3	3.8	36.7	100.0	160,313,000
November 1973	57.3	1.5	2.9	38.3	100.0	149,208,000
February 1964	54.4	2.2	3.1	40.4	100.0	126,440,000
May 1957	55.7	2.5	2.4	39.5	100.0	114,851,000
October 1952	55.1	3.3	1.7	40.0	100.0	109,164,000

Note: A sixth recovery period, beginning April 1958, lasted only twenty-four months and hence is omitted. The unemployment percentages shown above are much lower than the unemployment rates commonly used because the latter are percentages of the civilian labor force (employed plus unemployed) rather than of the total working age population. Otherwise they show much the same pattern. Starting with March 1978, the unemployment rates in the five recoveries are 6.1 percent, 4.8 percent, 5.4 percent, 4.1 percent, 3 percent.

Source: U.S. Bureau of Labor Statistics.

not seeking work are now doing so, shifting from the secondary to the primary reserve. Other former secondary reserve members have found jobs and are counted as employed. Under these circumstances, the unemployment rate does not accurately measure the tightness or ease in the labor market. Changes in the secondary labor reserve must also be considered. A reduction in this secondary reserve clearly affects the economy's capacity to expand employment. Hence it is important to take it into account when considering the subject of wage and price inflation.[3]

These observations demonstrate some of the analytical advantages of using the working age population as the base for an employment rate and an unemployment rate. It keeps the employment side of the picture in plain sight, with the rates comparable because they are figured on the same base, but not redundant because they are free to move independently. It does not, in my view, denigrate the unemployed, though it does make the percentage smaller, since the population is larger than the labor force. This simply means that a "high unemployment rate" will mean a figure of 4 or 5 percent rather than 7 or 8 percent, and a "low unemployment rate" will mean a figure of 2 or 2.5 percent rather than 3 or 4 percent.

Several other advantages attach to the use of the population base. One is that the population, as estimated, grows quite steadily from month to month and year to year, much more steadily than the labor force. Consider the month to month changes in both during 1977, as given in Table 7−2. Obviously, the labor force fluctuated far more widely than the population. Since it is also a smaller number, the differences in the relative fluctuations are even wider. This simply means that the labor force is an unstable base upon which to calculate rates. One reason for this is that the labor force, being the sum of the employed and the unemployed, is subject to the sampling fluctuations inherent in a survey. The population is largely an extrapolated estimate, not subject to sampling error. Another reason is that the labor force is subject to the uncertainty of identifying who is employed and who is unemployed. There is much less uncertainty about who is in the population.

The labor force columns in Table 7−2 point to another advantage of the population base—it doesn't have to be seasonally adjusted. Without seasonal adjustment the labor force would, of course, fluctuate even more widely, but since there is an inherent uncertainty in the measurement of seasonal variations, the adjusted figures are subject to this additional source of error. Each year, for example, the seasonally adjusted figures for the preceding year are revised. The fluctuations in the labor force as estimated during 1977 were differ-

Table 7−2.   **Changes in Labor Force and Population, 1977.**

Change from Preceding Month (thousands of persons)

	Civilian Labor Force, Seasonally Adjusted		Population
	A	B	
January	−444	−217	205
February	629	601	203
March	394	303	198
April	221	123	204
May	398	415	242
June	483	391	228
July	−336	−245	226
August	392	307	217
September	171	142	215
October	234	315	220
November	896	806	188
December	−72	42	214

A = before revision of seasonal factors in January 1978.
B = after revision of seasonal factors in January 1978.
Source: Bureau of Labor Statistics.

ent from what they were when reestimated in January 1978 (see A and B in table). These revisions are one source of revision in the unemployment rate as presently calculated—on the labor force base. The population figures, which are estimated in such a way as to exclude seasonal variations, are not subject to such revision.

Of course, since the seasonal in unemployment itself is subject to revision, the use of the population as the base for the unemployment rate does not eliminate revisions entirely. But it does not compound the problem by mixing it up with revisions in the seasonal for employment (the other component of the labor force). In this connection it should be noted that the revisions in the seasonal adjustment of employment data are usually smaller than those for unemployment. Hence the revisions in the percentage of the population that is employed are likely to be smaller than those in the percentage that is unemployed. The revisions made in January 1978 covering the preceding year provide a clear example of this point. The revisions in the seasonally adjusted number employed were smaller than those in the number unemployed in ten of the twelve months of 1977. The unemployment percentage was revised twice as frequently as the

employment percentage. Moreover, the revisions of the unemployment figures changed the pattern during the year from near stability
to rather steady improvement; the revisions of the employment
figures had no such effect. They showed steady improvement
throughout the year, apart from a slowdown in July and August,
both before and after revision.[4]

The working age population not only provides a firm statistical
base upon which to calculate employment and unemployment rates;
it is also readily understood by the public, far more so than the labor
force concept. "Jobs per capita," which is essentially what the percentage employed is, can be readily understood by everyone. The
statement that in June 1978, fifty-nine persons out of a hundred had
jobs, four were unemployed, one was in the armed forces, and thirty-
six were neither employed nor seeking work tells a simple but effective story. The improvement since the bottom of the recession, in
March 1975, when only fifty-five had jobs, five were unemployed,
one was in the armed forces, and thirty-nine were neither employed
nor seeking work is equally clear. Comparisons with previous periods
of high employment are more ambiguous, but the ambiguity is in the
situation, not in the complexity of the figures. In one of the most
prosperous years of 1950s, for example, fifty-five had jobs, two were
unemployed, three were in the armed forces, and forty were neither
employed nor seeking work. This was in 1953, when the unemployment rate was about half the 1978 figure. Relative to the population,
however, more people have jobs now than then. The difference is
that more are now unemployed—that is, seeking work—and fewer
are neither employed nor seeking work. The rise in unemployment
has not come about through a fall in employment, and that makes
the situation very different than if it had. The set of percentages recommended for attention here reveals the difference.

Although the nation as a whole has recently achieved a higher percentage employed than at any time since World War II, there is no
reason to regard this as a maximum. It is instructive to look at some
areas of the country where the number of jobs per capita is higher
than for the country as a whole. The Bureau of Labor Statistics has
published employment-population ratios for thirty large metropolitan areas for 1976, together with unemployment rates (labor force
based). Compared with a national employment ratio of 56.8 percent
in that year, the five cities with the highest ratios ranged from 64.6
percent in Dallas to 65.3 percent in Denver. In those same cities the
unemployment rate ranged from 4.6 percent to 6.5 percent, well
below the national unemployment rate of 7.7 percent in 1976. Careful study of these and other geographical data (for example, by

states) might provide valuable information on the conditions that are conducive to a higher national employment ratio and a lower unemployment rate.

The Bureau of Labor Statistics should also be encouraged to give prominent emphasis to both the employment and the unemployment percentages of the working age population for different age, sex, and racial groups. It is not widely known, for example, that in 1978 the percentage of adult women who were employed was higher than at any time since 1947 and that the percentage of teenagers who were employed also reached a record high. This situation is not disclosed by the unemployment rates, which for both groups were at relatively high levels in 1978. It reflects a much more favorable situation than if their relatively high unemployment rates had been accompanied by low employment percentages, as might be expected to happen during a recession. The high unemployment rates for women and teenagers give the impression that job opportunities for them are scarce; but the unusually high employment percentages tell us that this is not so. This does not imply that efforts to improve the access of women and teenagers to jobs should be relaxed. It does imply that the nature of the problem is different from what it would be if their employment percentages were low and declining, as they were during the 1973–1975 recession.

To take another example, although the unemployment rates for both whites and blacks in 1978 were higher than they were in 1973, at the peak of the previous business cycle, this information does not reveal that the percentage of whites employed in 1978 was considerably higher than it was at the earlier peak, while for blacks it was lower. Thus for whites the situation is mixed: more unemployed, but also more employed. But for blacks the situation is worse on both counts: more are unemployed, and fewer are employed.

Although the Bureau of Labor Statistics has taken some useful steps to provide the information described above, it should in my view be encouraged to go farther than it has, in the directions indicated.

A NEW REPORT: EMPLOYMENT CONDITIONS DIGEST

In any large statistical agency such as the Bureau of Labor Statistics, which produces figures that are avidly sought by a wide variety of users every month, there is a tendency to gear up to the essential task of getting the figures out promptly and accurately and describing their movements compared with the last month or year, but not to take the time to consider how to facilitate their use in a longer perspective. One of the best ways to do this is with charts, and the bureau has pioneered in the production of computer-plotted charts in its press releases, in *Employment and Earnings*, in the *Chartbook on Prices, Wages, and Productivity*, and in *Employment, Hours and Earnings: A Graphical Analysis*. This last document is a forty-page chartbook, issued on the same day as the current month's figures are released and covering the last ten years by months. For timeliness it has, to my knowledge, no equal, but it is not a regular publication of the bureau, and hence its circulation is limited.

The development of this document into a published chartbook, with little or no sacrifice of timeliness, would be a worthwhile enterprise, albeit a major one. It could become an *Employment Conditions Digest* (or *Labor Conditions Digest*), corresponding to the *Business Conditions Digest* of the Department of Commerce. The latter has made economic indicator information far more accessible to users, giving them a historical perspective, a wide range of data, and an analytical arrangement focused on current interpretation. *ECD* could do the same with respect to employment, unemployment, and related labor activities.

The chief features of the proposed *ECD*, as I see them, would be as follows:

1. Charts to cover a twenty-five year time horizon, showing monthly seasonally adjusted data. An alternative would be to cover twenty-five years for the principal series and ten years for others, since this would permit reproduction of more series in the same space.

One of the incidental but not unimportant advantages of such charts is that they could be reproduced for other purposes, either by the BLS for presentation before congressional committees or other audiences or by users themselves. There is a need for visual presentation of employment and unemployment data before large audiences, such as those generated by TV newscasts, newspapers, and news magazines. Many charts that are constructed hastily by people who do not know much about the subject matter are unintentionally misleading. The reproduction of charts from *ECD* could therefore serve a significant educational purpose, especially if those charts that are likely to be in most demand were designed with this end in view. One particular use that could be facilitated would be to design charts that give national figures in such a way that comparable charts could be prepared with state or local area data. Comparison of the local pictue with the national is often a useful way to give perspective, and the needs for local employment information have become so great that this kind of graphic presentation should be given careful attention.

2. Arrangement principally by subject, without regard to source of data (e.g., household survey, establishment survey, or other sources). An arrangement of selected series by cyclical timing should be given separately, and comparisons of the current recovery (or recession) with previous recoveries (or recessions) should also be shown, as discussed later in this chapter. The proposed content of the report is as follows:

a. Employment:

Number employed, percent of population, aggregate hours, new hire rates, diffusion indexes.

By age, sex, race, occupation, industry, state or region.

Help-wanted advertising (Conference Board) and anticipated employment changes (Dun & Bradstreet) should be included.

b. Unemployment:

Number unemployed, percent of population, percent of labor force.

By age, sex, race, occupation, reasons, duration, family relationship, industry, state or region.

Initial claims and insured unemployment should be included, as well as layoff and quit rates.

c. Hours of work:

Average workweek, overtime hours, full-time and part-time employment.

By industry, including diffusion indexes.

d. Persons not in the labor force:

Number, percent of population.

By age, sex, race, reasons for not seeking work, intentions to to seek work, work experience.

e. Leading, coincident, and lagging indicators of employment conditions (see below).

f. Recovery comparisons (see below).

g. International employment conditions:

Employment and unemployment series for the major industrial countries (presently compiled by BLS).

3. Business cycle shading should be a standard feature of the charts. Many users find this device helpful in reminding them when recessions occurred and what happened then, whether or not they use the business cycle chronology in any analytical way. In addition, a section of *ECD* should be devoted to charts comparing the current recovery (or recession, as the case may be) with earlier recoveries (see below).

4. Tables of monthly figures should be included in *ECD*, covering the last three years, together with annual averages for, say, five years. It is highly important to give the monthly data with the charts, so that current figures can be identified easily, recent trends studied with care, new figures added if they become available between publi: cation dates, and so forth. The monthly tables should include breakdowns of totals or of ratios given in the charts, since the breakdowns help to explain movements in the totals or ratios but may not be important enough to chart. Highly detailed breakdowns should, of course, be left to *Employment and Earnings*.

5. Historical monthly data back to 1947 for the same series covered in *ECD* should be made available once a year, either in appendixes to *ECD* or in a yearbook. The *Handbook of Labor Statistics* does not do this nor does *Employment and Earnings*. Probably *Employment and Earnings* would be the best place for this historical supplement of monthly data, but it should be clearly distinguished from the rest of the data, so that users can readily find the series that are shown in *ECD*. These series should be identified by numbers in the charts, in the current monthly tables, and in the historical monthly tables. An index in *ECD* should give the series titles, identification numbers, and page references showing where charts, monthly tables, historical tables, and series descriptions can be found.

6. *ECD* should contain a standard introductory section patterned after the "Notes on Current Labor Statistics" in the *Monthly Labor Review*. It should include a schedule of future release dates for the series shown in *ECD*, so that the user can bring series up to date prior to the next issue. The notes should cover the household survey, establishment survey, unemployment insurance data, and such privately compiled series as are included. References to sources of more detailed data or fuller descriptions should be given.

7. It would be useful, in each issue of *ECD*, to include the report on employment conditions prepared each month by the Commissioner of Labor Statistics for presentation to the Joint Economic Committee. This gives a brief interpretation of the current month's data and would be helpful to users of *ECD*.

Since the development of a publication such as *ECD* would be a major undertaking, it should probably start out on modest lines, with new features added as time goes on. It would be highly important not to let the publication process defeat the timeliness feature, since it is frustrating to users to receive a publication that does not contain data that have already been issued by the same agency. Since the employment data are nearly all released on the same date, the publication should be in the hands of users shortly after that release date and well before the next release date.

Some of the resources now devoted to other BLS publications could be devoted to *ECD*. *Employment, Hours and Earnings: A Graphical Analysis* would of course be completely replaced, and the charts in *Employment and Earnings* would be discontinued. The current labor statistics section of the *Monthly Labor Review*, which now covers nearly forty pages, might be reduced to around ten and still give representative coverage of the principal BLS series for the convenience of *MLR* readers. This would also provide more space for the types of analytical articles proposed in the next section.

LEADING, COINCIDENT, AND LAGGING LABOR MARKET INDICATORS

Students of business cycles have long recognized that recessions and recoveries do not affect all aspects of the labor market at the same time. The average workweek in manufacturing was identified as a leading indicator in 1937 in a study by Wesley C. Mitchell and Arthur F. Burns for the National Bureau of Economic Research and has remained on the list of selected leading indicators ever since. In many industries it is reasonable to expect that employers will change the length of the workweek more promptly than they will change the number of employees at work. While overtime work costs more, there is no long-term commitment, and the decision is easily reversed. Hence the average workweek is a leading indicator vis-à-vis the number of persons employed.

Similarly, there are good reasons to expect that the unemployment rate will start to rise before the number employed turns down in a recession, because slower growth in the number employed often precedes a decline, in which case the advance in employment may not keep up with the steadily rising population and labor force. Experience bears out this supposition. On the other hand, a decline in the unemployment rate is not likely to begin until some months after the pickup in employment begins, because the pickup may be slower at first than the continuing rise in the population and labor force. Thus unemployment is often a leading indicator at downturns in the business cycle, but a lagging indicator at upturns.

Again, one might expect the number of people unemployed for a long time, say fifteen weeks or more, to lag behind the turns in the total number of unemployed, since the rest have only recently become unemployed, and there is an obvious lapse of time involved before anyone can be classified as having been unemployed for fifteen weeks. Moreover, the recently unemployed are on the whole more likely to be recalled to work before those who have been seeking work for a long time without success. Long duration unemployment, therefore, is a lagging indicator.

Knowledge of these timing relationships is useful in understanding the movements in employment and unemployment and in anticipating what is likely to happen next. A classification of the chief labor market series into leading, coincident, and lagging groups, along the lines carried out in *Business Conditions Digest*, together with the historical record of leads and lags and an analytical statement explaining these relationships, would be helpful to the users of the data. To illustrate such a record, consider Table 7–3, which shows the leads of the average workweek in manufacturing industries at turns in employment and unemployment (see also Chapter 22).

Table 7–3. Workweek Turns Before Employment or Unemployment.

Dates of Cyclical Troughs			Lead (−) or Lag (+), in Months of Workweek versus	
Average Workweek, Manufacturing	Nonfarm Employment	Unemployment Rate, Inverted	Employment	Unemployment
4/49	10/49	10/49	−6	−6
4/54	8/54	9/54	−4	−5
4/58	5/58	7/58	−1	−3
12/60	2/61	5/61	−2	−5
9/70	11/70	8/71	−2	−11
3/75	6/75	5/75	−3	−2
Dates of Cyclical Peaks				
12/47	9/48	1/48	−9	−1
4/53	4/53	6/53	0	−2
11/55	3/57	3/57	−16	−16
5/59	4/60	2/60	−11	−9
10/68	3/70	5/69	−17	−7
4/73	9/74	10/73	−17	−6

Source: U.S. Bureau of Labor Statistics.

Charts of the early moving and later moving indicators of labor activity should be included in a section of proposed *Employment Conditions Digest*. At the same time, a report on the historical record and the rationale underlying it should be prepared and published.

RECESSION AND RECOVERY PATTERNS

One of the more widely used devices for measuring the state of the economic recovery that began in 1975 is to compare it with changes over corresponding periods during previous recoveries. A comparative picture of the relative strength or weakness of the current recovery, and of any unusual features that develop, is readily obtained by this device. Julius Shiskin, former Commissioner of Labor Statistics, used it frequently in presentations before the Joint Economic Committee, and comparisons of this type have been made in the *Economic Report of the President*, in news magazines and newspapers, and in many privately published reports and presentations. The comparisons have, of course, not been limited to employment and unemployment data, but have covered production, retail sales, capital investment, prices, profits, and other economic variables.

The record of what typically happens during periods of economic recovery from recessions is not widely known. There is often a long lag in public recognition even of the fact that a recovery is taking place. How far along it is at any point, what has happened in the later stages of previous recoveries (especially the developments that have helped to bring them to an end), and what factors appear to be especially strong or weak in the light of past experience are matters on which greater public enlightenment would be desirable. The same can be said of recessions, and the same comparative device can be and has been used during recessions.

To do this effectively, advance preparation and study of the historical record is essential. The BLS has been undertaking some of the preparatory analysis.[5] It should be encouraged to do this with respect to all the various types of data that it is responsible for (employment, prices, wages, productivity) and to publish the results so that they may be used by others.

Charts showing recovery patterns for the principal employment, unemployment, and hours of work series should appear in a separate section of the proposed *Employment Conditions Digest*, together with the relevant tabular material. From time to time analytical reports on the results should be issued. Similar provisions should be made in the event of a recession.

It is highly desirable that such charts be kept as simple as possible. The charts currently published in *The Conference Board Statistical Bulletin* are good examples of an effective way to do this (see Figure 7-1). The current expansion, starting from the low point of the business cycle in March 1975, is compared with the average of the five preceding expansions starting from their respective low points. The unemployment rate has persisted at a much higher level during the current expansion than in the previous expansions, but it has been declining at about the same pace as in the previous expansions. Nonfarm employment rose more slowly during the first two years than average experience during previous expansions indicated, but it caught up in the third year.

DEVELOPMENT OF NEW DATA

The development of new data on employment and unemployment is, of course, a topic warranting the most careful consideration. My discussion is limited to types of data that are not altogether new, but that are especially needed for improved presentation and analysis. One recommendation of this sort has been made earlier in this chapter—namely, the publication of employment, unemployment, and not in the labor force data as percentages of the total population of working age. Five additional recommendations follow.

Household versus Payroll Survey

A reconciliation between the employment figures as derived from the household survey and from the establishment (payroll) survey should be published currently. Many users do not know what the conceptual differences are or how to go about eliminating them from the published totals. The published household survey figure for nonfarm employment is much larger than the payroll survey figure, but it becomes smaller than the payroll survey figure when definitional differences are removed. A major reason for the remaining difference is that the payroll survey counts persons with more than one job more than once (if they appear on different payrolls), whereas they are counted only once in the household survey. These differences are, of course, well known to the BLS staff, and articles about them have been written from time to time.[6] But such articles are not widely read or easy to locate. Regular publication of a simple reconciliation table in the BLS press release and a more detailed table in *Employment and Earnings* would increase public awareness of the differences between the two surveys and their relative strengths and weaknesses.[7]

Figure 7–1. Tracking the Economic Expansion *(all data seasonally adjusted).*

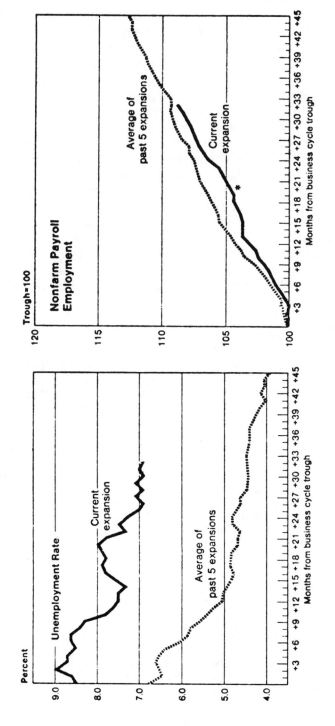

Note: Cycle trough dates (month, quarter): 1949 October, IV; 1954 May, II; 1958 April, II; 1961 February, I; 1970 November, IV; 1975 March, I.

*Denotes point in current expansion at which the series passed its prerecession peak.

Source: The Conference Board Statistical Bulletin, January 1978, p. 16.

An example of a partial reconciliation, based upon published seasonally adjusted totals, is in Table 7−4. The household survey figures for total civilian employment are larger than the payroll figures for nonfarm employment by eight or nine million, and the increase during 1977 was more than one million larger according to the household survey. But when the household survey figures are adjusted to exclude agricultural workers, the self-employed, and unpaid family workers, the figures become smaller than the payroll figures, and the difference in growth during the year is reduced to 600,000. Some further adjustments can be made from unpublished data to render the surveys more comparable in coverage, as indicated in the table's footnotes. The difference due to multiple job counting in the establishment survey can be approximated from the household survey data, however, only once a year (in May), when persons working on their second job as a nonagricultural wage and salary worker are counted. In May 1977 there were 2.9 million such people. A major step toward better reconciliation of the current figures, therefore, could be taken if this question were asked every month. Some further steps are suggested below.

Industry Employment

Although the BLS publishes monthly seasonally adjusted unemployment rates for a number of major industries, by classifying peo-

Table 7−4.   **Partial Reconciliation of Employment Figures from Household and Payroll Surveys** *(seasonally adjusted data, in thousands).*

	December 1976	December 1977	Change
1. Total civilian employment, sixteen and over, household survey	88,441	92,589	+4148
2. Less: agricultural workers	3,257	3,331	+74
self-employed, nonfarm	5,798	6,197	+399
unpaid family workers, nonfarm	460	438	−22
3. Equals: nonfarm wage and salary workers, household survey[a]	78,926	82,623	+3697
4. Nonfarm employment, payroll survey[b]	80,370	83,439	+3069

[a]Includes private household workers and workers absent without pay (due to bad weather or industrial dispute), who are not included in payroll survey.

[b]Includes fourteen and fifteen year olds, who are excluded from the household surveys, and agricultural service workers, who are counted as agricultural workers in the household survey. Persons with more than one job may be counted more than once in the payroll survey, but only once in the household survey.

Source: U.S. Bureau of Labor Statistics.

ple according to their last full-time job, monthly seasonally adjusted employment data for the same industries from the household survey are not published. In analyzing changes in total employment, therefore, it is not possible to determine readily what industries are supplying the jobs. Such information is, of course, provided by the establishment survey, and this is one of its major functions. But as we have seen, the establishment survey data do not reconcile fully with the household survey data and therefore cannot be used directly to account for movements in the latter.

Hence a twofold function would be served by regular publication of monthly seasonally adjusted employment data by major industry from the household survey. First, it would permit analysis of the industries in which employment is growing or declining. The unemployment figures, by industry of last job, do this only indirectly, and not accurately, because workers do not remain indefinitely in the same industry. For example, between December 1976 and December 1977 unemployment in the finance and service industries fell by about 200,000; employment in these industries increased by about 1.3 million. Surely the latter is an important piece of information on the source of the 4.1 million new jobs in 1977, but monthly seasonally adjusted figures of this sort are not presented in the BLS tables.

The second function served by such data would be to throw light on the differences between the two surveys. For example, the payroll survey reported an increase of about one million jobs in the finance and service industries during 1977 (December to December). Hence about 300,000, or half of the difference between the gains reported by the household and payroll surveys unaccounted for in Table 7-4 (cf. lines 3 and 4), can be attributed to this one industry sector. Much of the remainder can be attributed to wholesale and retail trade, where the household survey showed a gain of about 800,000, and the payroll survey, 600,000. It is probably significant that the differences are concentrated in these industries, because they are the industries in which it has always been difficult to locate, for purposes of the payroll survey, new and small employers. When there is a large increase in the number of retail and service establishments, the payroll survey may not pick them up immediately. When the figures are revised on the basis of additional information, the discrepancy may be reduced. In the meantime it is useful to know how consistent or inconsistent the two surveys are in what they report about industry employment, and this requires publication of the household survey figures.[8]

Employee Hours

The household survey provides the most comprehensive data available on the employment of the nation's work force. It also provides the most comprehensive data on the number of hours they work. Indeed, it is the only survey that purports to cover the number of hours actually worked, as distinct from the number of hours paid for—an important distinction in measuring productivity. Furthermore, the data on hours resolve, at least in principle, one of the chief differences between the household survey and the establishment survey—namely, the difference due to multiple job holding. If employed persons responding to the household survey report all the hours that they work at all jobs they hold, the aggregate hours reported should theoretically equal the aggregate hours reported on payrolls, where multiple job holders and the hours they work are counted on each payroll on which they appear.

Although the BLS publishes monthly figures on average hours worked per week from the household survey, the figures are not seasonally adjusted, nor are they combined with the employment figures to produce a series on aggregate hours worked. This is unfortunate. Such a series would represent the most comprehensive estimate of the amount of labor time utilized in the American economy. It would take account of the fact that a growing number of persons are employed part time—some of their own volition, some because full-time jobs are not available. The most comprehensive regularly reported figure of this sort is the aggregate hours of nonfarm wage and salary workers, an estimate developed largely from the establishment survey and used in the BLS estimates of productivity and labor cost.

To illustrate, in November 1977 this figure was 158 billion hours, seasonally adjusted at annual rate. It represents hours of work paid for, does not include the self-employed or unpaid family workers, and of course excludes agricultural workers. In comparison, the aggregate number of hours actually worked by all civilian workers, based upon the household survey, was 177 billion in November 1977, at annual rate but not seasonally adjusted. Seasonal adjustment would no doubt raise the November figure somewhat, but even so it is 12 percent higher than the 158 billion hours reported for nonfarm wage and salary workers. Furthermore, if those counted as employed but not actually working (some of whom are paid and some not) are credited with the same average workweek as those who were at work, the 177 billion figure becomes 184 billion hours (at annual rate), which is 16 percent above the 158 billion hours reported for nonfarm wage and salary workers, which also includes time paid for but not worked. Since only a portion of these differences can be accounted for in the published data (e.g., the part attributable to agricultural workers), it would be desirable for the BLS to publish regularly a reconciliation table in terms of aggregate hours similar to the one for number employed that was recommended in the preceding section.

The principal objective, however, should be to report the comprehensive aggregate hours worked information from the household survey and to give the results prominent attention in press releases and analytical articles. Not only do they represent the most comprehensive measure of labor input, but the trend that they show may differ appreciably from that shown by the establishment data. For example, in November 1977 the aggregate hours worked by all civilian workers was 4.1 percent above the year ago figure, and the hours worked by nonfarm workers, also from the household survey, showed an identical rate of increase. But the establishment survey estimate for nonfarm wage and salary workers was up by only 3.4 percent over the year. The deficiency may lie in the discrepancies noted earlier, but it is not negligible and should not be obscured by failure to publish the requisite numbers.

The availability of the comprehensive aggregate hours series from the household survey would make it possible to compute an improved measure of labor utilization.[9] One of the limitations of the ratio of the number of persons employed to the total population of working age is that it does not take account of the fact that an increasing number of those employed work only part time. Each part timer is counted the same as a full timer, and those who work overtime or at more than one job are also counted only once. Vacation periods have been getting longer, and more holidays are observed. The aggregate hours worked figure makes allowance for all these variations. It could therefore be expressed in terms of the number of full-time equivalent persons employed. If the full-time workweek is assumed to be 37.5 hours, the November 1977 number of full-time equivalent persons employed would be 177 billion hours divided by 37.5 times 52, or 90.8 million persons. This compares with the 92.5 million persons actually employed. Relative to the working age population, the full-time equivalent employment ratio is 57 percent for November 1977, slightly smaller than the 58 percent based on the actual number of persons employed. Since the average number of hours worked per person employed has been declining for many years, for the reasons mentioned above, the trend in the full-time equivalent ratio will not be as steep as the trend in the ratio based upon the actual number of persons employed.[10]

Job Vacancies

It has long been held that one of the aims of economic policy is to see to it that everyone who wishes to work has an opportunity to obtain a job. Indeed, this objective is explicitly stated in the Humphrey-Hawkins Full Employment Act, in which the Congress "establishes as a national goal the fulfillment of the right of all Americans able, willing, and seeking to work to full opportunities for useful paid employment at fair rates of compensation" (§102). In order to meet such a goal, to determine whether or not it is being met, and to evaluate the policies and programs adopted to meet it, it is surely necessary to have comprehensive information on the job opportunities that exist—where they are, what skills are required, whether the positions are full time or part time, how long they have been available, and what compensation is offered. There is not much point in having a goal if you cannot tell where the goal posts are. In short, a job vacancy survey is needed.

The Bureau of Labor Statistics developed such a survey in 1965–1966 and began publishing the results of it in 1970. It was discontinued as of December 1973. At that time it was still in a developmental stage, partly because of inadequate funding. National coverage was restricted to manufacturing industries; data for all nonfarm industries were published for only a few cities. Nevertheless, the survey did yield illuminating information bearing upon the number, location, industry, and duration of job openings.[11]

For example, during the course of the one business cycle covered by the data, the number of vacancies in manufacturing declined from a high of 280,000 in April 1969 to a low of 80,000 in March 1971 and then rose to a high of 200,000 in October 1973. Employment in manufacturing moved in the same direction, from 20.2 million to 18.5 million to 20.2 million on the same dates. Unemployment among persons whose last job was with a manufacturing concern rose from 680,000 to 1,420,000 and then fell to 840,000. Thus, at the bottom of the recession job opportunities with manufacturing companies were negligible relative to the number of unemployed. Even at the 1969 peak there were more than two persons seeking work for every unfilled job opening, and at the 1973 peak the ratio was more than four to one. Nevertheless, it is clear that a considerable number of job opportunities did exist at the peak dates, suggesting that a part of the problem, even in good times, is matching people with jobs. The extent of the need for special efforts of this sort and the direction they should take—whether toward better information, greater mobility, more training, and so on—can be quantified only by accurate and comprehensive statistics on job vacancies.

Regularly published sources of statistical information on job vacancies are almost nonexistent. An exception is the index of help-wanted advertising compiled by The Conference Board from newspapers in fifty-one cities. A national index is compiled as well as an index for each city (based upon a single paper in each city). The city indexes give a vivid picture of where the growth in jobs has taken place and where it has not (Figure 7−2). In February 1978, for example, the index for New York City was 52 and for Dallas, 227, both in terms of 1967 = 100. That is, in New York the volume of ads was about half what it was ten years before and in Dallas more than double. The difference surely seems related to the fact that the unemployment rate in New York in the spring of 1978 was around twice as high as the rate in Dallas. There is less occasion for employers to advertise in New York, since employment has been declining, and there are many job seekers around. The opposite is true in Dallas. Unfortunately, perhaps, Dallas newspapers are rarely read in New York.

Although the value of the help-wanted advertising indexes is limited because the geographic breakdown is the only one available (no information is gathered on the types of jobs, etc.), it would be desirable to exploit them further. There is considerable geographic mobility in the labor force, especially among younger persons, and yet most people have very little knowledge about job markets outside of their local area. What cities have shown the biggest increases in help-wanted ads during the past year? The past ten years? Knowledge that the volume of ads in Dallas in February 1978 was 55 percent larger than a year ago and more than double that of ten years ago might induce some unemployed persons to look into the possibilities there. Information of this sort, widely publicized in areas of considerable unemployment, could help to draw people to where the jobs are and away from where they are not. One special advantage of this type of information is that everyone knows what help-wanted ads are—they have a concrete, visual significance that a statistic like the unemployment rate does not. Nearly a third of the job seekers in the country during 1977—that is, nearly two million persons—used help-wanted ads as a means of finding work. Figure 7−2 illustrates one way of presenting this information without anything as complicated as an index number.

Despite the limited coverage of the job market provided by help-wanted ads, their general validity as an indicator of where the jobs are is supported by other information, such as the BLS reports on hiring rates in manufacturing. Between February 1977 and February 1978 the four cities with the largest increase in help wanted ads as

Figure 7−2.   Where the Jobs Are: Growth in Help-wanted Ads in Fifteen Cities.

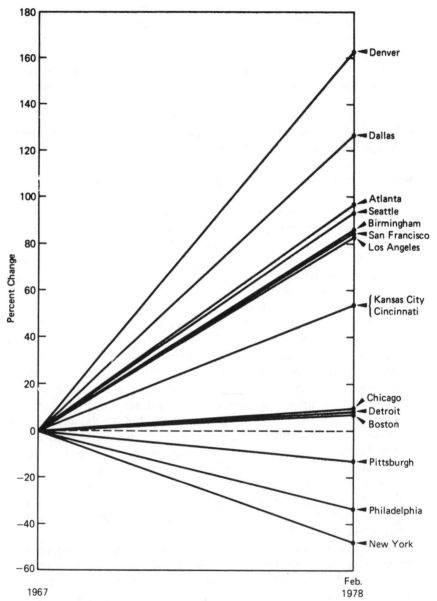

The Long-Run Picture: Rapid Growth in Some Cities,
Stability or Decline in Others

Source: *The Conference Board Statistical Bulletin*, April 1978.

Figure 7—2. continued

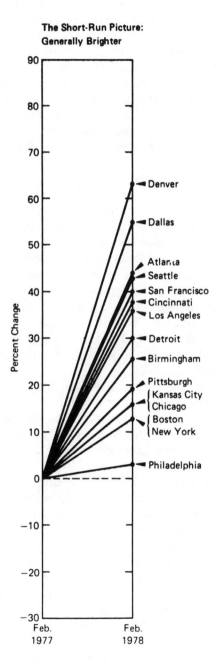

shown in Figure 7−2—Denver, Dallas, Atlanta, and Seattle—were also the cities with the largest increase in new hires per hundred employees.[12] In short, these incomplete or indirect sources of information on employment demand are supportive and useful and could be exploited more than they now are to improve the functioning of the job market. Because of its relatively low cost, it would be worthwhile to consider extending the help-wanted advertising survey to more cities and securing more information on the types of jobs offered. In this manner it would help fill the gap pending the implementation of a comprehensive monthly or quarterly survey of job vacancies that the country needs as part of its employment information system.

State and Local Employment

As noted in the preceding section, the variations across the nation in the demand for labor are enormous. Long-run growth trends are vigorous in some localities, sluggish in others. By 1970, for example, the three Pacific Coast states had 25 percent more people than they had in 1960. The three Middle Atlantic states had gained 9 percent. Two and a half million persons migrated to the Pacific Coast states during this period, while net migration to the Middle Atlantic states was 60,000. Partly because growth trends are different, but also for other reasons, recessions do not hit all parts of the country in the same way. During the 1974−1975 recession, the Middle Atlantic states lost about half a million jobs; in the Pacific Coast states the net loss was only 15,000.

Variations of this magnitude have great significance for the behavior of labor markets, the interpretation of current developments, and the policies that may be appropriate to deal with them. In consequence, the statistical system that yields information on state and local area employment and unemployment must be adequate to meet the demands placed upon it.

Something in this direction can be accomplished by enlargement of the household survey sample to provide better coverage of smaller areas. This is expensive, however, and in order to keep the cost burden down, it would be desirable to exploit less expensive alternatives. One of them is to make fuller use of the employment data collected in the establishment (or payroll) survey. This survey covers approximately 160,000 establishments each month, reporting on about 35,000,000 employees, or about 40 percent of the total number of nonfarm employees in the country. Because of its vast coverage (for example, the household survey covers directly only 54,000 households, less than 0.1 percent of the total number of households), the establishment survey provides much geographic detail. Estimates of employment, hours, and earnings are made monthly for all states and many cities and towns.

One specific use of these data, which has not to my knowledge been explored before, is to use the employment and hours estimates for a given locality to compute the number of full-time equivalent employees in the area and then to take this as a ratio to the area's population of working age. The change in this ratio during a recession might be expected to give a fairly accurate measure of the severity of the impact of the recession on that area, especially when compared with similar changes during previous recessions. This ratio has some of the merits of the employment-population ratio described in the first section of this chapter and perhaps some additional advantages as well. The definition of who is employed is based on a payroll report by an employer, and since the number of hours worked (actually, the number paid for) is also reported, an adjustment is automatically made for part-time workers and for those with more than one job, as well as for those working overtime. Conversion of total reported man hours to full-time equivalent workers is, of course, an arbitrary step, and the level of the resulting estimate will depend on the number of hours assumed to represent full-time work. But as long as this number is kept constant, the change over time in the resulting estimates will not be affected.

Hence the numerator of the proposed ratio—number of full-time equivalent employees—has the conceptual advantage of representing actual working time paid for by employers and the statistical advantage of a large sample base. As for the denominator—the population aged sixteen and over—there may be problems in providing a population estimate for local areas monthly or quarterly, but they are no different from the problems in providing a population base for a household survey, and such estimates present fewer conceptual difficulties than estimates of the labor force. Problems having to do with the place of residence of employees reported in the establishment survey would also have to be dealt with.

I have not explored this suggestion in detail, but Figure 7−3 compares the national figures for the proposed full-time nonfarm employee ratio with those for the total civilian employment-population ratio and the unemployment rate. It is evident that the long-run trends of the three series are rather different but that the cyclical movements, for the most part, are quite similar. Table 7−5 compares the changes in the three series during business cycle recessions. All three yield approximately the same picture of the relative severity of the six recessions and indeed are very highly correlated with one another.[13] If the full-time equivalent employee ratio is used to esti-

Figure 7−3. Two Employment-Population Ratios and the Unemployment Rate.

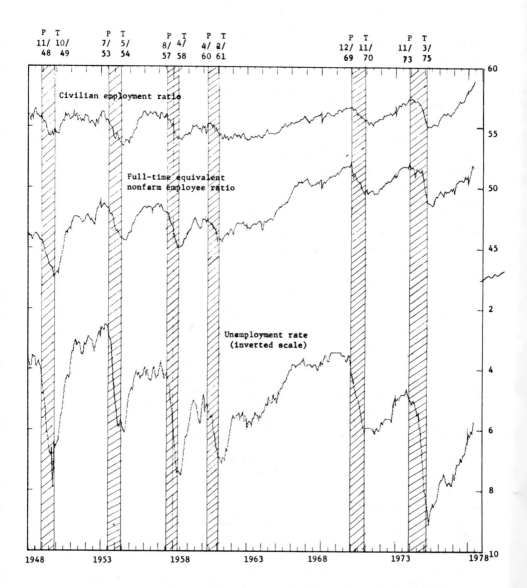

Note: Shaded areas represent business cycle contractions from peak (P) to trough (T).

Source: Compiled from data published by the U.S. Bureau of Labor Statistics.

Table 7–5. Three Measures of the Impact of Recessions upon Employment.

Business Cycle Recession		Change in Percentage Points from Business Cycle Peak to Trough			
Peak (1)	Trough (2)	Full-time Equivalent Nonfarm Employee Ratio (3)	Civilian Employment Ratio (4)	Unemployment Rate Actual (5)	Unemployment Rate Estimated (6)
November 1948	October 1949	−2.7	−1.3	+3.1	+3.1
July 1953	May 1954	−2.3	−1.7	+3.2	+2.6
August 1957	April 1958	−2.7	−1.6	+2.9	+3.1
April 1960	February 1961	−1.5	−0.5	+1.6	+1.7
December 1969	November 1970	−2.1	−1.0	+2.2	+2.4
November 1973	March 1975	−3.0	−2.1	+3.5	+3.5

Note: Entries in columns 3, 4, and 5 represent the difference between a three month average centered on the business cycle peak month (column 1) and a three month average centered on the business cycle trough month (column 2). Column 6 is calculated from a regression fitted to the entries in columns 3 and 5, namely:

Change in unemployment rate = −0.1 − 1.2 times change in full-time equivalent employee ratio.

Source: Derived from Bureau of Labor Statistics data, seasonally adjusted.

mate the change in the unemployment rate, as shown in the last column of the table, the errors in the estimates average only two-tenths of a percentage point, and the largest error, in 1953−1954, is six-tenths of a percentage point. At the national level, therefore, the ratio serves as an excellent proxy for estimating the change in unemployment during recessions. Unlike the unemployment rate, however, it focuses squarely upon the loss of work that recession brings. A careful examination of its value and limitations as an instrument for gauging the impact of recession upon state and local area employment is recommended. Such a study is eminently feasible because of the availability for a long historical period—covering several recessions—of the extensive collection of employment and hours data for states and metropolitan areas.

A CONTINUING AUDIT OF
EMPLOYMENT STATISTICS

Thoroughgoing reviews of employment statistics by such bodies as the Levitan commission and the previous Gordon Committee are highly desirable, but are bound to be infrequent. As a result, problems with the data accumulate, sometimes for years, when many of them could have been resolved much more quickly. The impetus provided by an authoritative monitoring or auditing agency, outside the statistical agencies themselves and responsive to problems seen by users of the data and those who supply the information, needs to be harnessed on a continuing basis. In particular, such an agency should be charged with seeing whether the recommendations that are made are being carried out.

The perception of this need is no criticism of the statistical agencies or of the functioning of the Office of Statistical Policy, now located in the Department of Commerce. Many improvements in the statistics originate in the agencies themselves, and the professional statisticians in charge of the work are usually fully aware of deficiencies that should be overcome or of new needs that have arisen. Nevertheless, they may not have the resources or the "clout" to do what should be done, especially when it involves the discontinuance of some types of data and the starting up of others or the changing of a definition or a concept. An outside group, available for consultation and support on such matters, can take an independent look from a broad point of view and can develop recommendations that will carry weight because of the process by which they were formulated and the auspices under which that process was conducted.

Continuity in such an auditing process is needed to insure timeliness and to secure attention to the little problems or new ideas that can be quickly taken care of as well as to the bigger ones that take longer. The work should be conducted with adequate safeguards to assure objectivity and professional competence. An agency such as the National Research Council would be an appropriate sponsor, operating on a committee level with a small permanent staff of experts, some of whom might be engaged on a part-time or consulting basis. A larger advisory group of data users from business, labor, government, and universities should be consulted regularly with regard to priorities, new areas for study, and review of preliminary results. It would be desirable for the auditing committee to issue an annual report to keep the Congress, the executive branch, and the public informed about its work. Reports on particular subjects should be published in professional journals or other suitable media.

A continuing audit of employment statistics organized along these lines would strengthen confidence in the employment and unemployment statistics, since there would always be an authoritative body to which questions about the data could be put. During 1978, for example, questions were raised about the validity of the seasonal adjustment of the employment and unemployment data. Some charges surfaced in the press suggesting that the figures were being manipulated. A watchdog group could investigate such charges promptly and issue an appropriate response. Sometimes it might anticipate the problems of credibility that can arise from a change in methodology or procedure. As it gained recognition, the auditing committee would be consulted directly by the press or others who had questions to raise.

An important matter that needs periodic investigation is to what extent data are being used. The auditing committee should conduct surveys of statistics users and evaluate the results, disclosing what types of data are little used and might be discarded as well as types that are needed. Regular consideration of this question would be helpful in the budgetary process and in assuring that the statistical dollar is being well spent.

The President's Commission on Federal Statistics, which reported in 1971, recommended that frequent "statistical audits" be organized covering a wide range of subjects and specialties. It also recommended that there be a "continuous review of federal statistical activities, on a selective basis, by a group of broadly representative professionals without direct relationships with the federal government."[14] The proposal just outlined combines both of these ideas—

a statistical audit and a continuing outside review—focusing on employment statistics.

NOTES TO CHAPTER 7

1. Congressional Record (Washington, D.C.: January 20, 1978) p. S 115.

2. The four-to-one ratio persisted during the first half of 1978. Between December 1977 and June 1978 the number employed increased 2.2 million while the number unemployed dropped by 0.5 million. The percentage of the population with jobs reached a record high in June 1978 of 58.9 percent, while unemployment still remained in the range experienced during the 1974 recession.

3. For further analysis evaluating the employment ratio as a factor in inflation in both Canada and the United States see Chapter 13, and Christopher Green, "The Employment Ratio as an Indicator of Aggregate Demand Pressure," *Monthly Labor Review*, April 1977, pp. 25-32.

4. Julius Shiskin, in "Measuring Current Economic Fluctuations," *Annals of Economic and Social Measurement* (NBER) 2, no. 1 (January 1973): 1–15, constructed measures of the revisions in eighteen economic indicators due to revision of seasonal factors, 1965–1969, including employment and unemployment. The average revisions in the monthly percentage changes of the seasonally adjusted data arising from revisions of seasonal factors, without regard to sign, was 0.12 percent for employment and 1.55 percent for unemployment. The average monthly change in the cyclical component (a smooth flexible moving average of the seasonally adjusted data) of the two series is 0.20 for employment and 1.13 for unemployment. Hence the "noise" due to seasonal revisions is only 60 percent as large as the "signal" in the case of employment, but 37 percent larger than the signal in the case of unemployment. Shiskin notes that the irregular component of the series, quite apart from revisions, also is smaller relative to the cyclical component for employment than for unemployment. The average month-to-month change in the irregular component is 0.22 for employment and 2.75 for unemployment. Finally, in a measure that combines both sources of noise (revisions and irregular movements), Shiskin computes a noise-to-signal ratio, which is 1.70 for employment, 3.81 for unemployment. Changes taken over longer spans than a month reduce the noise-to-signal ratio, but of course delay recognition of the signal. For employment the delay required for the signal to exceed the noise, on the average, is two months; for unemployment, four months. Presumably the same relationships hold for the employment and unemployment percentages, since the denominator (working age population) is the same for both.

5. See, for example, Robert W. Bednarzik, "Involuntary Part-time Work: A Cyclical Analysis," *Monthly Labor Review*, September 1975, pp. 12–18; and Bureau of Labor Statistics, *Employment in Perspective: A Cyclical Analysis of Gross Flows in the Labor Force*, Report 508 (Washington, D.C.: Bureau of Labor Statistics, 1977).

6. Gloria P. Green, "Comparing Employment Estimates from Household and Payroll Surveys," *Monthly Labor Review*, December 1969, pp. 9–20; Gloria P. Green, "Nonagricultural Employment as Measured by Two Series," *Employment and Earnings*, March 1978; Christopher G. Gellner, "A 25-Year Look at Employment as Measured by Two Series," *Monthly Labor Review*, July 1973, pp. 14–23; Joseph Antos and others, *Why Employment Estimates Differ*, Working Paper 65 (Washington, D.C.: Bureau of Labor Statistics, October 1976); Alexander Korns, "Coverage Issues Raised by Comparisons between CPS and Establishment Employment," *1977 Proceedings of the Social Statistics* Section (Washington, D.C.: American Statistical Association, 1978).

7. A detailed table was presented by the Commissioner of Labor Statistics, Julius Shiskin, in his December 2, 1977, statement before the Joint Economic Committee (Washington, D.C.: Bureau of Labor Statistics, mimeo).

8. See Gellner, "A 25-Year Look at Employment."

9. For further analysis of the household survey data on aggregate hours see Richard Ruggles, "Employment and Unemployment Statistics as Indexes of Economic Activity and Capacity Utilization," Background Paper No. 28 (Washington, D.C.: National Commission on Employment and Unemployment Statistics, April 1979).

10. For another full-time equivalent employment ratio, based on the establishment and survey figures for nonfarm workers, see the section below on state and local employment.

11. See Paul A. Armknecht, Jr., "Job Vacancies in Manufacturing," *Monthly Labor Review*, September 1975, pp. 12–18.

12. For further analysis of the validity of the series, consult Charlotte Boschan, "Job Openings and Help Wanted Advertising as Measures of Cyclical Fluctuations in Unfilled Demand for Labor," in *The Measurement and Interpretation of Job Vacancies* (New York: NBER, 1966).

13. The correlation (r) between the changes during the six recessions are:

Full-time equivalent employee ratio and unemployment rate: -0.92;

Civilian employment ratio and unemployment rate: -0.95; and

Full-time equivalent employee ratio and civilian employment ratio: $+0.89$.

14. Federal Statistics: A Report of the President's Commission, Vol. 1 (Washington, D.C.: 1971), pp. 171–175.

Chapter 8

The Federal Deficit as a Business Cycle Stabilizer

The federal surplus or deficit, or rather the change in it, has long been considered a stabilizing factor in business cycles. Its stabilizing properties are partly automatic, as when tax collections go down during a recession with a decline in incomes and profits or when expenditures go up because of a rise, say, in unemployment compensation. They can also be partly deliberate, as when tax rates are cut during a recession or the duration of unemployment benefits is extended and expenditures thereby increased. These stabilizing properties can also work in reverse during a business cycle expansion and help to dampen the inflation in the price level that usually accompanies rapid growth.

In order to determine how well or poorly the large deficits of recent years have worked in these respects, some consideration of the past record of deficits during business cycles is essential. To make this record meaningful, I think the commonly cited dollar figures should be adjusted to allow for the fact that the price level has risen substantially. A dollar of deficit now is not worth the same in real goods and services as a dollar of deficit ten or twenty years ago. It is desirable also to allow for the fact that the economy has grown substantially in real terms. A deficit of a billion dollars in a trillion dollar economy is not the same as in a half-trillion dollar economy, even if both the deficit and the economy are measured in constant prices.

Statement presented before the Committee to Investigate a Balanced Federal Budget, Democratic Research Organization, March 25, 1976.

The figures in Table 8–1, then, measure both the deficit and GNP in constant (1972) prices and compare the change in the real deficit with the change in real GNP.[1] They cover six recessions, starting with 1948–1949 and ending with 1973–1975.

Details apart, several points stand out:

1. The real deficit rose in every recession but one, 1953–1954.

2. The increase of $52 billion in the real federal deficit in the most recent recession was more than twice as large as in any of the five previous recessions. The allowance for rising prices makes a considerable difference—in current dollars, the 1973–1975 increase was more than six times as large as the increase in, say, 1948–1949.

3. Relative to the decline in GNP of $47 billion, however, the rise in the deficit was relatively modest compared with previous recessions. Allowing for the size of the recession makes a vast difference in how one views the size of the deficit.

4. The price level was relatively stable during the first four recessions, but rose sharply in the last two. Note that changes are measured over a two year interval in 1973–1975, but over one year in the earlier recessions because they did not last as long. Even though the rise in the real deficit in 1973–1975 was not large relative to the decline in real GNP, the rise in prices was extraordinarily great. In fact, it is clear from these figures as well as other price indexes that price increases during recessions have been getting progressively stronger since 1948.

Table 8–1. Changes in the Deficit, GNP, and Price Level during Six Recessions.

Recession, from Peak Year to Trough Year	*Change during Recession*		
	In Real Deficit	*In Real GNP*	*In GNP Price Level*[b]
	(billions of 1972 dollars)		*(percent)*
1948 to 1949	+21	+3[a]	−1
1953 to 1954	−2	−8	+1
1957 to 1958	+19	−1	+2
1960 to 1961	+10	+18[a]	+1
1969 to 1970	+23	−4	+5
1973 to 1975	+52	−47	+19

[a] On a quarterly basis, real GNP declined during these recessions, but the declines do not show up in the calendar year totals used here.
[b] Implicit price deflator.
Source: Table 8A–1.

So much for a quick review of recession experience. One cannot, however, determine whether the deficit moved in a stabilizing manner by looking at recessions alone. What happened during expansions is equally relevant, and the contrast at least as important. Table 8-2 presents the record for the six expansions that took place between the recessions.

Several points are worth noting:

1. The real deficit fell during every expansion but one, 1949-1953. Coupled with the result for recessions, we can say that the deficit has nearly always moved in a stabilizing manner, rising in recession, falling in expansion.

2. The declines in the real deficit during expansions have been picayune relative to the rise in real GNP. The real deficit has not acted nearly as powerfully to constrain expansion as to constrain recession.

3. The rise in the price level has generally been far greater in expansion than in recession. There are, of course, many reasons for this, including the obvious one that expansions are periods when demand is rising. But the point just mentioned may also be a factor. The small relative declines in the deficit during expansions probably contributed to the greater rise in the price level at those times.

4. Indeed, since the restraint on the price level imposed by a declining deficit has been getting relatively smaller, on the whole, since 1946, it is not implausible that this has carried over into the subsequent recessions, thus helping to explain the increasing vigor of price increases during recessions.

Table 8-2. Change in the Deficit, GNP, and Price Level during Six Expansions.

Expansion, from Trough Year to Peak Year	*Change during Expansion*		
	In Real Deficit	*In Real GNP*	*In GNP Price Level*
	(billions of 1972 dollars)		*(percent)*
1946 to 1948	−8	+12	+20
1949 to 1953	+7	+131	+12
1954 to 1957	−14	+67	+9
1958 to 1960	−20	+57	+4
1961 to 1969	−16	+324	+25
1970 to 1973	−7	+158	+16

Source: Table 8A-1.

To what extent is this record of countercyclical behavior of the federal deficit attributable to discretionary policy on the part of the Congress and the executive branch and to what extent has it been the automatic result of the cyclical swings in the economy? The estimates of the full employment budget help to answer this question, since they indicate roughly what the change in the deficit would have been had the economy remained at a high level instead of lapsing into recession every few years. They enable us to break down the change in the deficit into an automatic component and a "policy-determined" component, the latter being the estimated change in the deficit due to tax or expenditure changes other than those arising directly from recession or recovery. It is recognized, of course, that the so-called policy-determined changes (i.e., change in the full employment surplus or deficit) are adopted for a wide variety of reasons, many of which have nothing to do with stabilization. The figures are given in Table 8-3.

From this we learn that:

1. Stabilizing changes in the deficit (i.e., increases during recession and reductions during expansion) have been the rule for both the automatic and the policy-determined changes.

2. Movements in a stabilizing direction have generally been larger in the automatic than in the policy-determined components of the deficit. The four exceptions (out of eleven), where the policy-determined changes were larger—in the stabilizing direction—than the automatic changes all occurred before 1961. Since 1961, the automatic have far exceeded the policy-determined changes.

3. The policy-determined increase in the real deficit during the recession of 1973-1975 amounted to only $13 billion (in 1972 prices), a small figure compared with the decline of $47 billion in real GNP.

4. The policy-determined reduction in the real deficit during the expansion of 1970-1973 was miniscule, and in the expansion before that (1961-1969), the policy-determined component did not decline at all. The price level rose substantially during these expansion periods, and the policy-determined component of the deficit had no net restraining influence whatever. By contrast, in the two preceding expansions (1954-1957 and 1958-1960), the policy-determined reductions in the deficit were quite substantial, and the price level rose very little.

Let me now sum up these observations on the federal deficit as a business cycle stabilizer. As an automatic stabilizer, the deficit has

Table 8-3.   Changes in Two Components of the Deficit during Recessions and Expansions.

Recession	Changes in Real Deficit during Recession		Expansion	Changes in Real Deficit during Expansion	
	Automatic	Policy-determined		Automatic	Policy-determined
	(billions of 1972 dollars)			(billions of 1972 dollars)	
1948–1949	+8	+13	1949–1953	−13	+20
1953–1954	+7	−9	1954–1957	+1	−15
1957–1958	+11	+8	1958–1960	−2	−18
1960–1961	+4	+6	1961–1969	−17	+1
1969–1970	+17	+6	1970–1973	−6	−1
1973–1975	+39	+13			

Source: Table 8A–1.

almost always moved in the right direction, rising in recession, falling in expansion. The magnitude of these movements has been significantly large during recessions but insignificant during expansions, which is where the big increases in the price level have occurred.[2] We cannot, therefore, depend on automatic reductions in the deficit during expansions to have any appreciable effect in stabilizing prices. The policy-determined changes in the deficit have also, by and large, operated in a stabilizing direction, but here again, the antirecession changes have been more consistently consequential than the anti-inflation changes. Since we are now, once again, in the expansion-inflation phase of the business cycle, the question before policymakers is whether to enhance the automatic tendency of the economy to reduce the deficit.

(Note added August 4, 1978) During the two and a half years since this paper was presented, the United States has continued to enjoy an economic expansion, and the deficit has reacted in much the same way as in previous expansions. The real deficit (i.e., in 1972 dollars) has declined slightly, from $56 billion in 1975 to $38 billion in the first quarter of 1978 (at annual rate). The $18 billion drop in the real deficit compares with a $158 billion rise in real GNP during the same period. As in previous expansions, the decline in the deficit has been miniscule compared with the rise of GNP or compared with the increase in the deficit during the preceding recession. Meanwhile the price level (GNP deflator) has risen 15 percent, very nearly the same as the rise during the 1970–1973 expansion. The deficit has again failed to offset in any significant way the inflationary pressures that have been building up during the expansion.

(Note added February 16, 1982) Amen.

APPENDIX

(Tables 8A-1 through 8A-4)

Table 8A-1. GNP and Federal N/A Surplus or Deficit, in Current and in 1972 Dollars, at Business Cycle Peaks and Troughs, Calendar Years, 1946-1975.

Business Cycle Peak and Trough Years (1)	GNP in Current $ (billions) (2)	GNP in 1972 $ (billions) (3)	GNP Implicit Price Deflator (1972 = 100) (4)	Federal NIA Surplus or Deficit (−) in Current $ (billions) (5)	in 1972 $ (billions) (6)	Full Employment NIA Surplus or Deficit (−) in Current $ (billions) (7)	in 1972 $ (billions) (8)
Trough, 1946	209.6	475.7	44.1	3.5	7.9	n.a.	n.a.
Peak, 1948	259.1	487.7	53.1	8.3	15.7	10.2	19.2
Trough, 1949	258.0	490.7	52.6	−2.6	−5.1	3.1	5.9
Peak, 1953	366.1	621.8	58.9	−7.1	−12.0	−8.1	−13.8
Trough, 1954	366.3	613.7	59.7	−6.0	−10.2	−2.8	−4.7
Peak, 1957	442.8	680.9	65.0	2.3	3.4	6.3	9.7
Trough, 1958	448.9	679.5	66.1	−10.3	−15.7	1.4	2.1
Peak, 1960	506.0	736.8	68.7	3.0	4.5	13.8	20.1
Trough, 1961	523.3	755.3	69.3	−3.9	−5.6	9.8	14.1
Peak, 1969	935.5	1078.8	86.7	8.5	9.9	11.1	12.8
Trough, 1970	982.4	1075.3	91.4	−12.1	−13.2	6.1	6.7
Peak, 1973	1306.3	1233.4	105.9	−6.9	−6.6	7.5	7.1
Trough, 1975	1499.0	1186.4	126.4	−73.4	−58.1	−7.6	−6.0
Budget estimates for calendar							
1976				−64.4		−8.0	
1977 (1st 3 quarters)				−34.1		18.0	

Sources: Column 1. National Bureau of Economic Research, Inc.
Columns 2, 3, 4, 5. *Economic Report of the President,* January 1976, Washington, D.C., pp. 171, 172, 174, 249. Federal NIA surplus or deficit is defined according to the national income accounts.
Columns 6, 8. Obtained by dividing columns 5 and 7, respectively, by column 4, and multiplying by 100. Based on quarterly data averaged by fiscal years.
Column 7. 1948–1949: Federal Reserve Bank of St. Louis; 1953–1975: Council of Economic Advisers.

Table 8A–2.   GNP and Federal Budget Surplus or Deficit, in Current and in 1972 Dollars, at Business Cycle Peaks and Troughs, Fiscal Years Ended June 30, 1946–1975.

Business Cycle Peak and Trough Years (Fiscal) (1)	GNP in Current $ (billions) (2)	GNP in 1972 $ (billions) (3)	GNP Implicit Price Deflator (1972 = 100) (4)	Federal Budget Surplus or Deficit (−) in Current $ (billions) (5)	in 1972 $ (billions) (6)	Full Employment Budget Surplus or Deficit (−) in Current $ (billions) (7)	in 1972 $ (billions) (8)
Trough, 1946				−15.9			
Peak, 1948	245.9	476.2	51.6	12.0	23.3		
Trough, 1950	264.8	504.8	52.5	−3.1	−5.9		
Peak, 1953	360.1	614.8	58.6	−6.5	−11.2		
Trough, 1954	363.6	613.1	59.3	−1.2	−2.0		
Peak, 1957	433.3	676.2	64.1	3.2	5.1		
Trough, 1958	441.7	673.5	65.6	−2.9	−4.5		
Peak, 1960	498.3	731.1	68.2	0.3	0.4	8.5	12.5
Trough, 1961	509.0	738.3	68.9	−3.4	−4.9	10.7	15.5
Peak, 1969	904.2	1070.2	84.5	3.2	3.8	−0.4	−0.5
Trough, 1970	960.2	1077.2	89.2	−2.8	−3.2	3.0	3.4
Peak, 1974	1358.6	1230.8	110.4	−3.5	−3.1	14.9	13.5
Trough, 1975	1440.0	1180.9	122.0	−43.6	−35.7	5.9	4.8
Budget estimates for fiscal year ended:							
June 30, 1976				−76.0		−16.0	
September 30, 1977				−43.0		3.0	

Sources: Column 1. National Bureau of Economic Research, Inc.
Columns 2, 3, 4. Bureau of Economic Analysis, U.S. Department of Commerce.
Column 5. *Economic Report of the President*, January 1976, Washington, D.C., p. 245. Federal budget surplus or deficit is defined according to the unified budget.
Columns 6, 8. Obtained by dividing columns 5 and 7, respectively, by column 4, and multiplying by 100. Based on quarterly data averaged by fiscal years.
Column 7. Office of Management and Budget. These figures have not been adjusted to the 1976 benchmark revision of the national income accounts.

Table 8A–3.   Changes in Federal Budget Deficit and in GNP During Business Cycles, Fiscal Years, 1947–1975.

Business Recessions, Peak to Trough (fiscal years)	*Change During Recession*			Business Expansions, Trough to Peak (fiscal years)	*Change During Expansion*		
	Deficit (in billions 1972 $)	*GNP* (in billions 1972 $)	*GNP Price Deflator* (percent change)		*Deficit* (in billions 1972 $)	*GNP* (in billions 1972 $)	*GNP Price Deflator* (percent change)
1948–1950	+29.2	+28.6	+1.7	1950–1953	+5.3	+110.0	+11.6
1953–1954	−9.2	−1.7	+1.2	1954–1957	−7.1	+63.1	+8.1
1957–1958	+9.6	−2.7	+2.3	1958–1960	−4.9	+57.6	+4.0
1960–1961	+5.3	+7.2	+1.0	1961–1969	−8.7	+331.9	+22.6
1969–1970	+7.0	+7.0	+5.6	1970–1974	−0.1	+153.6	+23.8
1974–1975	+32.6	−49.9	+10.5				

Source: Based on Table 8A–2. An increase in the deficit (or reduction in surplus) is recorded with a positive sign. A reduction in the deficit (or increase in surplus) is recorded with a negative sign.

Table 8A-4.   Automatic and Policy-determined Changes in Federal Budget Deficit During Business Cycles, Fiscal Years, 1947-1975.

Business Recessions, Peak to Trough (fiscal years)	Change During Recession			Business Expansions, Trough to Peak (fiscal years)	Change During Expansion		
	Automatic	Policy-determined	Total		Automatic	Policy-determined	Total
	(in billions 1972 $)				(in billions 1972 $)		
1948–1950	n.a.	n.a.	429.2	1950–1953	n.a.	n.a.	+5.3
1953–1954	n.a.	n.a.	–9.2	1954–1957	n.a.	n.a.	–7.1
1957–1958	n.a.	n.a.	+9.6	1958–1960	n.a.	n.a.	–4.9
1960–1961	+8.3	–3.0	+5.3	1961–1969	–24.7	+16.0	–8.7
1969–1970	+10.9	–3.9	+7.0	1970–1974	+10.0	–10.1	–0.1
1974–1975	+23.9	+8.7	+32.6				

Source: Based on Table 8A–2. An increase in the deficit (or reduction in surplus) is recorded with a positive sign. A reduction in the deficit (or increase in surplus) is recorded with a negative sign. The policy-determined component is based on the change in full employment surplus or deficit (column 8, Table 8A–2). The automatic component is the change in deficit excluding the policy-determined component.

NOTES TO CHAPTER 8

1. The figures used in the Tables 8-1 through 8-3 and 8A-1 are for calendar years and pertain to the federal surplus or deficit as defined in the national income accounts. Corresponding figures for the unified budget, for fiscal years, are shown in the other tables of the Appendix.

2. It can be argued that a business-cycle-stabilizing mechanism like the deficit should not operate in a wholly symmetrical manner during expansions and recessions, because it is desirable to stimulate growth. Furthermore, fiscal stimulus may be desirable during the initial recovery phase of an expansion but not later. In a fuller analysis, one should take these points into account, but I do not believe that they would substantially alter the basic results presented here. For an alternative treatment see Chapter 15.

Chapter 9

Security Markets and Business Cycles

SUMMARY

From 1873 to 1970 the U.S. economy experienced twenty-three recessions or contractions in business activity and twenty-three expansions. With rare exceptions, the recessions were accompanied by a decline in stock prices. Moreover, there have been few sustained or substantial swings in stock prices that have not been closely associated with swings in the business cycle. An understanding of this association, therefore, is clearly of concern to anyone interested in the stock market.

The bond market also is closely attuned to the business cycle. Yields on corporate, municipal, and U.S. government bonds—as well as other interest rates—have nearly always risen during the later stages of upswings in business and fallen during downswings. Bond prices, of course, have moved in the opposite direction. As a rule, prosperity is good for stock prices but bad for bond prices, while depression is bad for stock prices and good for bond prices.

This does not mean, however, that a turn for the worse in business and in stock prices always occurs at the same time. Typically, the turn in stock prices occurs prior to the turn in business activity. Hence stock prices are said to lead the swing in the business cycle, and stock price indexes are "leading indicators." At the peak of the business cycle, it is characteristic that stock prices have already been declining for some months, and at the trough of the business cycle,

Reprinted from *Financial Analysts Handbook, I—Portfolio Management* (Dow Jones-Irwin Co., Homewood, Illinois, 1975).

stock prices usually have already started to rise. Bond yields, on the other hand, frequently continue to decline for some months after a business upswing has begun and occasionally continue to rise after a business recession has begun. Bond yields and other interest rates are generally classified as coincident or lagging indicators.

Business cycles also have marked influences on the volume of new issues of stocks and bonds and on the repayment and refunding of bonds. Rising stock prices and falling bond prices tend to encourage the issuance of common stock and to discourage bond financing, so a shift toward stock and away from bonds tends to occur during a business upswing. The opposite movements characterize the contraction phase of the business cycle.

A wide variety of factors, summed up in the term *business cycle*, bring about or are related to the regularities in the behavior of the securities markets just described. Among the factors associated with the regularities in the behavior of stock prices during business cycles, probably the most significant are profits and interest rates. Declines in the level or rate of growth of profits or in factors portending such declines—for example, declines in profit margins or in new orders—during the late stage of a business cycle expansion alter appraisals of common stock values and hence tend to produce a decline in stock prices before the downturn in business. At this stage also, a restricted supply of money and credit and the accompanying higher interest rates tend to lower capital values and may cause postponement of plans to exploit potentially profitable investment opportunities, make common stocks a less attractive security to hold, and diminish incentives to borrow for that purpose. Hence, these changes as well as those in profits depress stock prices in the later stages of business expansions. Both sets of factors operate to produce the "lead" in stock prices. Opposite changes occur during business contractions and help to explain the tendency for stock prices to begin to rise while business activity as a whole is still depressed.

But a wide variety of other factors play upon the market—shifts in investor confidence, fears of inflation, prospects for higher taxes or stiffer government regulation, changes in margin requirements, the flow of funds from abroad, a strike in a major industry, the failure of a large enterprise—and these make the underlying regularities more difficult to observe and to predict. Moreover, developments in the securities markets have repercussions of their own. A rise in capital values can lift the propensity of consumers to spend and encourage enterpreneurs to embark on new ventures; a collapse in capital values can do the opposite. Hence there is a feedback from the markets to business.

DEFINITION AND CHARACTERISTICS
OF BUSINESS CYCLES

Business cycles, according to a definition formulated in 1946 by Wesley C. Mitchell and Arthur F. Burns, are

a type of fluctuation found in the aggregate economic activity of nations that organize their work mainly in business enterprises; a cycle consists of expansions occurring at about the same time in many economic activities, followed by similarly general recessions, contractions, and revivals which merge into the expansion phase of the next cycle; this sequence of changes is recurrent but not periodic; in duration business cycles may last from more than one year to ten or twelve years; they are not divisible into shorter cycles of similar character with amplitudes approximating their own.[1]

This definition resulted from extensive observation of economic data for a number of countries over periods ranging back to the late eighteenth century and up to the 1930s. Studies of more recent data have, for the most part, confirmed the continued existence of business cycles conforming to the definition, and the chronology of cycles has been extended down to date. However, secular shifts in the character of economic activity, such as the shift toward greater employment in service industries, including government; the creation of new institutions such as bank deposit insurance and unemployment insurance; and the attention given by government to the use of fiscal and monetary policy to modify the business cycle, particularly to offset any tendency toward recession, have led to long-term changes in the character of the cycle. In general, cyclical fluctuations in recent decades, both in the United States and abroad, have been milder, with the contraction phase often characterized by a reduced rate of growth in aggregate economic activity rather than by an absolute decline. Hence the term *growth cycle* has come to be applied to these milder fluctuations. This shift has generally been accompanied by a higher rate of inflation during the expansion phase of the cycle, often extending into the contraction phase.

Chronologies of business cycles have been constructed for a number of countries. The one in common use for the United States was developed by the National Bureau of Economic Research, Inc. On an annual basis, it extends from 1834 to 1970 and covers thirty-two expansions and thirty-two contractions. The monthly and quarterly chronology begins in 1854 and covers twenty-seven cycles. The latest contraction extended from November 1969 to November 1970. (For later data see Appendix Table A–1.)

Table A-2 gives a record of the chief characteristics of all of the business cycle contractions (recessions) in the United States during the past sixty years. Most of the contractions have lasted about a year or less. Only two were substantially longer, the eighteen-month contraction during 1920–1921 and the forty-three-month contraction during 1929–1933. These intervals (the top line of the table) represent the consensus among a number of different measures of economic activity, some of which are also shown in the table.

Business contractions vary in length and depth. In the Great Depression after 1929, gross national product fell by nearly half, and even after allowance for the accompanying fall in the price level, the drop was nearly one-third. None of the contractions since then, or for that matter few before then, have approached this magnitude. The declines in real GNP have ranged from 1 to 4 percent. Similarly, the unemployment rate, which by 1933 had climbed to about 25 percent, has not gone higher than eleven percent in subsequent recessions.

Severe business contractions have wide repercussions throughout the economy, affecting not only production and employment, but also commodity prices, profits, interest rates, wages, stock prices, and many other aspects of economic life. Mild contractions are more scattered in their effects. This phenomenon of diffusion is illustrated in the bottom line of the table, in terms of the percentage of industries, out of those that cover the entire nonfarm sector, in which employment declined. Even in the milder contractions, like those of 1926–1927, 1960–1961, and 1969–1970, the percentage of industries registering declines ranged from seventy-one to eighty-three. In the severe contractions of 1920–1921, 1929–1933, and 1937–1938, the percentage reached as high as ninety-seven to one hundred, virtually encompassing all industries. These pervasive movements naturally have a vital bearing on conditions in security markets.

The growth cycle concept referred to above has not yet come into wide use in the United States, but it may do so if recessions continue to become milder and if concern about even the mildest continues to mount. Recent research has identified eight growth cycles during 1948–1970. Five of the periods of slowdown overlap the business cycle recessions of 1949, 1954, 1958, 1961, and 1970, beginning one or two quarters earlier but ending at about the same time. These five, of course, were the more serious episodes. The other three milder slowdowns occurred in 1951–1952, 1962–1963, and 1966–1967, interrupting the business cycle expansions of 1949–1953 and 1961–1969. A ninth slowdown appears to have begun in the spring of 1973 (see Chapter 5 and Appendix Table A-4).

During the five slowdowns that overlapped business cycle recessions, gross national product in constant dollars declined, though not in every quarter, at average rates of decline ranging from −0.5 percent per year in the mildest to −2.5 percent per year in the sharpest. In the other three slowdowns, real GNP continued to grow, in most quarters, at rates that averaged about 2.5 percent per year in 1951−1952, 3.5 percent in 1962−1963, and 3 percent in 1966−1967. During the eight intervening upswings, on the other hand, growth rates ranged from 4 to nearly 12 percent and averaged 6 percent per year. As will be seen, even the milder slowdowns in economic growth have had significant effects on security markets.

STOCK PRICES AND BUSINESS CYCLES

The chronology of business cycles in Table 9−1 makes it easy to answer the question of whether stock prices are higher at the top of a boom than at the bottom of a recession. The answer, surprisingly, is "most of the time but not always." On a few occasions, most recently in 1953−1954 and 1960−1961 [and 1982], Standard & Poor's index of 500 common stock prices was higher at the bottom of the business cycle contraction than it was when the recession began. The same was true of the Dow-Jones Industrials Index. In most cases, as Table 9−1 shows, the general level of stock prices has been much higher at the top of a boom than at the bottom of a recession. The average of twenty-two periods of business expansion, 1873−1970, shows the index rising 35 percent, or at an annual rate of 12 percent. The average of twenty-three periods of business contraction shows the index falling 8 percent or at 2 percent annual rate.

Clearly it is of importance from the investor's point of view to know when the turns in the business cycle occur. Since 1948 the four periods of business cycle expansion witnessed increases of 54, 54, 52, and 34 percent in the Standard & Poor's index. By contrast, during the five periods of business contraction the index never rose as much and on two occasions dropped around 10 percent. The average rate of appreciation during the expansions was 12 percent per year; during the contractions, only 4 percent.

The general correspondence between stock prices and business cycles does not mean that knowledge of the business cycle turns would enable one to pick out all the significant declines in stock prices. For example, substantial declines occurred in 1962 and 1966, when no business cycle contraction is identified (see Figure 9−1). In both cases, however, slowdowns in economic growth did occur. The sharp decline in the market during 1973 also corresponds with a

Table 9–1.   Changes in Standard and Poor's Index of Common Stock Prices During Business Cycles, 1873–1970.

Business Cycle		Index Standing[a] (1941–1943 = 10) at		Percentage Change During	
Trough	Peak	Trough	Peak	Contraction[b]	Expansion[c]
December 1870	October 1873	3.8	4.4		
March 1879	March 1882	4.5	6.0	−14	58
May 1885	March 1887	5.3	5.9	−25	31
April 1888	July 1890	5.1	5.7	−10	8
May 1891	January 1893	4.5	5.8	−11	14
June 1894	December 1895	4.4	4.6	−22	2
June 1897	June 1899	4.4	6.4	−4	45
December 1900	September 1902	7.1	9.1	11	28
August 1904	May 1907	7.5	8.4	−18	12
June 1908	January 1910	8.0	10.4	−5	30
January 1912	January 1913	9.5	9.6	−9	1
December 1914	August 1918	7.6	8.0	−21	5
March 1919	January 1920	8.6	9.1	8	6
July 1921	May 1923	6.9	9.2	−24	33
July 1924	October 1926	9.5	13.5	3	42
November 1927	August 1929	17.0	28.5	26	68
March 1933	May 1937	5.9	15.4	−79	161
June 1938	February 1945	10.4	13.8	−32	33
October 1945	November 1948	16.4	15.6	19	−5
October 1949	July 1953	15.8	24.3	1	54
August 1954	July 1957	30.8	47.3	27	54
April 1958	May 1960	42.7	56.1	−10	31
February 1961	November 1969	62.0	94.3	11	52
November 1970		86.3		−8	
Average, 1873–1970				−8	35
Average, 1873–1948				−12	32
Average, 1948–1970				4	48

Table 9-1. continued

Business Cycle		Length (in months) of		Annual Rate (in percent) of Change During	
Trough	Peak	Contraction[b]	Expansion[c]	Contraction[b]	Expansion[c]
December 1870	October 1873				
March 1879	March 1882	65	36	-3	16
May 1885	March 1887	38	22	-9	16
April 1888	July 1890	13	27	-9	3
May 1891	January 1893	10	20	-13	8
June 1894	December 1895	17	18	-16	1
June 1897	June 1899	18	24	-3	20
December 1900	September 1902	18	21	7	15
August 1904	May 1907	23	33	-10	4
June 1908	January 1910	13	19	-5	18
January 1912	January 1913	24	12	-5	1
December 1914	August 1918	23	44	-12	1
March 1919	January 1920	7	10	14	7
July 1921	May 1923	18	22	17	17
July 1924	October 1926	14	27	3	17
November 1927	August 1929	13	21	24	35
March 1933	May 1937	43	50	-35	26
June 1938	February 1945	13	80	-30	4
October 1945	November 1948	8	37	30	-2
October 1949	July 1953	11	45	1	12
August 1954	July 1957	13	35	-25	16
April 1958	May 1960	9	25	-13	14
February 1961	November 1969	9	105	15	5
November 1970		12		-8	
Average, 1873–1970		19	33	-2	12
Average, 1873–1948		21	29	-3	12
Average, 1948–1970		11	52	4	12

[a] Three month average centered on business cycle peak or trough month.
[b] From peak on preceding line to trough.
[c] From trough to peak.

Source: National Bureau of Economic Research, Inc.

Figure 9–1. Stock Prices, Profits, and Bond Yields, 1952–1973.

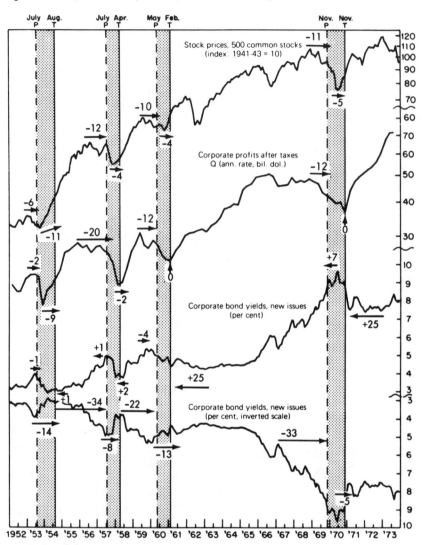

Note: Shaded areas are business recessions. Numbers and arrows indicate length of leads (−) and lags (+) in months from business cycle peaks and troughs.

Source: Standard & Poor's Corporation; U.S. Department of Commerce; First National City Bank of New York; and U.S. Treasury Department.

slowdown in growth. The only instances since 1948 of an economic slowdown where there was no substantial decline in stock prices were in 1951–1952 [and 1980].

In short, with these exceptions, the market has reflected all the slowdowns in the economy since 1948, and sustained declines in the market have not occurred at other times.[2]

The reason for most of the exceptions to the rule of higher stock prices at the peak than at the trough of the business cycle is not that stocks were not depressed by the business recession, but rather that they began to decline sooner and to recover earlier than business activity as a whole. For example, in 1953–1954, the Standard & Poor's index reached its highest monthly average (twenty-six) in January 1953, six months before the business cycle peak in July, by which time the index had dropped to twenty-four. The decline in the index continued for only two more months, reaching bottom in September 1953 at twenty-three. From then on it rose vigorously, so that by the time the August 1954 trough in the business cycle had arrived the index was thirty-one, nearly 30 percent higher than its level at the previous business cycle peak. The January–September 1953 decline in the index was evidently associated with the business recession but occurred much earlier (see Figure 9–1).

Table 9–2 shows that this tendency for stock prices to lead the business cycle is quite characteristic. Since 1873, it has happened at eighteen of the twenty-three business cycle peaks and at seventeen of the twenty-three troughs. Since 1948 there has been no exception to the rule. The average lead is around five or six months, but there have been wide variations around the average. Table 9–2 also shows that there have been only two occasions since 1873 when a business recession occurred but no cyclical decline in stock prices was associated with it. One was during the recession that briefly interrupted the boom of the 1920s, in 1926–1927; the other was in the short "reconversion" recession after World War II, in 1945. In both instances the decline in business activity was mild [as it was in 1980].

Does the systematic lead in stock prices mean that the stock market forecasts turns in the business cycle or that it is reacting to other developments that also lead? Possibly there are elements of both, but it is worth noting that two factors bearing on stock prices may help to account for the lead: profits and interest rates. Table 9–3 pulls together some relevant information on profits. Although the turning points in profits and in stock prices do not occur at precisely the same time (the leads would be identical if they did), the tendency is clearly in that direction.[3] It seems reasonable to suppose that promptly available information and astute guesses about profit

Table 9–2.   Leads and Lags of Common Stock Price Index at Business Cycle Peaks and Troughs, 1873–1970.

Business Cycle		Lead (−) or Lag (+) (in months) at		Business Cycle		Lead (−) or Lag (+) (in months) at	
Peak	Trough	Peak	Trough	Peak	Trough	Peak	Trough
October 1873	March 1879	−17	−21	January 1920	July 1921	−6	+1
March 1882	May 1885	−9	−4	May 1923	July 1924	−2	−9
March 1887	April 1888	+2	+2	October 1926	November 1927	n.s.	n.s.
July 1890	May 1891	−2	−5	August 1929	March 1933	+1	−9
January 1893	June 1894	−5	+9	May 1937	June 1938	−3	−2
December 1895	June 1897	−3	−10	February 1945	October 1945	n.s.	n.s.
June 1899	December 1900	−2	−3	November 1948	October 1949	−5	−4
September 1902	August 1904	0	−10	July 1953	August 1954	−6	−11
May 1907	June 1908	−8	−7	July 1957	April 1958	−12	−4
January 1910	January 1912	−1	−18	May 1960	February 1961	−10	−4
January 1913	December 1914	−4	0	November 1969	November 1970	−11	−5
August 1918	March 1919	−21	−15				

Summary

	1873–1970		1873–1945		1948–1970	
	Peaks	Troughs	Peaks	Troughs	Peaks	Troughs
Median lead, in months	−5	−5	−3	−6	−10	−4
Average lead, in months	−6	−6	−5	−6	−9	−6
Longest lead, in months	−21	−21	−21	−21	−12	−11
Shortest lead (or longest lag), in months	+2	+9	+2	+9	−5	−4
Number of						
Leads six months or longer	9	9	5	8	4	1
Leads five months or shorter	9	8	8	4	1	4
Exact coincidences	1	1	1	1	0	0
Lags	2	3	2	3	0	0

n.s.—No specific cycle.

Source: Standard & Poor's index of 500 common stocks, industrials, rails, and utilities. For 1873–1958, leads and lags are from *Business Cycle Indicators*, ed., G.H. Moore, (New York: NBER, 1961), pp. 674, 677. For 1948–1970, *Business Conditions Digest*, June 1973, p. 115.

Table 9–3.   Leads and Lags of Corporate Profits and Stock Prices at Business Cycle Peaks and Troughs, 1921–1970.

Business Cycle		Lead (−) or Lag'(+), in Months, at Business Cycle Peaks and Troughs			
		Corporate Profits after Taxes		Stock Price Index, Standard & Poor's 500	
Peak	Trough	Peak	Trough	Peak	Trough
May 1923	July 1921	0	−2	−2	+1
October 1926	July 1924	−2	+1	n.s.	−9
August 1929	November 1927	0	0	+1	n.s.
May 1937	March 1933	−6	−7	−3	−9
February 1945	June 1938	−12	−1	n.s.	−2
November 1948	October 1945	−6	+1	−5	n.s.
July 1953	October 1949	−2	−5	−6	−4
July 1957	August 1954	−20	−9	−12	−11
May 1960	April 1958	−12	−2	−10	−4
November 1969	February 1961	−12	0	−11	−4
	November 1970		0		−5

Summary

	1921–1970		1921–1945		1948–1970	
	Corporate Profits	Stock Prices	Corporate Profits	Stock Prices	Corporate Profits	Stock Prices
Median lead, in months	−2	−5	−1	−2	−6	−6
Average lead, in months	−5	−6	−3	−3	−7	−7
Longest lead, in months	−20	−12	−12	−9	−20	−12
Shortest lead (or longest lag) in months	+1	+1	+1	+1	0	−4
Number of						
Leads six months or longer	8	7	3	2	5	5
Leads five months or shorter	6	8	3	3	3	5
Exact coincidences	5	0	3	0	2	0
Lags	2	2	2	2	0	0

n.s. No specific cycle.

Source: Standard & Poor's index of 500 common stocks, industrials, rails and utilities. For 1873–1945 leads and lags are from *Business Cycle Indicators,* ed. G.H. Moore, (Princeton: Princeton University Press, 1961), pp. 674, 677. For 1948–1970, *Business Conditions Digest,* June 1973, p. 115.

trends would influence the market and help to account for its propensity to lead the business cycle. Since other leading indicators such as new orders, housing starts, defense contracts, and construction contracts also have a bearing upon profit prospects, they also influence the thinking of investors about the value of equities and contribute to the lead of stock prices.

Although increases in profits are likely to have a favorable effect on stock prices, increases in interest rates are likely to have an unfavorable effect. The higher the discount rate applied to future earnings, the lower the capital value of the equity. The higher the yield on bonds, the more attractive they become as an alternative to holding common stocks. Higher interest rates and the accompanying reduced availability of credit may diminish the propensity of investors to borrow in order to buy stocks. Higher interest rates increase the cost of doing business, notably the cost of holding inventory and of accounts receivable, and hence may adversely affect profit margins in certain trades. Thus, increases in interest rates tend to depress stock prices, and the sharper the rise, the greater this effect is likely to be.

Interest rates often do not begin to rise, or do not begin to rise rapidly, for some months after a business upswing gets underway. Often they rise fastest in the late stages of the upswing, as a result of restrictions on the supply of money and credit. Such a development can depress the market even though business activity itself is still expanding. If this surge in interest rates is coupled with a profit squeeze that also antedates the business downturn, as frequently happens, stock prices can drop sharply even while business is good and getting better.

A similar sequence of events can be described during a business cycle contraction to account for upturns in stock prices prior to the upturn in business. The fall in interest rates helps the market for stocks, and if the customary early upturn in profits also occurs, optimism among investors in common stocks is doubly justified even though business activity is still depressed and sliding downward.

BOND PRICES, INTEREST RATES, AND BUSINESS CYCLES

Among the interrelated factors that pull interest rates and bond yields upward during a business expansion are (1) the rising demand for business credit, both for operating purposes and for capital investment; (2) the rising demand for mortgage credit, both residential and nonresidential; (3) the rising demand for consumer credit; (4) the widening expectation of an increase in the rate of inflation, which makes lenders reluctant to lend at the same interest rate and borrowers more willing to pay a higher rate; and (5) the sluggish response of the supply of lendable funds to these pressures. During a business cycle contraction, all or most of these factors operate in reverse and bring interest rates down.

Certain types of interest rates reflect these forces more promptly and in larger degree than other types. Short-term rates on marketable securities such as treasury bills, federal funds, and commercial paper are the most sensitive. New issue yields on corporate bonds are more sensitive than yields on outstanding issues. Bank rates on business loans, mortgage rates, and rates on consumer loans are relatively sluggish. Not only do they typically move in a narrower range, they usually begin their moves later. As a rule, returns on securities traded in the open market move earlier, more frequently, and by larger amounts than rates on sparsely traded debt instruments.

Table 9—4 illustrates some of these differences for treasury bills and corporate bond yields. Bill yields have usually turned a month or two before or after the business cycle peak or trough, while yields on outstanding bonds (high grade) have usually turned later, especially at troughs. Yields on new issues of corporate bonds (shown in Figure 9—1) usually turn earlier than those on outstanding issues and hence at about the same time as bill rates. The basis point change from the peak to the trough of the business cycle has generally been much larger for bills than for bonds, as the table shows.

Although it is customary to look upon interest rates as being pulled up by a rising demand for funds operating against a sluggish supply during a cyclical expansion and as being pushed down by a declining demand during a contraction, it is also possible to look at them in a different way. Interest payments are a part of the cost of doing business, and an increase in rates can act as a deterrent to new investment. The cost of holding inventories and of accounts receivable is particularly sensitive to interest changes. High rates may make an industrial or commercial building project look less profitable and cause plans to be cut back or canceled. Tight money and the accompanying high mortgage rates have a particularly prompt and substantial depressing effect on new housing starts. Although high yields on bonds enhance their attractiveness as far as investors are concerned, they have the opposite effect on borrowers, and new issues of bonds may be postponed in the belief that yields will go lower.

From this point of view—that is, looking at the cyclical effects of changes in interest rates rather than their causes—it is useful to compare upturns in rates with subsequent downturns in business and downturns in rates with subsequent upturns in business.

Table 9–4. Leads and Lags and Rates of Change in Treasury Bill Rates and Corporate Bond Yields During Business Cycles, 1920–1970.

| Business Cycle | | Lead (−) or Lag (+), in Months, at Business Cycle | | | |
| | | Trough | | Peak | |
Trough (1)	Peak (2)	Treasury Bill Rate (3)	Corporate Bond Yield, Moody's Aaa (4)	Treasury Bill Rate (5)	Corporate Bond Yield, Moody's Aaa (6)
March 1919	January 1920		−1	+5	+5
July 1921	May 1923	+13	+14	−2	−1
July 1924	October 1926	+1		−11	
November 1927	August 1929	−2	+5	−3	+1
March 1933	May 1937	+35[a]	+46[a]	−1[a]	−1[a]
June 1938	February 1945	+31[a]	+30[a]		−35[a]
October 1945	November 1948		+6		−9
October 1949	July 1953		+8	−1	−1
August 1954	July 1957	−2	+1	−1	+1
April 1958	May 1960	+2	+2	−5	−4
February 1961	November 1969	−2	+25[b]	+2	+7
November 1970		+15	+25		
Average, 1920–1970		+4	+9	−2	0

Table 9-4. continued

Business Cycle		Lead (−) or Lag (+), in Months, of Bond Yields versus Bill Rates at		Change in Bill Rates and Bond Yields, in Basis Points per Month, during Business Cycle			
				Contraction		Expansion	
Trough (1)	Peak (2)	Trough (7)	Peak (8)	Bills (9)	Bonds (10)	Bills (11)	Bonds (12)
March 1919	January 1920		0				3.9ᵃ
July 1921	May 1923	+1	+1	2.4	1.8	−4.8	−4.2
July 1924	October 1926			−16.4	−1.5	5.9	−1.0
November 1927	August 1929	+7	+4	−3.4	−1.7	9.3	1.4
March 1933	May 1937	+11ᵃ	0ᵃ	−10.7	−0.3	−1.0	−2.6
June 1938	February 1945	−1ᵃ		−4.6	−0.8	0.4	−0.7
October 1945	November 1948			0.0	−0.4	2.1	0.0
October 1949	July 1953		0	−0.6	−1.9	2.4	1.5
August 1954	July 1957	+3	+2	−9.9	−3.3	7.8	3.2
April 1958	May 1960	0	+1	−26.4	−3.7	8.0	3.3
February 1961	November 1969	+27	+5	−0.8	−2.4	4.7	3.0
November 1970		+10		−16.3	3.7		
Average, 1920–1970		+8	+2	−8.7	−1.0	3.5	0.4

ᵃExcluded from average.

ᵇThis comparison ignores the minor rise in the series from September 1960 to September 1961.

Source: Phillip Cagan, "Changes in the Cyclical Behavior of Interest Rates," in Essays on Interest Rates, vol. II, ed. Jack M. Guttentag, (New York: National Bureau of Economic Research 1971), pp. 23–32. Bill rates are seasonally adjusted except 1931–1947; bond yields are seasonally adjusted 1948–1961 only. Updated 1969–1973 on basis of unadjusted data. The lag of bond yields at March 1933 trough (forty-six months) is included because the turn is comparable with that in bill rates.

For example, the peak in corporate bond yields in June 1970, which is treated in Table 9—4 as a lag of seven months behind the November 1969 business cycle peak, can also be looked on as a lead of five months before the November 1970 business cycle trough. Since bond prices move inversely to bond yields, this is equivalent to comparing the trough in bond prices with the trough in business. From some points of view this is a simpler way to put it, and Table 9—5 is drawn up on this basis. It shows not only that bond prices lead the business cycle but also that their leads are substantially longer than those of stock prices. Hence bond prices also lead stock prices. The leads vary greatly in length, averaging around a year at peaks and a half year at troughs.[4]

The average sequence during 1920—1970 that emerges from the records presented in Tables 9—4 and 9—5 is as follows:

	Months
From business cycle trough to bond yield trough (bond price peak)— Table 9-4, column 4	9
From bond yield trough to stock price peak—Table 9-5, column 8	15
From stock price peak to business cycle peak—Table 9-5, column 6	6
From business cycle peak to bond yield peak—Table 9-4, column 6	0
From bond yield peak to stock price trough—Table 9-5, column 7	6
From stock price trough to business cycle trough—Table 9-5, column 4	5

Although the order in which these turning points in financial markets and in business activity have occurred has been followed with considerable fidelity, the length of the intervals has varied enormously. Hence, the average intervals are of little or no value in pinpointing a future turning point. Moreover, as the blank spaces in the tables indicate, turning points in bond yields, stock prices, and business cycles do not always match, in which case the sequence cannot even be recorded. This means, of course, that many other factors play a part in the financial markets. Nevertheless, the sequence has occurred often enough over a long period—it can be traced back to the 1870s—and has survived severe disturbances like the Great Depression of the 1930s and the economic controls of World War II. Thus, one can be reasonably confident that it reflects persistent tendencies in the adjustment of financial markets to economic conditions.

Table 9-5. Leads and Lags of Corporate Bond Prices and Stock Prices During Business Cycles, 1920-1970.

Business Cycle		Lead (−) or Lag (+), in Months, at Business Cycle				Lead (−) or Lag (+) in Months, of Bond Prices versus Stock Prices at	
		Trough		Peak			
Trough (1)	*Peak (2)*	*Corporate Bond Prices (3)*	*Stock Prices (4)*	*Corporate Bond Prices (5)*	*Stock Prices (6)*	*Trough (7)*	*Peak (8)*
March 1919	January 1920			−11	−6		−5
July 1921	May 1923	−13	+1	−8	−2	−14	−6
July 1924	October 1926	−15	−9			−6	
November 1927	August 1929			−16	+1		−17
March 1933	May 1937	−9	−9	−4	−3	0	−1
June 1938	February 1945	−14	−2			−12	
October 1945	November 1948				−5		
October 1949	July 1953			−37	−6		−31
August 1954	July 1957	−14	−4	−34	−12	−3	−22
April 1958	May 1960	−8	−11	−23	−10	−4	−13
February 1961	November 1969	−13	−4	−33	−11	−9	−22
November 1970		−5	−5			0	
Average, 1920-1970		−11	−5	−21	−6	−6	−15

Source: Based on Tables 9-4 and 9-6. The peaks and troughs in bond prices correspond to the troughs and peaks in bond yields, respectively.

THE VOLUME OF STOCK AND
BOND FINANCING DURING
BUSINESS CYCLES

The most comprehensive study of corporate bond financing during business cycles was conducted during the late 1940s and early 1950s by W. Braddock Hickman for the National Bureau of Economic Research. He covered the period 1900 to 1938 and drew the following conclusions regarding the relationships of bond to stock financing over the various stages of the business cycle:

> While bond extinguishments (repayments plus refundings) usually rise through the expansion phase of the cycle and fall through the contraction phase, bond offerings are usually inverted, rising during most of the contraction phase and falling during most of the expansion. The net change in outstandings—the difference between offerings and extinguishments—consequently shows an inverse relationship to the rise and fall of general business activity. . . .
>
> The conclusion that, on balance, corporations obtain an increasing volume of funds through the bond market during periods of contraction and a decreasing volume during periods of expansion leads to the question, Where, then, do corporations obtain funds to meet the increasing monetary requirements of expansion phases? Among the alternative sources of capital funds employed by corporations, a principal one during the period studied was the stock market. The behavior of stock offerings shows that corporations typically obtain an increasing volume of funds in the stock market during expansion stages, when net bond financing declines, and a decreasing amount during contraction stages, when net bond financing expands. Stock and bond financing thus appear to complement each other over the various stages of the cycle. . . .
>
> From analysis of the cyclical movements in the net-change series and its components in relation to bond and stock prices, it appears that both the new-money component and total offerings tend to be directly associated with bond prices, while both repayments and total extinguishments are associated with stock prices (and stock offerings). Since the relation between bond and stock prices during business cycles is complex, and since the price factors do not play with equal strength on the components of net change in bond financing, no simple formula in terms of bond or stock prices seems adequate to explain the behavior of the net change. In general, however, when the ratio of stock to bond prices turns downward during the contraction stages of the business cycle, corporations tend to shift their financing from the stock to the bond market; and conversely, when the ratio of stock to bond prices turns upward during expansion stages, corporations shift from the bond to the stock market.[5]

Since 1938 there has been a vast growth in the volume of stock and bond financing, a sharply rising trend in stock prices and bond yields, and a fall in bond prices. To some extent these trends obscure the cyclical movements, especially because the business cycle contractions have been short. Nevertheless, Table 9–6 suggests that many of Hickman's conclusions regarding the behavior of the markets before 1938 have remained valid.

Common stock offerings rose during each of the five business expansions from 1946 to 1970 and fell in two of the contractions (1957–1958 and 1969–1970). Offerings of preferred stock (which Hickman did not distinguish) have behaved in the manner he described for bonds. They declined in three of the expansions and rose in four of the contractions, thus conforming inversely to the business cycle. The shift toward common and away from preferred stock financing during the business upswing and the reversal during the downswing appears to reflect cyclical shifts in investor confidence, with prosperity favoring the riskier security and recession favoring the safer.

Bond offerings, on the whole, have not shown as much inverse conformity to the cycle since 1946 as Hickman found for the earlier period. Nevertheless the average volume of offerings at the six business troughs was higher than the average at the five peaks. This was also true of preferred stock offerings, and from this point of view they belong with bonds. The ratio of common stock to bond offerings, therefore, usually rose during business expansions and fell during contractions.

In terms of the annual average figures used in Table 9–6, common stock prices declined in only two of the five business contractions. Corporate bond yields declined in all but one contraction, so bond prices rose in all but one. The ratio of stock to bond prices, dominated by the larger movements in stock prices, conformed positively to the business cycle as a rule.

We end up, then, with a picture resembling Hickman's description, with corporate financing shifting from stocks toward bonds as the price ratio of stocks to bonds becomes less favorable for stocks during the contraction phase of the business cycle and back toward stocks as the price ratio becomes more favorable for stocks during the expansion phase of the cycle. A similar and even more decisive cyclical shift occurs in the relative volume of offerings of common and preferred stock, with preferred stock taking on the character of bonds in this context. It seems fair to say, therefore, that the record of past experience in security markets during business cycles can serve broadly to illuminate current developments and prospects and can contribute to a better understanding of the factors that have a significant bearing on the outcome of security investments.

Table 9–6.   Stock and Bond Prices and the Volume of Offerings During Business Cycles, 1946–1970.

| Business Cycle | | Corporate Securities Offered for Cash ($ millions) | | | | | | Common Stock Price Index, S&P's 500 1941–1943 = 10 at | | Corporate Bond Yield, Moody's Aaa (percent) at | | Corporate Bond Price S&P's AAA (dollars) at | |
| | | Common Stock at | | Preferred Stock at | | Bonds and Notes at | | | | | | | |
Trough	Peak	Trough	Peak	Trough	Peak	Trough	Peak	Trough	Peak	Trough	Peak	Trough	Peak
1946	1948	891	614	1127	492	4882	5973	17	16	2.53	2.82	123	118
1949	1953	736	1326	425	489	4890	7083	15	25	2.66	3.20	121	112
1954	1957	1213	2516	816	411	7488	9957	30	44	2.90	3.89	117	101
1958	1960	1334	1664	571	409	9653	8081	46	56	3.79	4.41	103	95
1961	1969	3294	7714	450	682	9420	18348	66	98	4.35	7.03	95	69
1970		7240		1390		30315		83		8.04		62	
Average, 1946–1970		2451	2767	796	497	11108	9888	43	48	4.04	4.27	104	99
Conformity Index[a]		+40		−40		+20		+20		+80		−70	

| Business Cycle | | Ratio, Common to Preferred Stock Offerings at | | Ratio, Common Stock to Bond Offerings at | | Ratio, Preferred Stock to Bond Offerings at | | Ratio, Common Stock Price Index to Bond Price at | |
Trough	Peak	Trough	Peak	Trough	Peak	Trough	Peak	Trough	Peak
1946	1948	0.79	1.25	0.18	0.10	0.23	0.08	0.14	0.14
1949	1953	1.73	2.71	0.15	0.19	0.09	0.07	0.12	0.22
1954	1957	1.49	6.12	0.16	0.25	0.11	0.04	0.26	0.44
1958	1960	2.34	4.07	0.14	0.21	0.06	0.05	0.45	0.58
1961	1969	7.32	11.31	0.35	0.42	0.05	0.04	0.69	1.42
1970		5.21		0.24		0.05		1.34	
Average, 1946–1970		3.15	5.09	0.20	0.23	0.10	0.06	0.50	0.56
Conformity Index[a]		+60		+40		−90		+30	

[a]Number of positively conforming movements minus number of inversely conforming movements divided by the total (10). Positively conforming movements are increases from business cycle trough to following business cycle peak and decreases from peak to following trough. Inversely conforming movements are the opposite. If all movements conform positively the index is + 100; if all conform inversely, −100.

NOTES TO CHAPTER 9

1. Wesley C. Mitchell and Arthur F. Burns, *Measuring Business Cycles* (New York: National Bureau of Economic Research, 1946).

2. For further analysis of the relation between stock prices and growth cycles see Geoffrey H. Moore, "Stock Prices and the Business Cycle," *The Journal of Portfolio Management*, 1, 3 (Spring 1975): 59–64.

3. The correlation between the length of lead in stock prices and in profits, based on the figures in Table 9–3, is +0.7. This means that about half the variation in the length of leads in stock prices is associated with corresponding variations in the length of leads in profits.

4. The correlation between the length of lead in stock prices and in bond prices, based on the figures in Table 9–5, is +0.4. The relationship is not so close as that between the leads in stock prices and profits (see n. 3).

5. W. Braddock Hickman, *The Volume of Corporate Bond Financing since 1900* (New York: National Bureau of Economic Research, 1953), pp. 132–34.

REFERENCES

Burns, Arthur F. *Stock Market Cycle Research*. New York: Twentieth Century Fund, Inc., 1930.

Cagan, Phillip. "The Recent Cyclical Movements of Interest Rates in Historical Perspective." *Business Economics*, January 1972.

Conard, Joseph W. *The Behavior of Interest Rates: A Progress Report*. New York: National Bureau of Economic Research, Inc., 1966.

Friedman, Milton, and Anna Jacobson Schwartz. *A Monetary History of the United States, 1867–1960*. New York: NBER, 1963.

Guttentag, Jack M., and Phillip Cagan, eds. *Essays on Interest Rates*. Vol. I. New York: NBER, 1969.

_____. *Essays on Interest Rates*. Vol. II. New York: NBER, 1971.

Hamburger, Michael J., and Levis A. Kochin. "Money and Stock Prices: The Channels of Influence." *Journal of Finance*, May 1972, pp. 231–49; and "Discussion" by Merton H. Miller, pp. 294–98.

Hickman, W. Braddock. *The Volume of Corporate Bond Financing*. New York: NBER, 1953.

_____. *Corporate Bond Quality and Investor Experience*. New York: NBER, 1958.

Keran, Michael W. "Expectations, Money and the Stock Market." *Federal Reserve Bank of St. Louis Review*, January 1971.

Macaulay, Frederick R. *The Movements of Interest Rates, Bond Yields and Stock Prices in the United States since 1856*. New York: NBER, 1938.

Mennis, Edmund A. "Security Prices and Business Cycles." *Analysts Journal*, February 1955.

Mitchell, Wesley C. *Business Cycles and their Causes*. Berkeley: University of California Press, 1941.

_____. *What Happens during Business Cycles: A Progress Report*. New York: NBER, 1951.

Moore, Geoffrey H., ed. *Business Cycle Indicators.* New York: NBER, 1961.

Morgenstern, Oscar. *International Financial Transactions and Business Cycles.* New York: NBER, 1959.

Selden, Richard T. *Trends and Cycles in the Commercial Paper Market.* New York: NBER, 1963.

Sprinkel, Beryl W. *Money and Stock Prices.* Homewood, Ill.: Richard D. Irwin, Inc., 1964.

_____. *Money and Markets: A Monetarist View.* Homewood, Ill.: Richard D. Irwin, Inc., 1971.

Chapter 10

Some Secular Changes
in Business Cycles

Although industrialized countries continue to have business cycles, such cycles have changed significantly in character. In what follows some of these changes are described and their possible implications for research and policy are discussed.

Perhaps the most obvious change is that business recessions—periods of actual decline in economic activity—have become less frequent, shorter, and milder. Interruptions to a steady rate of growth are more often simply slowdowns rather than actual declines in aggregate economic activity. This kind of shift can be observed in the business recessions identified by the National Bureau of Economic Research. On the whole, the five recessions of 1948–1970 were shorter than the five recessions of 1920–1938; produced smaller declines in output, income, and employment; and were less widespread in impact. But recent recessions have been accompanied by higher rates of unemployment than might have been expected in view of other evidence attesting to their mildness.

One of the factors underlying this shift toward recessions of lesser severity, and one reason why it may be expected to persist, is the trend in the industrial composition of employment. Industries that normally experience larger percentage reductions in employment when recession hits are less important in the overall economic picture nowadays, while industries that often continue to expand right through recession have become more important.

Reprinted from *American Economic Review*, May 1974.

Of the eleven major industrial sectors that account for total employment, seven experienced reductions averaging 3 percent or more during the five recessions of 1948-1970 (Table 10-1). These seven sectors include manufacturing of durable goods like autos and appliances, with an average drop of 12 percent; mining, with an average drop of 10 percent; transportation and utilities, with an average drop of 5 percent; and farming, manufacturing of nondurable goods like textiles, construction, and federal employment, with drops of 3 to 4 percent. Employment in these seven sectors constituted more than half of total employment in 1955, but by 1972 their share had declined to about two-fifths. The other four major sectors—wholesale and retail trade; services; finance, insurance, and real estate; and state and local government—experienced much smaller declines or actual increases in employment during the five most recent recessions. They accounted for slightly less than half of total employment in 1955; by 1972, three-fifths. (For more recent data, see Appendix Table A-3.)

In short, the industries that have contributed most to reduced employment during recession have shown little or no growth during the past fifteen years or so, while those that have contributed least to recession have grown much faster. The added stability has reduced the impact of recession upon total employment by something like one-third. If the 1955 distribution of employment among the eleven sectors had prevailed in all five recessions of 1948–1970, the average reduction in total employment would have been 2.7 percent. With the 1972 distribution, the reduction would have been 1.7 percent.[1]

If the projections of industrial employment to 1985 that have recently been published by the Bureau of Labor Statistics are anywhere near the mark, this source of employment stability will endure.[2] In fact, aggregate employment in the four recession-proof sectors (trade, services, finance, and state and local government) is expected to grow between 1972 and 1985 just about twice as fast as in the seven recession-prone sectors. The former will, by 1985, contribute nearly two-thirds of total employment; the latter, only about one-third. More people will be working in jobs that are relatively secure. If the distribution of employment among sectors in 1985 corresponds to the projection, an average recession will reduce total employment by 1.4 percent—approximately half the estimated 2.7 percent reduction based on the 1955 distribution.

One of the implications of these employment trends is that future recessions are more likely to be in the nature of slowdowns in the rate of economic growth. This prospect has already led economists here and abroad to experiment with new methods—or to resurrect old methods—of identifying economic fluctuations. The interest in the GNP gap and other measures of capacity utilization, in rates of change in activity rather than levels, in trend adjustment techniques, and in spectral analysis, stems in part from this shift. At the National Bureau, Ilse Mintz has identified growth cycles in the economies of West Germany and the United States, and other students have done similar work for Japan, Canada, Great Britain, and other countries. For the United States, Mintz's chronology includes three "growth recessions" in addition to the five already included in the National Bureau's business cycle chronology.[3] These occurred in 1951–1952, 1962–1963, and 1966–1967. In each, real GNP growth dropped to an average annual rate in the range of 2.5 to 3.5 percent over periods of a year to a year and a half. Another such period of slow growth in real GNP began in the spring of 1973, well before the energy crisis came upon us.

The policy implication that I particularly would like to draw from all this is that it has become more important than ever for policymakers to support basic research into the causes and consequences of these interruptions to steady growth. Indeed, this implication holds for anyone who is trying to foresee the outcome of current trends and the effects of efforts to move them in a more favorable direction. The emergence of a relatively new phenomenon is apt to create all sorts of uncertainties, some of which can be dispelled by research.

Let me mention a few points that are important enough or intriguing enough to call for further exploration. First, I have already noted that the trend toward milder recessions does not seem to show up in the level of the unemployment rate. Curiously, while changes in the rate have become smaller, the rate itself has become higher in both recession and prosperity. Is this due to the shift in the composition of the labor force toward greater participation by women and young persons who are prone to higher rates of unemployment? Has the existence and wider scope of unemployment benefits increased the incidence of unemployment? If the risk of losing a job has diminished because of the shift in the industrial composition of employment, why hasn't the unemployment rate come down commensurately?

Second, federal employment is not very stable over the cycle. Federal employment has declined in every one of the five recessions since 1948 and by percentages that rival those in the private sector (Table 10–2). During the intervening expansions, federal employment has increased. Although opinions differ as to whether in the long run federal employment should go up or down, scarcely anyone would argue that it should be pro cyclical. Why has it been pro cyclical? How can the timing of changes in federal employment be better con-

Table 10-1.   Estimated Effect of Employment Trends to 1985 on Cyclical Stability of Employment.

	Annual Percent Change in Employment During Five Recessions, 1948–1970	Percentage Distribution of Total Employment in			Annual Percentage Rate of Change in Employment	
		1955	1972	1985	1955–72	1972–85
Sectors with substantial percentage declines in employment during recessions						
Durable manufactures	−11.9	14.9	13.0	13.2	0.7	1.9
Mining	−9.6	1.3	0.8	0.6	−1.5	−0.2
Transportation and utilities	−4.5	6.6	5.5	5.0	0.5	1.0
Agriculture	−3.8	9.8	4.0	1.8	−3.6	−4.5
Nondurable manufactures	−3.5	11.5	9.6	8.7	0.5	1.0
Contract construction	−3.1	5.4	5.1	4.8	1.2	1.4
Federal government	−3.0	3.3	3.1	2.6	1.1	0.4
Total		52.8	41.1	36.7	0.1	0.9
Sectors with small percentage declines or with increases in employment during recessions						
Wholesale and retail trade	−0.8	20.1	21.5	20.8	2.0	1.5
Services	+1.8	15.9	20.0	22.2	2.9	2.8
Finance, insurance, and real estate	+2.4	4.0	5.0	5.5	2.9	2.5
State and local government	+4.5	7.2	12.4	14.9	4.9	3.2
Total		47.2	58.9	63.4	2.9	2.3
All Sectors	−3.0	100.0	100.0	100.0	1.6	1.8
Estimated percent change during recession for all sectors,						
based on 1955 distribution of employment	−2.7					
based on 1972 distribution of employment	−1.7					
based on 1985 distribution of employment	−1.4					

Notes to Table 10-1

Source: Compiled by the National Bureau of Economic Research, Inc., from data published by the U.S. Bureau of Labor Statistics. The projection of employment to 1985 is given in Ronald E. Kutscher, "The United States Economy in 1985: Projections of GNP, Income, Output and Employment," *Monthly Labor Review*, December 1973, p. 39.

The percent changes in employment during recessions are computed from three month standings of seasonally adjusted data centered on business cycle peak and trough months, on the base of cycle averages running from trough to trough (except 1948-1949, where the cycle base runs from peak to peak). The peak to trough periods are: November 1948-October 1949; July 1953-August 1954; July 1957-April 1958; May 1960-February 1961; and November 1969-November 1970.

Note: Data used to compute recession changes are from the establishment survey (jobs) except for agriculture, where the household survey (persons) is used. The "all sector" series derived in this manner undergoes larger declines during recession than total civilian employment from the household survey, because of the greater sensitivity of the nonfarm establishment data than the household data to recession. The average declines during the five recessions, 1948-1970, are:

Nonfarm, household survey (persons)	−1.1 percent
Nonfarm, establishment survey (jobs)	−2.9 "
Farm, household survey (persons)	−3.8 "
Total, household survey (persons)	−1.4 "
Total, nonfarm establishment and farm household surveys	−3.0 "

The data for the distribution of employment in 1955, 1972, and 1985 are based on the jobs concept, but differ from those used to measure recession changes because of the inclusion in the former of self-employed, unpaid family workers, and paid household employment and because of other statistical and conceptual differences.

Table 10-2.   Changes in Private and Public Employment During Recession, 1948–1970 *(in thousands of persons; percentage change in parentheses).*

| Recession Period | | Private | | State and |
Peak	Trough	Total	Federal	Local
November 1948	October 1949	−2,514 (−5.3)	−58 (−2.7)	+168 (+4.1)
July 1953	August 1954	−1,862 (−3.9)	−120 (−5.5)	+289 (+6.9)
July 1957	April 1958	−2,675 (−5.3)	−39 (−1.8)	+176 (+3.5)
May 1960	February 1961	−1,054 (−2.1)	−55 (−2.5)	+177 (+3.0)
November 1969	November 1970	−1,218 (−2.2)	−65 (−2.6)	+419 (+5.2)

Sources: See Table 10-1 for source and method of computation. See also W.W. Ebanks, *"Public Employment and Post World War II Economic Fluctuations"* (Ph.D dissertation, New York University, 1973).

trolled with a view to offsetting rather than augmenting employment fluctuations in the private economy?[4]

Third, wholesale prices seem to have become less responsive to changes in final demand. During each of the five recessions of the 1920s and 1930s, industrial wholesale prices declined by rates exceeding 5 percent per year. In contrast, during the five recessions of the past twenty-five years, industrial wholesale prices declined on the order of 5 percent in only one instance, 1948–1949. In part, this is related to the fact that the postwar recessions were shorter and milder than the prewar ones. But this does not seem to account for the entire shift in price behavior.[5] What other factors are involved? Will they persist or intensify? What are their implications for the control of inflation over the longer run? (See Chapter 15.)

Fourth, financial markets have become increasingly sensitive to economic fluctuations. Interest rates have moved in far wider swings in recent recession–recovery periods than formerly.[6] Stock prices, too, have become more sensitive not only to the standard business cycle recessions but also to the milder growth recessions. Indeed, stock price movements have exaggerated the relative severity of recent recessions. Thus the common impression that declines in the market forecast recession may prove unduly pessimistic. What is the relation, if any, between the shifts in interest rate behavior and stock price behavior? What factors underlie the greater sensitivity of stock prices, and what implications do they have for this form of investment?

A fifth and final point is that growth recessions appear to be international in scope. It has long been known that the more severe business cycle contractions have been worldwide. The Great Depression of the early 1930s is the best known example, but the severe contractions of 1907, 1921, and 1938 are equally illustrative. It is now clear that the mild growth recessions of 1951–1952, 1962–1963, and 1966–1967 in the United States had counterparts in Europe. As a result, our exports, which used to fluctuate with demand conditions abroad and were more or less independent of domestic demand, now conform more closely to domestic conditions because foreign demand also is more nearly in tune with ours and is also now subject to wider cyclical fluctuation. As Mintz has noted, "The contrast between this shift and the dampening of the domestic business cycle is striking, and suggests that policies or structural changes conducive to international stabilization have been far less effective than those conducive to national stability."[7] This remark, though written in 1967, seems especially apt today.

But the full implications of a more closely integrated international business cycle, or growth cycle, remain to be explored and evaluated. Better current information in comparable form for different countries on the state of the business cycle is needed. A project launched in 1973 by the National Bureau on International Economic Indicators will, we hope, help to fill this need.[8] The subject has a bearing on international economic policy problems ranging over a very wide field—monetary relations, inflation, foreign trade, capital flows, migration, to say nothing of energy. All these topics seem likely to require a major share of policymakers' attention during the 1970s, and they will need all the help they can get from economic research.

NOTES TO CHAPTER 10

1. For an extension of this analysis to 1990, see Appendix Table A-3.

2. R.E. Kutscher, "The United States Economy in 1985: Projections of GNP, Income, Output and Employment," *Monthly Labor Review*, December 1973, p. 39.

3. Ilse Mintz, "Dating U.S. Growth Cycles," *Explorations in Economic Research* 1, 1 (Summer 1974).

4. For an analysis of the cyclical behavior of federal as well as state and local government employment, see Walter Ebanks, "Public Employment and Post World War II Economic Fluctuations" (Ph.D. dissertation, New York University, 1973).

5. Phillip Cagan has documented this change and explored some of its sources in "Changes in the Recession Behavior of Wholesale Prices in the 1920s

and Post-World War II," *Explorations in Economic Research* 2, 1 (Winter 1975): 54–104.

6. Phillip Cagan, "Changes in the Cyclical Behavior of Interest Rates," Occasional Paper 100 (New York: NBER, 1966); and Phillip Cagan, "The Recent Cyclical Movements of Interest Rates in Historical Perspective," *Business Economics* (January 1972).

7. Ilse Mintz, *Cyclical Fluctuations in the Exports of the United States Since 1879* (New York: NBER, 1967).

8. See Chapter 6.

REFERENCES

P. Cagan. "Changes in the Cyclical Behavior of Interest Rates." Occasional Paper 100. New York: National Bureau of Economic Research, 1966.

_____. "The Recent Cyclical Movements of Interest Rates in Historical Perspective." *Business Economics*, January 1972.

_____. "Changes in the Recession Behavior of Wholesale Prices in the 1920's and Post-World War II." *Explorations in Economic Research* 2, 1 (Winter 1975), pp. 54–104.

W.W. Ebanks. "Public Employment and Post World War II Economic Fluctuations: A Study of the Stabilizing Effects of Government Employment." Ph.D. dissertation, New York University, 1973.

R.E. Kutscher. "The United States Economy in 1985: Projections of GNP, Income, Output and Employment." *Monthly Labor Review*, December 1973, p. 39.

I. Mintz. *Cyclical Fluctuations in the Exports of the United States Since 1879*. New York: National Bureau of Economic Research, 1967.

_____. "Dating U.S. Growth Cycles." *Explorations in Economic Research*. Summer, 1974.

PART II

INFLATION

Chapter 11

Five Little-known Facts about Inflation

FACT ONE: INFLATION IS CLOSELY TIED TO THE BUSINESS CYCLE

Every downturn in the business cycle since 1948 has been associated with a downturn in the rate of inflation, and every upturn in the business cycle has been accompanied by an upturn in the rate of inflation, measured by the consumer price index (CPI). On only two occasions has a decline in the inflation rate occurred during an expansion in business, but in both instances there was a marked slowdown in the rate of economic growth. On the record, a slowdown or recession has been both a necessary and a sufficient condition to reduce the inflation rate. A business recovery and expansion has been both necessary and sufficient to raise the inflation rate.

The latest business cycle upturn came in March 1975 and the upturn in the inflation rate followed about a year later. Its low point was 4.7 percent, centered on April 1976. The latest rate, centered on February 1977 (covering the six months November 1976–May 1977), was 8.7 percent. Both rates are adjusted for seasonal variations; a six month interval is used in order to smooth out irregular fluctuations.

Reprinted from *The Morgan Guaranty Survey,* August 1977.

FACT TWO: FOOD PRICE INFLATION
IS CLOSELY TIED TO THE
BUSINESS CYCLE

All the major swings in the overall inflation rate (CPI) have been accompanied by similar swings in the rate of change of food prices. Although weather and crop failures have had important effects on food prices at times, most of the major swings in food price inflation have been closely tied to the business cycle. One of the reasons is that food prices respond quickly and sharply to the changes in demand associated with the business cycle. In recession, employment and incomes decline, and this holds food prices down. In prosperity, rising employment and incomes pull food prices up. Another reason is that foods, especially processed foods, contain a significant labor cost component, and this is likely to move up and down with the business cycle, regardless of food supply conditions. The food inflation rate reached its low point (virtually zero) in January 1976, ten months after the business recovery began and has been rising since. The latest rate, calculated in the same way as for the overall rate, was 12.1 percent (seasonally adjusted annual rate, November 1976–May 1977).

FACT THREE: THE WHOLESALE PRICE
INDEX IS NOT A GOOD FORECASTER
OF CONSUMER PRICES

Only a small part (about 30 percent) of the wholesale price index (WPI) is directly related to the prices paid by consumers. That is the part labeled "consumer finished goods." The rest—raw materials, machinery, and the like—is not bought by consumers. Moreover, the WPI for consumer finished goods, which includes things like foods and shoes, applies to only a part of what consumers buy—namely, commodities. Services such as housing (rent, mortgage interest) and medical care are not covered by the WPI at all, but are included in the CPI.

When the two comparable parts of the WPI and the CPI are compared (WPI consumer finished goods and CPI commodities) for the period covered by both (1956 to date), it turns out that the rate of change in the former typically leads the latter by a month. This happened at five of the ten upturns or downturns in the two rates since 1956. At two of the other five turns the two rates were very close together; at the rest they were rather far apart. Hence the WPI consumer finished goods component provides a good check on what the commodity price component of the CPI is doing or is about to do, but not much of a forecast.

As for the rest of the WPI, the most useful "leading indicator" vis-à-vis the consumer price index is the WPI for crude materials excluding foods, feeds, and fibers. This covers the materials and fuels that enter into the cost of production of many consumer products and is highly sensitive to shifts in demand and supply that later affect consumer prices. The rate of change in this index has led the rate of change in the CPI at fifteen of the sixteen turns in the latter since 1948, with an average lead of seven months. The latest upturn in crude materials preceded the upturn in the CPI rate by more than a year.

FACT FOUR: THE EMPLOYMENT RATIO IS A BETTER INDICATOR OF INFLATIONARY PRESSURES THAN IS THE UNEMPLOYMENT RATE

A high level of unemployment has not prevented the rate of inflation from increasing. For example, the current upswing in inflation began in the spring of 1976, when the unemployment rate was around 7.5 percent. During the next twelve months the inflation rate climbed sharply even though unemployment remained high, contrary to some predictions that the slack in the economy would hold down prices. This is not an isolated instance attributable to special circumstances. Arthur F. Burns, writing in 1951 about the results of business cycle studies at the National Bureau of Economic Research prior to World War II, summed it up in seven words: "Inflation does not wait for full employment." After twenty-five years of more recent experience he said the same thing (less succinctly) in testimony before the Senate budget committee, March 22, 1977: "The prices of final goods and services gather substantial upward momentum well before full utilization of resources is achieved."

Although the rate of inflation has not been closely correlated with the unemployment rate, it has been more closely correlated with another measure of labor market tightness—the employment ratio. This is simply the percentage of the population of working age that have jobs. Naturally it moves in the opposite direction to unemployment, but the significant difference is that it takes into account shifts in labor force participation as well. Sometimes, as in recent years, a high level of unemployment is accompanied by a high level of employment, which means that more persons are in the labor force and fewer outside of it. The result is that labor markets are tighter than the unemployment rate, taken by itself, suggests. For example, in late 1973 and early 1974 the employment ratio reached an all-time high, even though the unemployment rate, at 5 percent, was not especially low. The high demand for labor pushed up wage costs, and the higher earnings pushed up demand for goods; both factors pushed up the rate of inflation. Similar forces are at work during the present recovery. The employment ratio is at a higher level than at any time prior to 1973, and the inflation rate is at the level reached early in 1973.

FACT FIVE: FORECASTS OF THE INFLATION RATE HAVE BEEN A LAGGING INDICATOR OF THE ACTUAL RATE

Economists have been aware for many years that the rate of inflation tends to perpetuate itself. Once inflation gets going, it tends to keep going. Hence one can do pretty well by forecasting that next year's inflation rate will be the same as last year's. The forecaster simply takes advantage of the inertia in the price system. The trouble is that forecasts made on this plan inevitably lag behind events. When the actual rate of inflation accelerates, the upturn will be missed. When it decelerates, the downturn will be missed. That is, the turn will not be identified before or at the time it happens, but only after it happens.

A record of economists' forecasts of the rate of change in the consumer price index, compiled since 1947 by Joseph Livingston of the *Philadelphia Inquirer*, demonstrates this tendency. Only twelve of the sixteen turns in the inflation rate between 1947 and 1976 were recognized by the forecasters at all, and at ten of the twelve the forecasts lagged. The average lag was six months. At the latest upturn the forecasts were ten months late. Perhaps more attention to the relationships discussed above will help to improve the record.

Chapter 12

The Cyclical Behavior of Prices

PREFACE

The National Bureau of Economic Research celebrated its fiftieth anniversary in 1970. In those fifty productive years, the National Bureau has generated a large number of studies bearing upon the cyclical behavior of prices. The work of Wesley C. Mitchell, Frederick C. Mills, Arthur F. Burns, Thor Hultgren, Daniel Creamer, George Stigler, Solomon Fabricant, Milton Friedman, Irving Kravis, Robert Lipsey, and many others has provided new statistical information or better organized data about the price system, findings about its internal structure and network of relationships, and generalizations pertaining to the monetary, competitive, cost, and other economic factors that influence prices and are in turn shaped by them. The general tendency for the price level to move with, rather than against, changes in the level of output; the lags of retail prices behind wholesale prices; the lags in wage rates and in unit labor costs; the marked inverse influence of changes in unit costs upon profit margins—all these and many additional findings have stemmed from National Bureau studies.

On the statistical side, we are indebted to Mills for the development of price indexes for various classifications of commodities; to Hultgren for carefully matched price and cost indexes; to Creamer for indexes of wage changes in the 1920s and 1930s; to Fabricant and to Kendrick for comparable price and productivity indexes; to

Reprinted from Report 384, Bureau of Labor Statistics, 1971.

Kravis and Lipsey for prices of goods bought and sold in foreign commerce; to Stigler and Kendahl, most recently, for indexes of transaction prices at wholesale; and so on. These new statistics have not only illuminated the past, they have led to the continuing provision of and improvement in current statistics on prices, wages, costs, and productivity. For these and other reasons, our debt to the work of the National Bureau is not only large, but growing.

This report is a revised version of an address made at a colloquium on The Business Cycle Today held by the National Bureau of Economic Research in New York on September 24, 1970, in celebration of its fiftieth anniversary. I am indebted to John Layng, Nancy Leach, and Mildred Tweedy of the Bureau of Labor Statistics staff for their assistance in the preparation of materials for this report.

INTRODUCTION

Inflation is characterized by a general and widely diffused rise in prices and costs. However, all prices and factors affecting prices do not begin to rise or fall at the same time. In part, this is due to the existence of more or less regular sequences in the movement of different prices. Prices in some markets almost always begin to rise more promptly than in other markets. Similarly, some prices typically begin to fall sooner than others.

Moreover, prices do not all move at the same pace, and in particular, they do not necessarily move at the same pace as wages or costs of production. Prices of some types of assets, such as common stocks or land, rise or fall, while the money price of other assets, such as savings accounts or debt instruments, may not change at all. These differences in price behavior have significant consequences. Real wages—money wages adjusted for price changes—may rise or fall, with vital effects on the wage earner and his family. Profit margins, dependent on the difference between prices and costs, may rise or fall, thereby encouraging or discouraging expansion of production, development of investment plans, or shifts of resources from one activity to another.

This chapter sets forth the results of a study of the cyclical behavior of prices. It describes a chronology of fluctuations in the rate of change in the price level (particularly since 1946), considers the relationship between these fluctuations and those in economic activity in general, examines how price increases and decreases are diffused through the price system, measures the tendencies of some prices to lead and others to lag, shows how the rates of change in costs and prices alter their relationship to one another during a cyclical swing, and finally, examines the current price situation in the light of these historical findings.

A REFERENCE CHRONOLOGY
FOR PRICES

The National Bureau's reference chronology of peaks and troughs, created by Wesley Mitchell, is one of the simplest yet most effective devices for studying business cycles. It has become widely used. Nowadays almost every economic statistician knows what the "shaded areas" on charts of monthly time series represent. A similar device may be employed for studying movements in the price system. To do so, a number of questions must be faced. Should the chronology represent peaks and troughs in the level of prices or in their rate of change? If the latter, how should the rate of change be measured? What index or set of indexes of prices should be used to establish the chronology? What criteria should be set up to define the chronology and identify its turning points?

The business cycle chronology is based on the working definition of business cycles set forth by Mitchell in his 1927 volume, *Business Cycles—The Problem and Its Setting*, and later refined by Burns and Mitchell in their 1946 monograph, *Measuring Business Cycles*. In brief, the definition applied three criteria to the problem: the magnitude, the duration, and the diffusion of fluctuations in economic activity. One inquired how large the fall or rise in total activity was, how long it lasted, and how widely it was diffused over different economic sectors. Turning points were identified not by a single aggregate, such as gross national product, but by determining the consensus among a number of series, each of which had some claim to represent or reflect total economic activity.

A business cycle chronology was constructed not only for the United States, but also for Great Britain, France, and Germany. Still other countries, such as Canada, Japan, and Italy, have constructed business cycle chronologies along similar lines. Much is to be said for developing a price chronology in a similar manner. Whether it is the level of prices or their rate of change that is selected as the ultimate variable, attention should be focused upon swings that are of substantial size, last more than just a few months, and are widely diffused throughout the price system. A single general price index is most convenient for this purpose. Although the idea of an index of the general price level is an ancient one, today no single widely accepted measure exists. The three leading candidates would be the consumer price index, the wholesale price index, and the implicit price deflator for gross national product. Each of these has its merits and deficiencies for the purpose.

The deflator is quarterly and the other two indexes are monthly; other things equal, a monthly chronology is to be preferred. The deflator has the largest economic coverage, but that also means that it includes some dubious elements, notably "prices" in the government sector that—lacking good information on the price of government purchases—are really wage rates. For this reason, many consider the private GNP deflator a better price index. The deflator is affected not only by changing prices but also by changes in the composition of output, whereas the other two indexes use fixed weights and hence reflect price changes alone.

The wholesale price index, of course, does not cover one part of the price system (namely, services), has some gaps in its industrial coverage, and depends in part upon list prices rather than actual transaction prices. The consumer price index is the closest approximation of the three to an actual transaction price index, but is limited to prices paid by urban wage earner and clerical worker families. Unlike the other two, it includes prices for existing goods, such as houses and used cars, as well as for currently produced goods and services.

These considerations do not point to a clear-cut conclusion, except to suggest a real need for a monthly general price index. Lacking this, I have based the chronology in this chapter upon the rate of change in the consumer price index, using the GNP deflator and the wholesale price index and some of their principal components (e.g., the private deflator and the WPI for industrial commodities) to provide supplementary evidence. The CPI has risen almost continuously since 1954, but there have been sizable fluctuations in its rate of increase, and the chronology identifies these fluctuations. The rate of inflation is, of course, a matter of major concern. The chronology shows when this rate, as measured by the CPI, reached high points and low points since 1947.

For the identification of turning points, we are fortunate to have, again thanks to the National Bureau, a computer program recently developed by Charlotte Boschan and Gerhard Bry. This essentially reproduces, in an objective and mechanical fashion, most of the choices of "specific cycle" turning points that used to be entirely dependent upon the judgment of National Bureau staff. Of course, it uses criteria that are similar to those used by the staff. It bases its choices upon whether the fluctuations in the data are large enough and long enough to be reflected in various moving averages, but does not explicitly use any criterion as to the size of a swing. Despite this, it is rather uncanny in its ability to detect and identify turning points independently selected by experts—and, I might add, to uncover inconsistencies in judgment by the less expert. We have used the turns selected by the computer program in a large majority of instances. The exceptions are due to the occasional failure of the program to select a large movement because it is too short or (more frequently) to select very small movements simply because they last quite long. I dare say our entire analysis could have been carried out strictly in terms of the turning points identified by the computer program without major effect upon our conclusions.

After deciding upon the rate of change in prices as the variable that the chronology would represent, several other decisions remain. First, the rates of change must be seasonally adjusted or derived from seasonally adjusted indexes. During the past year (1970) the Bureau of Labor Statistics began reporting the seasonally adjusted rate of change in the CPI. The seasonal pattern has a relatively small effect upon the level of the index (currently the largest and the smallest seasonal factors are, respectively, 100.12 in July and 99.83 in January and February). Nevertheless, it has a substantial effect upon rates of change over short periods. For example, the rate of change from July 1969 to January 1970 is raised from an annual rate of 5.7 percent to 6.3 percent after seasonal adjustment, which is equivalent to dividing a seasonal index of 90 into the unadjusted rate. This seasonal effect has been powerful enough to cause the unadjusted July to January rates to be lower than either the preceding or the following January to July rates in four out of the past five years.[1]

Next, precisely how the rate of change is to be measured must be determined. The range of possibilities is wide. The interval over which a change is measured can be as short as one month or as long as twelve months or more. Monthly indexes can be averaged over calendar quarters or over moving three-month intervals and rates of change measured between these averages. More complicated smoothing formulas can be applied. Generally, month-to-month changes are highly erratic, so some form of smoothing is desirable. On the other hand, smoothing formulas can twist and distort cyclical patterns and timing relationships. After some experimentation I have concluded that the rate of change over a six-month span meets reasonably well such criteria as smoothness, simplicity, and limited distorting effects for the CPI and most other price and wage series. For series that are available only in quarterly form, quarter-to-quarter changes are used. (Although the interval between two adjacent quarters is only three months, the averaging over a quarter offsets the shorter interval, so the smoothing effect is similar to a six-month change.) Occasionally,

I use changes over twelve-month or four-quarter spans, when these are the only data available or when the six-month or one-quarter rates are unduly erratic.[2]

Taking into account the foregoing considerations, Figure 12-1 presents the reference chronology, based upon the rate of change in the consumer price index, together with the rates of change in the other comprehensive indexes mentioned above. Six contractions in the rate of change are identified: in 1947–1948, 1950–1952, 1953–1954, 1956–1958, 1959–1961, and 1966–1967. We have marked a tentative peak in February 1970. If confirmed [as it was], this will mark the beginning of the seventh contraction since 1947 (see below). Taking the twenty-three-year period between the 1947 and 1970 peaks, we find that expansions in the rate of change lasted 162 months in the aggregate, while contractions covered 106 months. That is, although the level of the consumer price index has been generally rising during this period, the rate of increase has declined over long stretches—aggregating nearly nine years (for a revised and updated chronology, see Appendix Table A-5).

The other indexes show broadly similar fluctuations, but with exceptions, especially in the period 1959–1964. In terms of these comprehensive indexes, therefore, the chronology seems to represent fluctuations that are spread widely throughout the price system. This matter will be examined more directly in the section on diffusion indexes.

Some interesting points emerge from the chart. During the first three contractions in the rate of change in the CPI, the rate fell below zero—that is, the index declined. But the rate barely reached zero in the next two contractions (1958 and 1961) and did not do so at all in the last one (1967). Indeed, the level of the rate at its successive low points becomes progressively higher throughout the period. There is a related tendency for the declines in the rate to become progressively smaller. In the first two contractions the rate dropped eighteen and fifteen percentage points; in the next two, three and four and one half percentage points; and in the last two, two and two and one half percentage points. However, the high points in the rate have not become progressively higher, nor have the expansions become progressively larger. If there has been a rising floor under the rate, there has not been a rising ceiling also. The peak rates form a U-shaped curve. One possible explanation, which needs further exploration, is that the rising importance of services and the diminishing importance of foods in family budgets have had the effect of preventing declines in the rate of change of the CPI from

Figure 12-1. Rates of Change in Comprehensive Price Indexes *(measured over six month or quarter-to-quarter span, seasonally adjusted, at annual rate, centered).*

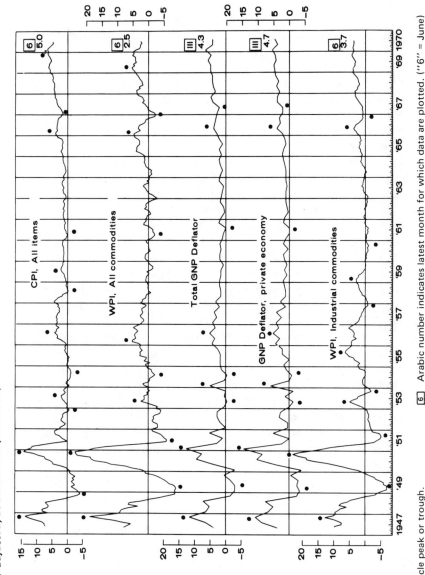

• Price cycle peak or trough.

Source: Bureau of Labor Statistics.

6 Arabic number indicates latest month for which data are plotted. ("6" = June)

III Roman numeral indicates latest quarter for which data are plotted. ("III" = third quarter)

reaching as low a level in recent years as it did earlier in the postwar period.

PRICE CYCLES AND BUSINESS CYCLES

How does the price chronology compare with the business cycle chronology? Four of the price contractions correspond with the four business contractions of 1948–1949, 1953–1954, 1957–1958, and 1960–1961. But the business expansion of 1949–1953 was interrupted by the price contraction of 1950–1952 during the Korean War, and the long business expansion that began in 1961 was interrupted by the price contraction of 1966–1967. Both of these interruptions were characterized by some hesitancy in business as well. Hence there is a notable degree of correspondence between the behavior of the rate of change in the consumer price index and general economic activity. Since World War II, every economic slowdown or actual recession has been accompanied by a cyclical contraction in the rate of change in the price level, and cyclical contractions in the rate of change in the price level have not occurred at other times.

This does not mean, however, that a business recession as defined by the National Bureau of Economic Research is a necessary condition for a reduction in the rate of inflation. As already noted, two such reductions since 1947 have occurred at times when the economy merely slowed down. Moreover, several of the declines in the rate of price rise that were associated with business cycle contractions began well before the contraction in business activity got underway. The 1947 and 1956 peaks in the rate of change in the consumer price index both came about a year before the business cycle peak, and the 1959 price peak came ten months before the business peak. In fact, in 1948, all of the decline in rate of change in prices—and it was substantial—took place before the recession began. In 1953, the two peaks coincided. More often than not, then, the CPI has begun to decelerate while business activity was still expanding.

On the other hand, low points in the rate of price change have coincided rather closely with business cycle troughs—at least on three out of four occasions. The 1948 upturn in the rate of price change (from a level of minus 4 percent) came eleven months before the business upturn, but the 1954 price upturn coincided with the business upturn, while the 1958 and 1961 price upturns followed the business turn by three months and one month, respectively. In short, declines in the rate of price change have typically started earlier and hence have continued somewhat longer than business cycle contractions.

However, the rate of price change has usually persisted at a low level, even a negative level, beyond the point of upturn. These tendencies are illustrated in Figure 12-2. Perhaps the most striking showing is that about a year after the business peak, the rates of price change have all been in the vicinity of zero, plus or minus one percent. The food price component of the CPI, highly sensitive to economic demand, is largely responsible for this result.

DIFFUSION OF PRICE CHANGES

One of the characteristics of business cycles that Wesley Mitchell deemed important and which he demonstrated empirically time and again, was their generality. "A business cycle consists of expansions occurring at about the same time in many economic activities, followed by similarly general recessions, contractions, and revivals . . . ," says the definition formulated by Burns and Mitchell in 1946. Among the many activities are prices, and we have just seen that the rate of change in the price level is clearly one of the participants in the ebb and flow of business cycles.

This observation does not, however, directly answer the question of whether the price chronology we have constructed reflects widespread similar movements among different prices. We can get at this question by examining diffusion indexes of prices, for such indexes report how many out of a given population of prices are rising at a particular time and how many are falling. In terms of the popular conception of whether or not the economy is experiencing inflation or whether inflation is getting worse or better, variations in the degree of generality of price increases are perhaps more significant than variations in the rate of change in a price index.

Figure 12-3 brings together several price diffusion indexes and illustrates several propositions. First, at all times some prices are falling and some are rising, but the proportions that are in the one category or the other vary greatly. Second, the most widespread increases in prices generally have occurred during the periods marked off as expansions in our price chronology, while the most widespread reductions in prices generally have occurred during the contractions. That is to say, the reason why the consumer price index increases more rapidly at some times than at others is partly that price increases are more widespread at those times, not only that the increases are larger.

Figure 12-2. Rates of Change in the Consumer Price Index before and after Business Cycle Peaks.

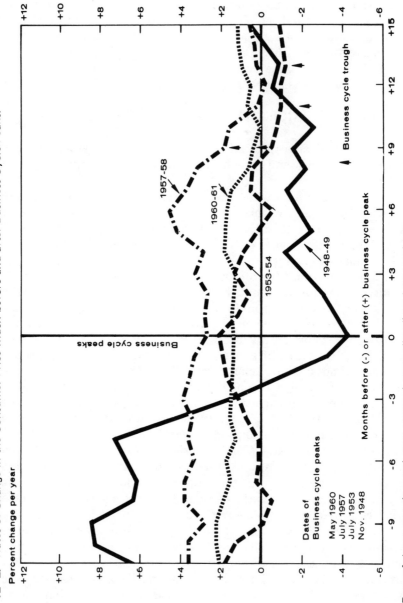

Note: Rates of change over six-month span, centered, seasonally adjusted at annual rate.

Source: Bureau of Labor Statistics.

Third, there are discernible sequences in the process whereby price changes spread through the economy. Prices of industrial materials take an early position, wholesale prices of manufactured goods move somewhat later, and retail prices of consumer goods and services come still later. The sequences among those parts of the price system that are shown in the figure are so long drawn out, in fact, that on several occasions (notably during 1957–1958) the most widespread declines in the early moving prices came almost at the same time as the most widespread increases in consumer prices. Unless the sequences in the price system are taken into account, one could be misled into thinking that the cyclical swings in prices are less general than they are in fact.

LEADS AND LAGS IN PRICES

The diffusion indexes in Figure 12-3 depict some of the sequences in the price system. But we can examine the matter more thoroughly by referring to the rates of change in a larger array of price indexes, using the price chronology as a reference frame in the same way that the business cycle chronology has been used to study leads and lags in economic activities generally. In this manner we can observe not only the leads and lags of other prices vis-à-vis the consumer price index, but also their leads and lags with respect to one another.[3]

Looking first at certain major components of the consumer price index, we find that the turns in the commodity component match those in the total index very closely (see Table 12-1). On five occasions since 1956 (when the commodity-service grouping first becomes available), the turns in the rate of change in the commodity index and in the total index came in exactly the same month, while on the remaining occasion the commodity turn was one month earlier. This correspondence is due more to food prices, whose volatile movements have a marked effect on both the commodities component and the total, than to commodities other than food. As for prices of services, their well-known tendency to lag is apparent. Perhaps less well known is the fact that the rate of change in service prices undergoes cyclical movements that correspond closely, except for the lag, to those in commodity prices. The lag of service prices behind commodity prices averages about three months. These relations are shown by Figure 12-4.

Turning to wholesale prices, we find that the total WPI exhibits a slight tendency to lead the total CPI (see Table 12-2). That is, it leads on five occasions, exactly coincides four times, and lags only

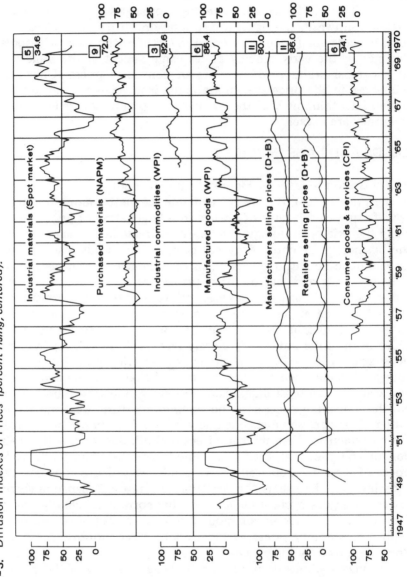

Figure 12-3. Diffusion Indexes of Prices *(percent rising, centered)*.

Notes to Figure 12-3

6⃞ Arabic number indicates latest month for which data are plotted. ("6" = June)

Ⅲ̲ Roman numeral indicates latest quarter for which data are plotted. ("III" = third quarter)

Notes: Figures are the percent of components rising over the spans indicated below (half of the unchanged components are considered rising). Data are centered within spans: one-month indexes are placed on latest month, six-month indexes are placed on the fourth month, nine-month indexes are placed on the fifth month, twelve-month indexes are placed on the seventh month, and four-quarter indexes are placed on the third quarter of the span.

Industrial materials (spot market), thirteen industrial materials, nine-month span, BLS. Component series are seasonally adjusted by Bureau of the Census.

Purchased materials, companies reporting higher buying prices, one-month span, National Association of Purchasing Management.

Industrial commodities, sixty-nine commodity group indexes covering the entire wholesale price index for industrial commodities, twelve-month span, BLS.

Manufactured goods, twenty-two industry indexes covering the entire wholesale price index for manufactured goods, six-month span, BLS.

Manufacturer's selling prices, companies reporting higher selling prices, four-quarter span, Dun and Bradstreet, Inc. This is a copyrighted series used by permission. It may not be reproduced without written permission from the source.

Retailer's selling prices, same.

Consumer goods and services, seventeen commodity and service group indexes covering about 92 percent of the content of the consumer price index, seasonally adjusted, six-month span, BLS.

Source: Bureau of Labor Statistics.

Table 12-1.   Leads and Lags in Rates of Change of Major Components of the Consumer Price Index.

Item	CPI, All Items	Dates of Corresponding Peaks and Troughs				Lead (−) or Lag (+) in Months, at Turns in CPI, All Items			
		CPI, Commodities[a]	CPI, Food	CPI, Other Commodities[a]	CPI, Services[a]	CPI, Commodities[a]	CPI, Food	CPI, Other Commodities[a]	CPI, Services[a]
Peak	10/47	—	10/47	—	—	—	0	—	—
Trough	11/48	—	11/48	—	—	—	0	—	—
Peak	11/50	—	11/50	—	—	—	0	—	—
Trough	11/52	—	2/53	—	—	—	+3	—	—
Peak	7/53	—	2/54	—	—	—	+7	—	—
Trough	8/54	—	10/54	—	—	—	+2	—	—
Peak	7/56	7/56	4/56	12/56	2/57	0	−3	+5	+7
Trough	7/58	7/58	7/58	7/58	9/58	0	0	0	+2
Peak	7/59	7/59	5/60	4/59	6/59	0	+10	−3	−1
Trough	3/61	3/61	3/61	5/60	5/61	0	0	−10	+2
Peak	1/66	1/66	12/65	—	6/66	1	−1	—	+5
Trough	1/67	12/66	1/67	—	4/67	—	0	—	+3
Peak	2/70[b]	3/69	11/69	—	—	—	—	—	—

Dates of Extra Peaks and Troughs[c]

Item		CPI, Commodities[a]	CPI, Food	CPI, Other Commodities[a]					
Peak		9/63	—	7/61					
Trough		4/64	10/56	10/62					
Peak		—	1/58	8/63					
Trough		—	—	4/65					

Table 12-1. continued

	Summary of Leads and Lags at Turns in CPI, All Items			
Item	CPI, Commodities[a]	CPI, Food	CPI, Other Commodities[a]	CPI, Services[a]
Number of:				
Leads	1	2	2	1
Exact coincidences	5	6	1	0
Lags	0	4	1	5
Total timing comparisons	6	12	4	6
Rough coincidences[d]	6	10	2	4
Median lead (−) or lag (+), in months:				
At peaks	0	0	+1	+5
At troughs	0	0	−5	+2
At all turns	0	0	−1.5	+2.5

[a] Data are not available before 1956.
[b] Tentative.
[c] Extra peaks and troughs are those that do not match turns in the CPI, all items.
[d] Rough coincidences include exact coincidences and leads or lags of three months or less.

Note: Dashes (−) indicate no timing comparison. Percent changes are computed over six-month spans, centered, seasonally-adjusted at annual rate.

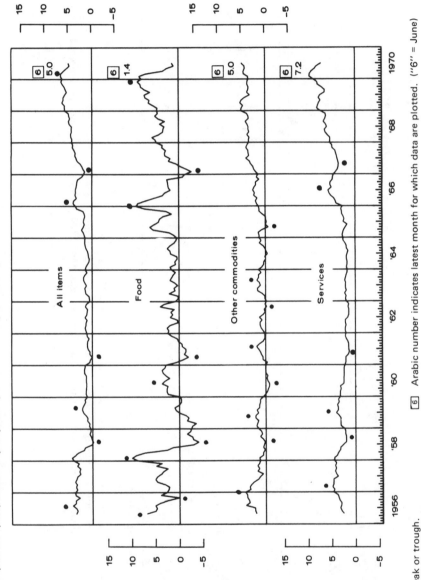

Figure 12–4. Rates of Change in the Consumer Price Index and its Major Components *(measured over six-month or quarter-to-quarter span, seasonally adjusted, at annual rate, centered).*

• Price peak or trough.

6 Arabic number indicates latest month for which data are plotted. ("6" = June)

Source: Bureau of Labor Statistics.

once. The lead appears to derive more from the industrial commodities in the WPI than from the farm products, processed foods, and feeds component. The latter component, however, matches the CPI quite closely and of course compares most directly with the food price component of the CPI, which, as we have seen, itself has a dominant effect on the CPI. The behavior of consumer prices depends, to an extent that most city dwellers are probably unaware of, on the behavior of farm prices.

The industrial commodities component of the WPI has turned before the CPI nine times since 1948, coincided once, and lagged twice. The tendency to lead is imparted primarily by the prices for crude and intermediate materials other than foods rather than for finished goods. Prices for crude materials other than food have led nine out of ten turns in the CPI since 1947, an average lead of about four months. This index is similar in its movements and timing to the weekly index of spot market prices of industrial materials prices. On most occasions the turns in the rates of change in these two materials price indexes have occurred within a month or two of each other. Prices for producer-finished goods—that is, machinery, equipment, trucks, office furniture, and the like—show about as much tendency to lag behind as to lead the movements in the CPI. Many of these relationships as well as others are depicted in Figures 12-5 and 12-6.[4]

The rate of change in the GNP deflator is a lagging indicator relative to the rate of change in the CPI (see Table 12-3). This is true also of the private deflator, since its turns usually coincide with those of the total. The deflators have lagged behind the turns in the CPI far more frequently than they have led or coincided with it, and the average lag has been about three months. The reason for the lag may lie in the fact that personal consumption expenditures—namely, the type of expenditure reflected in the CPI—constitute less than two-thirds of total GNP, and prices for the two largest elements in the remainder—fixed investment goods and government services—are relatively sticky. The fluctuating weights in the GNP deflator may also be a factor. When the deflator is computed with fixed (1958) weights, as the Department of Commerce has done since 1962, the 1966 peak and the 1967 trough in the rate of change are reached one quarter earlier, and the most recent high is two quarters earlier.

In this brief review we have, of course, only scratched the surface of the complex structure of leads and lags in the price system. In the vanguard are the wholesale prices of raw and semifabricated materials. At the rear are the retail prices of services. In between are

Table 12-2.   Leads and Lags in Rates of Change of Wholesale Price Indexes.

Peaks and Troughs (1)	CPI, All Items (2)	WPI, All Commodities (3)	WPI, Industrial Commodities (4)	WPI, Farm Products, Processed Foods and Feeds (5)	WPI, Crude Materials (6)	WPI, Crude Materials Less Food (7)
			Dates of Corresponding Peaks and Troughs			
Peak	10/47	10/47	10/47	10/47	10/47	8/47
Trough	11/48	2/49	4/49	11/48	11/48	4/49
Peak	11/50	11/50	10/50	11/50	11/50	7/50
Trough	11/52	6/51	8/51	11/52	5/51	8/51
Peak	7/53	4/53	4/53	2/54	2/54	4/53
Trough	8/54	7/54	10/53	9/55	9/55	10/53
Peak	7/56	2/56	8/55	3/56	2/56	9/55
Trough	7/58	—	11/57	12/58	7/59	—
Peak	7/59	—	2/59	2/60	—	—
Trough	3/61	3/61	9/60	3/61	—	8/60
Peak	1/66	1/66	4/66	11/65	11/65	12/65
Trough	1/67	12/66	10/66	12/66	12/66	10/66
Peak	2/70[b]	3/69	—	3/69	3/69	5/69
			Dates of Extra Peaks and Troughs[c]			
Peak	None	None	2/57	—	—	
Trough	—	—	12/57	2/57	10/57	
Peak	—	—	9/61	2/58	7/58	
Trough	—	—	12/62	—	—	
Peak	—	—	—	9/61	4/61	
Trough	—	—	—	12/62	4/62	
			Leads (−) and Lags (+) in Months, at Turns in CPI, All Items			
Peak	10/47	0	0	0	0	−2
Trough	11/48	+3	+5	0	0	+5
Peak	11/50	0	−1	0	0	−4
Trough	11/52	−17	−15	0	−18	−15
Peak	7/53	−3	−3	+7	+7	−3
Trough	8/54	−7	−10	+13	+13	−10
Peak	7/56	−5	−11	−4	−5	−10
Trough	7/58	—	−8	+5	+12	—
Peak	7/59	—	−5	+7	—	—
Trough	3/61	0	−6	0	—	−7
Peak	1/66	0	+3	−2	−2	−1
Trough	1/67	−1	−3	−1	−1	−3

Table 12-2. continued

		Dates of Corresponding Peaks and Troughs			
Spot Market Price Index, Industrial Materials[a] *(8)*	*WPI, Intermediate Materials (9)*	*WPI, Consumer Finished Goods (10)*	*WPI, Consumer Foods (11)*	*WPI, Other Consumer Goods (12)*	*WPI, Producer Finished Goods (13)*
—	10/47	10/47	10/47	10/47	8/48
—	2/49	11/48	11/48	2/49	7/49
8/50	10/50	9/50	9/50	10/50	10/50
6/51	7/51	11/52	1/53	10/51	9/52
3/54	4/53	2/54	2/54	4/53	—
—	7/54	7/54	7/55	10/53	—
—	7/55	12/57	12/57	11/56	8/56
9/57	11/57	8/58	12/58	3/58	5/58
8/58	2/59	2/60	2/60	2/59	12/58
9/60	7/61	2/61	3/61	2/61	6/60
8/64	4/66	12/65	12/65	—	10/66
11/66	11/66	12/66	12/66	—	4/67
6/69	—	12/69	12/69	—	—
		Dates of Extra Peaks and Troughs[c]			
2/61	7/63	10/61	12/61	None	None
4/62	3/64	12/62	12/62	—	—
—	—	—	—	—	—
—	—	—	—	—	—
—	—	—	—	—	—
—	—	—	—	—	—
		Leads (−) and Lags (+) in Months, at Turns in CPI, All Items			
—	0	0	0	0	+10
—	+3	0	0	+3	+8
−3	−1	−2	−2	−1	−1
−17	−16	0	+2	−13	−2
+8	−3	+7	+7	−3	—
—	−1	−1	+11	−10	—
—	−12	+17	+17	+4	+1
−10	−8	+1	+5	−4	−2
−11	−5	+7	+7	−5	−7
−6	+4	−1	0	−1	−9
−17	+3	−1	−1	—	+9
−2	−2	−1	−1	—	+3

(*Table 12-2. continued overleaf*)

Table 12-2. continued

(1)	Summary of Leads and Lags at Turns in CPI, All Items				
	WPI, All Commodities (3)	WPI, Industrial Commodities (4)	WPI, Farm Products, Processed Foods and Feeds (5)	WPI, Crude Materials (6)	WPI, Crude Materials Less Food (7)
Number of:					
Leads	5	9	3	4	9
Exact coincidences	4	1	5	3	0
Lags	1	2	4	3	1
Total timing comparisons	10	12	12	10	10
Rough coincidences [d]	8	5	7	5	4
Median lead (−) or lag (+), in months:					
At peaks	0	−2	0	0	−3
At troughs	−1	−7	0	0	−7
At all turns	−5	−4	0	0	−3.5

[a] Weekly index, not a component of the WPI.

[b] Tentative.

[c] Extra peaks and troughs are those that do not match turns in the CPI, all items.

[d] Rough coincidences include exact coincidences and leads or lags of three months or less.

Note: Dashes (−) indicate no timing comparison. Percent changes are computed over six months spans, centered, seasonally adjusted at annual rate.

the wholesale and retail prices of foods and many other commodities. We have dealt with fairly large groups of prices of goods and services and have not touched upon the prices of fixed assets, such as land or buildings, or the price of labor, or interest rates. There is a large amount of room for further investigation.

PRICES, COSTS OF PRODUCTION, AND PROFITS

During the past few years, a systematic body of statistics has been built up that connects the rate of change in the price level with rates of change in compensation per man hour, output per man hour, labor costs per unit of output, profits, and other costs per unit of output. The data are available quarterly for the private sector as a

Table 12-2. continued

Summary of Leads and Lags at Turns in CPI, All Items

Spot Market Price Index, Industrial Materials [a] (8)	WPI, Inter- mediate Materials (9)	WPI, Consumer Finished Goods (10)	WPI, Consumer Foods (11)	WPI, Other Consumer Goods (12)	WPI, Producer Finished Goods (13)
7	8	5	3	7	5
0	1	3	3	1	0
1	3	4	6	2	5
8	12	12	12	10	10
2	7	9	7	5	5
−7	−2	+5	−5	−1	+1
−8	−1.5	−.5	+1	−4	−2
−8	−1.5	−.5	0	−2	0

whole, as well as for certain major elements of the private sector. They tell us some things about the cyclical behavior of prices and the factors affecting them that hitherto could be inferred only indirectly, if at all.

The year-to-year rates of change in these data since 1947 for the total private economy are shown in Figures 12-7 and 12-8. They reveal that output per man hour has risen in every year and that hourly compensation has done likewise. In most years, the increase in compensation has exceeded the increase in productivity, so labor costs per unit of output have also risen. But the fluctuations in unit labor costs are wider than in productivity or compensation, and they also bear a closer relationship to price. The remaining costs (depreciation, interest, and indirect taxes) also fluctuate considerably per unit of output, in part no doubt because of their relatively fixed nature; but they have been generally increasing relative to output in the postwar period. The fluctuations in profits per unit of output are wider still, and for the most part they move inversely with unit labor costs and with total unit costs.

The relationships of costs and profits to price depend not only on how they fluctuate but also on their magnitude. The data enable us

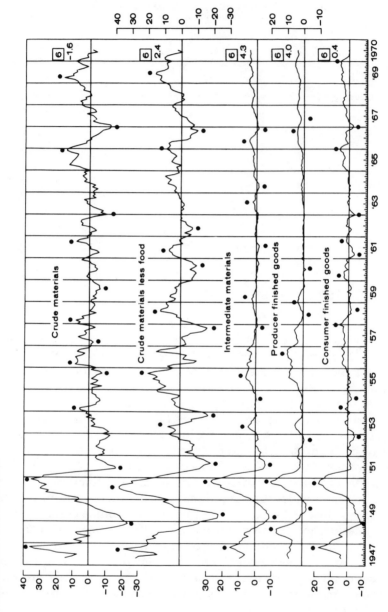

Figure 12–5. Rates of Change in Wholesale Price Indexes, by Stage of Process *(measured over six-month span, seasonally adjusted, at annual rate, centered).*

• Price cycle peak or trough.   ⬚ Arabic number indicates latest month for which data are plotted. ("6" = June)

Source: Bureau of Labor Statistics.

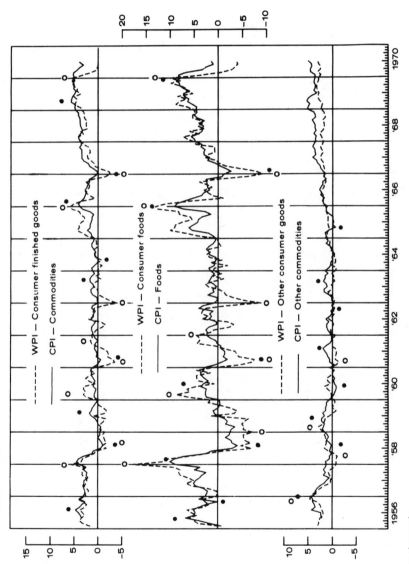

Figure 12-8. Rates of change in Wholesale and Consumer Price Indexes (measured over six-month span, seasonally adjusted, at annual rate, centered).

● CPI Peaks and troughs.

○ WPI Peaks and troughs.

Source: Bureau of Labor Statistics.

Table 12-3.   Leads and Lags in Rates of Change of GNP Implicit Price Deflators.

	CPI, All Items	Dates of Corresponding Peaks and Troughs		Lead (−) or Lag (+) in Months, at Turns in CPI, All Items	
		GNP Deflator		GNP Deflator	
		Total	Private Sector	Total	Private Sector
Peak	10/47	10/47	10/47	0	0
Trough	11/48	4/49	1/49	+5	+2
Peak	11/50	1/51	1/51	+2	+2
Trough	11/52	4/53	4/53	+5	+5
Peak	7/53	1/54	1/54	+6	+6
Trough	8/54	7/54	7/54	−1	−1
Peak	7/56	7/56	7/56	0	0
Trough	7/58	—	—	—	—
Peak	7/59	—	—	—	—
Trough	3/61	7/61	7/61	+4	+4
Peak	1/66	4/66	4/66	+3	+3
Trough	1/67	4/67	4/67	+3	+3
Peak	2/70 [a]	—	—	—	—

Table 12-3. continued

	Summary of Leads and Lags at Turns in CPI, All Items	
	GNP Deflator	
	Total	Private Sector
Number of:		
Leads	1	1
Exact coincidences	2	2
Lags	7	7
Total timing comparisons	10	10
Rough coincidences[b]	6	7
Median lead (−) or lag (+), in months:		
At peaks	+2	+2
At troughs	+4	+3
At all turns	+3	+2.5

[a] Tentative.
[b] Rough coincidences include exact coincidences and leads or lags of three months of less.
Note: Dashes (−) indicate no timing comparison.

Figure 12-7. Annual Percent Change in Prices, Productivity, Labor Compensation, and Unit Labor Costs, Total Private Economy, 1948–1970.

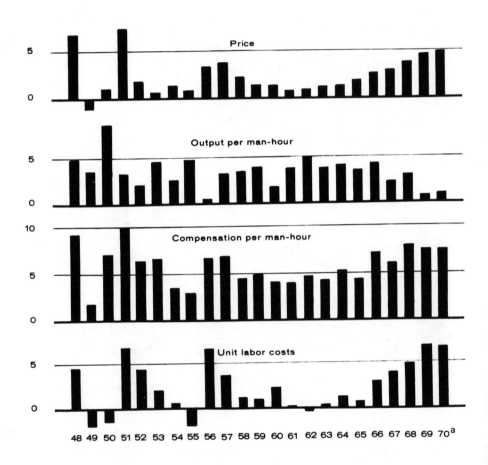

[a]Second quarter 1970 over second quarter 1969.

Compensation and labor costs include wages and salaries and supplemental payments for employees and an estimate of the salaries and supplements for the self-employed. Other (nonlabor) costs include depreciation, interest, and indirect taxes. Profits include corporate profits, estimated profits of unincorporated enterprises, and net rental earnings of owner-occupied dwellings.

Unit costs and unit profits are total costs and profits divided by total output.

Source: Bureau of Labor Statistics.

Figure 12-8. Annual Percent Change in Prices and Unit Costs, Total Private Economy, 1948–1970.

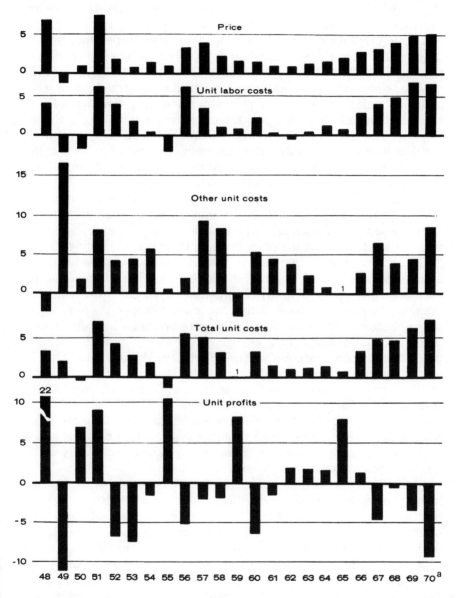

1. Indicates plotting at zero.
[a]Second quarter 1970 over second quarter 1969.
Note: For definitions see note to Figure 12-7.
Source: Bureau of Labor Statistics.

to take the magnitude into account and thereby to decompose the change in price into its constituent cost and profit components (see Figure 12-9). Thus in 1968-1969, for example, when the price index rose 4.5 percent, the share absorbed by increased unit labor costs was four percentage points: the share that went to pay increases in other unit costs was equivalent to 0.9 percent, while the decline in unit profits offset the rise in costs to the extent of 0.4 percent. In general, since payments for labor constitute the largest single cost and since unit labor costs have generally been rising, the share of unit labor costs usually has been positive and closely related to the change in price. The share of other costs is smaller, though usually positive, and less well correlated with the change in price. As often as not, the share of price change absorbed by unit profits has partly offset the increases in other costs (see Chapter 17).

A fairly characteristic picture of the behavior of costs and profits during a cyclical rise and fall in the rate of change in prices emerges from these data, particularly when use is made of the quarterly figures. At the bottom of the price cycle, with prices relatively stable or declining, the rate of increase in output per man hour is high, but after prices start rising, it diminishes as the upswing in prices continues. Rates of increase in hourly compensation, on the other hand, are usually at a moderate level during the initial phase of the upswing in prices, but soon begin to rise, partly in response to the price movement. As a joint result of the changing discrepancy between the rates of change in compensation and productivity, the rate of change in unit labor costs diminishes during the initial phase of the price expansion, but rises sharply in the later phase. Other unit costs follow somewhat the same path, so at the start of the price expansion costs are rising less rapidly than prices, while at its close they are rising more rapidly than prices, even though the price rise has in the meantime accelerated. Unit profits, therefore, typically rise rapidly at the start of a price expansion, but decline at the end.

As the downswing in the rate of price increase begins, output per man hour usually continues to show lower growth rates for a time, but shortly a recovery sets in. This reduction in physical costs is no doubt partly a consequence of the downswing in prices, as producers react to the profit squeeze, but it also serves to support it. Further support is provided by a decline in the rate of increase in hourly compensation. Both factors generate a decline in the rate of increase in unit labor costs. Other unit costs also show lower rates of growth as the price contraction continues. The upshot is that while the increase in total unit costs exceeds that of prices at the start of the

Figure 12-9.   Decomposition of Annual Rates of Change in Prices into Cost and Profit Components, Total Private Economy, 1948–1970.

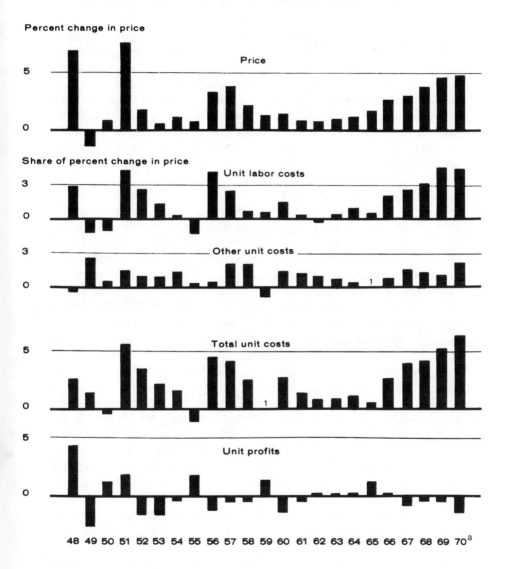

1. Indicates plotting at zero.
[a]Second quarter 1970 over second quarter 1969.
Note: For definitions see note to Figure 12-7.
Source: Bureau of Labor Statistics.

price contraction and unit profits are therefore declining, this situation is reversed before the end of the price contraction. Cost increases become sharply lower or actual cost reductions take place; the downswing in costs exceeds that in prices; and unit profits begin rising again.

This description of the interplay of costs and profits during a cycle in the rate of change in prices is, of course, highly generalized. Although it is based on recent data, it follows fairly closely the process that Wesley Mitchell described nearly sixty years ago in his classic treatise, *Business Cycles*, whereby costs rise relative to prices and encroach upon profits during an economic boom. I believe it can still help us to comprehend and to anticipate the developments experienced when inflationary pressures build up as well as when they subside (see Chapter 16).

THE CURRENT SITUATION

One of the purposes of the National Bureau's studies of business cycles was to enable men to make better judgments about the current economic situation. Improved statistical data, more precise knowledge of economic relationships, and better understanding of the changing nature of these relationships all serve this end. There is a reverse effect as well. The unfolding situation may, by adding one more observation so to speak, help to confirm, to contradict, or to modify what we thought we had learned from the past. It is well, therefore, to consider some recent developments in the cyclical behavior of prices to see whether they are illuminated by, or help to illuminate, our historical findings.

Our tentative peak date for the reference chronology of prices, based upon the rate of change in the consumer price index, is February 1970. This is the date when the seasonally adjusted rate of change over a six-month interval reached its highest level in the current upswing, 6.7 percent per year, and began to decline. February is simply the central month of that interval, which runs from November 1969 to May 1970. Several factors persuade me to call this a tentative rather than a definite peak. The most important, of course, is that the subsequent decline to 6 percent in March, 5.4 percent in April, 4.8 percent in May, and 5 percent in June and July has been brief, but at present writing the July figure (representing the change from April to October 1970) is the latest we have. The decline to date is shorter than any previous contraction in our chronology—the shortest was twelve months in 1966–1967. In magnitude, the decline (one and seven-tenths percentage points) is smaller than in 1966–1967 (two and four-tenths points). Unless the decline continues, therefore, it will not qualify as a contraction in our chronology.

Although we cannot, therefore, at this time consider the peak to be firmly established, there are a number of bits of evidence pointing in that direction. First, the rates of change in the CPI over shorter spans than six months show peaks around the turn of the year, with much larger declines since. Next, our observations upon leads and lags suggest that a peak in the rate of change in the CPI is apt to be matched closely by one in food prices and to be followed by one in service prices. In fact, food prices reached their highest rate of increase over a six-month interval, nearly 9 percent per year, in November 1969. The decline to the latest figure, about one percent at an annual rate, has been precipitous. As for services, their high point to date, about 9.5 percent, occurred in February 1970, some three months after the turn in food prices.

Third, corroboration is to be found in the behavior of other price indexes, notably the WPI, where we now have data through November. The total index reached its peak rate of increase (over a six-month span, seasonally adjusted at annual rate) in March 1969 at 5 percent and has declined since then to about 2 percent. The decisive drop occurred in the farm products, processed foods, and feeds component, from 8.5 percent in December 1969[5] to a negative figure currently. Industrial commodity prices, as usual, have shown a much milder movement, but nevertheless did decline from a 4 percent rate in October 1969 to about 3 percent currently. The drop in the rate of change in food prices at wholesale has been sharper than at retail, as has usually been the case in the past. The high month was December 1969 at 10 percent, and the latest figure is −2 percent.

The prices of crude materials at wholesale have played their traditional role by declining early and sharply. Their peak rate of increase, 16 percent per year, was attained in March 1969. The latest, and lowest, rate is −3 percent. The weekly industrial materials index has behaved in a similar, though more extreme fashion, by declining from a peak rate of increase of 25 percent per year in January 1969 to a current low of −14 percent, a drop of thirty-nine percentage points in the past year and a half. The GNP deflator reached its fastest rate of increase between the fourth quarter of 1969 and the first quarter of 1970—namely, 6.4 percent. The latest figure, for the second to third quarter, is 4.6.

Finally, all the diffusion indexes of Figure 12-3 have receded from their highs, which were reached during 1968 and 1969. The decline to date has been largest in the index that has typically moved earliest—industrial materials prices. In general, the rise in prices is no longer as widespread as it was, and price reductions are now somewhat more common.

All these developments are consistent with what has happened during past economic slowdowns. Although we must await further evidence to be confident that a decline of substantial dimensions in the rate of change in prices is underway, if this welcome development does take place, it will mark one more occasion when the price system has reacted to a reduction in demand pressures.

The long-continued upswing in the rate of change in prices and its recent subsidence have been accompanied by changes in costs and profits that bear a striking resemblance to earlier episodes. Table 12-4 tells the story. Between 1964 and 1969, unit labor costs accelerated steadily, partly as a result of the acceleration in compensation rates per hour and partly because of the retardation in output per man hour. Other costs also accelerated, but the big contributor to the advance in the rate of increase in total costs was labor cost. By 1966, costs were rising faster than prices, and they have continued to do so every year since. At the same time, unit profits began to decline, and they have also declined each year. Mitchell himself could not have asked for a better illustration of the process he described.

The annual time unit used in Table 12-4 is too crude to show changes during the past few months, but the quarterly data reveal an important shift. Between the first and second quarters of this year the rate of change in the price index for the private sector fell to 4 percent, the lowest rate since 1968. Output per man hour advanced at an annual rate of about 3 percent, also the best showing since 1968. Coupled with a decline in the rate of increase in hourly compensation to about 5 percent, this produced a sharp decline in the rate of increase in unit labor costs to around 2 percent. Quarter-to-quarter changes are, of course, erratic, but the directions that these changes began to take in the second quarter and continued to take in the third are in line with what previous experience suggests is likely when an inflationary boom comes to an orderly end and a downswing in the price cycle begins.

THE NEED FOR FURTHER WORK

In my former capacity at the National Bureau of Economic Research, one of my favorite pieces of advice to authors was to close their reports with suggestions for further research and for improved statistics. To follow my own advice on this occasion is surely fitting.

Table 12-4. Percent Change in Prices, Costs, and Profits, Total Private Economy, 1965–1970.

Year	Price (1)	Output (2)	Output per Man Hour (3)	Compensation per Man Hour (4)	Unit Labor Costs (5)	Other Unit Costs[a] (6)	Total Unit Costs (7)	Unit Profit[b] (8)
Change from preceding year:								
1965	1.7	6.6	3.4	4.1	0.7	0.0	0.5	8.0
1966	2.5	6.4	4.0	6.9	2.8	2.5	2.8	1.3
1967	2.9	2.3	2.1	5.8	3.7	6.2	4.4	-4.5
1968	3.6	4.9	2.9	7.6	4.6	3.7	4.3	-0.4
1969	4.5	2.9	0.7	7.2	6.5	4.1	5.8	-3.3
1970[c]	4.6	-0.2	0.9	7.3	6.3	9.2	7.1	-10.8
Change from preceding quarter, at annual rate:								
1969: 3d	4.5	2.5	1.6	8.2	6.5	5.5	6.2	-5.9
4th	4.7	-1.0	0.8	8.8	7.9	10.1	8.5	-17.5
1970: 1st	5.3	-3.0	-2.5	6.8	9.6	9.0	9.4	-20.0
2d	4.1	0.7	3.7	5.3	1.5	12.3	4.4	1.8
3d	4.5	1.6	4.6	7.7	3.0	9.6	4.8	2.4

[a]Includes depreciation, interest, and indirect taxes.
[b]Includes corporate profits, estimates profits of unincorporated enterprises, and net rental earnings of owner-occupied dwellings.
[c]Second quarter 1969 to second quarter 1970.
Source: Bureau of Labor Statistics.

I shall confine myself to a single general admonition, which is to pay more attention to the price side of economics. Over the past twenty-five years or so, this aspect has been relatively neglected. It is time, I think, for a change. A great concern has developed over the problem of inflation in this country and not only in this country but around the world. Our ability to cope with it depends on our ability to understand it, and the starting point for understanding is statistical information and research.

Statistical information and research have helped to resolve the problem of the business cycle. The cyclical behavior of prices is ripe for an equally thorough probing. The National Bureau of Economic Research and the Bureau of Labor Statistics, continuing a long and fruitful cooperative relationship, might well devote themselves to this end.

NOTES TO CHAPTER 12

1. The magnification of the seasonal effect on the rate of change compared with the level can be illustrated as follows. The increase in the seasonal factor from 99.83 in January to 100.12 in July is 0.6 percent at an annual rate. If the increase in the unadjusted index is at a 6 percent annual rate, the seasonal factor is accounting for about one-tenth of the rise. Of course, it has an equal and opposite effect on the increase from July to January. The ups and downs in the rate of increase that are attributable to seasonal factors can be quite misleading in judging trends in the rate of inflation. For example, the unadjusted rate of increase during the six months ending in July 1965 showed a sharp acceleration, but by January 1966 the rate had declined sharply again, largely for seasonal reasons. There was a similar acceleration in July 1966 and then a retardation again in January 1967. This time, however, the decline was reflecting both seasonal factors and the 1967 minirecession. In short, as the figures given below indicate, the seasonally adjusted rates show the onset of inflation in 1965, its interruption in 1967, and its continuation thereafter.

	Percent Change at Annual Rate, CPI, All Items	
	Unadjusted	*Seasonally Adjusted*
1964 — January-July	1.1	0.6
July-January	1.1	1.6
1965 — January-July	2.4	1.9
July-January	1.5	2.0
1966 — January-July	4.2	3.7
July-January	2.5	3.1
1967 — January-July	3.2	2.6
July-January	3.6	4.2
1968 — January-July	5.0	4.4
July-January	4.3	5.0
1969 — January-July	6.7	6.1
July-January	5.7	6.3
1970 — January-July	6.0	5.4

2. A question related to the length of span is whether the rates of change should be centered within the interval they cover or placed at the terminal month. Placing at the terminal month, while convenient for current analysis, tends to make the dates of historical peaks or troughs later the longer the interval over which change is measured. Thus, six month rates of change will typically turn down after month-to-month changes do; twelve-month changes turn still later. Centering eliminates this bias and is especially important when different spans are being used for different series. In this chapter we shall follow the convention of centering, and since we generally use a six-month span, this means that dates are three months earlier than they would be had they been set at the terminal month.

3. This is possible, and efficient, only when a large portion of the cyclical turns in the other price series can be matched with those in the CPI. This is generally, but not always, the case.

4. The study by Stigler and Kindahl (*The Behavior of Industrial Prices* [New York: National Bureau of Economic Research, 1970]) indicates that the substitution of an index of transaction prices for the present BLS index, which is based in large part on list prices, would, if anything, reduce the length of the leads of industrial commodity prices relative to the CPI. Their index of industrial prices covers about 19 percent of the content of the BLS industrial commodities index, and they construct an index of comparable coverage from BLS data. The turning points in the rates of change (over six-month spans, centered) correspond as follows with those in the consumer price index:

	Trough	Peak	Trough
CPI, all items	7/58	7/59	3/61
WPI, industrials			
Restricted coverage			
NBER	3/58	10/58	7/61
BLS	1/58	8/58	2/61
Total, BLS	11/57	2/59	9/60

	Lead (−) or Lag (+) in Months, at Turns in CPI		
WPI, industrials			
Restricted coverage			
NBER	−4	− 9	+4
BLS	−6	−11	−1
Total, BLS	−8	− 5	−6

The NBER index lags behind the comparable BLS index at each turn, apparently because of the inclusion in the former of long-term contract prices at the dates when deliveries were made rather than when the contracts were consummated. Otherwise the transaction price index might be expected to lead.

5. The cyclical peak is March 1969, at 9 percent.

Chapter 13

Employment, Unemployment, and the Inflation-Recession Dilemma

SUMMARY

An alternative way of viewing the unemployment-inflation trade-off yields more sensible and more decisive results than the customary way. It uses the ratio of employment to population of working age, instead of the unemployment rate, as the variable that measures the utilization of the potential labor force. This measure avoids the problem of variation in labor force participation rates, which to some degree respond to conditions of demand. It avoids the problem of discouraged workers, who are not counted as unemployed because they are not seeking work, even though they "want" work in some sense; obviously they are not employed. It avoids such definitional problems as the degree to which persons must actively be seeking work to be considered unemployed or whether they have realistic ideas about their individual employability, wage aspirations, and so on.

The record for the postwar period shows a fairly close relationship between movements in the employment-population ratio and in the rate of wage or price inflation. This is not the case with the unemployment rate, at least in its raw form. It appears that one of the factors explaining the persistence of inflation during the 1973–1975 recession, despite the high unemployment rate, was that the percentage of persons employed held up relatively well, and this provided support for wage income and consumer demand. In this regard, the

Reprinted from *Contemporary Economic Problems, 1976*, William Fellner, ed. (Washington, D.C.: American Enterprise Institute, 1976).

moderate decline in the inflation rate since 1974 was about in line with previous experience.

The implication is that policymakers and others concerned about the state of the labor market and its bearing on wage and price inflation should pay closer attention than they have to the percentage of the population employed. Wider reporting of this statistic on a current basis, along with the reporting of the unemployment rate and other labor market information, would make it easier for it to be given that closer attention.

EMPLOYMENT AND UNEMPLOYMENT DURING RECESSION

One of the clichés of the times is that the 1973–1975 recession was the longest and deepest since the Great Depression of the 1930s. Such an appraisal is commonly based on the fact that the unemployment rate averaged 8.5 percent during 1975, higher than in any year since 1941. But the employment ratio, which is the percentage of the population employed, gives a contradictory verdict. In so doing, it may help solve an economic puzzle—why, in the face of this "worst recession," wages and prices have continued to advance at near record rates.

Admittedly, history will probably continue to record the 1973–1975 recession as the worst since the 1930s, particularly since it was worldwide. Yet in several significant respects it was in the same family with the three recessions that occurred in the United States between 1948 and 1958 and not at all in a class with the Great Depression. For example, the decline in nonfarm employment lasted nine months (September 1974 to June 1975) and came to 3 percent, compared to declines of fourteen months and 4 percent in 1957–1958; sixteen months and 3 percent in 1953–1954; and thirteen months and 4 percent in 1948–1949. In 1929–1933 the drop in nonfarm employment lasted forty-three months and reached 32 percent. Industrial production fell 13 percent in 1973–1975 and 12 percent in 1957–1958, but 53 percent in 1929–1932. Real gross national product dropped nearly 7 percent in 1973–1975 and 4 percent in 1957–1958, but 33 percent in 1929–1932.[1]

A large part of the reduction in output in 1973–1975 was attributable to a reduction in inventory investment, which was what happened in the earlier postwar recessions but not in 1929–1932. This probably contributed to the brevity of the decline in employment, since inventory movements are usually quickly reversed and do not have the longer run implications of a decline in basic demand. The pecuniary volume of business scarcely declined at all in 1973–1975, nor did personal income, whereas they declined slightly in the earlier postwar recessions and dramatically in 1929–1932.

The unemployment rate and the employment ratio for the low years of each of the six recessions since 1949 are given in Table 13-1. According to the unemployment rate, the latest recession was by far the worst. According to the percentage of the population that continued to be employed, it was next to the mildest. Which of these characterizations is more accurate can be a matter of argument, but there is no question that they are different.

The two measures give more nearly similar verdicts when the lows are compared with the previous highs. The rise in unemployment in the first three recessions was larger than in the next two, and the decline in the employment ratio also was larger in the first three than in the next two. Moreover, the rise in unemployment and the decline in the employment ratio both were larger in the 1975 recession than in any of the previous five. This measurement of the severity of recession depends, of course, partly on the degree to which the economy enjoyed full employment when the recession began, and not only on the amount of slack there was when the economy hit bottom. Nevertheless, even by this measure, the unemployment rate puts the 1975 recession well in front of the others, whereas the employment ratio does not. According to the decline in the employment ratio, the 1973–1975 recession barely exceeded the worst of the earlier postwar recessions; according to the rise in the unemployment rate, it was much worse.

Table 13-1. Employment and Unemployment in Recession Years, 1949-1975 *(percentages).*

Business Cycle Low (1)	Unemployment Rate (2)	Employment Ratio (3)
1949	5.9	54.6
1954	5.5	53.8
1958	6.8	54.2
1961	6.7	54.2
1970	4.9	56.1
1975	8.5	55.3

Sources: Column (1): Business cycle trough years, National Bureau of Economic Research, Inc.; column (2): Unemployment as percentage of civilian labor force, U.S. Bureau of Labor Statistics; and column (3): Civilian employment as percentage of population sixteen years old and over, U.S. Bureau of Labor Statistics.

THE INFLATION TRADE-OFF

These alternative ways of looking at the employment situation are of more than academic concern. Not only do they tell us how people are faring in the job market, but they also have a bearing on the way we interpret the inflation that has accompanied the recession. If the percentage of the population employed is high, the total earnings of the population are likely to be higher than would otherwise be the case, and the same holds true for spending capacity. Under these circumstances, wage rates and prices are likely to remain higher than they otherwise would. If the unemployment rate is high, on the other hand, one might expect the opposite conditions: greater downward pressure on wages because of the large numbers seeking work and hence lower cost pressure on prices. Both propositions must of course be qualified, because many other factors besides employment and unemployment influence wages and prices. Moreover, the propositions do not tell what we should expect if employment and unemployment are both at relatively high levels.

In 1975, in fact, we had both a high unemployment rate and a moderately high employment ratio. The employment ratio seems more consistent with the inflationary conditions that existed than does the unemployment rate. Neither the rate nor the ratio can explain the whole situation, but the employment ratio does give a clue, which the unemployment rate alone does not, to determining why inflation persisted in 1975. Unemployment was a serious problem, but at the same time, a relatively high percentage of the population continued to be employed, and the fact that they were employed helped to sustain demand, wages, and prices. If we ignore this fact, and thereby treat employment and unemployment merely as opposite sides of the same coin, we may overlook one of the factors that can help explain the current dilemma of high unemployment and persistent inflation.

This dilemma has been growing more and more serious since World War II. Although reductions in the rate of inflation have continued to accompany recessions (sometimes with a short lag), each succeeding recession (with a partial exception in 1961) has left the rate of inflation in both prices and wages higher than it was left by the recession before. As Table 13-2 shows, the steady upward progression in the rate of increase in hourly compensation, from less than one percent at the trough of the 1949 recession to nearly 8 percent at the trough of the 1975 recession, has been matched by a similar progression in the rate of increase in consumer prices.

Table 13-2. **Prices and Wages in Recession Years, 1949–1975** *(percentages).*

Business Cycle Low (1)	Rate of Change in:	
	Consumer Prices (2)	Hourly Compensation (3)
1949	-1.8	0.6
1954	-0.5	3.1
1958	1.8	3.5
1961	0.7	4.3
1970	5.5	6.3
1975	7.0	7.7

Sources: Column (1): Business cycle trough years, National Bureau of Economic Research, Inc.; column (2): Percentage change in consumer price index, December of preceding year to December of current year, U.S. Bureau of Labor Statistics; column (3): Percentage change in average hourly compensation, fourth quarter of preceding year to fourth quarter of current year, private non-farm sector, U.S. Bureau of Labor Statistics.

If the figures on prices and wages in Table 13-2 are compared with those on employment and unemployment in Table 13-1, one can see why it is important to look at both measures. If the unemployment rate is taken as the measure of slack in the economy at business cycle lows, one would have to say that it bears virtually no relation to the rate of increase in either prices or wages. If, on the other hand, the employment ratio is taken as the measure of the degree to which there is full employment in the economy, the figures fall more nearly into place. The high rates of price and wage inflation in 1970 and 1975 correspond with relatively high employment ratios.

Data for years other than the six recession years covered in these tables support these results (see Figures 13-1 and 13-2). The two diagrams on the left-hand side of each figure relate unemployment to wage changes (Figure 13-1) and to price changes (Figure 13-2). The two on the right relate the employment ratio to the same wage and price data. One would expect diagrams using unemployment to show a scatter of points sloping downward to the right, in accordance with the so-called Phillips curve. It takes a close look to find any trace of this, though most of the lines connecting the peaks and troughs of the business cycles do slope downward. On the other hand, the diagrams using the employment ratio show a much tighter relationship, with the scatter of points clearly sloping upward to the

Figure 13-1.   Rate of Change in Hourly Compensation, Unemployment Rate, and Percentage of Population Employed, 1948–1975.

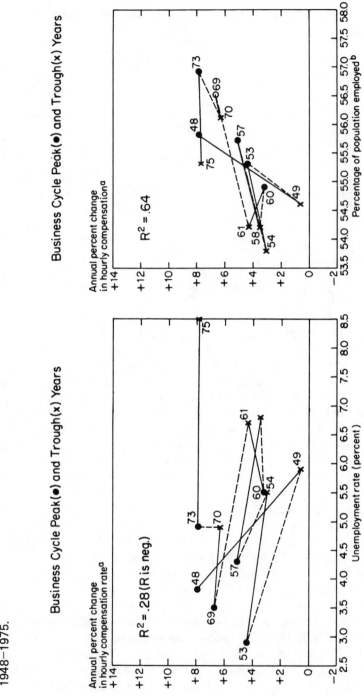

Figure 13-1. continued

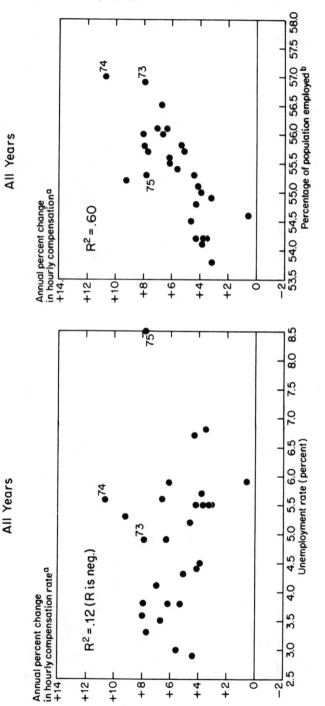

Note: The correlation (R^2) is based on data ending with 1974.
[a] Fourth quarter of preceding year to fourth quarter of current year, private nonfarm sector.
[b] Civilian employment as percent of noninstitutional population sixteen years of age and over.
Source: Table 13-5.

Figure 13–2. Rate of Change in Consumer Price Index, Unemployment Rate, and Percentage of Population Employed, 1948–1975.

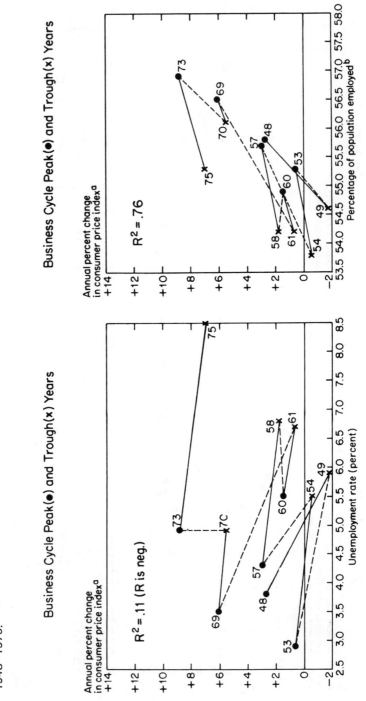

Figure 13-2. continued

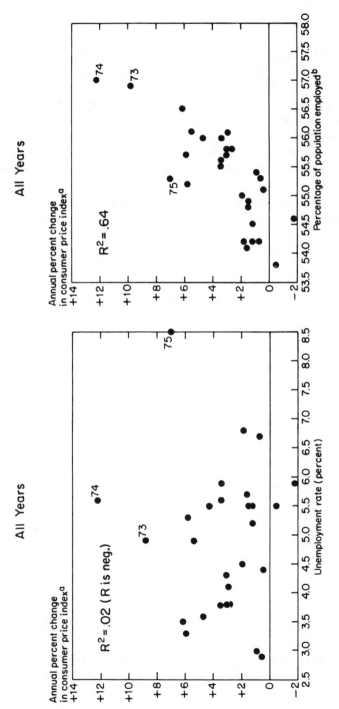

Note: The correlation (R^2) is based on data ending with 1974.

[a]December of preceding year to December of current year.

[b]Civilian employment as percent of noninstitutional population sixteen years of age and over.

Source: Table 13-5.

right. The correlation coefficients, which are nearly zero for unemployment but moderately high for employment, confirm this impression. (For further discussion, see Technical Note 1, below.)

Another way to depict the relation between employment, unemployment, and the rate of inflation is shown in Figure 13-3. The employment ratio and the rate of change in the consumer price index have followed nearly parallel courses. The unemployment rate (plotted on an inverted scale) has deviated from both, notably in the early 1950s and again in recent years. Especially noteworthy is the moderate decline in the employment ratio during the recent recession and

Figure 13-3. Unemployment Rate, Employment Ratio, and the Rate of Change in the Consumer Price Index, 1948–1976.

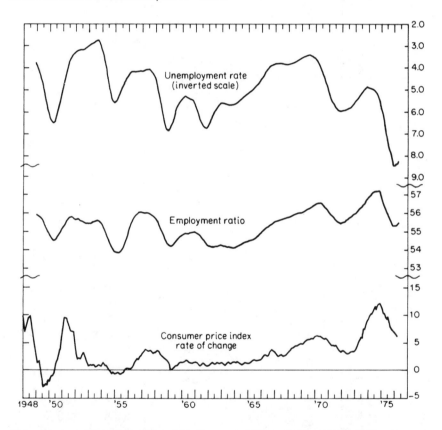

Note: The unemployment rate and employment ratio are twelve month moving averages; the rate of change in the consumer price index is the percent change over twelve months. All series are plotted at end of the twelve month period.

Source: U.S. Bureau of Labor Statistics. For annual data see Table 13-5.

the similarly moderate decline in the rate of inflation, in sharp contrast with what was happening to the unemployment rate.

One cannot deduce cause and effect from these or any other sets of numbers: they merely make one or another hypothesis more or less plausible. In this instance, since alternative measures of slack in the economy behave quite differently, and one (the employment ratio) bears a plausible and fairly consistent relationship to rates of price and wage inflation, while the other (the unemployment rate) does not, we would be well advised to reconsider our hypotheses about the way slack in the economy affects the rate of inflation. The employment ratio shows that sometimes there may be less slack than would meet the eye of one who looks only at the unemployment rate.

This is indeed the case during the current recovery, which at present writing (May 1976) is about one year old. The unemployment rate in April 1976 was 7.5 percent. By historical standards, such a rate suggests an enormous amount of slack in the economy, more than in any previous postwar recession year except 1975. It is more than one and a half times as high as the average unemployment rate during 1948–1974, which was 4.8 percent. The employment ratio, on the other hand, was 56.2 percent in April 1976. It is well above the average ratio for 1948–1974, which was 55.3 percent. It is also well above the level of any postwar recession year and, indeed, higher than in four of the six peak years in the business cycle (1948, 1953, 1957, and 1960). The economy, after a year of recovery, is providing employment for a relatively large fraction of the population of working age, though many are still seeking work. Under these conditions, judging from past experience, we should not find it surprising that the pace of wage and price inflation is still a worrisome problem.

NATURE OF THE EMPLOYMENT RATIO

The employment ratio used in this chapter is not the only available measure of employment nor even the only employment ratio. It takes the total population sixteen years of age and over as the potential labor supply, ignoring the fact that there are many in the population who—because of age, illness, affluence, or preoccupation with other duties—are not likely to become employed under any circumstances. It does not count those who are in the armed forces as employed, but does count them in the population. By using "civilian employment" in the numerator, it conforms to customary usage in reports of the number employed. By using total population in the denominator, it makes a simple allowance for the trend in the population of the country or, more specifically, the trend in the number of persons (apart from children under sixteen) who are largely supported by those who are employed. Since the size of the armed forces is subject to noneconomic considerations, the alternative treatments (either adding the armed forces to the employed or subtracting them from the population) do not seem to yield as satisfactory a ratio for economic analysis as the one adopted, though opinions may differ on this point. (For further discussion, see Technical Note 2, below.)

The employment ratio avoids some of the definitional questions that beset measures of unemployment. For example, the so-called "discouraged worker," who is not counted as unemployed because he or she is not seeking work even though he wants work, is obviously not counted as employed. Young people whose principal activity is going to school, but who are counted as unemployed if they are seeking part-time work, are not counted as employed unless they actually have a job. Unlike the unemployment rate, the employment ratio does not depend implicitly on the degree to which a person must actively seek work to be considered unemployed, nor does it depend on whether his ideas are realistic or unrealistic as to employability, earning capacity, the suitability of working conditions, and so on. If he does not have a job, he is not counted as employed. Hence it is both a more objective and a more neutral measure (as well as being, one hopes, less controversial) than the unemployment rate. For example, when the definitions of employment and unemployment were revised in 1967 in response to the recommendations of the Gordon Committee (which in turn arose out of a controversy regarding the measurement of unemployment), the revisions altered the unemployment count in 1966 by 3.4 percent but altered the employment count by only 0.06 percent.[2]

If the employment ratio is to receive due attention, however, it must be reported promptly and prominently, together with other statistics on the employment situation. At present, it is not so reported. The Bureau of Labor Statistics does not refer to it in its monthly press release, though it does report both the numerator and the denominator. The bureau does show an employment ratio (the ratio of civilian employment to civilian population) in its monthly *Chartbook on Prices, Wages and Productivity* and in its monthly *Employment and Earnings*. Although such notices are helpful, they are not likely to receive much public attention, because they do not appear as promptly as the figures in the monthly press releases.[3]

(Postscript: The BLS press releases now report the employment ratio.)

IMPLICATIONS

The principal implication of the findings described above is that in the conduct of economic policy, careful attention should be paid to the level and change in the percentage of the population employed. This is not to say that unemployment should be ignored. It is simply to say that evaluations of the labor market based upon employment data are not always consistent with those based upon unemployment data and it is therefore essential for us to analyze the difference and its implications for wage and price trends.

A high level of unemployment not accompanied by a low level of employment (relative to population) may not imply a deficiency of demand. It may, on the contrary, imply that large numbers of workers are seeking jobs, or seeking to change jobs, because employment opportunities are plentiful. The existence of numerous vacancies, satisfactory wage levels, and good working conditions induce persons to seek jobs, or to leave jobs that they have in order to search for better ones, or to take more time than they might otherwise take to find the best job they can. For example, many persons, particularly married women with small children and young people who are attending school, can accept only part-time employment. The fact that there are many more part-time jobs available today than there were twenty or thirty years ago, partly because of the growth of service industries, induces many to enter the labor force who would not otherwise have done so. Initially, they are likely to be counted as unemployed. Such changes in both supply and demand have tended to raise the unemployment rate, but they are not a symptom of inadequate demand, and they do not necessarily call for measures to stimulate demand.

More appropriate policies in such instances may be those that help to place people in jobs or to train them for jobs that are available or those that improve productivity and reduce costs, increasing incentives to employ people without at the same time putting upward pressure on prices. By means of such policies, the employment ratio may be raised and unemployment reduced without the usual inflationary consequences.

TECHNICAL NOTE 1: LONG-RUN CHANGES IN EMPLOYMENT, UNEMPLOYMENT, AND INFLATION RATES

In the unemployment diagrams (left-hand panels of Figures 13-1 and 13-2), there is clear evidence that the unemployment rate associated with a given rate of wage or price inflation has become higher in recent years than it was formerly. This is one way of accounting for the apparent lack of association between the two: the Phillips curve has shifted to the right. This means, of course, that some factor has caused the unemployment rate to drift upward relative to the rate of wage or price change. The employment ratio diagrams (right-hand panels of Figures 13-1 and 13-2) show some evidence of a similar shift, but to the left. This shift is much less pronounced than that for unemployment, but insofar as it is present it means that some factor has caused the employment ratio to drift downward relative to the rate of wage or price change.[4]

The employment ratio has tended to drift downward because of the declining proportion of adult men in the population and the rising proportion of adult women and teenagers. Since the adult men have much higher employment ratios than either adult women or teenagers, a decline in their relative numbers tends to reduce the overall employment ratio. For example, between 1948 and 1973 (both prosperous years in the business cycle), the proportion of adult males in the working age population fell from 45 percent to 42 percent, while adult women and teenagers rose from 55 to 58 percent (see Table 13-3). The percentage of adult males employed in 1948 was eighty-four compared to thirty-three for adult women and teenagers; by 1973 the former had dropped to seventy-six, and the latter had risen to forty-three. As a net result of these offsetting changes the overall employment ratio rose from 56 to 57 percent, but other things equal, it would have risen to 58 percent had the composition of the population remained the same. The shift in composition caused a downtrend of one percentage point in twenty-five years. This factor, incidentally, cannot bear any responsibility for the positive correlation between the employment ratio and the rate of inflation, since the latter has moved upward over the years.

The unemployment rate was affected not only by these demographic changes but also by the changing propensity of different groups to enter or leave the labor force. Adult men comprised 67 percent of the labor force in 1948, but only 56 percent in 1973; adult women and teenagers, entering the labor force in large numbers, increased from 33 to 44 percent. These were much larger shifts than those in the population, and they had a substantial effect on the overall unemployment rate, which rose from 3.8 to 4.9 percent from 1948 to 1973. Without the shift in labor force composition, the rate would have risen only half as much, to 4.4 percent. The higher unemployment rates for adult women and teenagers (4.9 percent in 1948 and 6.9 percent in 1973) than for adult men (3.2 percent in

Table 13-3.   Employment and Unemployment, 1948 and 1973.

	Noninstitutional Population, 16 and Over		Civilian Employment		Unemployment	
	1948	1973	1948	1973	1948	1973
	Number (in thousands)					
Males, 20 and over	46,958	62,843	39,382	47,946	1,305	1,594
Females, 20 and over	48,716	69,289	14,937	29,228	564	1,485
Teenagers, 16–19	8,853	16,130	4,028	7,236	407	1,226
Total	104,527	148,263	58,344	84,409	2,276	4,304
	Percent of Total					
Males, 20 and over	44.9	42.4	67.5	56.8	57.3	37.0
Females, 20 and over	46.6	46.7	25.6	34.6	24.8	34.5
Teenagers, 16–19	8.5	10.9	6.9	8.6	17.9	28.5
Total	100.0	100.0	100.0	100.0	100.0	100.0
	Percent of Noninstitutional Population					
Males, 20 and over	100.0	100.0	83.9	76.3	2.8	2.5
Females, 20 and over	100.0	100.0	30.7	42.2	1.2	2.1
Teenagers, 16–19	100.0	100.0	45.5	44.9	4.6	7.6
Total	100.0	100.0	55.8	56.9	2.2	2.9

(Table 13-3, continued overleaf)

Table 13-3. continued

	Civilian Labor Force		Armed Forces		Not in Labor Force	
	1948	*1973*	*1948*	*1973*	*1948*	*1973*
Number (in thousands)						
Males, 20 and over	40,686	49,539	1,041	1,901	5,231	11,404
Females, 20 and over	15,500	30,713	16	40	33,200	38,536
Teenagers, 16–19	4,435	8,461	402	386	4,016	7,283
Total	60,621	88,714	1,459	2,326	42,447	57,223
Percent of Total						
Males, 20 and over	67.1	55.8	71.3	81.7	12.3	19.9
Females, 20 and over	25.6	34.6	1.1	1.7	78.2	67.3
Teenagers, 16–19	7.3	9.5	27.6	16.6	9.5	12.7
Total	100.0	100.0	100.0	100.0	100.0	100.0
Percent of Noninstitutional Population						
Males, 20 and over	86.6	78.8	2.2	3.0	11.1	18.1
Females, 20 and over	31.8	44.3	0.0	0.1	68.2	55.6
Teenagers, 16–19	50.1	52.5	4.5	2.4	45.4	45.2
Total	58.0	59.8	1.4	1.6	40.6	38.6

Note: The unemployment rates (percent of civilian labor force), 1948 and 1973, are: total, 3.8, 4.9; males, 20 and older 3.2, 3.2; females, 20 and older, 3.6, 4.8; teenagers, 9.2, 14.5

Source: U.S. Bureau of Labor Statistics.

both years), coupled with their sharp rise in the labor force, added about half a percentage point to the unemployment rate over the twenty-five year period. This was a much bigger proportionate shift than in the employment ratio, since the unemployment rate is a much smaller figure.

This points to one of the merits of an unemployment ratio (unemployment as a percentage of population of working age) as compared with the unemployment rate (unemployment as a percentage of labor force): the population is less affected than is the labor force by changes in age-sex composition. Short-run as well as long-run changes in labor force participation affect the behavior of the unemployment rate. In the population, the long-run changes dominate; they are generally smaller than in the labor force; and some of them are predictable. Some consideration might well be given, therefore, to more extensive use of the unemployment ratio (see also Technical Note 2, below; and see Chapter 7).

TECHNICAL NOTE 2: CORRELATION ANALYSIS OF EMPLOYMENT, UNEMPLOYMENT, AND INFLATION RATES

Some of the factors underlying the fact that the employment ratio is more closely associated with inflation rates than is the unemployment rate are illuminated by a correlation analysis involving both measures.

The total population aged sixteen and over can be divided into the following groups: (1) civilian employed, (2) armed forces, (3) unemployed, and (4) not in the labor force. If we divide each of these by the population sixteen and over and multiply by 100, the four ratios, which we designate E/P, A/P, U/P, and NL/P, add to 100. The employment ratio, E/P, is equal to 100 minus $(A/P + U/P + NL/P)$. When the rate of change in prices or wages is regressed upon these variables, we can determine what each contributes to the result.

The simple correlation matrix, based upon annual data, 1948–1974, is given in Table 13-4. From this we learn that the employment ratio is more highly correlated with the rate of change in consumer prices or hourly compensation than are any of the other ratios. The armed forces ratio has a slight inverse correlation with the price and wage variables. The unemployment ratio is slightly correlated inversely with the price and wage variables.[5] The not in the labor force ratio has a substantial inverse correlation with the price

Table 13-4.   Correlation Matrix.

	ΔCPI	ΔHC	E/P	A/P	U/P	NL/P
Consumer price index (ΔCPI)[a]	+1.0					
Hourly compensation (ΔHC)[b]	+0.8	+1.0				
Employment ratio (E/P)	+0.8	+0.8	+1.0			
Armed forces ratio (A/P)	−0.3	−0.2	−0.2	+1.0		
Unemployment ratio (U/P)	−0.1	−0.3	−0.4	−0.6	+1.0	
Not in labor force ratio (NL/P)	−0.7	−0.6	−0.8	0.0	0.0	+1.0

[a]Percent change from December to December.
[b]Percent change from fourth quarter to fourth quarter.

and wage variables. In terms of these simple correlations, therefore, it appears that the ratios involving the armed forces, unemployed, and those not in the labor force belong together in that each appears to be (if anything) inversely correlated with the rates of change in prices and wages.

This is confirmed by multiple regressions using the three variables simultaneously (fitted to annual data, 1948–1974):

$$\Delta HC = \begin{array}{cccc} 88.17 & - & 2.28\,A/P & - & 2.05\,U/P & - & 1.81\,NL/P \\ (5.04) & & (3.59) & & (4.04) & & (4.11) \end{array}$$

$$R^2 = 0.62 \qquad (13.1)$$

$$\Delta CPI = \begin{array}{cccc} 143.51 & - & 2.98\,A/P & - & 1.66\,U/P & - & 3.39\,NL/P \\ (7.11) & & (3.92) & & (2.75) & & (6.43) \end{array}$$

$$R^2 = 0.73 \qquad (13.2)$$

The regression coefficients are all negative and statistically significant. The regressions were also computed with a time trend variable, but the time trend variable was not significant. Since the regression coefficients are substantially similar in magnitude, the multiple correlations are not greatly different from those obtained from the employment ratio alone:

$$\Delta HC = -\begin{array}{cc} 100.77 & + & 1.92\,E/P \\ (5.78) & & (6.09) \end{array} \qquad R^2 = 0.60 \qquad (13.3)$$

$$\Delta CPI = -\begin{array}{cc} 149.89 & + & 2.76\,E/P \\ (6.45) & & (6.58) \end{array} \qquad R^2 = 0.63 \qquad (13.4)$$

The multiple regressions indicate that the reason the employment ratio is more highly correlated with price and wage changes than is the unemployment rate is that the employment ratio implicitly takes account of two other factors that contribute to the relationship, these being the percentage of the population not in the labor force and the percentage in the armed forces. The influence of the not in the labor force ratio is, on the whole, more powerful than that of the unemployment ratio, as the following regressions testify:

$$\Delta HC = 84.24 - 1.02\,U/P - 1.92\,NL/P \qquad R^2 = 0.41 \qquad (13.5)$$
$$ (3.95) \quad (2.00) \qquad (3.56)$$

$$\Delta CPI = 143.38 - 0.32\,U/P - 3.52\,NL/P \qquad R^2 = 0.54 \qquad (13.6)$$
$$ (5.44) \quad (0.51) \qquad (5.29)$$

The armed forces ratio contributes significantly (and inversely) to the correlation, when treated as one of the three sectors outside civilian employment, as is shown by a comparison of equations (12.5) and (12.6) with (12.1 and (12.2). On the other hand, treating the armed forces as a sector to be included with civilian employment does not significantly improve the correlation, as the following regressions show:

$$\Delta HC = -98.22 + 1.89\,E/P - 0.27\,A/P \qquad R^2 = 0.60 \qquad (13.7)$$
$$ (5.34) \quad (5.76) \qquad (0.51)$$

$$\Delta CPI = -140.06 + 2.63\,E/P - 1.07\,A/P \qquad R^2 = 0.67 \qquad (13.8)$$
$$ (5.96) \quad (6.29) \qquad (1.54)$$

The persistence of the negative sign on the armed forces ratio is puzzling, and it is not clear what the reason for it may be. But it does suggest that nothing is to be gained in interpreting price and wage behavior by using an employment ratio defined to include the armed forces, which of course would then be counted positively. Similarly, from this point of view, nothing is to be gained by using an employment ratio defined to exclude the armed forces from the population, since this also would have the opposite effect to what the regressions suggest (compare columns 3 and 4 of Table 13-5).

Table 13-5. Annual Data on Employment, Unemployment and Inflation Rates, 1948–1975 (percentages).

Year	E/P (1)	A/P (2)	$\frac{E+A}{P}$ (3)	$\frac{E}{P-A}$ (4)	U/P (5)	UR (6)	NL/P (7)	ΔCPI (8)	ΔHC (9)
1948	55.8	1.4	57.2	56.6	2.2	3.8	40.6	2.7	7.9
1949	54.6	1.5	56.1	55.4	3.4	5.9	40.4	-1.8	0.6
1950	55.2	1.5	56.8	56.1	3.1	5.3	40.1	5.8	9.2
1951	55.7	2.9	58.5	57.3	1.9	3.3	39.6	5.9	7.7
1952	55.4	3.3	58.7	57.3	1.7	3.0	39.6	0.9	5.6
1953	55.3	3.2	58.5	57.1	1.7	2.9	39.8	0.6	4.4
1954	53.8	3.0	56.8	55.5	3.2	5.5	40.0	-0.5	3.1
1955	55.1	2.7	57.9	56.7	2.5	4.4	39.6	0.4	4.1
1956	56.1	2.5	58.6	57.5	2.4	4.1	39.0	2.9	7.0
1957	55.7	2.4	58.1	57.1	2.5	4.3	39.4	3.0	5.1
1958	54.2	2.3	56.4	55.4	4.0	6.8	39.6	1.8	3.5
1959	54.8	2.2	57.0	56.0	3.2	5.5	39.8	1.5	4.2
1960	54.9	2.1	57.0	56.1	3.2	5.5	39.8	1.5	3.2
1961	54.2	2.1	56.3	55.4	3.9	6.7	39.8	0.7	4.3
1962	54.2	2.3	56.5	55.5	3.2	5.5	40.3	1.2	3.7
1963	54.1	2.2	56.3	55.4	3.3	5.7	40.4	1.6	3.8
1964	54.5	2.2	56.6	55.7	3.0	5.2	40.4	1.2	4.6
1965	55.0	2.1	57.1	56.2	2.6	4.5	40.3	1.9	3.9
1966	55.6	2.4	57.9	56.9	2.2	3.8	39.9	3.4	6.2
1967	55.8	2.6	58.4	57.3	2.2	3.8	39.4	3.0	5.3
1968	56.0	2.6	58.6	57.6	2.1	3.6	39.3	4.7	8.0
1969	56.5	2.5	59.1	58.0	2.1	3.5	38.9	6.1	6.7

Year									
1970	56.1	2.3	58.4	57.4	2.9	4.9	38.7	5.5	6.3
1971	55.5	2.0	57.5	56.6	3.5	5.9	39.0	3.4	6.1
1972	56.0	1.7	57.7	57.0	3.3	5.6	39.0	3.4	6.6
1973	56.9	1.6	58.5	57.8	2.9	4.9	38.6	8.8	7.9
1974	57.0	1.5	58.5	57.8	3.4	5.6	38.2	12.2	10.6
1975	55.3	1.4	56.7	56.0	5.1	8.5	38.2	7.0	7.8
Average, 1948–1974	55.3	2.3	57.6	56.6	2.8	4.8	39.6	3.0	5.5

Definitions:

P = Noninstitutional population sixteen years of age and over;
E = Civilian employment;
A = Armed forces;
U/P = Unemployment ratio (percentage of population);
UR = Unemployment rate (percentage of civilian labor force);
NL = Not in labor force;
ΔCPI = Percent change in consumer price index, December of preceding year to December of current year;
ΔHC = Percent change in average hourly compensation, private nonfarm sector, from fourth quarter of preceding year to fourth quarter of current year.

Source: U.S. Bureau of Labor Statistics.

NOTES TO CHAPTER 13

1. In general, measures of activity obtained by deflating dollar values by price indexes (such as real GNP) showed 1973–1975 declines sharper in relation to those in previous recessions than did measures of activity expressed in physical units (such as man hours, units sold, and so on). Hence it is possible that the deflation procedure, which is especially hazardous when prices are rising rapidly and forcing extensive adjustments in spending habits, contract terms, and accounting procedures, has exaggerated the recent declines in the deflated (constant dollar) aggregates of sales, output, inventories, and incomes. (For revised data on these measures, see Appendix Table A-2.)

2. See Robert L. Stein, "New Definitions for Employment and Unemployment," *Employment and Earnings and Monthly Report on the Labor Force* (U.S. Bureau of Labor Statistics), February 1967, Table 1.

3. A useful analysis of the employment ratio in comparison with the unemployment rate and related measures is Julius Shiskin (Commissioner of Labor Statistics), "Employment and Unemployment: the Doughnut or the Hole?" *Monthly Labor Review* 99, no. 2 (February 1976): 3–10. See also Chapter 7.

4. Linear regressions fitted to the annual data used in the charts, 1948–1974, show that a time trend (T), has a significant positive influence on the relationships with the unemployment rate (UR) and a positive but not significant influence on those with the employment ratio (E/P):

$$\Delta HC \quad = \quad \begin{matrix} 1.11 \\ (0.38) \end{matrix} \quad - \quad \begin{matrix} 0.52\,UR \\ (-1.61) \end{matrix} \quad + \quad \begin{matrix} 0.11\,T \\ (2.57) \end{matrix} \quad R^2 = 0.25,$$

$$\Delta CPI \quad = \quad \begin{matrix} -7.33 \\ (-1.81) \end{matrix} \quad - \quad \begin{matrix} 0.62\,UR \\ (-1.36) \end{matrix} \quad + \quad \begin{matrix} 0.22\,T \\ (3.51) \end{matrix} \quad R^2 = 0.35,$$

$$\Delta HC \quad = \quad \begin{matrix} -86.57 \\ (-4.87) \end{matrix} \quad + \quad \begin{matrix} 1.64\,E/P \\ (4.87) \end{matrix} \quad + \quad \begin{matrix} 0.02\,T \\ (0.60) \end{matrix} \quad R^2 = 0.58,$$

$$\Delta CPI \quad = \quad \begin{matrix} -134.35 \\ (-5.73) \end{matrix} \quad + \quad \begin{matrix} 2.39\,E/P \\ (5.37) \end{matrix} \quad + \quad \begin{matrix} 0.09\,T \\ (1.84) \end{matrix} \quad R^2 = 0.68.$$

The unemployment rate is not significant in either equation, though it has the appropriate sign; the employment ratio is significant in both equations.

5. The unemployment ratio differs from the unemployment rate in that the latter uses labor force (employment plus unemployment) as the denominator rather than population. Nevertheless, the ratio and the rate are highly correlated because of the dominant influence of the numerator upon their fluctuations.

Chapter 14

Recession Slows Inflation

Over and over again lately the refrain is heard: A recession will not cure inflation. It is a theme with variations. Some say it would take a disastrous depression to have any effect on inflation—and who wants that? Others say that a slowdown might have some effect but only if it lasted five or ten years. Still others take a "positive" view: the only way to stop inflation is with wage and price controls. Once in a while there is an appeal to "history": since the inflation rate kept right on rising during the last recession, which was the worst since the 1930s, what can another recession be expected to do?

The record of recessions and inflation does not support any of these positions. It does support this statement: no significant decline in the rate of inflation has occurred that was not associated with a slowdown or recession, and virtually every slowdown or recession has been accompanied by a reduction in the rate of inflation. The statement holds not only for the United States, but also for Britain, West Germany, and Japan (see Figure 14-1). Taking all four countries together, there have been twenty-seven instances of slowdown or recession in economic growth between 1950 and 1975, and twenty-six instances of significant declines in inflation rates. There is virtually a one-to-one correspondence between the slowdowns or recessions and the declines in the rate of inflation.

In view of this record it seems to me reasonable to expect that another recession will be accompanied by another significant decline in the inflation rate. When something has happened twenty-six times

Reprinted from *The New York Times*, Sunday, November 18, 1979.

Figure 14–1.   Does Recession Slow Inflation? Evidence from Four Countries.

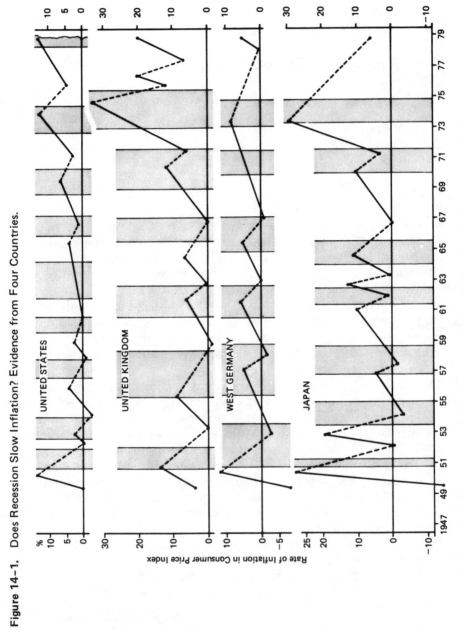

Note: Shaded areas are growth slowdowns or recessions. Declines in inflation rate are marked ------.

it is quite likely to happen again. It also seems reasonable to assume— since the four countries have tried almost everything—that nothing else will do it.

This is not to say, however, that a recession will "cure" inflation, that is, bring the rate down to zero. Some recessions have done this, but many have not. Nor is it to say that the inflation rate will start moving down as soon as a recession starts. In some cases the inflation rate has lagged, and not started down until a recession was well under way or indeed almost over. In other instances, however, it has not lagged. As a matter of fact, again taking the record for all four countries as a whole, downturns in the rate of inflation have started at just about the same time, on the average, as downturns in the economy.

To understand this, look at some of the factors at work. In a recession, businesses try to cut costs, and are often successful. They are forced to shave profit margins and give discounts to get rid of heavy inventories. The cost of holding even a normal inventory—in terms of interest charges—is likely to prove excessive. Some businesses fail, and sell out for what they can get. Overtime work is cut back or eliminated, which not only reduces costs but reduces the incomes of workers who have been earning the higher overtime rates. Layoffs occur, wage increases are deferred, and the uncertainty about jobs and earnings makes people cautious about spending for frills, postpone big ticket purchases, seek ways to economize, borrow less. Construction projects get postponed, delayed, or stretched out. Banks take a hard look at new loans, and may urge repayment instead of refinancing of existing loans.

All these factors make it more difficult to raise prices and more difficult to get wage increases. More prices remain steady and some fall. The price indexes go up less rapidly; that is, the rate of inflation declines.

This process usually begins in one or more lines of business before recession strikes the economy as a whole. If the influence of these sectors on the price level is significant enough, the overall rate of inflation may decline before the onset of recession. If not, there will be a lag.

The effects of recession on inflation show up at the grocery store, at the haberdashery, at the auto dealer's. Look for markdowns and discounts. Some of this price cutting, like the coupons in newspaper ads, does not get into the statistics. The coupons are a form of paper money, and their supply is apt to increase in a recession. Unlike real paper money, however, they reduce inflation.

Look at the wholesale commodity markets, where things like scrap steel, hides, print cloth, and lumber are sold. These markets react quickly to weakness in demand, and if the weakness is widespread the reaction will be widespread, too. Buyers of merchandise and materials for manufacturers, wholesalers, and retailers are always aware of such trends. The National Association of Purchasing Management surveys its members every month on whether the prices they are paying are going up, remaining the same, or going down. The percentage reporting price increases is a highly sensitive indicator of what is happening in these markets—perhaps surprisingly so, since the survey does not even ask how big the price changes are or what prices are changing. It is really a report on the buyers' feel of the market, but they are experts and are paid to know.

Another sensitive indicator of these commodity markets is the Bureau of Labor Statistics' weekly index of spot market prices of thirteen industrial materials. This index has declined in every recession since 1948, and in every economic slowdown as well. The declines in this index have preceded the declines in the rate of inflation, as measured by the Consumer Price Index, in every instance. One should look not only at the index, but also at its thirteen components, to see whether weakness is running across the board, or affecting only one or two commodities.

When price reductions in these markets become the rule rather than the exception, and if other signs of recession have also multiplied, a declining rate of inflation in consumer prices will probably not be far off.

Chapter 15

Cyclical Fluctuations
and Secular Inflation

The proposition that recessions slow inflation is now well established. In the United States as well as in other industrial countries there has been a virtual one-to-one correspondence between the occurrence of recessions or economic slowdowns and substantial reductions in the rate of price inflation. It is equally true that periods between recessions, when economic growth is more rapid, are the times when inflation accelerates.[1] A complex network of interrelations among economic variables operates to produce this result.

Although short-run "cyclical" movements in the inflation rate are of great concern, probably even greater significance attaches to the long-run trends in inflation. From 1960 to 1980 the rate of increase in the U.S. consumer price index climbed to successively higher cyclical peaks. The declines that occurred during and immediately after recessions failed to bring the rate down to as low a level as it had reached after the preceding recession. The inflation rate ratcheted upward. Recessions have slowed inflation but have not, during the past twenty years, cured it.

One of the possible reasons for the underlying trend—the changing nature of the business cycle itself—has not received much attention in recent years. In the 1920s, Wesley C. Mitchell and Willard Thorp (1926) suggested a simple hypothesis about long swings in the level of wholesale prices, namely, that they were associated with the relative length of business cycle expansions and contractions. A period during which expansions were much longer than contractions would generate more inflation than a period when expansions were relatively short. They showed that between 1790 and 1920 there had been a regular alternation of such periods, each one lasting twenty or thirty years, corresponding with the upswings and downswings in the wholesale price index (WPI).

Some twenty years later Mitchell and Arthur F. Burns (1946) examined the same hypothesis with a different set of measurements, extended the record to the 1930s, and found a similar result. We can now add another chapter. Continuing the same chronology of long swings in wholesale prices, the entire period from 1932 through 1981 must be classified as an upswing. In only a few years have prices been lower than the year before.[2] Encompassing five decades, it is by far the longest period of rising prices in the entire record back to 1790. It is also the largest upswing: In 1981 the WPI was more than eight times its level in 1932. We find that the Mitchell-Thorp-Burns hypothesis is supported once again. The expansion phases of business cycles outlasted the contraction phases throughout the period 1932-1981, and by a margin that had not even been approached in earlier times. There were five years of expansion for every year of recession. Figure 15-1 shows the long-standing association between the rate of price inflation and the relative length of the prosperous phases of business cycles.

In these exhibits we use the wholesale price index to identify and date the long swings, as Mitchell, Thorp, and Burns did originally. In addition, we measure the changes in the consumer price index during the same intervals, even though it is based on very slender evidence in the early years (see note to Table 15-1). The dates of the long swings would be somewhat different if based on the consumer price index itself, but taking the whole period, the wholesale price index provides firmer evidence.

What the results seem to mean is that the success the nation has had in moderating the business cycle since the 1930s—specifically, shortening recessions and lengthening expansions—has been achieved only at a price, namely an ever-rising price level. The current as well as the previous manifestations of this relationship, a kind of long-run Phillips curve, were doubtless brought about by monetary, fiscal, labor market, and other factors that produced both the shifts in cycle-phase durations and the accompanying shifts in inflation. Episodic factors were at work also, such as wars, gold discoveries, oil price explosions, and new legislation or administrative procedures. Here we shall not review this long history but will instead concentrate upon some aspects of the most recent upswing, especially the period since 1948.

One aspect that is especially intriguing is the possible emergence of a new phase beginning around 1980. The business cycle expansion

Figure 15-1. Long Swings in Prices and the Business Cycle, 1789–1981.

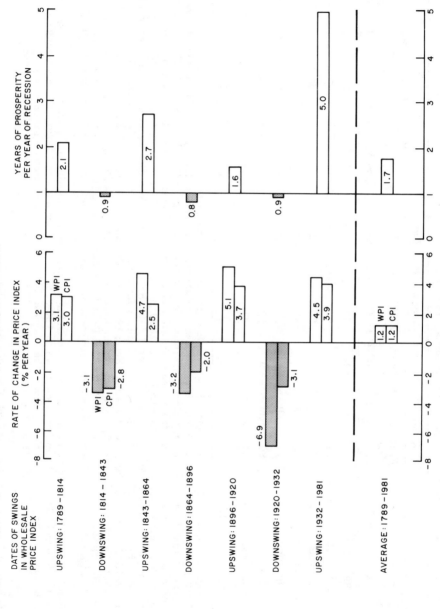

Source: Center for International Business Cycle Research, Rutgers University.

Table 15-1.   Inflation and Business Cycles, United States, 1789-1981.

Trend in Wholesale Prices			Wholesale Price Index			Consumer Price Index			State of the Business Cycle		
Direction	Dates	Number of Years	First Year (1967=100)	Last Year (1967=100)	% Change Annual Rate	First Year (1967=100)	Last Year (1967=100)	% Change Annual Rate	Years of Expansion	Years of Contraction	Ratio, Expansion Contraction
Rising	1789–1814	25	30	64	3.1	30	63	3.0	17	8	2.1
Falling	1814–1843	29	64	26	-3.1	63	28	-2.8	14	15	0.9
Rising	1843–1864	21	26	68	4.7	28	47	2.5	16	6	2.7
Falling	1864–1896	32	68	24	-3.2	47	25	-2.0	15	18	0.8
Rising	1896–1920	24	24	80	5.1	25	60	3.7	14	9	1.6
Falling	1920–1932	12	80	34	-6.9	60	41	-3.1	6	7	0.9
Rising	1932–1981	49	34	293	4.5	41	272	3.9	40	8	5.0
Total or average		192			1.2			1.2	122	71	1.7

Note: The periods of rising and falling trends in wholesale prices are those designated by Moore. The periods are substantially the same as those given by Mitchell and Thorp (Thorp 1926: 66), except that Burns and Mitchell placed the trough in wholesale prices in 1843 rather than 1849. The wholesale price index from 1896 to 1981 is the U.S. Bureau of Labor Statistics' all commodities index. From 1789 to 1864 the index constructed by Warren and Pearson is used, spliced to the BLS index at 1890.

The consumer price index from 1800 was estimated by the Bureau of Labor Statistics by splicing several indexes together, namely: 1800–1851, Index of Prices Paid by Vermont Farmers for Family Living; 1851–1890, Consumer Price Index by Ethel D. Hoover; 1890–1912, Cost of Living Index by Albert Rees; 1913–date, Bureau of Labor Statistics. See *Handbook of Labor Statistics* (1971: 253). We estimate the 1789 figure by splicing the Warren and Pearson wholesale price index to the Vermont price index at 1814 (see *Historical Statistics of the United States*, U.S. Department of Commerce 1975: 201–202). In these early years the figures give only a rough indication of what was happening to consumer prices and cannot pretend to be comparable with more recent figures.

The classification of business cycle expansions and contractions into periods of upswing and downswing in wholesale prices follows Burns and Mitchell 1946: 437 and 538, from 1843 to 1932. All business cycles from 1932 to 1981 are included in the latest upswing. The monthly business cycle chronology of the National Bureau of Economic Research is used. From 1789 to 1843 the classification is based upon Thorp (1926: 94) and Mitchell (1927: 444–445), with years of revival and prosperity classified as "expansion," and recession and depression as "contraction."

Source: Center for International Business Cycle Research, Rutgers University.

from July 1980 to July 1981 was not only one of the shortest on record (twelve months) but was also short relative to the recession that preceded it, which lasted only six months. This two-to-one ratio had not occurred in any of the eight business cycles since the Great Depression of the 1930s. Before then, ratios of two to one or less were frequent, as Table 15-1 shows. Another way of looking at the same information is to say that the recession of 1980 was followed unusually quickly by the recession of 1981-1982. It would not be unreasonable to expect, in light of the long historical record, that the consequence of two recessions back to back will be a more substantial reduction in the inflation rate than would have been produced by the usual sequence of brief recessions and long expansions. Indeed, it is already clear that the decline in the inflation rate since 1980 has been unusually large. Whether this marks a new trend or is just an episode depends largely on the persistence with which policies that will promote real growth without inflation are pursued in the future. Nonetheless, it is an auspicious beginning.

A second aspect of the most recent upswing that deserves attention is the evidence that the tendency for long business cycle expansions and brief recessions to promote inflation can be materially modified by appropriate monetary and fiscal policies. Table 15-2 divides the period since 1948 into business cycle segments running from the peak of one business cycle to the peak of the next. In every cycle the contraction phase was relatively brief, the subsequent expansion phase much longer. In every cycle the consumer price index rose, as did the gross national product implicit price deflator. This is what our 200-year history has taught us to expect: Long expansions and short recessions make for a rising trend in prices.

Nevertheless, the *rate* at which the price indexes advanced during each cycle had little or nothing to do with the relative length of expansion versus contraction. In the two cycles between 1953 and 1960 the rate of inflation was very moderate, just over 1 percent per year, even though the recessions were just as short relative to the expansions as in the 1973-1980 cycle, when the rate of inflation averaged 9 percent per year. What happened was that the growth in the stock of money and in the supply of credit accelerated sharply in the intervening twenty years. This had no apparent effect on the rate of growth of real output, which was virtually the same in 1973-1980 as in 1953-1960. It did not reduce unemployment, which was somewhat higher in the later period. The money and credit went into inflation and into higher interest rates.

Table 15-2 contains an important lesson for fiscal policy as well as for monetary policy. The rates of inflation in the seven cycles

Table 15–2.   Trends during Successive Business Cycles, 1948–1981.

	Business Cycles, Peak to Peak							Entire Period Nov. 48–July 81
	Nov. 48–July 53	July 53–Aug. 57	Aug. 57–Apr. 60	Apr. 60–Dec. 69	Dec. 69–Nov. 73	Nov. 73–Jan. 80	Jan. 80–July 81	
Business cycle durations								
Months of contraction (number)	11	10	8	10	11	16	6	72
Months of expansion (number)	45	39	24	106	36	58	12	320
Ratio, expansion to contraction	4.1	3.9	3.0	10.6	3.3	3.6	2.0	4.4
Rate of inflation (% per year)								
Consumer price index	2.2	1.3	1.2	2.6	5.2	9.0	10.9	4.2
GNP implicit price deflator	2.1	2.6	1.8	2.7	5.2	7.5	9.2	4.0
Prime rate (%)	2.5	3.4	4.3	5.3	6.7	9.1	16.7	6.0
Nominal GNP growth rate (% per year)	7.1	5.1	4.4	7.0	9.4	10.5	10.0	7.6
Real GNP growth rate (% per year)	4.9	2.5	2.6	4.2	3.9	2.8	0.6	3.5
Unemployment rate (%)	4.2	4.4	5.8	4.8	5.3	6.7	7.2	5.3
Money supply growth rate (% per year)								
M1	3.1	1.4	1.8	4.0	6.6	6.6	6.3	4.3
M2	3.3	2.7	5.0	7.3	10.0	10.0	9.4	6.8
Growth in debt (% per year)								
Private nonfinancial debt[a]	10.9[b]	9.7	8.8	8.8	10.5	11.2	8.9	9.9
Federal debt	1.2[b]	-0.5	2.2	2.1	4.9	11.3	11.8	4.1
Total nonfinancial debt	5.8[b]	5.4	6.5	7.0	9.4	11.2	9.4	7.8

[a] Total nonfinancial less federal debt.

[b] December 1948–December 1953 (year-end data).

Source: Center for International Business Cycle Research, Rutgers University.

were very closely associated with the growth in total debt of non-financial borrowers—business enterprises, consumers, state and local governments, and the federal government. Indeed, the relation between inflation and the growth of debt is about as close as that between inflation and the growth of money. It should be noted, however, that the table does not allow for lags. With time units as long as a business cycle, however, lags of a year or so might not make much difference. In any case debt and inflation are closely associated, a result that bolsters the argument of those who contend that credit is an appropriate target for monetary policy.

The interesting observation for fiscal policy is that it is the behavior of federal debt that is largely responsible for the close relation between credit and inflation. Privately held debt grew almost as rapidly in the earlier cycles as in the later ones. What varied widely in its growth rate was federal debt, starting with modest growth in the 1948-1953 cycle, which encompassed the Korean War, going down to no growth in the next cycle, 1953-1957, and accelerating ever since. After 1957 the acceleration in federal debt largely produced the acceleration in total debt and hence produced the close association of total debt with the rate of inflation.[3] Federal debt did not crowd out private debt. It was an add-on of increasing size, producing the wherewithal to finance a rising rate of inflation. Since the growth of federal debt is primarily determined by the size of the deficit, the current concern about the long-run trend in the deficit is clearly justified by the record.

Table 15-2 gives a bit of support to the possibility of a turning point in the trend of inflation, referred to previously. The most recent cycle, January 1980-July 1981, was not only unusual with respect to the brevity of the expansion phase (twelve months), but also because for the first time in nearly three decades the rates of growth in money and credit were smaller than in the preceding cycle. If these rates work down below their average levels for the 1948-1981 period as a whole, to say 3 percent for M1, 5 percent for M2, and 7 percent for total debt, the simple regressions between these rates and the inflation rates, based on the seven cycle observations, suggest an inflation rate in the 3 percent range. Judging from the record in the early years of the period, this is an attainable goal. It can be attained with output growth in the 3 to 4 percent range, unemployment in the 3 to 5 percent range, and with three or four years of expansion to every year of recession.

NOTES TO CHAPTER 15

1. For a brief review of the U.S. evidence see Geoffrey H. Moore, "Will the slowdown reduce the inflation rate?" *Across the Board*, The Conference Board Magazine, 26, no. 9 (September 1979): 3-7. The international evidence is summarized in Chapters 6 and 14 of this volume.

2. In terms of annual averages, the declines in the wholesale price index (from the preceding year) came in 1938, 1939, 1949, 1952, 1953, 1961, and 1963. The consumer price index registered declines in 1933, 1938, 1939, 1949, and 1955.

3. It is true that even if federal debt had continued to grow as slowly as it did, say, in 1957-1960 (2.2 percent per year) the growth of total debt might still have accelerated, because the effect of the slower growing federal component would have diminished as it got to be a smaller part of the total. But in fact the annual rate of borrowing by the federal government grew more than sixteenfold between 1957-1960 and 1980-1981, while borrowing by the private sector (including state and local governments) merely quadrupled. Hence the acceleration in growth of total debt was largely attributable to the increasing fraction of total borrowing done by the federal government. I am indebted to Arthur Broida for bringing to my attention the interesting point that a slow-growing component of a total can cause the total to accelerate even if none of the components does so.

REFERENCES

Thorp, Willard. *Business Annals.* New York: NBER, 1926.

Burns, Arthur F., and Wesley C. Mitchell. *Measuring Business Cycles.* New York: NBER, 1946.

Mitchell, Wesley C. *Business Cycles: The Problem and Its Setting.* New York: NBER, 1927.

Chapter 16

Trends and Cycles in Productivity, Unit Costs, and Prices: An International Perspective

Geoffrey H. Moore and John P. Cullity

This chapter examines short-run cyclical changes in productivity, costs, prices, and profits in the United States and other industrialized countries in recent decades, as well as in the current recession. It also analyzes long-term trends in productivity, compensation, costs, and prices for their implications about levels of inflation and real earnings.

Theoretical speculation into the causes of business cycles has often centered on the notion that imbalances among productivity, cost, and price changes are a significant part of the process of cumulative change by which one set of business conditions transforms itself into another set. That these factors were important to an understanding of cyclical changes in market-oriented economies was the subject of discussion as far back as 1913. Many decades elapsed before statistics that securely supported this insight arrived on the scene. In recent years, however, several of the larger industrial countries have begun to publish quarterly data on productivity, costs, prices, and profits. The section on short-run cyclical changes summarizes the salient findings on the relationships among these key variables.

The chapter also considers in more detail the disinflation processes currently affecting U.S. economic activity. Movements in hourly compensation, output per hour, and various measures of costs, prices, and profits during the 1981–1982 recession are compared with the

This chapter was presented at the American Enterprise Institute's conference on "International Comparisons of Productivity and Causes of the Slowdown." Washington, D.C., September 30, 1982.

The authors wish to thank Ted Joyce and Joyce Geiger for their valuable statistical assistance.

average of changes for the six recessions from 1948 to 1980. Recessions start out with an imbalance between costs and prices that grows worse for a time and damages the outlook for profits. However, the recession itself brings about a realignment as business enterprises strive to reduce costs. Once costs are rising less rapidly than prices, the outlook for profitable expansion of sales and output improves, and this sets the stage for recovery. All of this suggests that economic recovery hinges as much on an upturn in price/labor cost ratios as upon the much talked about decline in interest rates.

The section dealing with short-run cyclical changes also reveals a close link between movements in productivity and movements in the leading indicators. One can think of causal links running in both directions. For example, an upswing in new orders, one of the leading indicators, is likely to lead to an improvement in output per hour, because the additional output generated by the orders can often be ~roduced without a commensurate increase in labor input. One the other hand, an improvement in productivity, generated by new capital investment, can reduce costs and prices and thereby stimulate orders. Statistics depicting this linkage are provided for the United States, United Kingdom, West Germany, and Japan.

Productivity gains in the industrial countries were generally slower in the 1970s than in the 1960s or before. Statistics are provided documenting this trend, using 1973 as the dividing line. Data on trends in wages, labor costs, prices, and real earnings are presented for seven countries. It is plain that the international productivity slowdown did not retard the gains in nominal wages in most countries. In five of the seven countries studied, wage gains in manufacturing industries were higher, not lower, after 1973. The exceptions were West Germany and Japan. The consequence, except for those two, was an extraordinary acceleration in labor costs per unit of output. The statistics reveal that countries with the largest increases in unit labor costs generally had the largest increases in prices, especially during 1973–1980. Growth rates in real earnings were lower in the 1973–1980 period in every country except the United Kingdom.

Additional evidence about these long-term relationships is developed by measuring growth rates from one business cycle peak to the next. The data cover the nonfarm business sector in the United States since 1948. In every one of the business cycles, the gains in nominal hourly compensation exceeded the gain in output per hour. The differential diminished in the first three cycles, but increased afterwards, reaching dramatic heights in the last two cycles. This growing disparity showed up, of course, in unit labor costs. A tight relation between inflation in costs and inflation in prices was maintained throughout.

Finally, this chapter examines the long-lasting marriage of real earnings and productivity. Official statistics suggest that in the last two cycles, those since 1973, changes in real compensation were negative, even though productivity increased slightly. This discrepancy, however, may reflect a problem with the consumer price index used to calculate real earnings. When nominal hourly compensation is deflated by three other price indexes that have some claim to relevance, the rates of increase in real compensation match those in productivity growth more closely than when the consumer price index is used. The results cast doubt on the widely accepted view that real earnings have declined in recent years.

Sustained long-term economic growth has been the most striking feature of U.S. business history. Growth in labor and capital resources fueled a substantial part of this growth. Secular improvements in the use of these resources also accounted for a large part. Americans have generally taken these productivity improvements for granted. A cursory examination of the economic record of the 1970s, however, is sufficient to dispel anyone's continuing inclination to complacency on this matter. That decade was the worst since 1901–1910 in terms of the growth in output per hour. Specifically, from 1971 to 1980, labor productivity in the private, nonfarm business sector grew only 9 percent, which was well below its growth in any of the preceding six decades. This development constituted a cruel irony, since in the 1960s some of the nation's ablest economists had thoroughly analyzed the problem of economic growth and put together extensive menus on how to stimulate faster growth. The consequences of the dismal productivity performance made an impression on the growth of output, on the growth of real earnings, and on the behavior of costs and prices. The poor productivity performance was not a problem unique to America. The same ailment afflicted every major industrial economy. In this chapter, we first examine short-run cyclical changes in productivity, costs, prices, and profits in the United States and other industrialized economies in recent decades, as well as in the current recession. We then analyze long-term trends in productivity, compensation, costs, and prices for their implications about levels of inflation.

CYCLICAL MOVEMENTS

Mitchell's Generalizations and Recent U.S. Business Cycles

Theoretical speculation into the etiology of the business cycle has often centered on the notion that imbalances among productivity, cost, and price changes are a significant part of the process of cumulative change by which one set of business conditions transforms itself into another set. Wesley C. Mitchell, for instance, recognized as far back as 1913 that these factors were important to an understanding about cyclical changes in market-oriented economies.[1] His theoretical insights were widely discussed in the United States but many decades elapsed before statistics that securely supported his position arrived on the scene.[2] In 1972, the U.S. Bureau of Labor Statistics began to publish quarterly data on costs and profits per unit of output for all nonfinancial corporations along with comparable prices received. The BLS series were carried back to 1948 and they now cover seven full business cycles. In each of these cycles, the changes in these variables bear a family resemblance to those which Mitchell described almost seventy years ago.

Let us summarize Mitchell's views and then look at what has happened during recent business cycles. Mitchell suggested that in the later stages of economic expansion an encroachment of costs on prices occurred which paved the way for an eventual squeeze on aggregate profits. These developments were crucial to an understanding of the reluctance of business firms to commit themselves to new investment projects. This hesitancy to undertake new investments itself then contributed to the forces responsible for turning expansion into recession. In contrast, a reversal of this occurs during recessions and this helps to brake the cumulative process of contraction and bring about an upturn.

Figure 16-1 offers us a glimpse of the movements of these statistics in recent decades. The salient findings on this subject as they now appear to stand are as follows:

1. For nonfarm businesses as a whole, the rates of increase of unit labor costs and of prices received have generally tracked one another closely. (See Figure 16-1a.)

2. There have been important divergences, however. Shortly before and during each of the recessions (shaded area), unit labor costs rose more rapidly than prices, whereas in the early stages of each of the recoveries, unit labor costs rose more slowly than prices. The arithmetic differences between the growth rates in prices and unit labor costs are shown in Figure 16-1b.

3. The differences between price changes and unit labor cost changes follow a cyclical pattern, which is reflected in corporate profit margins (Figure 16-1b). In general, profit margins tend to fall late in economic expansions and during recessions, as businesses fail to pass through to prices some of the sharp increases they experience in unit labor costs. In contrast, margins tend to recover early in expansions.

Figure 16-1. Growth Rates in Labor Costs, Prices, Profits, and Productivity, Nonfarm Business—United States.

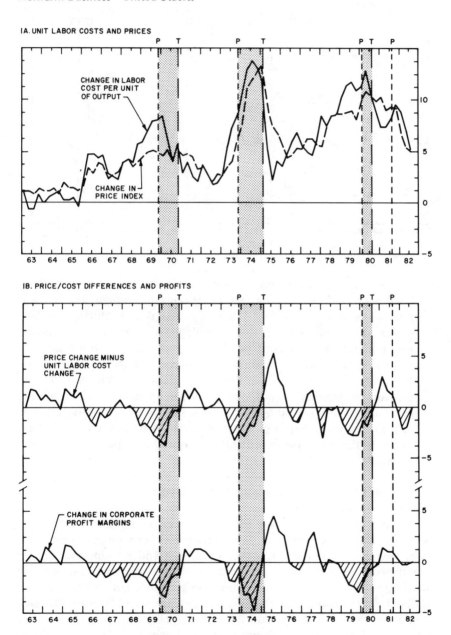

(Figure 16-1. continued overleaf)

Figure 16-1. *continued*

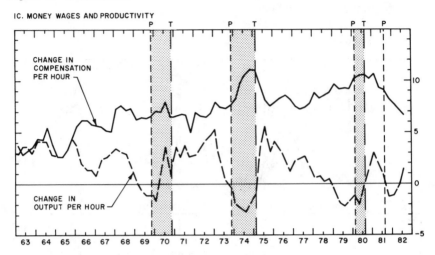

Note: Shaded areas are recessions, from peak (P) to trough (T).

4. The reasons for the behavior of unit labor costs can be seen when cost is subdivided into its two components: average hourly compensation and output per hour (Figure 16-1c). During the late states of contraction and the early stages of economic expansions rapid increases in output per hour occur along with a relatively slow rise in hourly compensation. Hence, changes in labor costs per unit of product fall. In contrast, as the economy approaches a peak, changes in output per hour usually decline. (For details, see Table 16-1.) At about that time, hourly compensation generally grows more rapidly. When growth in hourly compensation exceeds the increase in output per hour, changes in unit costs advance.

Mitchell's Generalizations and Growth Cycles
In Europe and Japan

Another test of the power of Mitchell's generalizations, which has both scientific value and practical advantages, can be made by compiling relevant statistics in other countries and conducting similar experiments with them. If similar relationships are revealed, the case for the theory would obviously be strengthened. However, finding a similar testing ground for the theory elsewhere is a bit more difficult than it might at first appear. As noted earlier, the U.S. tests were conducted inside the framework of the business or classical cycle.

Table 16-1. **Productivity Changes over Business Cycles, United States** (*percent*).

	Business Cycle Contractions		Business Cycle Expansions	
	1st Half	*2nd Half*	*1st Half*	*2nd Half*
Averages				
1919–1961 (10 cycles)	0.8	2.8	5.3	3.0
1961–1982 (4 cycles)	-1.9	1.4	3.2	0.7
Individual cycles				
1961–1969 (E)[a]			3.6	1.6
1969–1970 (C)[b]	1.2	1.4		
1970–1973 (E)			3.9	1.9
1973–1975 (C)	-2.9	-0.4		
1975–1980 (E)			3.4	-0.1
1980–1980 (C)	-2.8	3.2		
1980–1981 (E)			2.0	-0.2
1981–1982 (C)	-3.2			

[a]E = Expansion.
[b]C = Contraction.
Source: The data for 1919–1961 relate to the manufacturing sector and are monthly; see Solomon Fabricant, *A Primer on Productivity* New York: Random House, 1969), p. 91. The data for 1961–1982 are for the nonfarm business sector and are compiled quarterly by the Bureau of Labor Statistics.

This framework involves an absolute rise and fall in aggregate economic activity. In the 1950s and 1960s, however, many countries did not experience actual declines in activity but did experience varying rates of growth. When the work on international economic indicators now being conducted at the Columbia Center for International Business Cycle Research was first launched at the National Bureau of Economic Research in 1973, the task was to learn more about these fluctuations. To examine these growth cycles, therefore, methods of measuring and eliminating long-run trends were developed. From the trend-adjusted data, chronologies of growth cycles were derived in the same manner that had been used in the United States to derive the business cycle chronology. The growth cycle then is simply a trend-adjusted business cycle. The expansion phase is a period when the short-run growth rate of aggregate economic activity is greater than the long-run rate, whereas in the contraction phase the short-run growth rate is less than the long-run rate.

Figures 16-2, 16-3, and 16-4 disclose information about labor costs, productivity, and prices for the United Kingdom, West Germany, and Japan within a growth cycle framework. The peak (*P*) and trough (*T*) dates identify periods of slowdown in economic

Figure 16-2.   Growth Rates in Labor Costs, Prices, Profits, and Productivity in Manufacturing—United Kingdom.

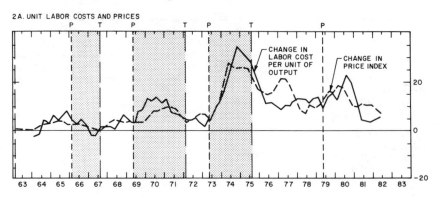

2A. UNIT LABOR COSTS AND PRICES

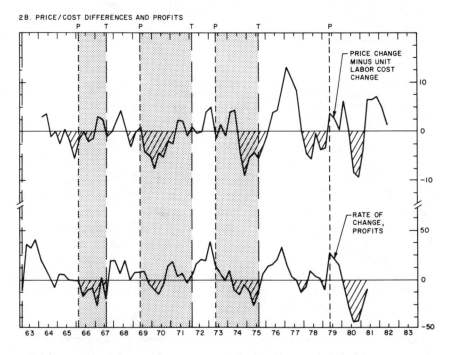

2B. PRICE/COST DIFFERENCES AND PROFITS

growth in each country, not necessarily periods of recession. The salient findings for the three countries are as follows:

1.   Although each country has its own pattern, the close relationship between rates of change in labor cost per unit of product and in prices is as visible in these three countries as in the United States.

Figure 16-2. *continued*

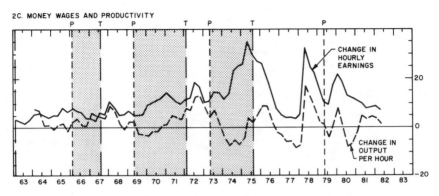

2C. MONEY WAGES AND PRODUCTIVITY

Note: Peak (P) and trough (T) dates identify periods of slowdown in economic growth.

2. For the three countries, unit labor costs rose faster than prices during each of the growth recessions since 1963. The encroachment process, however, started to take hold *before* the growth recessions in only seven of the twelve episodes.[3] Although this differs from the universal drop before U.S. business cycles it should be borne in mind that growth cycle peaks typically occur before business cycle peaks.

3. Changes in profit margins in Japanese factories since 1963 moved downward before each of the *growth* cycle peaks and reached negative values—that is, margins were falling—no later than one quarter after the growth cycle peak in any case. Moreover, lows of changes in profit margins preceded each of the growth cycle troughs. For the United Kingdom and West Germany we have unfortunately been unable to locate data on profit margins. As a proxy, we have computed changes in total profits for the United Kingdom and in total entrepreneurial and property income for Germany. In the United Kingdom highs in the rate of change in profits preceded each of the growth cycle peaks, and lows occurred before growth cycle troughs. At about the same time growth cycle lows were reached, total profits were again rising. Corresponding statistics on changes in the West German series are more erratic, and it is difficult to find more than traces of the cyclical pattern that shows up clearly in the price/cost differences.

4. During the early stages of growth cycle expansions, rapid increases in output per hour occur, along with a slowing of the rise in compensation; hence, increases in unit costs fall. In contrast,

Figure 16-3. Growth Rates in Labor Costs, Prices, Profits, and Productivity in Manufacturing—West Germany.

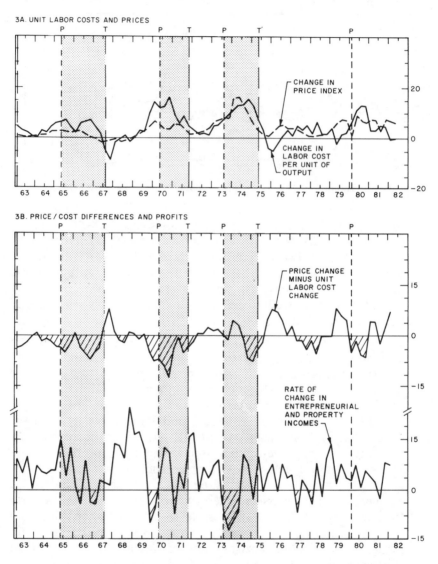

changes in output per hour typically decline as a growth cycle peak is approached, while hourly compensation grows more rapidly. When the growth in hourly compensation exceeds that in output per hour, changes in unit costs advance.

Figure 16-3. *continued*

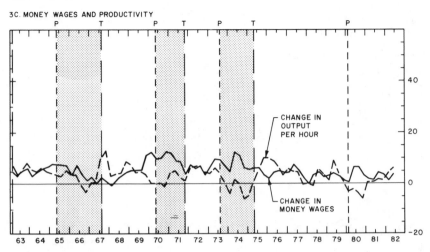

Note: Peak (P) and trough (T) dates identify periods of slowdown in economic growth.

Summing up these relationships, costs are generally rising more rapidly than prices when a slowdown or recession begins, but their differences diminish during recessions. By the time a recovery begins they are usually in much closer alignment.

A principal function of economic history, which studies changes under various sets of institutional arrangements, is to test the relevance of economic generalizations and to ask which are the more widely and which are the more narrowly applicable. The historical analysis we have summarized covers a long span of U.S. history and goes far beyond our boundaries to discover new testing grounds in the United Kingdom, West Germany, Japan, and other countries. Few economic generalizations have been accorded as much testing as Mitchell's views on the cyclical behavior of costs and profits. Still fewer have been able to survive tests of this sort for so long a period.

Recession-Recovery Patterns

We now turn to materials that disclose a few of the features of the disinflation processes currently affecting U.S. economic activity. Figure 16-5 depicts the movements of hourly compensation, output per hour, and various measures of costs, prices, and profits for the months before and after the business cycle peak in July 1981. The data are plotted in what is known as a recession-recovery format.[4]

Figure 16-4. Growth Rates in Labor Costs, Prices, Profits, and Productivity in Manufacturing—Japan.

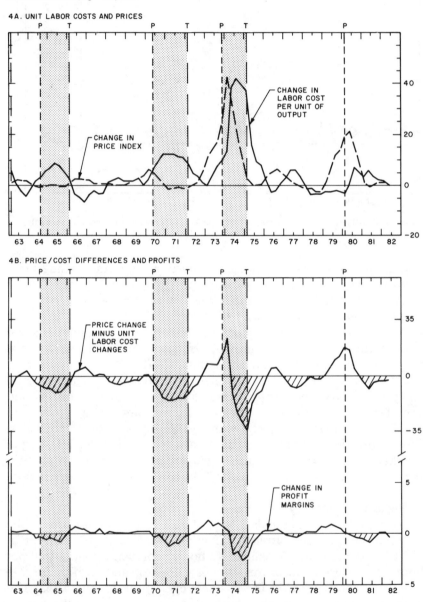

Figure 16-4. *continued*

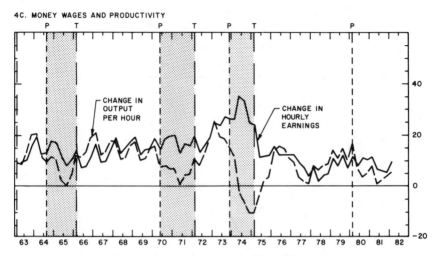

4C. MONEY WAGES AND PRODUCTIVITY

Note: Peak (P) and trough (T) dates identify periods of slowdown in economic growth.

The growth rates displayed are two-quarter smoothed changes; that is, the growth rate is derived from the ratio of the current quarter's index to the average index for the four preceding quarters. This calculation is designed to smooth out the irregularities in the short-term movements of the various statistics. The railroad track line displays the average pattern of the series during six preceding recessions, 1948–1980. The solid line represents the movements of the respective series during the current recession.

It is plain that the rate of gain in nominal hourly compensation during the 1981–1982 downswing has fallen more sharply than during earlier contractions. Hourly compensation was rising at a 9 percent annual rate at the 1981 peak. A year later, it was increasing at a less than 7 percent rate. The decline to date has been more than twice as large as the average decline in previous recessions.

The slowdown in the growth of hourly pay has helped to slow the growth of labor cost per unit of product. At first, however, unit labor costs rose more rapidly, owing to the sharp decline in productivity growth when the recession got underway. The decline in private nonfarm productivity was much sharper than the typical change that occurs in the early stages of economic contraction. Hence, unit cost accelerated during the first six months of the downswing. Since then, however, unit cost changes have followed a path similar to that during comparable phases of earlier recessions.

Figure 16-5.   Recession-Recovery Patterns: Productivity, Costs, Prices and Profits.

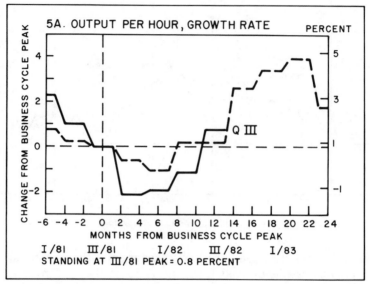

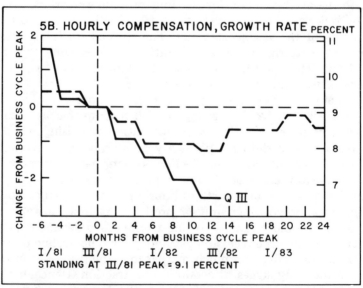

Figure 16-5. *continued*

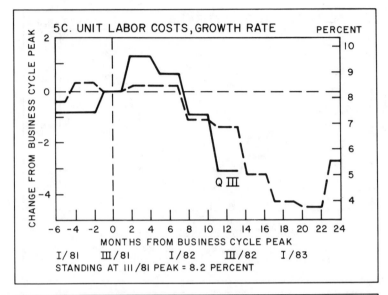

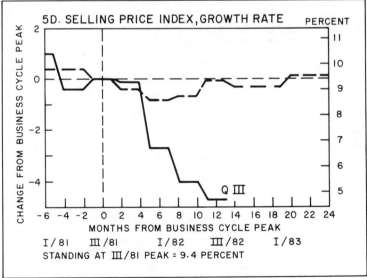

(Figure 16-5. continued overleaf)

Figure 16-5. *continued*

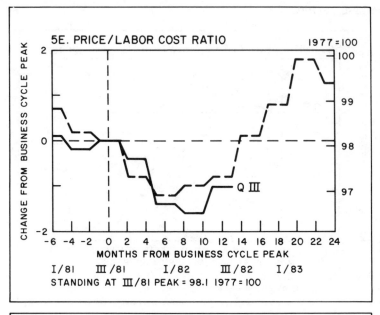

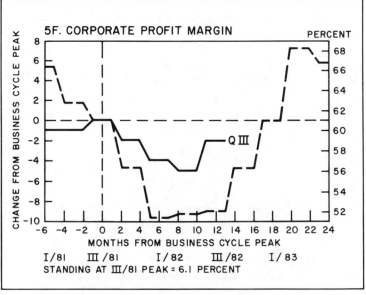

Figure 16-5. *continued*

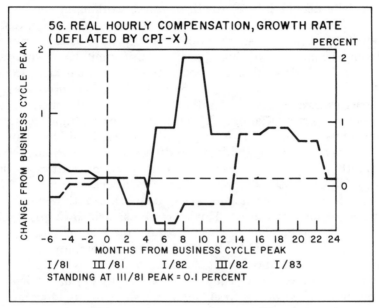

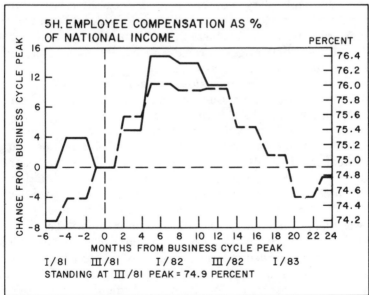

Note: Data pertain to the nonfarm business sector except for f (all nonfinancial corporations) and h (entire employed population).

The charts also reveal the striking changes in prices that occurred early in the economic slide. At that time, the inflation rate fell like a rock. The decline in the growth of prices working in conjunction with the stickiness of the cost changes served to prolong and intensify the encroachment of costs on prices that began, as usual, during the preceding economic upswing. Thus, the price/unit labor cost ratio continued its downward slide through the second quarter of 1982, a big factor in the decline of profit margins. Since then, both the ratio and margins have increased. Another implication of the sharp decline in the rate of price inflation, which affected the economic well-being of the close to 100 million employed persons, is disclosed in the movements of the changes in real hourly earnings. A sharp increase in real hourly compensation occurred about six months after the business cycle peak in the summer of 1981 (see discussion on page 272). Normally, real earnings do not start to increase until about a year after a recession has started. This increase has helped to offset some of the decline in income produced by the drop in employment, since real income has increased for those who remained employed.

Every economist knows that there are only two ways to increase the real earnings of labor. They can be raised by (1) increasing output per hour of work, or (2) enlarging the share of total income that goes to wage and salary workers. The first of these two sources is basic and will be addressed in our discussion of long-term trends. In the short run, however, business firms in the aggregate may not be able to increase their prices as rapidly as hourly rates of pay are rising. Hence, real hourly earnings will increase.

During the 1981-1982 recession, although real hourly compensation fell slightly at the start, there was a rapid quickening of real compensation afterward. In the second quarter, this series rose at a 2 percent annual rate. Not only that, as suggested earlier this is associated with an enlargement of the share of total income that goes to the workers. The latter effect can be seen in the lagging economic indicator, compensation of employees as a percent of national income, which has risen of late (see Figure 16-5h). Indeed, in the first half of 1982, workers' share in the national income, at 76 percent, was higher than in any preceding six-month period save one.

In his masterpiece on business cycles published in 1939, Joseph Schumpeter propounded the remarkable proposition that periods of recession are times when the harvest is gathered after the strenuous efforts of the expansion.[5] Sympathetic students of his work have usually looked at this proposition with bemusement, as something better overlooked since it would only detract from the respect that his work rightfully deserves. But Schumpeter's formulation is at least a reminder to us that business cycle recessions are not catastrophes in all respects. The data on changes in real hourly earnings just cited provide some perspective on this matter.

The figures tell still another story that perhaps has not received the attention it deserves. During the past year, the public's attention has been focused on the high level of nominal and real interest rates. There has been enormous speculation about the impact of these rates on the prospects for economic recovery. There is justification for this position. However, scant attention if any is focused on the behavior of unit labor costs and their relation to prices. Judging from past experience, economic recovery hinges as much on an upturn in price/labor cost ratios as upon a decline in interest rates.

The Link between Productivity and the Leading Indicators

We have seen that short-run movements in productivity are closely linked to costs, prices, and profits, which in turn have long been viewed as crucial factors in the generation of business cycles. One might expect, therefore, that productivity movements would show a close affinity to the so-called leading indicators, which for a variety of reasons anticipate business cycle peaks and troughs. One can think of causal relationships running in both directions. For example, an upswing in new orders, one of the leading indicators, is likely to lead to an improvement in output per hour, because the additional output generated by the larger volume of orders can usually be produced without a commensurate increase in labor input. On the other hand, an improvement in productivity generated, say, by new capital equipment, can reduce costs and prices and thereby stimulate orders.

Figure 16-6 supplies a test of the strength of this two-way relationship, comparing growth rates in leading indexes with growth rates in productivity in four countries. In each country there is a general correspondence between the movements of the two series. Thus, faster growth in a country's leading index is likely to be accompanied by faster growth in output per hour. Slower growth or decline in the leading index and in productivity also go together. Both lead general business activity, and by about the same amount of time; that is, the movements of the leading indexes and productivity are roughly coincident with one another. More often than not, in fact, the turns in productivity growth have preceded those in the leading index growth rates by a few months, again attesting to the significant role of productivity in the business cycle.

One of the practical values of this relationship is that the leading indexes can help appraise current movements in productivity. For

Figure 16-6. Growth Rates in Productivity and in the Leading Indexes—
Four Countries.

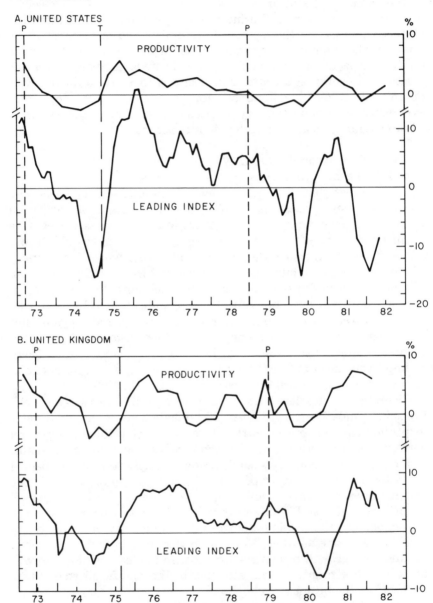

Figure 16-6. *continued*

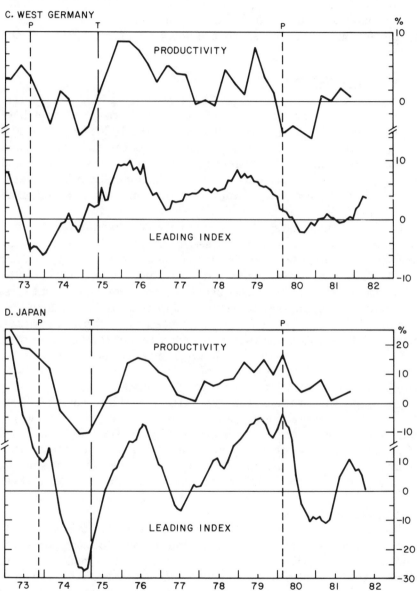

Note: Peak (P) and trough (T) dates identify periods of slowdown in economic growth.

example, the striking improvement in productivity growth in the United Kingdom since 1980 seems to be firmly based, since the growth rates in the U.K. leading index have risen substantially from their low at the end of 1980. In most countries, the leading indexes are available several months before productivity data are published, so the former give some advance indications of movements in the latter.

LONG-RUN TRENDS

As noted earlier, productivity gains in the industrial countries have been generally slower in the 1970s than in the 1960s or before. Figure 16-7 documents this trend, using 1973 as the dividing line, and displays the concommitant trends in wages, labor costs, prices, and real earnings, along the lines developed in John Kendrick's recent work.[6] Except for prices, where we use the consumer price index, all the data pertain to the manufacturing sector.

One thing the international productivity slowdown did not do was to retard the gains in nominal wages. In five of the seven countries, wage gains in manufacturing industries were higher, not lower, after 1973. Only in West Germany and Japan did wage gains follow the productivity trend. The consequence, in every country except West Germany and Japan, was an extraordinary acceleration in labor cost per unit of output. A further consequence was a faster rise in prices, because labor costs constitute a big proportion of total costs in most industries. Although reductions in profit margins and other costs can temporarily offset some of the increases in labor costs, in the long run, rising labor costs get passed through to prices.[7]

A comparison of the bars in Figure 16-7c and d reveals that countries with the largest increases in unit labor costs generally had the largest increases in prices, especially during 1973-1980. The United Kingdom and Italy are well above the rest in both cost and price increases. West Germany and Japan share the honors for the smallest increases in both costs and prices. They were the countries whose wage trends during the past eight years came closest to matching their reduced productivity growth.

As for real hourly earnings, growth rates were lower in the 1973-1980 period than in the previous period in every country except the United Kingdom (Figure 16-7e). The reduction in real wage gains for the United States and Japan were conspicuously sharp. The enormous acceleration in money wages did not pay off in real terms. As has been established time and again, productivity growth holds the key to growth in real earnings in the long run.

Figure 16–7. International Reactions to the Productivity Slowdown.

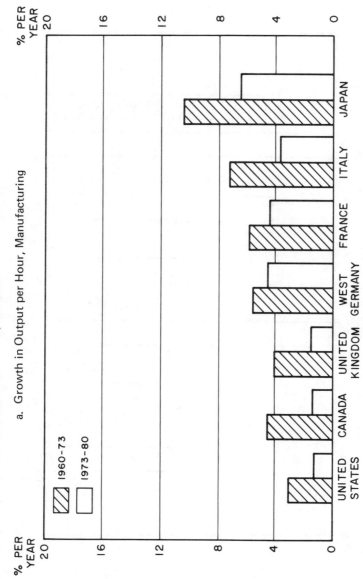

a. Growth in Output per Hour, Manufacturing

The productivity slowdown has been international in scope . . .

Figure 16–7. *continued*

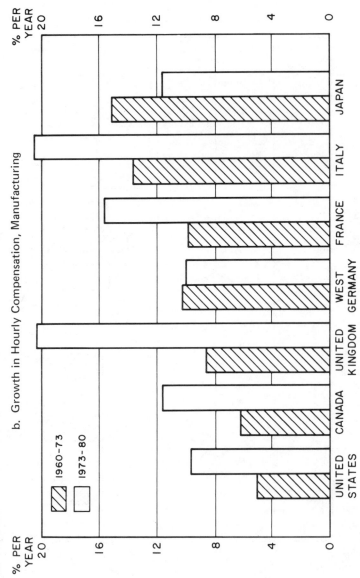

b. Growth in Hourly Compensation, Manufacturing

but hourly compensation accelerated everywhere except in Germany and Japan, far exceeding productivity growth.

Figure 16-7. *continued*

c. Growth in Unit Labor Cost, Manufacturing

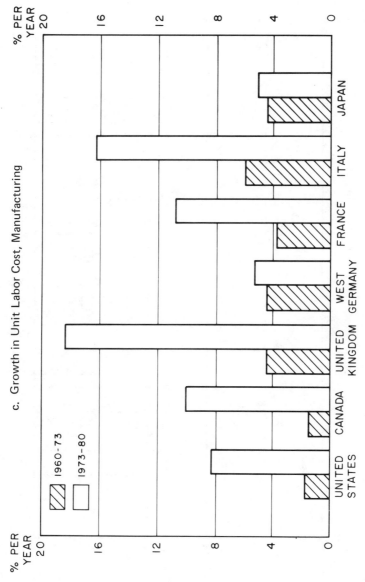

So labor cost per unit of output accelerated, though only a little in Germany and Japan . . .

Figure 16-7. continued

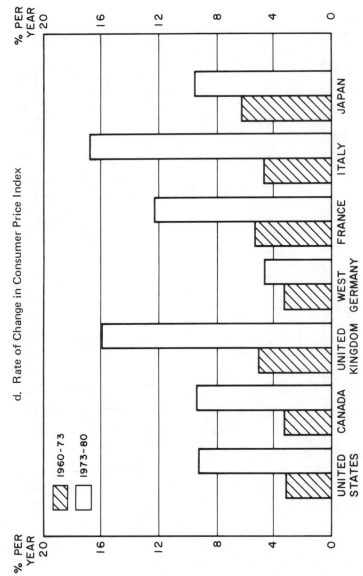

d. Rate of Change in Consumer Price Index

while prices accelerated also, but least in Germany and Japan . . .

Figure 16–7. *continued*

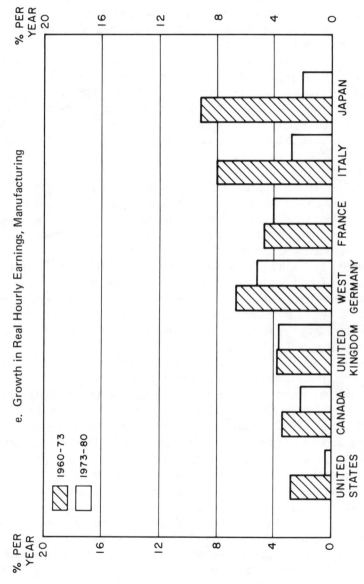

e. Growth in Real Hourly Earnings, Manufacturing

and gains in real hourly earnings slackened, like productivity.

Further evidence buttressing those long-run trend relationships is displayed in Figure 16-8. Here the method of putting to one side the short-run cyclical changes is to measure growth rates from one business cycle to the next. The data cover the nonfarm business sector in the United States since 1948. Hence the industry coverage and time span is wider than in the preceding charts, while the geographic coverage is narrower.

In every one of the seven business cycles, the gains in hourly compensation in nominal terms exceeded the gains in output per hour (Figure 16-8a). In the first three cycles, from 1948 to 1960, the differential diminished. Then it increased, reaching dramatic heights in the last two cycles, 1973-1980 and 1980-1981. Over the entire period the relationship between growth in hourly wages and in productivity was, if anything, inverse. Perhaps "perverse" would be a better word.

This growing disparity between wages and productivity in the 1960s and 1970s showed up, of course, in unit labor costs (Figure 16-8b). The tight relation between inflation in costs and inflation in prices was maintained throughout. Whatever the ultimate source of inflation, costs and prices go together.

Finally, in Figure 16-8c, we return once again to the long-lasting marriage of real earnings and productivity. As productivity goes, so go real earnings. This time, however, there is a slight twist. In the first two cycles, real earnings growth exceeded productivity growth. In the last five cycles, since 1957, real earnings growth fell short of productivity growth.

The reasons for this twist are worth further exploration. On the face of it, the inflation in nominal wages had a negative payoff. Not only did the gains in real earnings decline as productivity slowed, they did not even keep up with productivity. In fact, in the last two cycles, since 1973, changes in real earnings were negative, even though productivity increased slightly. This decline in real earnings, however, may reflect a problem with the consumer price index, which is used to calculate real earnings. To examine this matter, we have deflated hourly earnings with three other price indexes that have some claim to relevance, with the results shown in Figures 16-8d, e, and f. We find that in all three instances, the rates of increase in real compensation match those in productivity growth more closely than when the consumer price index is used. Moreover, all three of the alternative measures show that real earnings increased since 1973, albeit slowly.

One can argue, of course, about the relative merits of the various price deflators. CPI-X measures housing costs in terms of a rental

Figure 16-8. Growth Trends in Productivity, Compensation, Costs and Prices, Nonfarm Business Sector, United States, 1948–1981.

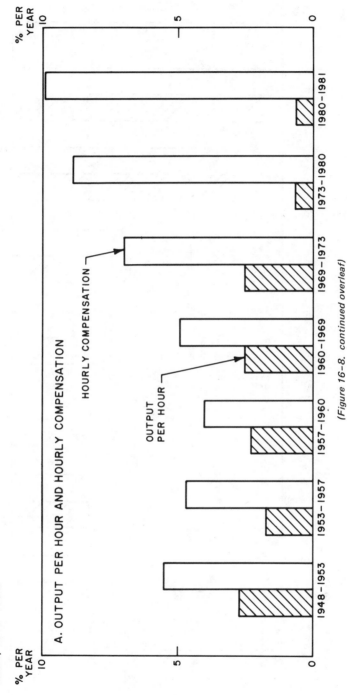

A. OUTPUT PER HOUR AND HOURLY COMPENSATION

(Figure 16-8. continued overleaf)

Figure 16-8. continued

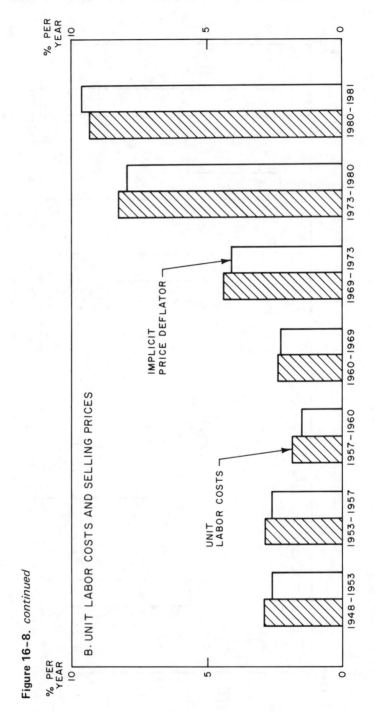

B. UNIT LABOR COSTS AND SELLING PRICES

Figure 16-8. *continued*

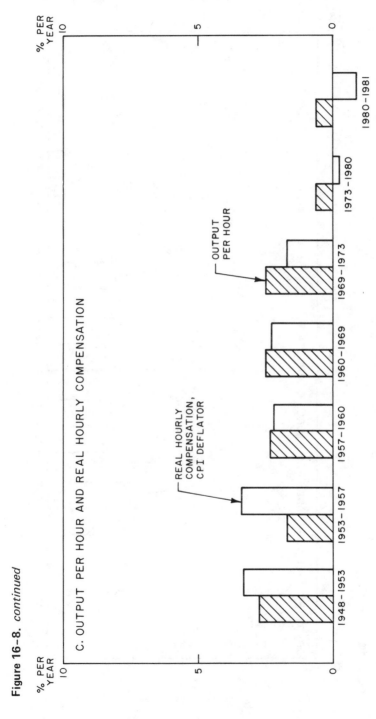

C. OUTPUT PER HOUR AND REAL HOURLY COMPENSATION

(Figure 16-8. continued overleaf)

Figure 16–8. continued

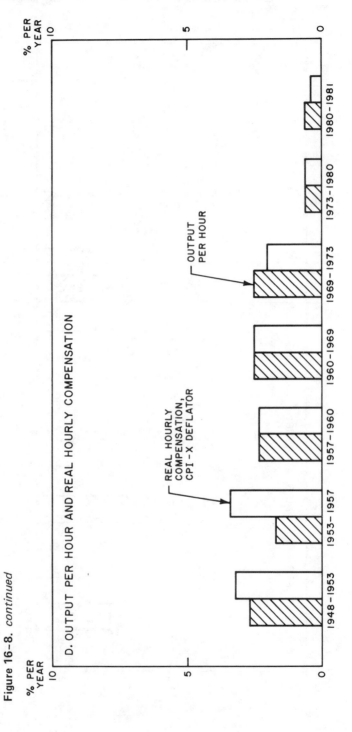

D. OUTPUT PER HOUR AND REAL HOURLY COMPENSATION

Figure 16-8. *continued*

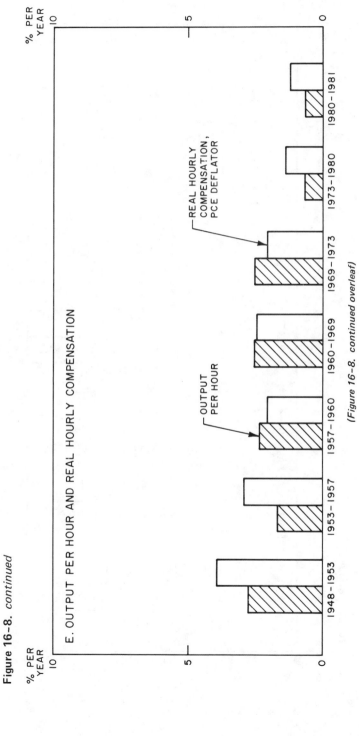

E. OUTPUT PER HOUR AND REAL HOURLY COMPENSATION

(Figure 16-8. continued overleaf)

Figure 16-8. *continued*

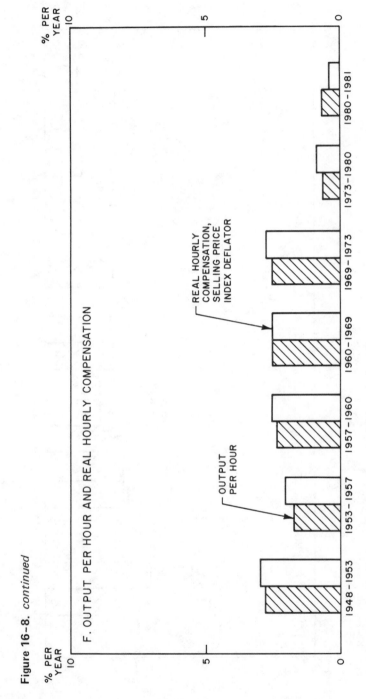

F. OUTPUT PER HOUR AND REAL HOURLY COMPENSATION

Note: Growth rates are measured between successive business cycle peaks.

equivalent concept, and is to be adopted by the BLS as the official CPI for the urban population after January 1983. The personal consumption expenditures deflator also uses a rental equivalent concept. In addition, it is affected by changes in the composition of consumer spending. The selling price index, which is the implicit price deflator for nonfarm business output, is the same deflator that is used to derive the productivity estimates. These prices are not the prices that wage earners pay, but this measure of real earnings does represent the amount of industry's output that could be purchased with an hour's compensation. All of the alternative price deflators support the conclusion that real earnings have increased in recent years about in line with productivity growth.

NOTES TO CHAPTER 16

1. Wesley C. Mitchell, *Business Cycles and Their Causes*, (Berkeley: University of California Press, 1941).

2. Empirical support for the hypothesis was first developed by Thor Hultgren in "Cyclical Diversities in the Fortunes of Industrial Corporations," *Occasional Paper 32* (New York: National Bureau of Economic Research, 1952). Stronger support was then provided in Thor Hultgren, *Costs, Prices, and Profits: Their Cyclical Relations*, Studies in Business Cycles, no. 14 (New York: 1965). The results of still other tests were disclosed in Geoffrey H. Moore's "Tested Knowledge of Business Cycles," *42nd Annual Report*, (New York: National Bureau of Economic Research, 1962), as well as in Moore's "Productivity, Costs, and Prices: New Light From an Old Hypothesis," *Explorations in Economic Research* 2, no. 1, (Winter 1975). See also Anthony T. Cluff's doctoral dissertation, "Prices, Unit Labor Costs, and Profits—An Examination of Wesley C. Mitchell's Business Cycle Theory for the Period 1947-1969," (George Washington University, June 1970). Findings about the validity of the hypothesis beyond U.S. boundaries are found in Philip A. Klein and Geoffrey H. Moore, "Monitoring Profits During Business Cycles," in Helmut Laumer and Maria Ziegler, eds., *International Research on Business Cycles* (Aldershot: 1981). Gower Publishing.

3. Three of the five exceptions occurred at the start of the 1973-1975 worldwide downturn when the price runups associated with the activities of the OPEC cartel doubtless were a contributing factor to the deviation from the usual sequence.

4. For further information on recession-recovery patterns, see *Recession-Recovery Watch*, a bimonthly publication of the Center for International Business Cycle Research, Rutgers University. See also Gerhard Bry and Charlotte Boschan, *Cyclical Analysis of Time Series: Selected Procedures and Computer Programs*, National Bureau of Economic Research, (New York: Columbia University Press, 1971), pp. 151-199.

5. Joseph A. Schumpeter, *Business Cycles*, vol. 1, (New York: McGraw-Hill, 1939), p. 142.

6. John Kendrick, "International Comparisons of Recent Productivity Trends," in *Contemporary Economic Problems, 1981–1982 Edition*, William Fellner, Project Director, (Washington, D.C.: American Enterprise Institute, 1981), pp. 125–170.

7. Some students of economic policy drew a distinction between demand-pull and cost-push inflation that suggested that the former was a monetary phenomenon while the latter was nonmonetary. In reality, both types of inflation are monetary in the important sense that they require monetary expansion. Either M, the quantity of money, or V, its velocity of circulation, must go up. Demand-pull, as well as cost-push inflations, are phenomena that can be stopped or prevented by monetary restrictions. In modern industrial economies, price and wage policymakers often operate on the basis of an important tacit assumption that monetary policy will accomodate pricing or wage bargains that they arrange. The notion that their actions might be incompatible with moderate rates of expansion in the money supply is not often considered.

Chapter 17

Inflation and Profits

Does a high rate of inflation improve the profit situation of business enterprises? Or to put it the other way around, do rising profits contribute to inflation? Although the experience of individual industries will differ, the record for business enterprise as a whole suggests that the answer to both these questions is no. Indeed, profit margins during the past twenty years have, on balance, acted more as an offsetting than as an intensifying factor with respect to inflation. Profit margins were higher, on the whole, when the rate of inflation was low and lower when the rate of inflation was high.

The record since 1948 is in Figure 17-1, based upon figures published by the Bureau of Labor Statistics. The top line in the figure shows the rate of change in the consumer price index during successive six month intervals, after adjustment for seasonal variation. This is the basis for the monthly chronology of the rate of inflation, marked off by vertical lines representing peak rates and trough rates.[1] The next line is the rate of change in the CPI over four-quarter intervals. Both rates are centered in the middle of the interval to which they pertain, and on this basis they show similar movements, although the quarterly series is smoother. The next pair of lines pertain to the rates of change in prices and in profits per unit of output for all nonfinancial corporations, also expressed as rates of change over four-quarter intervals. Corporate prices, it will be seen, are closely related to consumer prices. The consumer, by and large, pays what the corporations charge.[2]

Reprinted from *NBER Reporter*, December 1977.

Figure 17-1. Prices and Profits per Unit of Output; Rates of Change, 1948–1977.

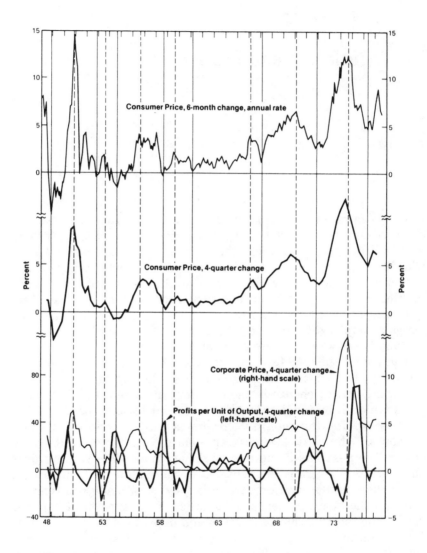

Note: Vertical Lines are peaks (P) and troughs (T) in Inflation Chronology (consumer price, six-month change). Rates are centered in middle of period covered.

Source: *U.S. Bureau of Labor Statistics.*

During the Korean War period and for several years thereafter, the rates of change in corporate profits per unit of output were, on the whole, positively related to the rates of change in corporate prices. But since 1955 or so an inverse tendency has developed. In 1972, for example, when corporate prices were rising at a modest 3 percent annual rate, profits per unit of output rose at an 18 percent clip. By 1974, when the rate of increase in corporate prices reached 13 percent, unit profits were falling at a 29 percent annual rate. In the following year, when the inflation rate dropped to 8 percent, profits per unit of output rose at a phenomenal 67 percent rate.

Table 17-1 shows the rates of change in unit profits when corporate prices were rising most rapidly and when they were rising least rapidly or falling. The first swing in prices, 1949 to 1951 to 1953, was accompanied by a similar swing in unit profits. Since then, profits have swung in the opposite direction to prices, declining when prices were rising most rapidly, rising when prices were rising least rapidly. In general, the fluctuations in profits, both up and down, are far wider than in prices: the scale for profits in Figure 17-1 is eight times as large as the scale for prices. The profit line and the price line have not always moved in the opposite direction by any means, but in recent years the tendency has been that way. High rates of inflation have not been good for profits.[3]

In view of the close relation, mentioned above, between corporate prices and consumer prices, the relations between corporate profits and corporate prices carry over to consumer prices (see Table 17-1). That is, the highest rates of increase in consumer prices have been associated in recent years with low rates of increase (or a decline) in corporate profits per unit of output and vice versa.[4]

How does this come about? To make sense of it, one has to look at the behavior of costs of production and at the changing relationship between costs and prices during the course of the business cycle. Costs and prices in the economy as a whole have a peculiar, yet characteristic, relationship during the business cycle. During a business expansion the rate of increase in prices generally rises and so does the rate of increase in costs—labor costs as well as other costs. But the cost curve rises faster. Whereas at the beginning of an expansion prices are typically rising faster than costs, at the end costs are typically rising faster than prices. Somewhere around the middle of an expansion costs per unit of output rise at about the same rate as prices, but from there on costs rise faster than prices, putting a squeeze on profits even though prices may still be rising faster than before. The upshot is that the rates of change in profits per unit of output are rising

Table 17-1. Corporate Prices, Consumer Prices, and Unit Profits, 1949–1977.

Dates of High and Low Rates of Change in Corporate Prices		Rates of Change (percent) in					
		Corporate Prices		Consumer Prices		Unit Profits	
High (1)	Low (2)	At High (3)	At Low (4)	At High (5)	At Low (6)	At High (7)	At Low (8)
	I/49–I/50						
II/50–II/51		6.3	−0.7	9.2	−1.5	7.3	−4.4
	IV/52–IV/53						
I/56–I/57		4.4	−0.9	3.4	0.8	−1.8	−26.2
	III/62–III/63						
II/69–II/70		4.9	−0.1	6.1	1.4	−21.9	7.4
	III/71–III/72						
I/74–I/75		14.6	2.3	11.1	3.1	−18.0	12.4
	I/76–I/77		4.6		5.9		−8.3

Note: The corporate price figures are based upon the implicit price deflator for gross domestic product of all nonfinancial corporations. Unit profits are corporate profits before taxes but with inventory valuation and capital consumption adjustments, per unit of gross domestic product of nonfinancial corporate business. All percent changes are computed from the same quarter year ago, for the intervals in columns 1 and 2.

Source: U.S. Bureau of Labor Statistics.

less rapidly, or even declining, at the end of a business expansion—
the peak of prosperity—than at the beginning, even though prices
are rising faster at the end than at the beginning.

NOTES TO CHAPTER 17

1. See Chapter 11 for a discussion of this chronology and Appendix Table
A-5 for the dates.

2. This is not strictly correct. For one thing, many things that corporations
sell are not sold to consumers. They may sell machinery to other corporations,
to the government, or to buyers in other countries, for example. Also, consumers buy some products or services from noncorporate sources. But the prices
paid by consumers, overall, are very closely correlated with the prices received
by corporations. The correlation coefficient (r), 1948–1977, based upon four-
quarter changes, is +0.90.

3. The correlation coefficients (r) between the four-quarter changes in corporate prices and unit profits are: 1948–1954, +0.40; 1955–1977, −0.07.
Neither of these coefficients are statistically significant, which means that by
this test the data do not refute the hypothesis that there is no relation between
the rates of change in unit profits and prices. It is clear, however, that since 1955
the relation has not been positive. It should be noted that because both the unit
profits and the price (implicit price deflator) indexes are obtained by dividing
dollar aggregates by an index of output, errors in the latter tend to produce a
spurious positive correlation between unit profits and prices, in which case an
observed inverse correlation would be understated (cf. n. 4, below).

4. The correlation coefficients (r) between the four-quarter changes in consumer prices and unit profits are: 1948–1954, +0.26; 1955–1977, −0.15. Since
the CPI is statistically independent of unit profits, the influence of spurious positive correlation is not present in these coefficients (cf. n. 3), which may explain
why the positive coefficient before 1955 is smaller and the negative coefficient
after 1955 is larger than when the corporate price series is used. Neither of them,
however, refute the hypothesis that the true correlation is zero.

Chapter 18

Inflation and Statistics

Inflation is having serious effects on our statistical intelligence system. The wide disparity in the rates of increase in different prices makes price indexes less reliable and more controversial. To illustrate the phenomenon, this study analyzes the respective merits of the consumer price index (CPI) and the deflator for personal consumption expenditures (PCE), and explores the reasons for the more rapid advance in the former. A new treatment of the weights in the CPI is suggested. The insidious effects of inflation on the use of price/labor cost ratios as a proxy for profit margins, on the interpretation of inventory/sales ratios, and on the validity of measures of spendable weekly earnings are also considered. Since these are only a sample of the problems that inflation is creating, the need for a major, continuing effort to deal with the matter is stressed.

THE NATURE OF THE PROBLEM

Inflation is widely recognized as a major economic problem. Less widely recognized are the statistical problems inflation has been creating. Because of inflation we are less certain about where the economy is going and less certain even about where it has been. Because inflation not only raises the general price level but raises some prices very much faster than others, we are less certain about how much inflation there is. Because sales and incomes are in current dollars, the uncertainty attaching to our price statistics increases the uncer-

This chapter is reprinted from *Essays in Contemporary Problems 1980* © 1980 by the American Enterprise Institute for Public Policy Research, Washington, D.C., and London.

tainty about the real level of sales and incomes. Because inventories and other assets are often measured in terms of what they originally cost rather than what they are currently worth, and since inflation makes the date to which the historical cost figures pertain very important, and since these dates are difficult to keep track of, estimates of the real value of inventories and other assets are subject to wider margins of uncertainty. Because inflation changes the incentive structure under which the economy operates—by raising interest rates, making capital gains and losses a bigger factor in decisions, making fixed incomes less desirable, increasing the profitability of tax avoidance, and opening new channels through which goods and services are bought and sold—the traditional sources of statistical information become less complete and less reliable.

Some of these problems have recently become highly visible. The consumer price index has been attacked for overstating inflation. The accounting profession has formally recognized the need to take account of inflation in measuring costs and profits. Even the index of lagging indicators, which rarely gets any attention at all, has been criticized because some of its components are inflated, whereas others are deflated. One result of this visibility is that some criticisms are ill-informed and some of the proposed remedies not well-considered. But the problems do need to be aired, and potential solutions should be explored. Even without solutions we can achieve a better understanding of the statistics and how they can be interpreted in an inflationary environment. That is the objective of this chapter. It will not solve the problem of inflation, but it may illuminate some of its unfortunate consequences.

PROBLEMS WITH THE PRICE INDEXES

Rapid inflation usually brings with it greater disparity in the rates of advance of different prices. During periods of rough stability in the general price level, some prices go up and some come down but the divergence as a rule is not very large. Double-digit inflation, on the other hand, is characterized by enormous advances in some prices and much smaller advances in others. One of the consequences of the divergence is that the actual extent of inflation becomes more difficult to measure, and measurement becomes more affected by the decisions about how to do it. In short, measures of inflation become more controversial.

Index numbers such as the consumer price index are affected by the sample of prices that go into them, by the quantities that are assumed to be bought at those prices, and by the conceptual framework that determines what the index measures and how it is done.

Table 18-1. Changes in Consumer Prices, by Major Expenditure Classes (*percent*).

Expenditure Class and Relative Importance, December 1979[a]	1967-1968	1978-1979
Food and beverages (19)	3.6	10.8
Housing (45)	4.0	12.2
Apparel and upkeep (5)	5.4	4.4
Transportation (18)	3.2	14.3
Medical care (5)	6.1	9.3
Entertainment (4)	5.7	6.7
Other goods and services (4)	5.2	7.3
All items (100)	4.2	11.3
Smallest change	3.2	4.4
Largest change	6.1	14.3
Range	2.9	9.9
Average deviation[b]	1.1	3.1
Standard deviation[b]	1.2	3.8

[a] Figures in parentheses are percentages of the total cost of the CPI market basket at December 1979 prices.
[b] Computed from the all-items figure rather than from the simple arithmetic mean of the seven group figures.
Source: U.S. Bureau of Labor Statistics.

Obviously, if all prices went up 10 percent, these things would not matter. The index would go up 10 percent. It is the variation that makes them matter, and the more variation, the more they matter. Table 18-1 makes a simple comparison between 1967-1968, when the consumer price index was going up at a 4 percent rate, and 1978-1979, when it went up at an 11 percent rate. In the first period prices in some of the major expenditure categories rose about 3 percent, whereas others rose as much as 6 percent. The overall index, which rose 4 percent, was quite representative, because there was a close consensus among the seven categories. In 1978-1979 the situation was very different. The increases were spread across a range running from 4 percent for apparel to 14 percent for transportation. The 11 percent increase in the overall index was far less representative, because there was little or no consensus among the price increases in the seven categories. Similar figures for the intervening years show that, as a rule, as the overall rate of inflation increased, the variation among the price increases in the different categories also increased (as shown in Figure 18-1).

This phenomenon opens the way for criticism of the price indexes. One of the more elementary lines of commentary that it provokes focuses upon the areas that are rising fastest and shows what the

Figure 18-1. Variability of Price Changes and the Rate of Inflation, 1967–1979.

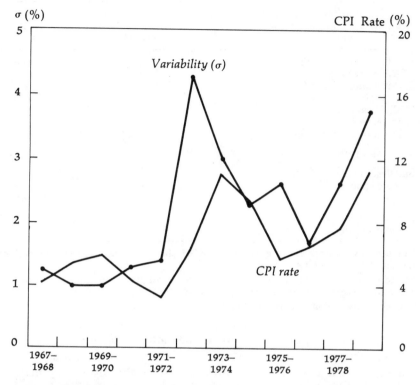

Note: The CPI rate is the percentage change between annual averages of the all-items index. The variability measure is the root-mean-square deviation of the year-to-year percentage changes in the seven major component indexes from the CPI rate. The seven components are listed in Table 18-1.
Source: U.S. Bureau of Labor Statistics.

index would do if they were omitted. Naturally the index then rises less rapidly. The lower rate is sometimes called the basic or underlying rate of inflation. The consequence of removing prices that are at the other end of the spectrum, rising least rapidly or declining, is usually disregarded. Sometimes the argument is more sophisticated, based on the special circumstances that affect the high-rising prices or upon the reasons for believing that the measurement of the high-rising prices is defective. Yet it is curious that the special circumstances or the measurement difficulties that are stressed always pertain to the high-risers rather than the low-risers. Also, the "special circumstances" argument, usually applied to food or energy, ignores the question of whether the behavior of those prices affects the others. If food or energy prices had not risen so fast, would other prices have risen faster, because money not spent on food or energy might then have been directed to driving up prices of other goods and services?

The measurement problems are more fundamental. Those that have surfaced in recent months mostly pertain to the differences between the consumer price index and the deflator for personal consumption expenditures. The latter is derived in the process of constructing the estimates of gross national product and represents the value of consumption expenditures in current prices divided by their value in constant (1972) prices. There are a very large number of differences between the two indexes, but perhaps the three most important are the following:

1. The CPI refers to the urban population (or, alternatively, to urban wage earners and clerical workers), whereas the PCE covers the entire population including, of course, the rural and farm population. The PCE also covers the expenditures of private nonprofit institutions, such as hospitals, universities, and churches.

2. The CPI refers to a fixed market basket of goods and services, determined by a survey of consumer expenditures in 1972–1973. Hence the movements in the CPI are determined solely by price changes, not by changes in quantities purchased. The PCE refers to a constantly changing market basket, determined by what consumers are buying currently. Hence it is influenced both by changes in prices and by changes in quantities. Some of the quantity changes may be in response to efforts by consumers to buy less of goods that are rising rapidly in price and more of goods that have become relatively cheap, but other shifts in expenditure patterns may reflect changes in tastes, in the availability of goods, in affluence, or other factors.

3. The CPI treats the cost of owner-occupied housing as an expense consisting of the net amount spent for new houses in 1972–1973 by the small fraction of the urban population that bought houses then, the amount committed to be spent on mortgage interest payments for these new houses, and the amounts spent by all homeowners for repairs and maintenance, property taxes, and property insurance. The PCE treats the cost of owner-occupied housing as an expense to be estimated by the rent that might be paid for such housing, using the rent index from the CPI for this purpose.

The difference in the population coverage of the two indexes means that the PCE is influenced by prices and expenditures that are not included in the CPI, notably prices paid by rural families and by nonprofit institutions. For some purposes, such as deflating total personal income or disposable income, the broader coverage of the PCE is desirable. For other purposes, such as measuring real wages of urban workers, the narrower coverage of the CPI is desirable. The CPI also is available for different areas of the country, while the PCE is not.

The issue of the fixed or changing market basket is complicated. One argument is that the use in the CPI of quantity weights pertaining to 1972–1973, before the sharp increase in oil prices began, means that cost-saving shifts in fuel consumption and in types of automobiles purchased are not allowed for. The result, so the argument goes, is that the CPI exaggerates the effective increase in prices, whereas the PCE, by using current quantity weights, avoids this bias.

In measuring the change in prices between a base period, say 1972, and the current period, an index using quantity weights pertaining to the base period will usually show a larger increase than an index using quantity weights pertaining to the current period. That is, the cost of the base period's market basket will ordinarily increase faster than the cost of the current period's market basket. Neither index, however, shows the increase in cost of a market basket that is best adapted to the price situation in *each* period. The use of base period quantities generally overestimates this increase, whereas the use of current period quantities generally underestimates it.[1]

Hence this factor alone tends to give the PCE a downward bias, whereas it gives the CPI an upward bias. This tendency, however, pertains only to comparisons with the base period. Much of the time these are not the comparisons of interest. Attention is usually focused on the rate of inflation over short periods, such as a month, or six months, or a year. The base period is not involved (directly), and it becomes impossible to say, on theoretical grounds, which type of index will show higher rates of increase. All that is clear, in this case, is that the PCE does not measure price change alone, since the quantities change (in an undefined way) as well as the prices, whereas the CPI measures only the change in prices, because the market basket stays fixed in all periods.

In any case, the numerous studies that have been made of the fixed versus changing weights issue have generally shown that the matter is not of much practical consequence. The PCE provides a convenient illustration of this, because the Commerce Department computes an alternative PCE with fixed weights (as of 1972). From 1972 to 1979 the PCE deflator increased by 63.3 percent, the PCE fixed-weight index by 66.2 percent. The equivalent annual rates over the seven-year period are 7.3 percent for the deflator, 7.5 percent for the fixed-weight index, hardly a consequential difference. This result has a bearing on the argument that the CPI is biased upward because its weights are based upon 1972–1973, before the fuel price rise made consumers use less fuel. The same argument applies to the PCE fixed-weight index, which uses 1972 weights. The foregoing comparison shows that it is an argument over two-tenths of 1 percent per year over the entire seven-year period.

In comparisons of the two indexes over shorter intervals the differences are often larger, but not always in the same direction, as Table 18–2 shows. Since 1976 the fixed-weight index has been rising faster, with a difference of eight-tenths of 1 percent during 1979. Evidently the changing quantities implicit in the PCE deflator have been causing it to show a smaller rate of increase. If this has come about because the changing market basket has deteriorated in terms of its real worth to consumers, the deflator would be understating the rise in prices. No one has demonstrated whether this is so or not.[2] The point is worth stressing because in a fixed-weight index the fact that the quantities in the market basket remain the same provides some assurance that the real worth of the market basket also has remained approximately the same.

In view of the uncertainty attaching to the propriety of using base year or current year weights, it might be well to return to a solution that was proposed years ago by Irving Fisher and others, namely calculating both indexes in a comparable manner and averaging the two indexes. This requires the development of estimates of current year weights; but since this is already being done in the PCE, it

Table 18–2. Rates of Change in Two Price Indexes Based upon Personal Consumption Expenditures, 1972–1979 (*percentage change from same quarter of preceding year*).

Year and Quarter	PCE Deflator	PCE fixed-weight Index[a]	Difference	Average
1972: 4	3.5	3.4	-0.1	3.4
1973: 4	7.5	7.8	0.3	7.6
1974: 4	11.9	12.0	0.1	12.0
1975: 4	6.1	6.5	0.4	6.3
1976: 4	4.8	4.5	-0.3	4.6
1977: 4	5.7	6.1	0.4	5.9
1978: 4	7.6	8.0	0.4	7.8
1979: 4	9.9	10.7	0.8	10.3
Average, 1971: 4–1979: 4	7.1	7.3	0.2	7.2

[a] The weights are for 1972.
Source: U. S. Department of Commerce.

would not appear to be an insuperable obstacle for the CPI. Index numbers are not very sensitive to errors in weights, and this would be especially true of an average of base-year and current-year weighted indexes. Since the Bureau of Labor Statistics (BLS) recently began a quarterly survey of consumer expenditures, some experimentation along these lines may soon prove to be practicable. The advantages of this type of index have long been recognized in making place-to-place comparisons of prices, where it is generally impossible to say whether the quantities purchased in city A are more appropriate than the quantities purchased in city B in judging whether prices are higher or lower in A than in B. If the BLS would compute both indexes currently we would know at least what difference it makes.

The measurement of housing costs has attracted more attention and probably created more misunderstanding than any of the other issues regarding the CPI and the PCE deflator. A common, but incorrect, assertion is that in computing the CPI the Bureau of Labor Statistics assumes that all homeowners buy a new home every month. The current price of houses does enter into the calculation, but not in such a ridiculous manner. New houses are treated like other purchases, such as automobiles or furniture, and the price enters the index in proportion to the amounts purchased in the base period, 1972–1973. Approximately 6 percent of homeowners bought new houses then; the other 94 percent were out of the market. The weights applied to house prices are based upon the 6 percent who purchased houses, just as the weights applied to automobile prices are based on the purchases of those who bought autos. The cost of the existing stock of houses or of autos or of anything else does not enter into the calculation of what the current price level is.

Mortgage interest payments are treated in a rather similar manner. The amount of interest the borrower commits himself to pay at the time a new mortgage contract is signed is treated as the price, and the total volume of such new commitments made during the base period is the weight. The interest payment depends upon the interest rate, the number of years the mortgage remains outstanding, and the dollar amount of the mortgage (which in turn depends upon the price of the house and the percentage that is borrowed). It is assumed that mortgages remain outstanding for about half the term written into the contract. As a result, the mortgage interest component of the CPI increases with the current level of mortgage interest rates and also with the current level of house prices (which determine the amount of the mortgage).

Other costs of homeownership, such as maintenance and repairs, property taxes, and insurance are also included in the CPI. In regard to these items all homeowners are included, since they all incurred such costs in the base period. Here is where an alternative treatment of mortgage interest costs presents itself. Since the great majority of homeowners make mortgage interest payments, why should the current payments not be treated like rents or property taxes or insurance? Only the annual interest payment would be included in the weight (not the total amount to be paid over the life of the mortgage), but all homeowners who made such payments in the base period would be included in the weights. The current interest rate would be an average of the rates on existing mortgages. It would represent a price previously contracted for but currently in effect, much like the rental on a leased apartment.

Most economists think house prices are not treated appropriately in the CPI. They regard the purchases of durable goods, such as houses and automobiles, as different from other goods and services, because the product is not consumed in a brief period. What is purchased is a continuing series of services that the durable good will render, and only the cost of what is consumed currently should be included in a consumer price index. The rest is an investment, not consumption.

This is the view taken in the PCE deflator, at least with regard to houses (not autos or other durables). The current services rendered by owner-occupied houses are measured by the rent that might be paid for them, and the index of rent that is used is the rent index in the CPI. Hence the price of new houses is not included at all in the PCE, nor are maintenance and repair costs, property taxes, insurance, or mortgage interest costs. These items are covered by the rent. The cost of newly constructed houses, however, is included in another component of the national product accounts, namely residential construction expenditure, which is a part of gross private domestic investment. If this were to be treated as an expenditure by or on behalf of consumers, the result would be more nearly comparable with the CPI (see Table 18-3).

Although the use of rental equivalents has much to be said for it conceptually, there are significant questions about the appropriateness of the CPI rent index for this purpose. It is designed to measure the rents of those who live in rented dwellings, and a large proportion of these are apartments located in the larger cities. The average apartment is smaller than the average owner-occupied house, some of them are under rent control, and many are occupied by persons with a low or fixed income seeking to minimize their housing costs.

Table 18-3.   Rates of Change in Selected Price Indexes, 1972–1979 (percentage change from same quarter of preceding year).

| Year and Quarter | CPI Rent (1) | CPI Homeownership | | | | CPI, All Items (6) | PCE Deflator (7) | Residential Construction Expenditures Deflator (8) | PCE Plus Residential Construction Expenditures Deflator (9) |
		Home Purchase (2)	Mortgage Interest Cost (3)	Taxes, Insurance, Maintenance and Repairs (4)	Total (5)				
1972: 4	3.4	3.4	2.1	6.4	4.1	3.4	3.5	6.4	3.7
1973: 4	4.8	3.0	17.8	5.6	7.3	8.3	7.5	11.3	7.7
1974: 4	5.3	9.4	20.3	9.9	12.8	12.2	11.9	10.4	11.7
1975: 4	5.2	11.1	8.2	6.8	8.5	7.3	6.1	6.8	6.1
1976: 4	5.4	4.4	1.5	6.5	4.5	5.0	4.8	8.8	5.0
1977: 4	6.4	7.9	9.1	8.8	8.5	6.7	5.7	12.7	6.3
1978: 4	7.3	11.0	21.1	7.1	12.8	9.0	7.6	14.0	8.0
1979: 4	8.1	15.5	32.5	6.2	18.3	12.7	9.9	10.1	9.7
Average 1971: 4– 1979: 4	5.7	8.1	13.6	7.2	9.5	8.0	7.1	10.0	7.2

Source: U.S. Bureau of Labor Statistics and Department of Commerce.

Owner-occupied houses are generally located in the suburbs and relatively few are offered for rent, so that few owners are aware of what rent they might pay or obtain for the premises. Hence a large element of uncertainty attaches to the assumption in the PCE deflator (and in the PCE fixed-weight index) that the CPI rent index closely approximates the equivalent rental cost of owner-occupied dwellings.

Another question about the CPI rent index pertains to its accuracy as a measure of rents. It is subject to a downward "aging" bias because rents are collected for identical apartments or houses with no allowance for the usual deterioration that occurs over time. A study of the effect of this, in which census data were used to allow for the changing quality structure of rented dwellings, showed a very much larger increase in rents than was recorded by the CPI.[3] For the decade 1950 to 1960, the adjusted rent index rose 49 percent, whereas the CPI rent index rose 30 percent. For 1960 to 1970 the adjusted rent index went up 31 percent, whereas the CPI rent index went up 20 percent. If the adjusted index is correct, the CPI rent index may understate the rate of increase in rents by as much as 1 or 1.5 percentage points per year. A more recent study covering 1974–1976 gave a similar result, with the quality-adjusted rent index rising 13.2 percent over the two years, while the CPI rent index rose 11.1 percent.[4]

In view of these considerations it is not clear whether owner-occupied housing costs are measured more accurately in the PCE deflator (or the PCE fixed-price index) or in the CPI. The latter has been rising much more rapidly, as is evident from a comparison of the CPI rent index (used in both the CPI and the PCE) with the CPI home-ownership index (Table 18-3), columns 1 and 5). The residential construction expenditures deflator has been rising more rapidly than the PCE deflator, so that including this element generally produces a faster rising index.[5] But residential construction expenditures are small relative to total personal consumption expenditures, so the effect is not great.

The rapid increase in home purchase prices and the even more rapid increase in mortgage interest costs provide a striking illustration of the fixed versus changing weight issue discussed earlier. One of the economic consequences of credit stringency and the accompanying rapid rise in mortgage interest rates is to reduce the construction and sale of new homes. Since summer 1979 new housing starts have declined from an annual rate of 1.8 million to 1.0 million as of March 1980. This has no effect on the fixed quantity weights in the CPI, of course, so the consequence is that the rising mortgage interest rates continue to boost the CPI, even though the volume of transactions to which they pertain has sharply declined. The use of current weights would produce the opposite effect. The small volume of current transactions, when applied to the sharply lower level of mortgage interest rates in the base period, would minimize the effect of those lower rates on the CPI in that period and hence reduce the rise in the CPI from the base period to the present. The current weights would be as unrepresentative of the base period as the base period weights are of the current period. Here again the merits of the compromise solution suggested earlier—using both types of weights— might be considered.

The questions examined here of course are not the only issues that have arisen concerning the validity of our price indexes. Problems pertaining to the treatment of quality changes, servicing and repair costs, improvements in efficiency, new products, the disappearance of old products, product changes that are mandated by government regulations, and the substitution of income taxes for sales taxes are as important as ever.[6] Indeed, they are more important in view of the wider use of price indexes in escalating wages and retirement benefits. Inflation not only makes price indexes more fallible; it makes errors more costly and raises the price tag on alternative procedures.

PROBLEMS WITH OTHER STATISTICS

Price/Cost Ratio

Since price indexes are used to create other statistical measures, uncertainties regarding their validity are passed along to the other measures that they affect. Price/cost ratios are an example. The ratio of the wholesale price index for manufactured goods to the labor cost per unit of output of manufactured goods served for many years as a proxy for movements in profit margins. The figures were available monthly and more promptly than profit margin reports based upon corporate accounts. Historical studies had traced their behavior back to the 1920s and not only confirmed their close relation to directly reported profits per dollar of sales but demonstrated their value as a leading indicator in business cycles. The price and cost figures, moreover, enabled one to account for the tendency of profit margins to decline in the later stage of a cyclical expansion: Prices fail to keep up with the sharp advance in costs. In a recession, on the other hand, margins decline initially but then begin to improve as costs are cut more sharply than prices. It was also evident that over the long run, prices and labor costs moved very closely in step. Apart from business cycles, the ratio followed a horizontal trend.

But this state of affairs began to change in the mid-1960s. The price/cost ratio failed to decline as much as the profit margin figures indicated it should, and in the 1970s the ratio rose rapidly when margins fell. The proxy was not behaving as a proxy should.

It is still not clear why this happened. Inflation had somehow affected the comparability of the numerator and the denominator of the price/cost ratio. Prices appeared to be rising more rapidly than labor costs, but the boost that this would normally give to profit margins did not show up in the profits numbers. Various hypotheses were looked into to explain it, but none provided a fully satisfactory answer. Nevertheless, a way out was provided by a deflator.

Figure 18-2 shows the monthly price/cost ratio described above (series 17) and also a quarterly price/cost ratio that, since 1965 or so, has behaved in a very different way. Both ratios pertain to manufacturing, but the numerator of the quarterly series is the implicit price deflator used to convert gross product originating in manufacturing from current to constant prices. The denominators differ also because of the different measures of output used to compute labor cost per unit of output. The upshot is that the quarterly ratio moves in a manner far more consistent with the trend and fluctuations in profits per dollar of output, also shown in the figure.

The quarterly price/cost ratio for manufacturing is not published currently, but a similar ratio for the private nonfarm sector is, and it shows a close relation to the movements in profit margins of nonfinancial corporations. It becomes available sooner than the profits figures and hence gives an advance clue to the change in profits. But the principal advantage of the monthly ratio—timeliness—has been lost, a victim of inflation.

Inventory/Sales Ratio

Another kind of ratio that has been significantly affected by inflation is the inventory/sales ratio. For many years it seemed adequate to compute this ratio by dividing the book value of inventories by the dollar value of sales. A low or declining ratio was interpreted as a favorable sign, indicating that inventories were not unduly burdensome or becoming so. But this interpretation implicitly assumed that the ratio of the two figures, both expressed in dollars, was a good approximation to a ratio computed from the physical quantity of inventories on hand and the physical volume of sales. It is the physical quantities of inventories that need to be replenished when they are low in relation to sales, or disposed of when they are high. The dollar form of ratio, which is generally the easiest to compute, can be misleading if the prices entering into the book value of inventories

Figure 18-2. Price/Cost Ratios and Profit Margins, Manufacturing.

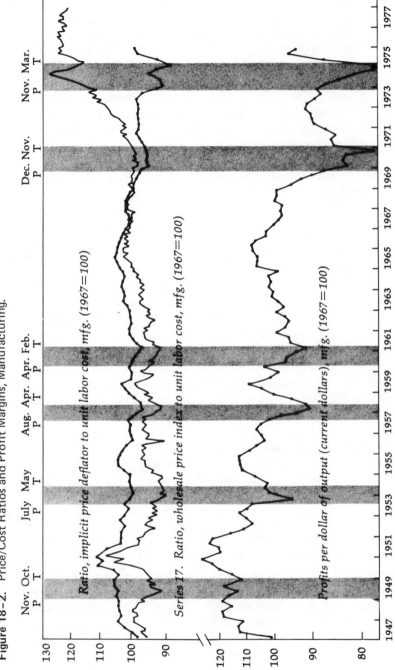

are moving differently than the prices involved in the current value of sales.

Inflationary conditions produce such differences, or rather make them far more important. When inventories are valued at cost, the costs are incurred at an earlier date. In the meantime prices have changed, and the prices in terms of which sales are being made may be very different, due to the lapse in time, from the prices used to enter inventories on the books. The appropriate deflator for inventories will be different from the appropriate deflator for sales, and this means that the ratio of the physical volumes will move differently from the ratio of the current dollar values. The greater the rate of inflation, the greater the difference will be.

Other sorts of complications enter as well. Inflation induces companies to change their system of accounting for inventories, from first-in-first-out to last-in-first-out, for example, and this changes the price component of inventories without changing the price component of sales. The mix of goods held in inventory differs from the mix of goods sold, due to different rates of turnover. With wider differences in the rate of price change under inflation, the measurement of prices in inventories and in sales becomes more difficult and generally less accurate, so that meaningless divergences between the two price components are more likely to occur. Revisions are likely to be larger.

Hence inflation causes trouble for the user of inventory/sales ratios. An illustration is provided in Figure 18-3. Notice that during the second half of 1973 and early 1974, the ratio based on current dollar figures remained at a relatively low level, whereas the ratios based on constant dollar figures began climbing sharply. This was the beginning of recession, and there was virtually no clue in the current dollar ratio, which is the one most commonly used, that inventories were beginning to be a problem. A similar divergence began toward the end of 1978. By the end of 1979 the constant dollar ratio was higher than at any time since 1975, whereas the current dollar ratio was hovering around a very low level. Has inflation again misled those who use the current dollar ratio as a guide?

Real Spendable Earnings

Between 1947 and 1965, according to the Bureau of Labor Statistics, the spendable weekly earnings of a married worker with three dependents nearly doubled, rising from $45 to $87. At the same time, the consumer price index increased about 40 percent. Hence the married worker with three dependents kept well ahead of inflation. In dollars of 1967 purchasing power, his weekly earnings rose

Figure 18–3. Inventory/Sales Ratios, Manufacturing and Trade.

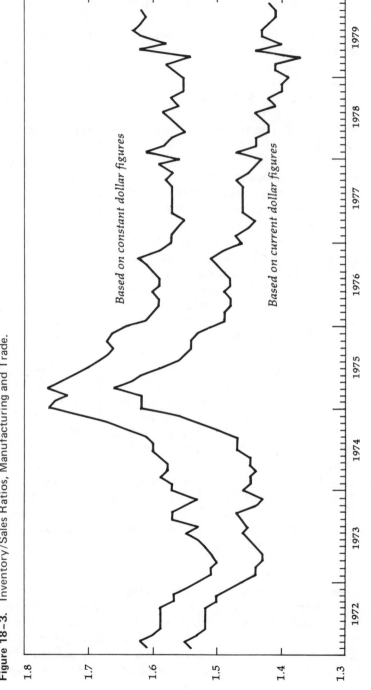

Source: U. S. Department of Commerce.

from $67 to $92, leaving him 37 percent ahead of where he was in 1947—in real terms, after taxes. That is a gain of nearly 2 percent per year during the eighteen years.

Between 1965 and 1979, according to the same statistics, the spendable weekly earnings of this worker rose from $87 to $195, more than doubling again. This time, however, the consumer price index more than doubled too. As a result, the married worker with three dependents was no better off in 1979 than he was in 1965. His weekly spendable earnings in 1979 came to $90 in 1967 dollars, not quite up to the $92 he was making in 1965. Inflation had taken away all of his gains in money income during the past fourteen years. The more he got ahead, the more he slipped behind.

If this situation were indeed typical, it would be a sorry state of affairs. But the Bureau of Labor Statistics is careful to note, in publishing the numbers, that they apply only to the worker who earns the average earnings. The hasty reader might think that this means the average worker; that is, that the average married worker with three dependents really does earn the average earnings. In fact, however, the average married worker with three dependents earns far more than this, and, moreover, his earnings have been going up faster too. Even after taxes, he is still far better off than the worker who earns the average earnings.

These statistics, in short, have become one of the most misleading series published by the federal government. Inflation is at least partly responsible for their misleading quality.

To see why this is so, consider the following hypothetical example: Joe Smith, a married worker with three dependents, earns $200 a week, working a full-time forty-hour week. Feeling the pinch of inflation, his wife decides to get a part-time job, and earns $80 for a twenty-hour week. The family income goes up to $280. But since two persons are working, the average earnings per worker goes down to $140. Furthermore, suppose Joe decides that $280 is not enough and does some moonlighting weekends with another employer, picking up $50 a week that way. The family's income is now $330, but since Joe is now listed on two payrolls and his wife on a third, the earnings of three workers are reported, and the average goes down to $110. Mr. and Mrs. Smith's attempt to beat inflation has made the average earnings per worker completely unrepresentative. I hesitate to suggest what would happen to the average if their teenager also takes on a job.

Fortunately, since this case is somewhat exceptional, and there are many married workers who are their family's sole source of support, the statistics do not behave as disastrously as in the example.

But it happens often enough to affect seriously the overall figures, and the problem has been getting worse with the rapidly rising numbers of part-time workers. Their earnings on part-time jobs significantly reduce the average earnings per worker.

Figure 18-4 gives some evidence. All the figures shown pertain to the real after-tax earnings of production and nonsupervisory workers, and all are published by the Bureau of Labor Statistics. The lowest curve (4) is the spendable earnings series described before (expressed at annual rate), which is based upon the average earnings per worker reported on private nonfarm payrolls and uses no information about the actual family status of the worker. The other figures shown in the chart come from a survey of households that provides

Figure 18-4. Four Estimates of Real After-Tax Earnings, Production and Nonsupervisory Workers.

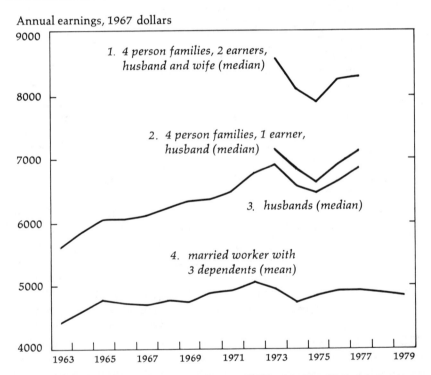

Annual earnings, 1967 dollars

1. 4 person families, 2 earners, husband and wife (median)
2. 4 person families, 1 earner, husband (median)
3. husbands (median)
4. married worker with 3 dependents (mean)

Sources: 1 and 2: Monthly Labor Review (August 1979), table 3, p. 45. Based upon household survey conducted in March of the following year. 3: Monthly Labor Review, (August 1979), table 4. Includes only full-time, year-round workers. 4: Monthly Labor Review (October 1979), table 20, p. 98. Based upon establishment survey of weekly earnings of all workers on private nonagricultural payrolls. Weekly figures are multiplied by fifty-two to obtain annual figures.

information on the marital status of the workers as well as their earnings. Line 3 refers to the earnings of husbands and includes only full-time, year-round workers. Also, it is a median rather than an arithmetic mean. In earnings figures the median, which separates the upper half of the number of earners from the lower half, is generally lower than the mean, because the total earnings of the upper half generally exceed the total earnings of the lower half. Hence if line 3 were a mean, as line 4 is, it would be even farther above line 4 (see note 7). On the other hand, not all husbands have full-time, year-round jobs, so this tends to lift line 3 as compared with a median for all husbands.

There are other differences as well between the type of family covered by lines 3 and 4, since the husband (line 3) may not head up a family with three dependents, and the married worker (line 4) may be a wife rather than a husband. The first of these differences is taken care of by line 2, which pertains to the earnings of husbands in four-person families in which the husband is the sole earner. This increases the disparity with line 4. Finally, line 1 covers the earnings of four-person families in which both the husband and wife are wage earners. Here the figures pertain to their combined earnings, whereas the rest of the figures shown on the chart pertain to the earnings of one person.

Although the data plotted in lines 1, 2, and 3 of the figure are not precisely comparable with those in line 4, for the reasons indicated, they are sufficiently comparable to show the scale of the bias in line 4. Every one of them gives a very different picture of the level and the trend of real after-tax earnings. In 1977 the earnings reported by husbands exceeded the earnings for married workers with three dependents by 40 percent. On a weekly basis husbands earned $238 after taxes, whereas married workers with three dependents were estimated to have earned $170 (both figures in current dollars). Either husbands are massively overstating their earnings or the estimates of married workers' earnings are seriously understated. From 1965 to 1977 the real after-tax earnings of husbands rose 13 percent, whereas the real after-tax earnings of married workers with three dependents rose 3 percent. Either husbands are getting to be bigger liars or the estimates for married workers are seriously understating the growth in earnings of this type of worker.

From the nature of the estimates it is clear that the latter are subject to a large and increasing downward bias. In 1979 there were 19.7 million employed husbands whose wives were not employed, 1.4 million wives whose husbands were not employed, and 20.1 million couples where both husband and wife were employed. Two-earner families have become the mode. In 1979, of the 97 million persons employed, 17 million or 18 percent were employed part-time. Back in 1965 only 15 percent were employed part-time. Part-timers obviously do not work as long a work-week as full-timers, and usually they earn less per hour. Average weekly earnings per worker are reduced by this factor, and its effect has been getting bigger.[7] Another factor is age. The average married worker with three dependents is older than the average of all workers, and has more experience, seniority, training, and skill. Family responsibilities usually are not undertaken until a certain level of earnings has been attained. For all these reasons the assumption that married workers with three dependents earn the average weekly wage of all job holders is ludicrous and has been becoming less and less tenable as inflation impels workers to supplement their incomes. Other factors have been at work as well.[8]

The Bureau of Labor Statistics has been aware of this situation for some years but nevertheless continued to issue the indefensible spendable weekly earnings figures every month until December 1981. The more defensible survey data on annual earnings are available only once a year and are far out of date by the time they appear. Since the household survey is in fact conducted monthly (it is the source of the unemployment figures), it is obviously practicable to obtain earnings figures from it more promptly. They could be used either to replace or at least to correct the level and trend of the existing spendable weekly earnings figures. The BLS began in 1979 to collect survey data on "usual weekly earnings" every month, but will release only quarterly figures. The first release, covering the four quarters of 1979, was issued in March 1980 but referred only to gross earnings for various types of family, not to spendable earnings. A calculation of spendable earnings from these figures (Table 18-4) shows the same enormous discrepancy that we have already seen from the annual earnings data.

The National Commission on Employment and Unemployment Statistics has recommended that the BLS develop a spendable earnings series on a quarterly basis from the survey data on usual weekly earnings and drop the monthly series.[9] An alternative, namely to benchmark the monthly series to another series that is more accurately defined, might be considered. One such benchmark is provided by the 1972–1973 survey of consumer expenditures which is currently used as the weight base for the consumer price index for urban wage earners and clerical workers. The survey covered income as well as expenditures, reported income after taxes, tabulated wage and sal-

Table 18-4. Three Estimates of Spendable Weekly Earnings, 1979.

	Gross Earnings (Current Dollars per Week)	Spendable Earnings		
		Current Dollars per Week	1967 Dollars per Week	1967 Dollars per Year
Estimated average weekly earnings of: Production or nonsupervisory workers on private nonfarm payrolls, married worker with three dependents	220	195	89	4,628
Reported median usual weekly earnings of: Full-time wage and salary earners (husbands)	324	273	125	6,500
Married couple, families with one earner (husband)	322	272	125	6,500

Source: U.S. Bureau of Labor Statistics, except that the spendable usual weekly earnings were calculated by the author using the BLS formula for married workers with three dependents.

ary earnings separately from other income, classified families by size and type, and calculated mean earnings rather than medians.

Table 18-5 shows the 1972-1973 survey figures for husband-and-wife families with children, from which we have derived average weekly earnings after taxes. They compare as follows with the average of the monthly series for 1972-1973:

	Urban and Rural Husband-Wife Families with Children	Private Nonfarm Production and Nonsupervisory, Married Worker with Three Dependents
Before taxes		
In current dollars	$239	$141
In 1967 dollars	185	109
After taxes		
In current dollars	202	125
In 1967 dollars	156	96

The monthly series in 1972-1973 was running at a level about 40 percent below the survey figures for approximately the same type of family. The coverage of course is not identical, since rural and farm

Table 18-5. Spendable Earnings from the Consumer Expenditure Survey,
1972-1973.

Urban and rural families	
Husband and wife, with children (number)	28,433,000
Other husband-and-wife families (number)	19,403,000
One-parent, single-person, and other families (number)	23,383,000
Total	71,220,000
Husband-and-wife families, with children:	
Average family size (number of persons)	4.2
Average age of family head (years)	41
Average family income	
Annually before taxes ($)	15,192
Annually after taxes ($)	12,835
Effective tax rate (%)	15.5
Average money wages and salaries, civilians	
Annually, before taxes (current $)	12,420
Weekly, before taxes (current $)	239
Annually, before taxes (1967 $)[a]	9,613
Weekly, before taxes (1967 $)[a]	185
Annually, after taxes (current $)[b]	10,495
Weekly, after taxes (current $)[b]	202
Annually, after taxes (1967 $)[a]	8,123
Weekly, after taxes (1967 $)[a]	156

[a] Calculated by dividing current dollar figure by the average consumer price index (1967 = 100) for 1972 and 1973 (129.2).

[b] Estimated by applying effective tax rate on total income to money wages and salaries.

Source: U.S. Bureau of Labor Statistics, *Consumer Expenditure Survey: Integrated Diary and Interview Survey Data, 1972-73*, Bulletin 1992, table 10.

families are included in the survey as well as families with more or fewer children, and the survey covers government employees, supervisory, and self-employed individuals. No doubt it would be possible to derive more nearly comparable tabulations from the survey data, covering urban residents only and omitting professionals and managers and the self-employed, and hence obtain a better benchmark for the monthly series. This would correct its level, which is one of its major deficiencies. To correct the trend would require additional benchmarks. Perhaps the recently started quarterly survey of consumer expenditures will provide earnings data for this purpose.

We have by no means exhausted the subject of the effect of inflation on our statistical intelligence system. Inflation has produced the anomaly of a trade balance that is in deficit when expressed in current dollars but in surplus when expressed in constant dollars. Inflation has produced confusing differences in the behavior of measures of output that are derived from physical quantity data as compared with those derived by adjusting value data for price changes. These differences, in turn, have produced uncertainty about the accuracy of measures of productivity.[10] Inflation has made it more difficult to interpret the unemployment rate by forcing many who would not otherwise be in the labor market to seek jobs. Their actions have increased both the number employed and the number unemployed and changed the nature of unemployment, since more are seeking part-time or temporary jobs.

Inflation has made an enormous difference in the level of profits reported to stockholders and the level of profits reported in the national accounts. Inflation has increased the divergence between different measures of the money supply, because it has changed the profitability of holding various types of "money." Inflation has made it more difficult to measure the nominal level of interest rates (because of the wider spread among different rates) and more important to measure the "real" level of interest rates.

Inflation is a number one statistical problem. Now more than ever we need a watchdog commission or agency with a continuing responsibility to uncover perplexing discrepancies in economic data, explain their significance to users of statistics, recommend solutions, and follow up on their implementation.

NOTES TO CHAPTER 18

1. A hypothetical example may clarify this point. Suppose a family buys only two commodities, beef and chicken, paying two dollars a pound for beef and one dollar for chicken, and buys a ten pounds of each in period 1. In period 2 the price of beef goes to three dollars whereas the price of chicken remains the same, and the family decides that in the new circumstances it would be just as well off as before by buying somewhat less beef (say, eight pounds) and a good deal more chicken (say, fifteen pounds). The increase in the total number of pounds of meat purchased (from twenty to twenty-three) compensates for the fact that the mix is a less desirable one. The family's expenditures rise from thirty dollars in period 1 to thirty-nine dollars in period 2. How much have prices increased?

Using the CPI method, prices in period 2 are weighted by period 1 weights, in which case the bill in period 2 would come to forty dollars (thirty dollars for beef and ten dollars for chicken). The CPI index would be 40/30 or 133. Using the PCE deflator method, prices in period 1 would be weighted by period 2 weights, and the bill in period 1 would come to thirty-one dollars (sixteen dollars for beef and fifteen dollars for chicken). The PCE index would be 39/31 or 126. Since we have assumed the family in fact adjusted its purchases so as to feel equally well off in the two periods, the true cost of living index is measured by the actual change in what they spent, namely 39/30 or 130. The CPI shows a larger increase than this, the PCE a smaller increase.

Note that we have simplified the example by assuming that the family bought a market basket of equal worth in both periods. Actual expenditures can, of course, change in other ways, in which case the true cost-of-living index corresponding to the basket purchased in period 1 may differ from that corresponding to the basket purchased in period 2. If the latter index exceeds the former, the PCE might exceed the CPI.

2. In addition to the two indexes shown in Table 18-2, the Commerce Department also constructs a PCE chain-price index, which holds the quantity weights constant between adjacent quarters.

3. Rafael Rom Weston, "The Quality of Housing in the United States, 1929-1970," Ph. D. dissertation, Harvard University, 1972.

4. James R. Follain and Stephen Malpezzi, *Dissecting Housing Value and Rent: Estimates of Hedonic Indexes for Thirty-Nine Large SMSA's*, Report 249-17 (Washington, D.C.: Urban Institute, 1979), tables 20 and 21.

5. In 1979 it produced a slightly less rapidly rising index (compare columns 7 and 9 of Table 18-3). This illustrates one of the anomalies of deflators, due to the changing weights. The real volume of residential construction expenditures declined during 1979, so that despite the fact that construction costs rose more rapidly than the PCE deflator, the combined deflator rose *less* rapidly. With changing quantity weights an index can rise less rapidly (or more rapidly) than any of its components—a possibility that surely would create credibility problems.

6. For an illuminating review of these issues, see Jack E. Triplett, "The Measurement of Inflation: A Survey of Research on the Accuracy of Price Indexes," in Paul H. Earl, ed., *Analysis of Inflation* (Lexington, Mass.: D.C. Heath, 1975).

7. The effect can be shown by the following calculation based upon the "usual weekly earnings" reported in the Current Population Survey in May of each year. In May 1978 the median weekly earnings of 12,473,000 part-time workers was $61. The median for 53,775,000 full-time workers was $195. The mean earnings for each group are not reported but can be calculated approximately from the distributions by amount of earnings. They are $75 and $265 respectively. The mean for both groups combined is $229. This calculation not only shows the effect of averaging part-timers with full-timers but also the difference between means and medians. The median full-time earnings ($195) is 26 percent lower than the mean ($265). For the basic data see Janice Hedges and Earl Mellor, "Weekly and Hourly Earnings of U.S. Workers, 1967-1978," *Monthly Labor Review* (August 1979): 32-34.

8. The other factors include the entrance into the labor force of the "baby boom" generation of the late 1940s and 1950s and of women pursuing career opportunities. See Paul M. Ryscavage, "Two Divergent Measures of Purchasing Power," *Monthly Labor Review* (August 1979).

9. National Commission on Employment and Unemployment Statistics, *Counting the Labor Force* (Washington, D.C., 1979), pp. 206-208. The BLS did discontinue the monthly series after December 1981. See Paul O. Flaim, "The Spendable Earnings Series: Has It Outlived Its Usefulness?" *Monthly Labor Review* (January 1982).

10. See L. J. Fulco, "Productivity Reports," *Monthly Labor Review* (February 1979): 43; George Terborgh, "A Quizzical Look at Productivity Statistics," *Capital Goods Review of the Machinery and Allied Products Institute* (August 1979); and Joel Popkin, "A Comparison of BEA and FRB Measures of Industry Output," in National Research Council Panel to Review Productivity Statistics, *Measurement and Interpretation of Productivity* (Washington, D.C.: National Academy of Sciences, 1979).

Chapter 19

Inflation and Statistics—Again

Three of the more serious effects of inflation upon our statistical intelligence system are explored in this chapter. The first concerns the method of allowing for changes in export and import prices in the calculation of real gross national product (GNP) and the GNP implicit price deflator. Because of the way this is handled in the U.S. Department of Commerce estimates, the faster rise in the prices of imports, especially oil, than in the prices of exports has converted a modest trade surplus in current dollars into a much larger surplus in 1972 dollars. As a result, the foreign trade sector of the accounts has been pushing up the growth of real GNP and holding down the implicit price deflator. An alternative method of deflating net exports of goods and services, which does not have this effect, is presented. Some striking differences in the recent history of real economic growth and inflation are revealed.

The second topic deals with the lag in the availability of inflation-adjusted estimates of retail sales, inventories, and certain other widely used monthly series. The delay has various consequences, including a lack of public awareness of what is happening to the real level of economic activity. An effort should be made to release inflation-adjusted estimates simultaneously with figures in current dollars, so that the effect of inflation on the latter is readily discerned.

Finally, an improved measure of the rate of inflation embodied in the consumer price index (CPI) is needed. The measure that is most

This chapter is reprinted from *Essays in Contemporary Economic Problems: Demand, Productivity, and Population.* © 1981 by the American Enterprise Institute for Public Policy Research, Washington, D.C., and London.

commonly used, the percentage change from the preceding month, seasonally adjusted, is highly erratic in its movements. Other measures, such as those that cover a three-, six-, or twelve-month span, have various advantages and disadvantages with regard to their stability, timeliness, and ease of understanding. A new measure, which achieves considerable stability, is reasonably up-to-date, and is fairly simple, is proposed for consideration. The same measure can be applied to quarterly or weekly data and to rates of change in wages, money supply, and so on.

A PERENNIAL PROBLEM

Statistical problems pertaining to the measurement of inflation and its consequences continue to plague us. Who would have forecast, in March 1980, that the 18 percent rate of inflation that the consumer price index was registering would hit zero briefly in July? How many are aware that the rising price of imported oil has *reduced* our most comprehensive measure of inflation? Why is it that, after fifteen years of experience with a worsening inflation problem, statistical agencies still release many of the numbers without, at the same time, allowing for the effect of changes in the value of the dollar?

INFLATION, THE TRADE BALANCE, AND REAL GNP

Inflation has been playing tricks with the trade balance. The trade balance—net exports of goods and services—is the only component of GNP that is larger in terms of 1972 dollars than in terms of current dollars.[1] In 1980, for example, the net export surplus was $23 billion in current dollars. One might suppose, since the dollar is not worth as much now as it was in 1972, that the surplus would be smaller than $23 billion when expressed in 1972 dollars. It was not. It was $52 billion in 1972 dollars. For the rest of GNP the relation is, of course, just the opposite. The 1980 figure for GNP excluding net exports was $2,602 billion in current dollars, but only $1,481 billion in 1972 dollars. The implicit price deflator for net exports last year was only 45 (1972 = 100), while the price deflator for the rest of GNP was 182. Many of us have thought we would never live to see a price index less than 100, but here it is.

One result of this anomaly is that net exports have been contributing a much larger percentage to real GNP (3.5 percent in 1980) than to current dollar GNP (less than 1 percent). The net export figures have also been exerting a more potent influence than might have been expected on the rates of change in real GNP and its implicit price deflator.

From the fourth quarter of 1980 to the first quarter of 1981, for example, the implicit price deflator for total GNP rose at the annual rate of 10.0 percent. If net exports are excluded, however, and only the rest of GNP considered, the implicit price deflator rose at the rate of 9.4 percent. That is, for the great bulk of GNP (99 percent of the total, in fact) the price level was rising somewhat more slowly than for the total. To put it differently, the 1 percent of GNP constituting net exports was causing the total deflator to rise more rapidly than it otherwise would have. The 1 percent tail wagged a big dog because *its* implicit price deflator rose very rapidly between the fourth quarter of 1980 and the first quarter of 1981. The reason for this rapid rise in the price deflator for net exports was that the prices of exports rose faster than the prices of imports. Hence the surprising consequence: The overall GNP price deflator, the most comprehensive measure of inflation that we have, was *pushed up* by the relatively slow rise in the prices we pay (for imports) as compared with the prices we receive (for exports).

Correspondingly, the movement of real GNP was also significantly affected by net exports. According to the official figures, real GNP rose at the annual rate of 8.4 percent in the first quarter of 1981. Excluding net exports, the rate was 7.1 percent. That is because real net exports, as officially measured, shot up at the annual rate of 53 percent. Thus, because net exports affect the statistics so markedly, an appraisal of inflation and the performance of the real economy hinges to a large extent on how net exports are treated in the national accounts.

The official method of deflating the numbers, and a proposed alternative, are displayed in Tables 19-1 and 19-2. In the official method, export values are deflated by prices of exports, and between 1979 and 1980 this deflator rose at the annual rate of 10 percent (Table 19-1, line 2, last column). Imports are deflated by import prices, which rose at the annual rate of 18 percent (line 3, last column). Since 1972 import prices have gone up much faster than export prices, largely because of the enormous rise in the price of oil. Consequently, when the export and import values are expressed in 1972 dollars, import values are reduced much more than export values, creating a large export surplus in 1972 dollars. In the first quarter of 1981 (Table 19-2), the export surplus in 1972 dollars was $54 billion at the annual rate, nearly half again as large as the $37 billion current dollar figure.

Table 19-1.   Alternative Methods of Deflating Net Exports: Effect on Real GNP and Implicit Price Deflator, 1979-1980.

	Current Dollars (billions)				1972 Dollars (billions)				Implicit Price Deflator (1972 = 100)		
			Change, 1979-1980				Change, 1979-1980				Change, 1979-1980
	1979	1980	$	%	1979	1980	$	%	1979	1980	(%)
1. GNP, official	2,413.9	2,626.1	212.2	8.8	1,483.0	1,480.7	-2.3	-0.2	162.8	177.4	9.0
2. Exports	281.3	339.8	58.5	20.8	146.9	161.1	14.2	9.7	191.5	210.9	10.1
3. Imports	267.9	316.5	48.6	18.1	109.2	109.1	-0.1	-0.1	245.3	290.1	18.3
4. Net exports	13.4	23.3	9.9	73.9	37.7	52.0	14.3	37.9	35.5	44.8	26.2
5. GNP less net exports	2,400.5	2,602.8	202.3	8.4	1,445.3	1,428.7	-16.6	-1.1	166.1	182.2	9.7
6. Net exports, directly deflated[a]	13.4	23.3	9.9	73.9	8.1	12.8	4.7	58.0			
7. GNP, including net exports directly deflated[b]	2,413.9	2,626.1	212.2	8.8	1,453.4	1,441.5	-11.9	-0.8	166.1	182.2	9.7
8. Terms of trade effect[c]					-29.6	-39.2	-9.6				

[a] Net exports (line 4) deflated by price deflator for GNP less net exports (line 5).
[b] Line 5 plus line 6.
[c] Line 6 minus line 4 (or line 7 minus line 1).
Source: Center for International Business Cycle Research, Rutgers University.

Table 19-2.   Alternative Methods of Deflating Net Exports: Effect on Real GNP and Implicit Price Deflator, Fourth Quarter, 1980-First Quarter, 1981.

	Current Dollars (billions)			1972 Dollars (billions)			Implicit Price Deflator (1972 = 100)		
	Fourth Quarter, 1980	First Quarter, 1981	Percent Change (Annual Rate)	Fourth Quarter, 1980	First Quarter, 1981	Percent Change (Annual Rate)	Fourth Quarter, 1980	First Quarter, 1981	Percent Change (Annual Rate)
1. GNP, official	2,730.6	2,853.8	19.3	1,485.6	1,516.0	8.4	183.8	188.2	10.0
2. Exports	346.1	376.8	40.5	157.4	166.8	26.1	219.9	225.9	11.4
3. Imports	322.7	339.8	22.9	108.9	112.9	15.5	296.3	301.0	6.5
4. Net exports	23.3	37.0	535.9	48.5	53.9	52.5	48.0	68.6	317.2
5. GNP less net exports	2,707.3	2,816.8	17.2	1,437.1	1,462.1	7.1	188.4	192.7	9.4
6. Net exports, directly deflated[a]	23.3	37.0	535.9	12.4	19.2	474.8	188.4	192.7	9.4
7. GNP, including net exports directly deflated[b]	2,730.6	2,853.8	19.3	1,449.5	1,481.3	9.1	188.4	192.7	9.4
8. Terms of trade effect[c]				-36.1	-34.7				

[a] Net exports (line 4) deflated by price deflator for GNP less net exports (line 5).
[b] Line 5 plus line 6.
[c] Line 6 minus line 4 (or line 7 minus line 1).
Source: Center for International Business Cycle Research, Rutgers University.

It is the difference in the deflators that causes net exports in 1972 dollars to be larger than in current dollars. If the import and export deflators were at about the same level, then the usual relationship would hold, with the 1972 dollar figures for net exports smaller than the current dollar figures. It is ironic that the oil price explosion should have an arithmetic effect on the official GNP numbers that is just the opposite of what the economic effect is usually presumed to be. The arithmetic effect of the higher import price deflator is to reduce the implicit deflator of net exports, reduce the overall GNP deflator, and increase real GNP. This is because imports have a negative impact on GNP. The more rapidly they rise in price, the less rapid the rise in the GNP deflator. The slower the rise in import volume, the more rapid the rise in real GNP.

This result is a consequence of the method chosen to deflate net exports. It is true that, to measure the physical growth in exports, deflation by an export price index is appropriate. Similarly, to measure the physical growth in imports, deflation by an import price index is appropriate. But it does not follow that the difference between these two deflated numbers is the appropriate measure of the real value of the trade balance. If the trade balance in current dollars is negative, it is difficult to think of any real counterpart that would make it positive. Yet this can happen unless the balance is deflated directly, and until the latest (December 1980) revision of the GNP accounts, it was happening regularly (because the previous estimates of exports were much smaller than the revised ones). Quite apart from this, however, the separate deflation of imports and exports can and does produce movements in the trade balance that are very different from what they would be if the balance were deflated directly. Since the balance itself can be considered to be a component of GNP (it is net foreign investment), it is not unreasonable to deflate it directly, thus treating this component in the same manner as the other components, such as domestic investment or consumption expenditures.

A method for doing this that has been advocated for many years by Solomon Fabricant and other students of this subject is to deflate the trade balance (net exports) by a general price index and incorporate the resulting real balance in real GNP.[2] A general price index that seems suitable for this purpose is the price deflator derived from total GNP exclusive of net exports. This is a measure of general purchasing power—it covers virtually the whole of GNP—and its use for this purpose leaves the deflator of total GNP unaffected by the trade balance itself. That is, since the deflator used for net exports is the same as for the rest of GNP, the overall deflator is the same also. The calculation for net exports and GNP is shown in Tables 19-1 and 19-2, and the effect on net exports in recent years is shown in Figure 19-1. The level and trend of the real balance derived by this method (bottom line) is very different from that shown by the official method (middle line) and corresponds more closely to the current dollar measure (top line).

Lately, the use of this method makes a remarkable difference in the level and growth of real GNP, and an equally remarkable difference in the inflation rate. During 1979 and early 1980 the growth in real GNP is reduced to zero, whereas the official figures rose gradually until the peak level of real GNP was reached in the first quarter of 1980 (see Figure 19-2). That is to say, the impact of the recession on real GNP developed sooner and more plainly in the modified figures than in the official numbers. In both the official and the modified figures the recession low was reached in the second quarter of 1980, and both show a substantial recovery since then, though it is more marked in the modified figures.

As for inflation, the alternative calculation shows that considerably higher rates were reached during 1979 and that there was a much sharper decline during the recession itself (see Figure 19-3). Between the first and third quarters of 1980 the inflation rate dropped from 11.5 percent to 6.5 percent according to the modified measure, whereas the official measure remained around the 9.5 percent level. In general, excluding the influence of net exports on the measure of inflation shows it to conform more closely to business cycle downswings as well as upswings.

What all this means is that the way the real trade balance is measured can substantially alter the behavior of the nation's most comprehensive measure of real economic activity and of inflation. This finding will not come as a surprise to students of national income accounting. They have argued about it for years and not only in this country, since in many countries foreign trade is a more important factor than in the United States. But the method of deflating the trade balance has recently become more important, partly because rates of inflation are higher and partly because trade balances are now greatly affected by imports or exports of oil.

In the United Kingdom, for example, the Central Statistical Office has since 1975 regularly published a measure, called "real national disposable income," which is distinguished from their real gross domestic product (GDP) chiefly by the fact that the trade balance is deflated by a single price index (the price of imports) whereas in real GDP, exports are deflated by export prices and imports by import prices (as in the United States).[3] At the time this measure was con-

Figure 19-1. Net Exports in Current and in Constant Dollars, 1968-1981, (*billions of dollars*).

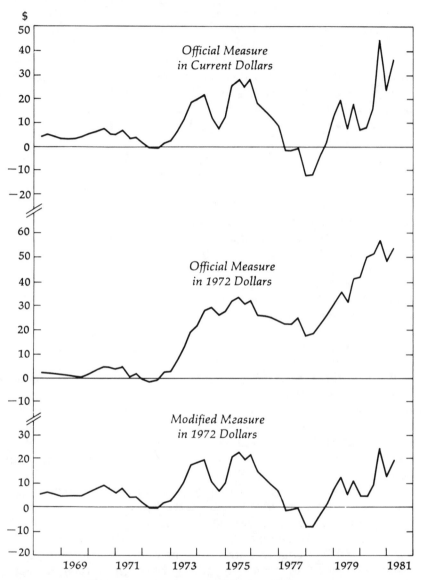

Note: In the official measure exports are deflated by export prices and imports by import prices. In the modified measure net exports are deflated by the GNP implicit price deflator excluding net exports.

Source: Center for International Business Cycle Research, Rutgers University. Based upon revised GNP data released in January 1981.

Figure 19-2. Real GNP with Alternative Measures of Net Exports, 1978-1981 (*billions of 1972 dollars*).

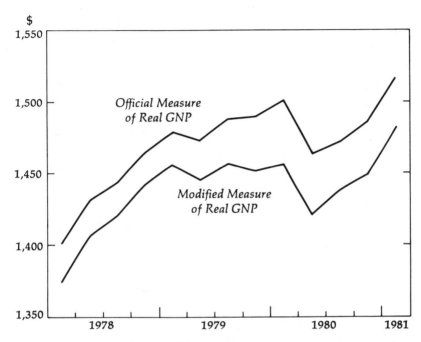

Note: In the official measure exports are deflated by export prices and imports by import prices. In the modified measure net exports are deflated by the GNP implicit price deflator excluding net exports.

Source: Center for International Business Cycle Research, Rutgers University.

structed in 1973-1974, the effect of directly deflating the trade balance was similar to what it has been in the United States: it reduced the measure of real output. Recently, however, the effect in Britain has been just the opposite, with the directly deflated measure exhibiting greater real growth and implying less inflation. This is because Britain is now exporting North Sea oil and getting the benefit of high oil prices, a benefit that is not reflected in the usual measure of real output (GDP).

Economists have usually discussed this issue in terms of whether a change in the terms of trade should or should not be considered to affect the nation's real output or income. If the same physical quantity of exports will no longer buy as large a physical quantity of imports, has the nation's real output been diminished? When exports are deflated by export prices and imports by import prices, a change in the terms of trade has no effect on the measure of output. When

Figure 19–3. Alternative Measures of the GNP Implicit Price Deflator, 1968–1981 (*percentage change from preceding quarter at annual rate*).

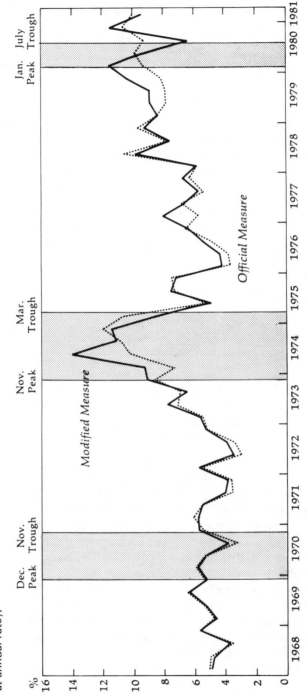

Note: The modified measure excludes net exports. Shaded areas indicate business cycle contractions; the end of the most recent contraction is tentatively set at July 1980.

Source: Center for International Business Cycle Research, Rutgers University.

both are deflated by the same price index a change in the terms of trade is reflected in the measure of output. Probably the most widely accepted view is that a nation's real *income* is diminished when imports become more expensive relative to exports, but that its real *output* is not affected. That is why the British have two measures, one referred to as income, the other as output.

It can be argued, however, that a nation's output and income are conceptually the same. Virtually no one disputes this when both are measured in current prices. Indeed, from the outset of national accounting this position has been accepted and estimates based on measures of income and on measures of output (or expenditure) have been viewed simply as different ways of estimating the same total, the differences being referred to as a statistical discrepancy. Why then should real output be different from real income? Is a dollar's worth of output different from a dollar's worth of income when both are measured in relation to the general level of prices? Or is the general level of prices different when it is to be used to measure real output than when it is to be used to measure real income? In particular, which is the more relevant measure of the general price level, an index that goes up faster when the prices we pay for imported oil go up faster than the prices we get for exported wheat, or an index that goes up more slowly in that event?

By the time this chapter appears in print the U.S. Department of Commerce may have enlightened us on these matters by producing a measure of real national product in which net exports of goods and services will be deflated directly by a price index, namely the price index for imports (as the British have already done).[4] The results, to judge from past experience, are not likely to differ much from those based on the method proposed here, where net exports are deflated by the price index for the rest of GNP. Whichever method persists, inflation will have stirred up an important issue.

DEFLATE NOW, REVISE LATER

One of the merits of the national accounts statistics is that estimates expressed in constant prices are released at the same time as estimates in current dollars. Hence one can see what has happened to the physical volume of GNP and its components and at the same time observe the current dollar magnitudes and the implicit change in the price level. With many of our monthly statistics, on the other hand, deflated data are released only later. This is true, for example, of retail sales, of total manufacturing and trade sales, of inventories, and of new orders. One of the consequences is that the press gives almost exclusive attention to the current dollar figures, since these are up to date, despite the fact that the deflated numbers may give a very different impression of the trend of business (see Figure 19-4).

Another consequence is that analysts make their own estimates of the deflated numbers, often on the basis of much less information than is available to the statistical agency. Of course, the agency does not have as much information on prices as it would like to have or will have at a later date, but this simply means that its preliminary estimates will have to be revised. The question is whether the preliminary estimates are sufficiently accurate to be useful. Judging from the efforts of analysts to provide their own preliminary estimates, the answer seems to be yes. When one is seeking evidence of recession or of recovery, under conditions of double-digit inflation, even rough estimates of the physical volume of sales, orders, and inventories are welcome. In appraising the effect of policies to fight inflation, promptly deflated statistics are a necessity. If the quarterly GNP figures can be deflated when they are first released, so can the monthly figures on which they are based.

Our statistical arsenal requires attention in another respect as well. Some figures are reported only in current dollars and are not published in deflated form at all. Examples are the monthly statistics on inventories by stage of processing, the stock of unfilled orders, and the volume of credit. Each of these can be linked, conceptually, with other statistics that are published in deflated form. Hence for analytical purposes they should be deflated also. The physical volume of materials inventories is needed to compare with output and to assess the extent of speculative buying in commodity markets. The physical stock of unfilled orders indicates how fully utilized capacity is and to what extent changes in inventories on order are offsetting or augmenting changes in inventories on hand. The flow of credit is related, of course, to both the physical volume of transactions and the price level. Adjusting the credit aggregates to allow for inflation distinguishes the physical component and facilitates comparison with other physical measures such as output and employment. How much credit is simply being used to pay higher prices?

WHAT IS THE RATE OF INFLATION?

Probably the most popular conception of the rate of inflation is a figure that is not even published by the statistical agency responsible for it. It is the seasonally adjusted month-to-month percentage change in the consumer price index, expressed at an annual rate. The Bureau of Labor Statistics (BLS) does publish the monthly percen-

Figure 19-4. Deflated and Undeflated Statistics Prior to, During, and After the 1980 Recession (*billions of dollars*).

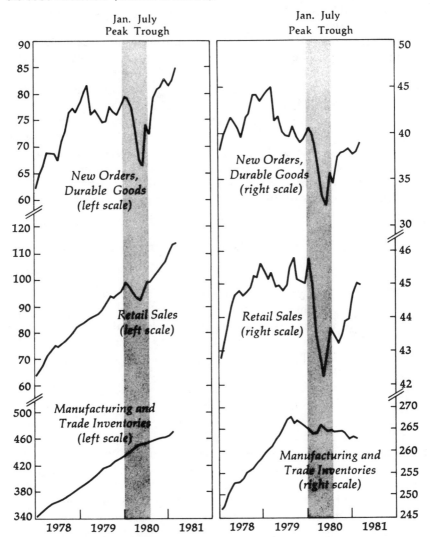

Note: The shaded area is the business cycle contraction beginning January 1980; the end of the contraction is tentatively set at July 1980.

Source: Center for International Business Cycle Research, Rutgers University.

tage change, but does not express it at an annual rate. News writers and TV commentators usually prefer the annual rate, and convert the monthly rate to that basis. On the other hand, the BLS does publish several other rates in annualized form, over a three-month span, a six-month span, and a twelve-month span (that is, from the same month a year ago).

The BLS's reason for not annualizing the monthly rate was, and is, that monthly changes are highly erratic and, consequently, the assumption implicit in the annualizing procedure—namely, that the annual rate is what would be realized if the monthly rate persisted for twelve months—is very unlikely to hold true. Experience in 1980 vividly illustrated this point. In January, February, and March, the seasonally adjusted monthly rate was 1.4 percent. Annualized, this worked out to a rate of 18 percent. But these monthly rates did not persist and indeed dropped to zero by July. The zero rate was an extreme in the opposite direction and was widely recognized as such. Nevertheless, the monthly rates continue to receive much attention, and they continue to be highly unrepresentative of the persistent rate of inflation.

In the long run, I hope, statistical data disobey Gresham's law. Good statistics do drive out bad. But the law has a certain power in the short run, and in the case of the rate of change in the CPI a single "bad" statistic has driven out a variety of "good" ones. It is easy to show that the three-month rate, or the six-month rate, or the twelve-month rate is less erratic than the one-month rate, and hence offers a better guide to what the underlying rate of inflation is. All these rates are published and available, but they rarely make headlines. Perhaps there are too many of them.

An alternative would be for the BLS to select and emphasize a single rate, which might become known as "the" rate of inflation. It would become known in the same way that "the" rate of unemployment is known. Naturally, other rates could be computed and used by analysts, but the public would be better informed than by a rate that swings from 18 percent to zero in the course of five months.

The candidate that I would propose for this honorable post is not now published by the BLS, nor is it widely used anywhere. But its newness may give it a novelty that existing rates do not have, and it has superior properties of stability. It is a rate determined by dividing the current month's CPI (seasonally adjusted) by the average CPI for the preceding twelve months. The span covered by such a rate is 6.5 months—the twelve-month average precedes the current month by that length of time. Hence the annual rate of change is roughly twice the percentage change between the twelve-month average and the current month's index.

When, for example, the CPI in March 1981 was 265.5 (1967 = 100) on a seasonally adjusted basis, the average for the preceding twelve months (March 1980 through February 1981) was 251.5. The rate of inflation, therefore, was $[(265.5 \div 251.5)^{12/6.5} - 1]\,100 = 10.5$ percent. What this method does is take the average of the preceding twelve months as a base, and compare the current month's index with it to see how much inflation has raised the current index. The twelve-month average is a stabler figure than any single month, such as the preceding month, which is the base for the month-to-month change. Last month's index may be affected by some special factor that raised or lowered the index in that month. The twelve-month average is much less subject to the influence of special factors. It is also not subject to revision because of changes in seasonal adjustment factors (which are revised every year), since over a twelve-month period the seasonal factors balance out.[5]

How stable the new rate is can be seen in Figure 19-5, which compares the month-to-month rate (annualized) with the proposed rate (also annualized). The wild fluctuations in the former are largely eliminated in the latter. The 18 percent rates in January, February, and March 1980 are reduced to about 15 percent, and the zero rate of July 1980 is raised to about 11 percent. Similarly, during the rise and fall of the inflation rate in 1972-1976, the new rate makes it much easier to see what was happening. In 1973, for instance, the monthly rate dropped as low as 1 percent (annualized, in July) and climbed as high as 24 percent (in August). In the same months, the new rate was 6 percent and 9 percent, respectively.

It is true that, if the month-to-month rate rose smoothly to a peak and then smoothly down again, the new rate would be likely to continue rising a month or two longer. That is, it would lag. Something like this happened in 1974, when the high in the monthly rate was reached in August (17 percent) while the high in the new rate was not reached until September (12 percent). A better example of the lag occurs at the next trough, in 1976, where the monthly rate hits its low (1 percent) in February while the new rate continued to drop until June (5 percent). But the fluctuations in the monthly rate make it very difficult, at any given time, to tell whether a true low has been reached or just a false bottom (as in 1973 or in 1975). The new rate is not perfect in this respect either, but it is surely better.

By computing and publishing a rate such as the one proposed (or one with equally good credentials) and eliminating all the other rates

Figure 19-5.   Rates of Change in the Consumer Price Index, 1972–1981.

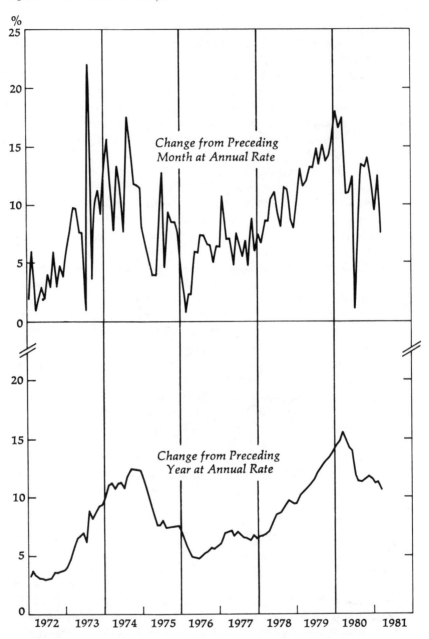

Source: Based upon seasonally adjusted consumer price index for urban households, from the Bureau of Labor Statistics. Center for International Business Cycle Research, Rutgers University.

it publishes, the Bureau of Labor Statistics would be doing the public a service. It would tell the nation what the rate of inflation is, in terms of the most widely known price index, the CPI. With inflation finally recognized as a number one economic problem, we need a number one inflation rate to tell us how we are getting on with it.

NOTES TO CHAPTER 19

1. For brevity I shall use the terms "trade balance" and "net exports of goods and services" interchangeably. The merchandise trade balance is, of course, more limited in coverage, excluding the services component.

2. See Solomon Fabricant, "Capital Consumption and Net Capital Formation," in Conference on Research in Income and Wealth, *A Critique of the United States Income and Product Accounts*, Studies in Income and Wealth, vol. 22 (New York: NBER, 1958), p. 447. Fabricant discussed this method in an unpublished memorandum, prepared for the NBER's Capital Requirements Study, June 1951, "Deflation of Foreign Investment." Simon Kuznets used the measure in the final report of the study, *Capital in the American Economy* (Princeton, N.J.: Princeton University Press, 1961); see p. 492 for annual data, 1919-1955.

3. J. Hibbert, "Measuring Changes in the Nation's Real Income," *Economic Trends*, 255 (London: Central Statistical Office, January 1975): xxviii-xxxv.

4. I am indebted to Edward Denison of the Bureau of Economic Analysis for allowing me to examine his manuscript on this subject prior to publication. See his "International Transactions in Measures of the Nation's Production," *Survey of Current Business* (May 1981): 17-28.

5. It would be possible, and indeed preferable, to use original data rather than seasonally adjusted data to compute the moving twelve-month average, though ordinarily there will be little difference between the two averages. But the current month's index *must* be seasonally adjusted since the objective is to obtain a seasonally adjusted inflation rate.

Chapter 20

How to Fix the CPI

Phillip Cagan and Geoffrey H. Moore

The consumer price index has been widely criticized for its inadequacies as a measure of inflation, primarily because of how it measures the cost of housing. But the criticism often arises out of ignoramce of how it is actually constructed and why. Statements are made, for instance, that the index assumes that all homeowners buy a new house every month and pay the current mortgage interest rate. That is not true. Almost as fallacious is the view that one could readily correct what is wrong with the CPI by substituting another index for it—without recognizing that every known alternative is beset with problems of its own. In short, there are trade-offs, and any proposal to change the CPI should recognize that the benefit to be gained is almost bound to be at the expense of some other valuable consideration, which should be weighed. Nevertheless, we believe the CPI can be improved.

HOMEOWNERSHIP COSTS

Since the CPI aims to measure the current price level of goods and services bought by consumers, it is hardly unreasonable that the current price of houses and the current level of mortgage interest rates should enter into it. It is also obvious that only a small fraction of

Phillip Cagan, Professor of Economics, Columbia University, and Geoffrey H. Moore were asked by the Business Roundtable to study the problems of the CPI and recommend solutions. This chapter, a synopsis of their full report published by the American Enterprise Institute, is reprinted from *Across the Board*, The Conference Board Magazine (April 1981).

people are currently in the market for houses or mortgages. Furthermore, in order that the CPI reflect only movements in prices, not changes in the amounts purchased, it is based on the concept of a *fixed market basket*, representative of what consumers bought during a certain period, namely 1972–1973. Consequently, the index measures the total expenditure on house purchases (net of sales) that would be incurred currently by the same small fraction of households that acquired houses in 1972–1973. It also measures the total interest payment that would be currently committed by these households over the average life of a mortgage at the time of purchase. The great majority of homeowners, who had already purchased houses before the 1972–1973 survey, of course, are not included in this computation, since the prices and interest rates involved in *their* transactions had already been included in the index at the appropriate dates. Their continuing current expenses for upkeep (insurance, repairs, and taxes) are covered in the CPI.

Nonetheless, the housing component has contributed significantly to recent increases in the CPI because of the rapid rise of house prices and mortgage interest rates. These two items contributed three percentage points to the 14 percent rise in the index for the fiscal year ended June 1980. For those who were not buying houses or borrowing on mortgages during this period, this may seem to be an unwarranted impact, and for them it is. But a single market basket cannot represent every individual family, and it may not even represent the average family beyond the period for which the survey was made. These are problems that no index can meet perfectly.

Another difficulty is that, although the current prices of houses, like the prices of hamburgers and haircuts, are among the prices that consumers pay, buying a house is also a long-term investment, unlike the hamburger or haircut. Viewed as an investment, homeownership provides a continuing series of services at a cost—not only maintenance and financing costs, which are now included, but also the capital costs of the homeowner's equity, adjusted for capital gains or losses. As a theoretical proposition, the CPI should allow the capital gains on houses to offset some of the other costs, and include as the true cost the alternative rate of return the homeowner could obtain by investing his equity somewhere else. But this alternative cannot be identified with any quoted rate of return in the market, and the capital gains can only be measured when realized—when the house is sold. Hence, such a measure would be highly speculative and at least as controversial as what is now being done.

An alternative would be to determine, through a broad survey, whether rents on houses representative of owner-occupied housing can be obtained to provide a valid measure of what this housing would rent for. The existing CPI rent index is designed to cover only rental housing, largely apartments in urban centers, and contains a serious downward bias, so that using it as the rental equivalent for owner-occupied housing is not a reasonable solution. We believe that the development of a valid rental-equivalent measure deserves high priority, for it would avoid all the questions of how to treat house prices and mortgage interest. They would no longer be needed in the index. The Bureau of Labor Statistics (BLS) has announced that it would design an appropriate rental survey to measure home ownership costs. (Postscript: The BLS has since adopted the method.)

In view of the time required to establish a valid rental-equivalent measure, the present treatment should. in the meantime, be modified in several respects. For mortgage interest costs we would use the actual interest paid currently on *all* mortgages instead of the interest committed to be paid on new mortgages. This means treating mortgage interest payments the same way that other long-term commitments, such as rental payments on leases, are now treated in the CPI. That is, of the two ways to handle such commitments— when they are committed and when they are paid—we would choose when they are paid. Then the rates for all mortgage borrowers would enter into the calculation and the impact on the CPI of sharp fluctuations in current rates, both upward and downward, would be greatly diminished. In 1979, for example, this modified treatment of mortgage interest rates would have reduced the rate of increase in the CPI from 13.3 percent to 11.7 percent (December to December).

At the same time, we would make other modifications in housing cost measures. Land should be eliminated from the house purchase price and from the property tax component, because land is a non-depreciable investment-good like stocks, bonds, and other assets whose purchase is excluded from the CPI. Similarly, we would exclude the portion of house purchases that reflects increased home-ownership per household. The combined effect of these two changes in 1979 would have been to reduce the weight of house purchases by 28 percent.

A CHANGING MARKET BASKET

Oil price increases and other developments have produced changes in the typical market basket since the survey that determined its content was taken in 1972-1973. With fixed quantity weights, prices that rise faster than others become relatively more important in the index, even though consumers tend to shift their expenditures in favor of lower priced products. Many consumers have shifted from heating oil to wood (where it is less expensive), or have conserved energy in other ways. An index that measures the cost of a given standard of living would allow for such substitutions while holding the standard constant. By comparison, the present index tends to be biased upward because it does not allow for these substitutions.

Past studies indicate that this bias has been quite small. Still, it should be monitored. In 1978 the BLS instituted a quarterly survey of consumer expenditures that, though less comprehensive than the major surveys made every dozen years or so, can provide the basis for more frequent revisions of weights. In addition, this makes it possible to construct an index weighted by current expenditures and to extend it back in time for comparison with the present base-weighted index. This would show how much difference frequent updating of the weights would make.

Under ordinary circumstances a current-weighted and a base-weighted index bracket an index that measures the cost of a constant standard of living. Hence, economists have long advocated an average of these two indexes as the best approximation to an index of the true cost of living. We recommend that the Bureau of Labor Statistics construct, on an experimental basis, such an average index.

A related problem with the CPI, especially in connection with its use as an escalator of wages and retirement benefits, is that it records price changes that reflect a change in the standard of living of the entire population, and it is not clear that such price changes should be escalated. OPEC, for example, has raised the price we pay for imported oil in exchange for our exports. This reduces our real national income. Instead of everyone's sharing this burden, indexed wages and benefits compensate for it.

In early 1980 Denmark removed imported oil from its consumer price index as part of a compromise to hold down wage escalation. That is not a desirable solution, however, because the deletion of particular items from the index is arbitrary. Instead, such foreign shocks to the economy can be removed from indexation by adjusting for changes in the cost of total imports relative to exports (the terms of foreign trade). The adjustment can be estimated by changes in a price index for imports relative to one for exports, weighted by the ratio of imports to GNP. From 1973 to 1979 this adjustment called for a reduction of indexation by about three-tenths of 1 percent a year. It is not large, because it has been held down by the large price increases of some exports and because imports are less than 10 percent of GNP. If the terms of trade improve, of course, the adjustment would be upward.

In principle, also, adjustments can be made in escalation agreements to allow for changes in real national income that are of domestic as well as foreign origin. Some of these reduce real national income, such as depletion of resources, higher costs of controlling pollution, or declining productivity. Others increase real income, as was true of productivity changes over most of our history. These are not matters that can be handled by the CPI or by any price index, however, without completely departing from the concept of a measure of general price change. The problem requires explicit recognition in escalation agreements themselves, by specifying how changes in real national income are to affect the escalation, whether of wages, pensions, or other types of payments. Some practicable formulas for doing this need to be worked out.

QUALITY BIAS

Product improvements are widely believed to bias the CPI upward. If the quality of a product improves, its effective price has been lowered even if its nominal price is unchanged. An example is the occasional medical finding that the proper dosage of a drug should be reduced, thus cutting the cost of its services even if the price per ounce remains the same. The Bureau of Labor Statistics, however, already makes many adjustments for such changes. If the detailed specification of any item in the index changes, the item is taken out of the index, unless the change can be attributed to a change in production costs and information on the latter is provided by the manufacturers, in which case the BLS adjusts the price. Such adjustments are applied to automobile prices when optional equipment becomes standard or when safety items or antipollution devices are mandated by the government. When items that change are left out of the index, the index is biased only if the prices of the items removed tend to rise more or less than the remaining prices.

Hence, the quality bias in the index is not necessarily upward. In fact, two major sources of downward bias have been identified. In the rent index the disregard of deterioration due to aging of the same rented unit produces a substantial downward bias. In house purchase prices, where the BLS relies on FHA quotations, there is a downward bias because of ceilings that prevent more expensive houses from being financed under these programs. The BLS is conducting studies to correct these two items.

REVISIONS

Unlike most other economic statistics, the CPI, once published, is not revised. This is a deliberate policy, and has much to recommend it in view of the wide use of the index in contracts. It is, however, a drawback whenever a substantial conceptual or other change in the index is made, since it can perpetuate inconsistencies between what was done prior to and subsequent to the change. For example, when the new market basket was adopted as a result of the 1972–1973 survey, the index as of December 1977 was left unchanged. In effect, the old basket was used until that date, the new basket only after that date. But this means that the index after December 1977 does not strictly represent the increase in cost since 1967 (the base of the index) of the 1972–1973 basket. That increase would probably be less than what the index shows, because any difference that might have existed as of December 1977 was wiped out. The increase to that point represents the increase in the cost of the old (1960–1961) basket, which very likely exceeded the increase in cost of the new one. Thus, the index lacks a straightforward interpretation.

Another example would occur if our proposal to change the mortgage interest component were adopted. Up to the time of the change, current mortgage interest rates would have been used in the index. Beyond that time, an average of past rates would be used, which of course includes the current rates already employed in the index. If the new index is simply linked on to the old, the increases in current rates that have already been counted in the index would be counted again in the future. The index would continue to reflect increases that had already been included. This can only be avoided by computing the index by the new method up to the date the revision is to start and allowing the level of the new index to reflect the effect of the change in method.

Since the principle of no historical revisions of the CPI should probably be preserved, and since sharp changes as of the date of revision should doubtless be avoided, we believe that a new principle is required. This would incorporate the effect of any revision gradually in the index over a period of months, at a fixed rate of, say, one-tenth of 1 percent per month. Thus if the total effect of a revision were to reduce the index, say, by 2 percent as of the date of revision, this would be incorporated by reducing the calculated rate of change in the index by one-tenth of 1 percent per month for the next 20 months. This would, it is true, introduce a small distortion into the index during that period, but it would be of known amount, and, once the adjustment period was over, the index would be at its correct level. Under present procedures the index never reaches its correct level. That is an unfortunate thing to have to say about an index that is as carefully constructed as the CPI.

PART III

FORECASTING

Chapter 21

Why the Leading Indicators Really Do Lead

In August 1972 a headline proclaimed that 43 percent of the public believed that the country was no longer in a recession. For the
first time in two years more people believed the country was not
in recession than believed it was. The verdict was correct, but it took
a long time to reach it, and even then the margin was only 43 to 41
percent. Meanwhile, an index of leading indicators, especially designed to tell when a recession is over, had been rising vigorously
ever since October 1970. Most of the citizens participating in the
survey had, of course, never heard of this index, and still fewer were
aware of the reasons for relying upon what it had been saying.

That was 1972. Today, the leading index is much more widely
known, but the reasons for its performance in anticipating recessions
and recoveries still are probably obscure to many. Why do the leading indicators lead?

The most familiar type of indicator is what we call "coincident."
These are measures of economic performance, such as gross national
product, industrial production, employment, unemployment, personal income, and retail sales. They show how well the economy is
faring, because they measure aggregate economic activity. They rise
and fall more or less together, in roughly coincident fashion, and tell
us whether the economy is currently experiencing a recession or a
slowdown, a recovery or a boom. They are used to identify and date,
after the fact, the peaks and troughs in the business cycle.

Reprinted from *Across the Board*, May 1978.

The leading indicators, on the other hand, anticipate movements in the coincident. Their function is to consistently provide advance warning of changes in economic activity. Many of them reflect commitments to activity in the near future: new orders for machinery or housing starts are examples. The placing of an order implies some future activity, as does starting construction on a new house.

Still another type of indicator is described as "lagging," because their fluctuations usually follow those of the coincident indicators. Examples are labor cost per unit of output, the level of inventories, and interest rates on mortgage loans. They are not mere followers, however. Cost factors, as we note below, have significant implications for the subsequent performance of the leading indicators. Many of the indicators classified in this group can, in economic terms, be described as measures of excesses and imbalances.

The leading indicators have a noteworthy record. The composite index of twelve indicators now published by the Department of Commerce has turned down before every business cycle peak and turned up before every business cycle trough since 1948. Further, if the definition of a recession is extended to include retardations in growth, then the leading index shows a one-to-one match at every peak and trough since 1948; it leads at nearly every turning point and does not lag at any. Thus, while a sustained decline in the leading index has always signaled a weakening of the economy, sometimes these signals have been followed by retardations in growth rather than by recession (see Figure 21-1). It is also to be noted that the 142 peaks and troughs in the twelve individual series that are used to compile this index led the business cycle peaks and troughs in 92 percent of the instances between 1948 and 1975.

The scientific method requires that systematic empirical behavior be supported by a convincing explanation if it is to be credible. We must therefore ask not only what the leading indicators forecast and how well they do it but also why they have this capacity? If we know the reasons, we can have more confidence in their future performance. We can also set the stage for observing the conditions that, in effect, lead the leading indicators.

One major reason why the leading indicators successfully anticipate changes in the economy is that many of them represent the decisions or commitments to economic activity in the months ahead, and economic decisions take time to work out their effects. For example, new orders for machinery and equipment, a leading indicator, reflects decisions of business firms to buy new machinery. It takes time to convert the orders into machines. Hence, such orders

Figure 21-1.   Indexes of Leading, Coincident, and Lagging Indicators *(index: 1967 = 100; ratio scale).*

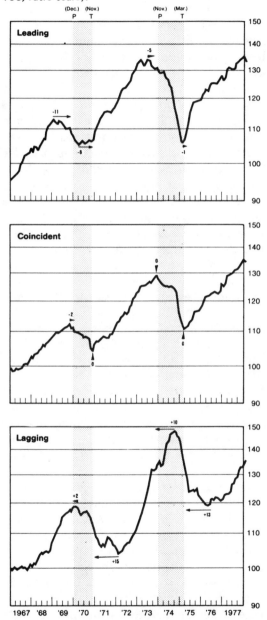

Note: Shaded areas represent the business recessions of December 1969–November 1970 and November 1973–March 1975. Numbers and arrows represent leads or lags in months.
Source: U.S. Department of Commerce.

tend to precede, or lead, machinery production, as well as the production of the goods the machinery later helps to produce.

A similar kind of decision is reflected in obtaining a permit to build a house. After a permit is taken out, the building can be started and is eventually completed and sold. This sequence of events takes time. Hence new building permits and housing starts lead residential construction expenditures (see Figure 21-2, panel 1). Similarly, a decision to start a new business often involves an application to a state office for permission to incorporate. Since establishment of a new business is, in turn, followed by new hirings and purchase of new equipment, series on new incorporations also tend to lead employment and investment expenditures. Again, the decision to construct a new commercial or industrial building usually involves a construction contract and new orders for equipment. Consequently, contracts and orders for plant and equipment lead commercial and industrial construction expenditures (see Figure 21-2, panel 2). The earliest phase of the sequence of events given in these examples is represented by a leading indicator and the final phase by some measure of economic performance such as production, sales, or employment.

These are the kinds of everyday relationships that are taken advantage of in other walks of life. For example, we know that heavy snowstorms reduce both maneuverability of automobiles and the road space available for driving and that, therefore, traffic jams follow snowstorms. This timing relationship can be explained in a straightforward manner and does not need to be built into a complex theory of traffic engineering. Hence, when snowstorms are predicted, alert city managers activate prompt snow removal and often prevent or at least reduce the traffic jams that would otherwise occur. In economics, also, we can rationalize familiar patterns of behavior and modify the usual sequences by appropriate and well-timed economic policies.

The explanation of the lead in some economic indicators, however, is more complex. For example, the series on the average workweek tends to lead the employment series. A reasonable hypothesis is that employers can increase hours of work more promptly than they can hire new employees. While overtime work costs more, there is no long-term commitment, and the decision is easily reversed. Experience has shown that this reasoning is borne out in most manufacturing industries: the average length of the workweek usually begins to increase or decline before the number of workers employed follows suit (see Figure 21-2, panel 3). However, this relationship is not evident in such industries as construction or retail trade. Hence the workweek for manufacturing is the selected leading indicator. Even though it is limited to manufacturing, it bears a close relation to movements in total employment, in part because of the many economic ties between manufacturing industries and the rest of the economy.

In many ways the most exciting of the leading indicators is stock prices, perhaps because so many Americans own stocks. Another reason is that indexes of stock prices are available hourly and can be followed as closely as baseball or football scores. Preoccupation with hourly or daily fluctuations in individual stocks, however, may hide the consistent lead in the broad stock price indexes (see Figure 21-2, panel 4). Although opinions differ on the reason for this, a plausible explanation of the lead can be constructed from the fact that stock prices are influenced by profits and by interest rates. The tendency for profits to decline prior to a peak in output depresses stock prices and so does the tendency for interest rates to rise briskly under such circumstances.

The fact that profits are a leading indicator does more than help to explain the behavior of stock prices; it helps to explain—and this is more important—how the business cycle itself comes about. For the prospect of profits is, of course, a powerful motivating force in a private enterprise economy. When this prospect dims, business decisions to expand are canceled or postponed. Cost cutting and layoffs become the order of the day. Capital expansion projects are deferred. So it is not hard to see why a decline in profits leads to a decline in investment, production, and employment.

But why does the decline in profits usually begin when business as a whole is still expanding? A major factor is the behavior of a lagging indicator—unit costs of production. A period of prosperity brings with it developments that raise production costs: the tight labor market and rising cost of living lift wage demands, productivity slackens, inventories rise as do interest rates and other costs of holding the inventories, and so on. Although prices go up, they are sometimes constrained by previous commitments, by international competition, or by an intensification of efforts to maintain a share of the market. The upshot is that prices begin to rise less rapidly than costs, putting a squeeze on profit margins. When the squeeze on margins is sufficient to offset the continued rise in output, profits decline. This story has been repeated many times in the history of business cycles. It demonstrates the importance of looking at the lagging indicators— measures of excesses and imbalances—for the first sign of developments that may bring about a reversal in the leading indicators.

Figure 21-2.   Leading Indicators and the Activities They Lead.

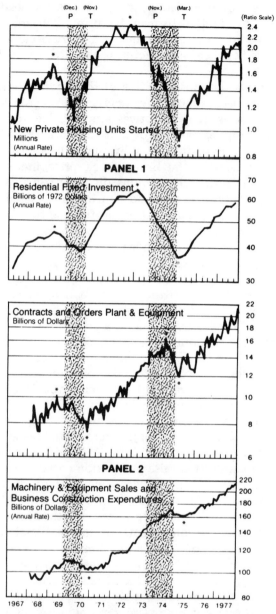

Note: Asterisks identify the cyclical peak and trough months for each series. Shaded areas represent the business recessions of December 1969—November 1970 and November 1973—March 1975.

Source: U.S. Department of Commerce. *Business Conditions Digest.*

Figure 21-2. continued

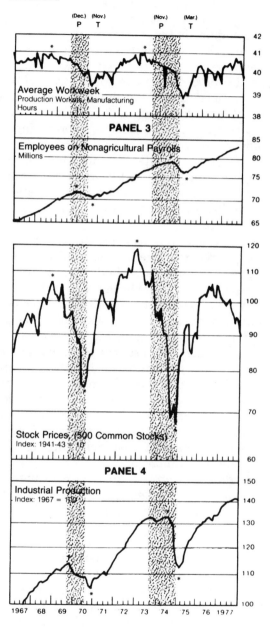

As this brief analysis suggests, the selection of particular indicators for each of the composite indexes has been guided by our still incomplete understanding of the causes of business cycles. Many different explanations of the underlying causes have been advanced. Some lay primary stress on the relations between investments in inventory and fixed capital on the one hand and final demand on the other. Others assign a central role to the supply of money and credit; or to government spending and tax policies; or to relationships among prices, costs, and profits (as in the preceding example). All these factors undoubtedly influence the course of business activity, and some may be more important at one time than another, but there is no consensus on which is the most important. Hence it is prudent to consider a variety of indicators that reflect all the processes, and the full list of indicators of which we have shown some examples does just that.

An equally important consideration in selecting indicators has been their empirical record. Careful studies of the behavior of indicators over long periods have been conducted before their selection. In addition, repeated studies have been made of the behavior of indicators after they have been selected. Many of the indicators have repeatedly survived such testing. For example, the average workweek, construction contracts, and stock prices were in the original 1937 list as well as in the 1975 list. The same lists of indicators have also been tested by their performance in other countries, notably Canada, the United Kingdom, West Germany, and Japan. Every new recession or economic slowdown provides some additional evidence against which the indicators can be assessed. As a result of this continued examination and reexamination, a large amount of empirical evidence has been accumulated that demonstrates both the value of the indicators and their limitations.

Reading the leading indicators to divine the future is not a simple, straightforward matter. No leading indicator moves on a straight and narrow path, and the coincident indicators are not glued to the leaders. The leading indicator index will, however, aid the observer in this effort. The index is smoother than most of its components, hence easier to follow, and of course, it summarizes their movements. But the components are essential to an understanding of the economic developments under way, because the economic rationale applies to the components rather than to the composite index. In a similar way the coincident and lagging indexes are useful summaries of their components, but an understanding of their interaction with the leading index requires an examination of the components themselves. The indexes are simply aids to this end.

Like other tools for economic forecasting, the leading indicators, and their index, seldom hit the bull's eye. But they have an enviable record.

AN NBER READING LIST ON WHY THE LEADING INDICATORS LEAD

The index of leading indicators released each month by the U.S. Department of Commerce is, according to the usual press notices, "believed to anticipate future changes in the economy." What is the basis for this belief? Since the NBER originated the idea of leading indicators in 1937 and since over the years the Bureau has issued a large number of reports that explain and document their behavior, a classified list of NBER references may be helpful to those who wish to gain a better understanding of why the leading indicators lead.

The following list contains general references that cover a large number of different indicators and explain their interconnections as well as specialized references that explain the behavior of particular indicators. The latter are organized according to the list of twenty-six indicators issued by the Bureau in 1966, which was used by the Department of Commerce from 1967 to 1975, but most of the entries serve equally well to document the 1975 list presently used by the Department of Commerce. The references are limited to reports either published by the National Bureau or prepared by members of its staff for publication elsewhere.

GENERAL REFERENCES
Burns, 1961, 1969a; Clark, J.M., 1934; Mitchell and Burns, 1961; Moore, 1961b, c, 1962, 1975a; Moore and Klein, 1977; Moore and Shiskin, 1967; Shiskin, 1961; Zarnowitz, 1972; Zarnowitz and Boschan, 1975, a, b.

SPECIFIC REFERENCES, BY TYPE
OF INDICATOR [1]

LEADING INDICATORS
1. Average Workweek, Manufacturing Industries. Bry, 1959, 1961.
2. Initial Claims, Unemployment Insurance. Moore, 1961a, 1973; O'Dea, 1975.
3. New Business Formation. Evans, 1948; Zarnowitz, 1961a.
4, 5. Durable Goods, New Orders; Plant and Equipment, Contracts and Orders. Zarnowitz, 1961b, 1973.

---

1. The list of indicators is the 1966 list, published in Moore and Shiskin, 1967.

6. Building Permits, Housing. Burns, 1938; Clark, 1934; Grebler, 1960.

7. Inventory Change, Manufacturing and Trade. Abramovitz, 1950; Mack, 1967; Stanback, 1962.

8. Industrial Materials Prices. Mack, 1967; Moore, 1972; Zarnowitz, 1962.

9. Common Stock Prices. Hickman, 1953; Macaulay, 1938; Moore, 1975c; Morgenstern, 1959.

10, 11. Corporate Profits; Ratio, Price to Unit Labor Cost. Hultgren, 1965; Moore, 1962, 1975b; Zarnowitz and Lerner, 1961.

12. Consumer Instalment Credit, Change in. Haberler, 1942; Kisselgoff, 1952; Klein, 1971.

ROUGHLY COINCIDENT INDICATORS

13, 14. Nonagricultural Employment; Unemployment Rate. Bry, 1959, 1961; Burns, 1969b; Moore, 1961a, 1973; O'Dea, 1975.

15, 16. Gross National Product, in current dollars; in constant dollars. Kuznets, 1941, 1946.

17. Industrial Production. Mitchell and Burns, 1936; Zarnowitz, 1973.

18. Personal Income. Creamer, 1956.

19, 20. Manufacturing and Trade Sales; Retail Sales. Burns, 1952; Clark, 1934; Friedman 1957; Mack, 1956.

LAGGING INDICATORS

21. Unemployment Rate, 15 weeks and over. Moore, 1973; Moore and Shiskin, 1967; O'Dea, 1975.

22. Plant and Equipment Expenditures. Hastay, 1954; Zarnowitz, 1961b, 1973.

23. Manufacturing and Trade Inventories. Abramovitz, 1950; Mack, 1967; Stanback, 1962.

24. Unit Labor Cost, Manufacturing. Fabricant, 1959; Hultgren, 1965; Moore, 1961a, 1962, 1975b.

25. Commercial and Industrial Loans Outstanding. Moore, 1969; Moore and Shiskin, 1967.

26. Bank Rates on Short-Term Business Loans. Cagan, 1966, 1969; Conard, 1966.

AUTHORS AND TITLES

Abramovitz, Moses. 1950. *Inventories and Business Cycles, with Special Reference to Manufacturers Inventories.* New York: NBER.

Bry, Gerhard. 1959. *The Average Workweek as an Economic Indicator.* New York: NBER.

_____. 1961. "The Timing of Cyclical Changes in the Average Workweek." In *Business Cycle Indicators,* ch. 15. New York: NBER.

Burns, Arthur F. 1938. "The Cyclical Behavior of Construction Activity." New York: NBER manuscript.

_____. 1952. "The Instability of Consumer Spending." In *32d Annual Report.* New York: NBER.

_____. 1961. "New Facts on Business Cycles." In *Business Cycle Indicators*, ch. 2. New York: NBER.

_____. 1969a. "The Nature and Causes of Business Cycles." In *The Business Cycle in a Changing World*, ch. 1. New York: NBER.

_____. 1969b. "The Problem of Unemployment." In *The Business Cycle in a Changing World*, ch. 7. New York: NBER.

Cagan, Phillip. 1966. *Changes in the Cyclical Behavior of Interest Rates.* New York: NBER.

_____. 1969. "The Influence of Interest Rates on the Duration of Business Cycles." In *Essays on Interest Rates*, vol. I. New York: NBER.

Clark, John Maurice. 1934. *Strategic Factors in Business Cycles.* New York: NBER.

Conard, Joseph W. 1966. *The Behavior of Interest Rates: A Progress Report.* New York: NBER.

Creamer, Daniel. 1956. *Personal Income during Business Cycles.* New York: NBER.

Evans, George Heberton, Jr. 1948. *Business Incorporations in the United States, 1800–1943.* New York: NBER.

Fabricant, Solomon. 1959. *Basic Facts on Productivity Change.* New York: NBER.

Friedman, Milton. 1957. *A Theory of the Consumption Function.* New York: NBER.

Grebler, Leo. 1960. *Housing Issues in Economic Stabilization Policy.* New York: NBER.

Haberler, Gottfried. 1942. *Consumer Instalment Credit and Economic Fluctuations.* New York: NBER.

Hastay, Millard. 1954. "The Cyclical Behavior of Investment." In *Regularization of Business Investment.* New York: NBER.

Hickman, W. Braddock. 1953. *The Volume of Corporate Bond Financing since 1900.* New York: NBER.

Hultgren, Thor. 1965. *Costs, Prices, and Profits: Their Cyclical Relations.* New York: NBER.

Kisselgoff, Avram. 1952. *Factors Affecting the Demand for Consumer Instalment Sales Credit.* New York: NBER.

Klein, Philip A. 1971. *The Cyclical Timing of Consumer Credit, 1920–67.* New York: NBER.

Kuznets, Simon. 1941. *National Income and Its Composition, 1919–1938.* New York: NBER.

_____. 1946. *National Income: A Summary of Findings.* New York: NBER.

Macaulay, Frederick R. 1938. *Some Theoretical Problems Suggested by the Movements of Interest Rates, Bond Yields and Stock Prices in the United States since 1856.* New York: NBER.

Mack, Ruth P. 1956. *Consumption and Business Fluctuations: A Case Study of the Shoe, Leather, Hide Sequence.* New York: NBER.

_____. 1967. *Information, Expectations, and Inventory Fluctuation: A Study of Materials Stock on Hand and on Order.* New York: NBER.

Mitchell, Wesley C., and Arthur F. Burns. 1936. *Production during the American Business Cycle of 1927–1933.* New York: NBER.

_____. 1961. "Statistical Indicators of Cyclical Revivals." In *Business Cycle Indicators,* ch. 6. New York: NBER.

Moore, Geoffrey H. 1961a. "Business Cycles and the Labor Market." In *Business Cycle Indicators,* ch. 16. New York: NBER.

_____. 1961b. "Leading and Confirming Indicators of General Business Changes." In *Business Cycle Indicators,* ch. 3. New York: NBER.

_____. 1961c. "Statistical Indicators of Cyclical Revivals and Recessions." In *Business Cycle Indicators,* ch. 7. New York: NBER.

_____. 1962. "Tested Knowledge of Business Cycles." In *42d Annual Report.* New York: NBER.

_____. 1969. "Generating Leading Indicators from Lagging Indicators." *Western Economic Journal,* June, pp. 137–44.

_____. 1972. "The Cyclical Behavior of Prices." In *The Business Cycle Today.* New York: NBER.

_____. 1973. *How Full is Full Employment?* American Enterprise Institute, Washington, D.C.

_____. 1975a. "The Analysis of Economic Indicators." *Scientific American,* January.

_____. 1975b. "Productivity, Costs, and Prices: New Light from an Old Hypothesis." *Explorations in Economic Research* (NBER) Winter, pp. 1–17.

_____. 1975c. "Security Markets and Business Cycles." In *Financial Analyst's Handbook.* Homewood, Illinois: Dow Jones-Irwin, Inc.

Moore, Geoffrey H., and Philip A. Klein. 1977. "Monitoring Business Cycles at Home and Abroad." New York: NBER manuscript.

Moore, Geoffrey H., and Julius Shiskin. 1967. *Indicators of Business Expansions and Contractions.* New York: NBER.

Morgenstern, Oskar. 1959. *International Financial Transactions and Business Cycles.* New York: NBER.

O'Dea, Desmond J. 1975. "The Cyclical Timing of Labor Market Indicators in Great Britain and the United States." *Explorations in Economic Research* 2, no. 1 (Winter), pp. 18–53.

Shiskin, Julius. 1961. *Signals of Recession and Recovery, An Experiment with Monthly Reporting.* Occasional Paper 77. New York: NBER.

Stanback, Thomas M., Jr. 1962. *Postwar Cycles in Manufacturers Inventories.* New York: NBER.

Zarnowitz, Victor. 1961a. "Cyclical Aspects of Incorporations and the Formation of New Business Enterprises." In *Business Cycle Indicators,* ch. 13. New York: NBER.

_____. 1961b. "The Timing of Manufacturers' Orders during Business Cycles." In *Business Cycle Indicators,* ch. 14. New York: NBER.

_____. 1962. *Unfilled Orders, Price Changes, and Business Fluctuations.* New York: NBER.

_____. ed. 1972. *The Business Cycle Today.* New York: NBER.

_____. 1973. *Orders, Production, and Investment: A Cyclical and Structural Analysis.* New York: NBER.

Zarnowitz, Victor, and Charlotte Boschan. 1975a. "Cyclical Indicators: An Evaluation and New Leading Indexes." *Business Conditions Digest*, May.

_____. 1975b. "New Composite Indexes of Coincident and Lagging Indicators." *Business Conditions Digest.* November.

Zarnowitz, Victor, and Lionel J. Lerner. 1961. "Cyclical Changes in Business Failures and Corporate Profits." *Business Cycle Indicators*, ch. 12. New York: NBER.

Chapter 22

A New Leading Index
of Employment
and Unemployment

One of the composite leading economic indicators published by
the U.S. Commerce Department is the "marginal employment adjustments" index. Its title derives from the fact that its components
reflect employment adjustments typically made by employers and
employees during an early stage of the business cycle. Three of the
four components pertain to manufacturing: the average workweek,
the accession rate, and the layoff rate. The fourth, initial claims for
unemployment insurance, is broader in scope. The workweek reflects
changes in the amount of overtime or in the number of workers
employed part time; such adjustments can usually be made more
promptly, and are easier to reverse when necessary, than decisions to
hire and fire. The accession rate includes persons newly hired as well
as those rehired after layoff, and the layoff rate includes both temporary and permanent layoffs. Initial claims represent the number of
persons currently applying for unemployment compensation, rather
than those who are already receiving it.

Each of the four series typically leads at business cycle peaks and
leads or is roughly coincident at troughs. Thus, the composite of the

The author wishes to thank Richard Conger, who did the statistical work underlying this chapter. Research for the project was supported by a grant from the
Economic Development Administration of the U.S. Department of Commerce;
however, that agency bears no responsibility for the content of the chapter. For
further details on the new index, including historical and current data, please
contact the Center for International Business Cycle Research, Rutgers University.

Reprinted from *Monthly Labor Review* (June 1981).

four series has led at every one of the seven business cycle peaks and six troughs between 1948 and 1980. The leads at troughs, however, have been short; for four of the six troughs, the lead was only one month. At peaks, the leads averaged twelve months, and none was shorter than eight months.

One reason the leads are long at peaks and short at troughs is that the index, as well as each of its components, displays virtually no long-term growth. At its earliest peak, in January 1948, the index was 102.5 (1967 = 100). At its latest peak, in December 1978, the index stood at 99.1. Because the marginal employment adjustments index does not reflect the substantial growth of the economy during the intervening thirty years, its flat trend tends to produce early peaks and late troughs when compared with aggregate economic activity. This characteristic is a disadvantage for some purposes and an advantage for others. Warnings of a recession one year or more ahead are apt to be discounted, in view of the inevitable uncertainties, while signs of recovery one month ahead of the event are of limited value. On the other hand, the marginal employment adjustments index can be expected to be symmetrical in its behavior with respect to the peaks and troughs of some important economic indicators, such as the unemployment rate, the employment ratio, or the capacity utilization rate, which are also largely trendless.

There is a need, therefore, for a leading index in two forms, one with a trend corresponding to the growth in the economy, the other without. The trend requirement can be met by the same procedure used in the Commerce Department's comprehensive leading index, namely, reverse trend adjustment. Here the long-term trend in the index is set equal to a "target trend" observed over a certain period, and the current figures are adjusted by the same monthly increment required to achieve the target trend in the given period. In addition, it would be desirable to take advantage of component series that are available promptly, and at the same time reduce the considerable weight given to manufacturing in the existing index (three out of four series). Less emphasis on a single sector may reduce the size of subsequent revisions of the index and smooth out erratic fluctuations, especially if the expanded sector coverage is provided by series from different sources.

With these objectives in mind, the Rutgers Center for International Business Cycle Research has constructed a new index based upon four components. Two are included in the existing index: average workweek and initial claims. The third series is average weekly overtime hours in manufacturing. This is a component of the average workweek, but is included as well because it is smoother and less frequently affected by holidays. The fourth series is the ratio of voluntary to involuntary part-time employment. The cyclical movements in this ratio are attributable primarily to the denominator, which reflects employers' decisions to shorten work hours in response to current or anticipated adverse business conditions. It behaves as a leading indicator at peaks and is roughly coincident at troughs.[1] It is based on data from the Current Population Survey of households and hence is statistically independent of the other series in the index, which are based on the Bureau of Labor Statistics establishment survey (average workweek and overtime hours) or unemployment insurance records (initial claims). Also, it covers all sectors of the economy, not just manufacturing.[2]

Hence the new index includes two series that are restricted to manufacturing (average workweek and overtime hours) and two that are broader in scope (initial claims and part-time employment ratio). Only two of the series are from the same data source. Moreover, all the components are usually available by the end of the first or second week of the month following the month to which they refer. As a result, the new leading index is compiled by the Rutgers Center concurrently with other employment data, and about three weeks earlier than the existing index. In its original form the index has virtually no long-run trend, but it is also compiled with a growth trend equal to that used in the Commerce Department's leading, coincident, and lagging indexes, namely 3.3 percent annually, or 0.272 percent per month.[3]

The new index without the target trend factor yields results very similar to those from the present index. Five of the turning points are in the same month in both indexes, one is six months earlier in the new index, six are a month later, and one is two months later. Thus the new index is often not quite as prompt as the existing one in reaching its high and lows. However, the new index is somewhat smoother. Its relation to the unemployment rate is shown in Table 22-1. It reaches its highs and lows prior to the corresponding turns in unemployment in every instance except the January 1948 peak, and the average lead is about six months. Hence the new index should prove to be a useful leading indicator of unemployment, especially if, as we expect, it is less subject to revision than the present index.

Not only does the new index lead, but the magnitude of its changes are rather closely correlated with subsequent changes in the unemployment rate. (See Figure 22-1.) For example, a regression of the year-to-year change in unemployment on the change in the new index during the last six months of the preceding year yields a corre-

Table 22-1. Relationship of the Unemployment Rate and the New Leading Index of Employment (without Target Trend) to the Business Cycle, 1948–1980 (*in months*).

| Business Cycle | Lead (–) or Lag (+) at Business Cycle Turns | | Lead (–) or Lag (+) of New Index at Turns in Unemployment Rate |
	Inverted Unemployment Rate	New Leading Index of Employment without Target Trend	
Peak November 1948	–10[a]	–10[a]	0[a]
Trough October 1949	0	–5	–5
Peak July 1953	–1	–8	7
Trough May 1954	+4	–1	–5
Peak August 1957	–4	–21	–17
Trough April 1958	+3	0	–3
Peak April 1960	–2	–11	–9
Trough February 1961	+3	–2	–5
Peak December 1969	–7	–14	–7
Trough November 1970	+9	0	–9
Peak November 1973	–1	–7	–6
Trough March 1975	+2	0	–2
Peak January 1980	–6	–13	–7
Mean lead or lag			
At peaks	–4	–12	–8
At troughs	–4	–1	–5
At both turns	–1	–7	–6

[a]Initial month of series. Hence peak might have been earlier and index might have led the unemployment rate.

lation coefficient of – 0.90 during the period 1949–1980 (thirty-one observations). Thus, by this simple method, the unemployment rate was forecast for the year ahead with an average error of about one-half percentage point.[4]

The new index with the target trend bears a fairly close relationship to nonfarm employment. (See Figure 22-2.) However, the trend is steeper because the trend rate of growth in nonfarm employment is 2.2 percent annually, compared with the 3.3 percent target trend in the new index; the latter figure was selected to permit comparison with series other than nonfarm employment. The new index leads employment at twelve of the thirteen peaks and troughs between 1948 and 1980, and is coincident once. The average lead is three months and the leads are about as long at troughs as at peaks (Table 22-2).

Figure 22-1. Relation of New Leading Index of Employment to the Unemployment Rate, 1972-1980.

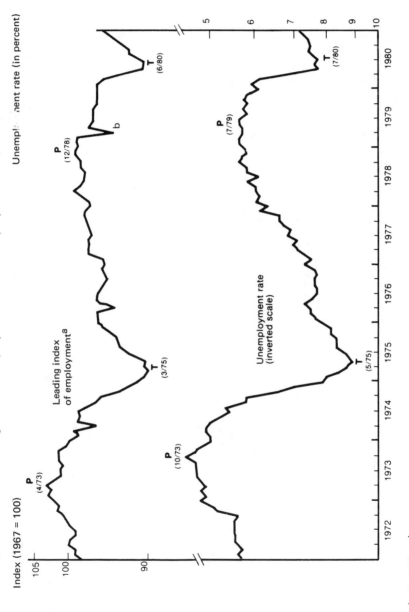

a Excludes target trend.

b April 1979 data affected by trucking strike and holidays.

Note: P indicates series peaks; T indicates troughs.

Figure 22-2. Relation of New Leading Index of Employment to Nonfarm Employment, 1972-1980.

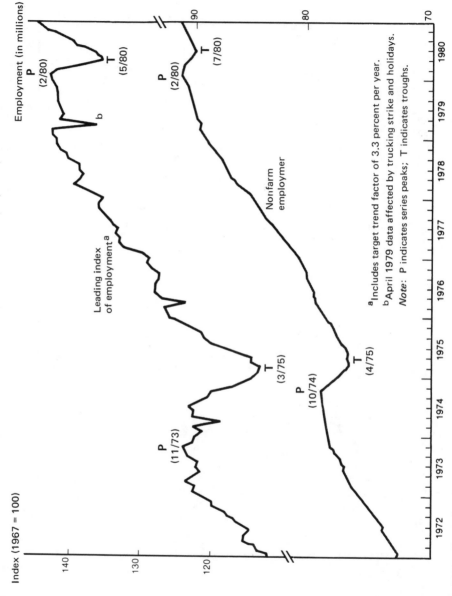

Table 22-2. Relationship of Nonfarm Employment and the New Leading Index of Employment (with Target Trend) to the Business Cycle, 1948–1980 (*in months*).

	Lead (-) or Lag (+) at Business Cycle Turns		Lead (-) or Lag (+) of New Index at Turns in Employment
Business Cycle	Nonfarm Employment	New Leading Index of Employment with Target Trend[a]	
Peak November 1948	-2	-4	-2
Trough October 1949	0	-6	-6
Peak July 1953	-1	-3	-2
Trough May 1954	+3	-2	-5
Peak August 1957	-5	-8	-3
Trough April 1958	+1	0	-1
Peak April 1960	0	-3	-3
Trough February 1961	0	-2	-2
Peak December 1969	+3	0	-3
Trough November 1970	0	0	0
Peak November 1973	+11	0	-11
Trough March 1975	+1	0	-1
Peak January 1980	+1	0	-1
Mean lead or lag			
At peaks	+1	-2	-4
At troughs	+1	-2	-2
At both turns	+1	-2	-3

[a] Target trend is that used in *Business Conditions Digest* composite indexes, 0.272 percent per month.

Compared with the existing index of this type, the new leading index of employment and unemployment has a broader economic coverage and is available more promptly. In its trendless form the new index is comparable with other series that are essentially trendless, such as the unemployment rate, employment ratio, or capacity utilization rate. It consistently leads the unemployment rate at both peaks and troughs by about six months on average. The index is also constructed with a trend, in which form it is comparable with series that grow with the economy, such as the employment level, which it leads by two or three months at both peaks and troughs. The new index, therefore, offers an early warning of cyclical shifts in employment and unemployment.

POSTSCRIPT: AN UPDATE ON LEADING AND COINCIDENT EMPLOYMENT INDEXES

Two additional components have been included in the leading employment index. The *layoff rate* is the ratio of the number of job losers on layoff to total civilian employment. The *short-duration employment rate* is the percentage of the labor force who has been unemployed for less than fifteen weeks. Both these series, treated invertedly in the index, have usually led downturns and upturns in the business cycle, as well as in employment and unemployment. Data for these as well as the other four components are available for a given month on the first Friday of the following month. Prompt availability is one of the hallmarks of this leading index.

A coincident employment index is also constructed on the same date. It contains three series pertaining to employment and two to unemployment (treated invertedly). The selection takes advantage of all three of the major sources of information about labor market conditions. The household survey produces figures on the *total number employed* and the *unemployment rate.* The establishment survey provides the *number of nonfarm jobs on payrolls* and *nonfarm employee hours* (which avoids double counting persons on more than one payroll). The *insured unemployment rate* pertains to the very large fraction of the experienced workforce covered by insurance. The definitions, concepts, and sample size of these sources vary. By lumping the five series into an index, the result is a less erratic and more reliable indicator of the ease or tightness of the labor market, whose turning points have been very nearly coincident with the business cycle. In this respect it differs from two of its components, the total and insured unemployment rates, which have tended to lag at business cycle troughs and to lead at peaks.

NOTES TO CHAPTER 22

1. See Chapter 18 of the first edition of this book (Cambridge, Mass.: Ballinger, 1980).

2. Since this was written a fifth leading indicator has been included in the index: the layoff rate. It is based upon household survey data on the number of job losers on layoff divided by total civilian employment.

3. The trend rates are compound monthly rates between average levels during the peak-to-peak specific cycles 1948–1953 and 1974–1979. The target trend is the average for the four components of the coincident index: nonfarm employment, real personal income less transfer payments, industrial production, and real manufacturing and trade sales. It is almost the same as the rate for real gross national product. See *Business Conditions Digest* (March 1979): 107 for more details.

4. See also Geoffrey H. Moore "Forecasting Unemployment with a Leading Index," *Monthly Labor Review,* 1983.

Chapter 23

When Lagging Indicators Lead:
The History of an Idea

On Tuesday, February 14, 1978, the *Wall Street Journal* ran a front page news story on the "lagging indicators." It was a high water mark in terms of public interest in these series after four decades of relative neglect. Attention is usually riveted on the leading indicators. Who cares about the followers? The leaders tell us where we're going.

This view is understandable and is fostered by the terms used to classify the indicators. Nevertheless it is unfortunate because it neglects the problem of who or what it is that tells the leaders where to go. We live in an interdependent world, and the business cycle is one of the manifestations of that interdependence. A downturn in a leading indicator—say an index of stock prices—is not the beginning. It is a result of something else. The something else is where the lagging indicators come in.

This idea has had a long history. My first acquaintance with it began when I read Mitchell and Burns's "Statistical Indicators of Cyclical Revivals" in 1938. In that study some seventy economic series were arrayed according to the length of their average lead or lag at business cycle troughs. Several series on bond yields were placed at both the top and the bottom of the list. The authors explained that bond yields, as well as some other series, could be considered either to conform positively to business cycles, in which case their upturns generally lagged behind the revival in business, or to

Reprinted from the *NBER Reporter*, Winter 1978. This chapter also appeared in the *New York Statistician* (New York Area Chapter of the American Statistical Association), March-June 1978.

conform inversely, in which case their downturns generally preceded the revival in business. After a while, a business revival tended to pull interest rates up as demand for loans expanded and pressure on reserves mounted. But the prior decline in interest rates facilitated revival by reducing costs of borrowing and indicating that credit was easier to get. From one point of view, bond yields were a lagging indicator of revival; from the other point of view, a leading indicator.

In my 1950 paper, "Statistical Indicators of Cyclical Revivals and Recessions," I pushed this idea a bit further by showing that it applied to both recessions and revivals and that it applied to the entire group of indicators that I classified as lagging. Tracing the record back to 1885, I noted that the downturns in the laggers had consistently preceded the upturns in the leaders, while upturns in the laggers had consistently preceded downturns in the leaders. Considered on an inverted basis, the laggers were the longest of leaders. The lengths of their leads varied from one business cycle to another, but these variations were positively correlated with those in the leads of the leading indicators. Such consistency over a fifty year period bespoke a causal connection.

Subsequent studies of the indicators revealed that this relationship had persisted. In 1969 I wrote "Generating Leading Indicators from Lagging Indicators" in an effort to put more meat on the bones of the argument. I noted that there were good economic reasons to expect that rapid increases in certain types of lagging indicators—interest rates, costs of production, inventories, and outstanding debt—would have deterrent effects on certain types of leading indicators—new commitments to invest, profit margins, inventory accumulation, new credit extensions, and so forth. One way to determine what was a "rapid increase" was to compare the increase in the laggers with that in the coincident indicators, since the latter represented the rate of growth in aggregate economic activity. The ratio of coincident to lagging indicators quantified this comparison. Several such ratios, notably the ratio of sales to inventories, already existed and behaved in the expected manner.[1]

Phillip Cagan contributed a useful study on this theme in 1969, "The Influence of Interest Rates on the Duration of Business Cycles." He showed that the lengths of the lags in interest rates after business cycle turns had a bearing upon the length of the business expansion or contraction in which they occurred. A delayed upturn in rates indicated a long expansion, and a delayed downturn indicated a long contraction. He also pointed out that this connection may operate through the relation between interest rates and the money supply and through the effect of interest rate changes upon decisions to invest. He developed evidence that supported this hypothesis by examining the behavior of such leading indicators as the rate of change in the money supply and contracts for residential, commercial, and industrial construction.

In 1971 my daughter, Kathleen Moore (with a little nudge from her father), took up the question. Do lagging indicators in other countries display the same properties vis-à-vis the leading indicators as they do in the United States? In "The Comparative Performance of Economic Indicators for the United States, Canada, and Japan," she found that they did. Philip Klein and I followed this with studies not only for Canada and Japan, but also the United Kingdom and West Germany. We found the relationship substantially confirmed in all these countries.[2] The British in their own work on indicators at the Central Statistical Office, now published regularly in *Economic Trends*, also find that interest rates and unit labor costs, treated invertedly, behave as leading indicators.

Victor Zarnowitz and Charlotte Boschan, in their study of indicators for the Bureau of Economic Analysis, recommended that the ratio of the coincident to lagging indexes be regularly published in *Business Conditions Digest*. This has been done since November 1976. In the *Fifty-Seventh Annual Report* (September 1977) of the National Bureau of Economic Research, Zarnowitz and Boschan showed how the lagging index (treated invertedly) consistently led the leading index in an analysis of growth cycles during the period 1948–1975. In a paper presented before the American Statistical Association in August 1977, Zarnowitz and Beatrice Vaccara demonstrated that the lagging indicators (treated invertedly) could be used to extend the forecast span of the leading indicators in quantitative forecasts of real GNP and other coincident indicators.

The new list of indicators that is now used in *Business Conditions Digest* enables us to update the historical record on the relationship between cyclical turns in the leading and lagging indicators. The table on the median leads and lags of seventy-five leading series and thirty lagging series in my 1950 paper that covered the period 1885–1938 can be extended from 1948 to 1975 by using the medians for the twelve leading series and six lagging series in the *BCD* list. The results (see Table 23-1) show that the turns in the lagging group have persistently preceded the opposite turns in the leading group during the entire ninety year period. Usually the turns are close enough to suggest a plausible relationship. The exceptions pertain to the unusually long business cycle expansions ending in 1937, 1953, and 1969 and to the long contraction ending in 1933. Apart from these unrepresentative instances, the median upturn in the lagging group has preceded

Table 23-1. Cyclical Timing of Leading and Lagging Indicators, 1885–1975.

Business Cycle Peak	Lead (−) or Lag (+) in Months at Business Cycle Peak		Interval in Months (trough in lagging to peak in leading)
	Median Trough, Lagging Group	Median Peak, Leading Group	
March 1887	−20	−3	17
July 1890	−14	−5	9
January 1893	−8	−5	3
December 1895	−14	−5	9
June 1899	−6	−1	5
September 1902	−15	−4	11
May 1907	−27	−16	9
January 1910	−11	−4	7
January 1913	−14	−3	11
August 1918	−34	−20	14
January 1920	−9	−2	7
May 1923	−13	−4	9
October 1926	−24	−11	13
June 1929	−15	−5	10
May 1937	−50	−2	48
February 1945	n.a.	n.a.	n.a.
November 1948	n.a.	−10	n.a.
July 1953	−39	−5	34
August 1957	−31	−21	10
April 1960	−19	−12	7
December 1969	−99	−9	90
November 1973	−24	−8	16
Averages:			
All observations	−24	−7	17
Excluding 1937, 1953, 1969	−18	−8	10

Note: n.a., data not available.

Sources: 1885–1938: Geoffrey H. Moore, "Statistical Indicators of Cyclical Revivals and Recessions," Occasional Paper 31 (New York: NBER, 1950), Table 11. Based on seventy-five leading and thirty lagging series.

1948–1975: *Business Conditions Digest*, October 1977, Appendix F. Based on twelve leading and six lagging series.

Table 23-1. continued

Business Cycle Trough	Lead (−) or Lag (+) in Months at Business Cycle Trough		Interval in Months (peak in lagging to trough in leading)
	Median Peak, Lagging Group	Median Trough Leading Group	
May 1885	n.a.	−6	n.a.
April 1888	−7	−2	5
May 1891	−5	−4	1
June 1894	−11	−4	7
June 1897	−13	−9	4
December 1900	−8	−5	3
August 1904	−9	−9	0
June 1908	−6	−6	0
January 1912	−17	−13	4
December 1914	−14	−1	13
April 1919	−7	−3	4
July 1921	−12	−5	7
July 1924	−10	−6	4
November 1927	−14	−4	10
March 1933	−43	−5	38
June 1938	−10	−4	6
October 1945	n.a.	n.a.	n.a.
October 1949	−11	−5	6
May 1954	−6	−6	0
April 1958	−6	−2	4
February 1961	−5	−2	3
November 1970	−9	−2	7
March 1975	−4	−1	3
Averages:			
All observations	−11	−5	6
Excluding 1933	−9	−5	5

the median downturn in the leading group by ten months on the average, while the median downturn in the lagging group has preceded the median upturn in the leading group by an average of five months. The record since 1948 does not seem to differ greatly from that prior to 1938. Long leads in the inverted lagging group, relative to the business cycle, are associated with long leads in the leading group, and vice versa.[3]

All this is relevant in 1978 because of recent advances in the lagging indicators, and this was the reason for the *Wall Street Journal* story. *BCD*'s lagging index began rising more rapidly than the coincident index after April 1977, and hence the coincident to lagging ratio declined.[4] The leading index, meanwhile, continued to rise, but not so vigorously as the lagging index. The question in the summer of 1978, therefore, was how long the upward trend in the leading index would persist in the face of factors that over many years have foreshadowed its decline.

NOTES TO CHAPTER 23

1. So far as I know, Edgar Fiedler, then at Bankers Trust Company, was the first to compute a ratio based upon composite indexes of coincident and lagging indicators. He did this in 1964 to test the view expressed by Leonard Lempert (1964) that cyclical imbalance should be measured by comparing the rates of increase in the laggers with those in the coincident. Another early (1968) experimenter with such ratios was John H. Merriam of Idaho University.

2. See Chapter 6 in this book.

3. The correlation coefficients (r) between the leads of the inverted lagging group and those of the leading group in the table are as follows:

	1887–1938		1948–1975		1887–1975	
	N	r	N	r	N	r
All observations	30	+0.33	11	+0.38	41	+0.35
Omitting four long phases (ending 1933, 1937, 1953, 1969)	23	+0.76	9	+0.90	37	+0.81

4. Edgar Fiedler recently observed that since two of the six lagging indicators included in the lagging index are expressed in current dollars, it is more affected by inflation than the coincident index whose four components are all expressed in physical units or in constant dollars. To rectify this, the two lagging indicators—unit labor cost and commercial and industrial bank loans—could be deflated by using man hours per unit of output (the reciprocal of the usual productivity measure) as the physical counterpart of unit labor cost and deflating loans by the wholesale price index for industrial commodities.

REFERENCES

Cagan, Phillip. "The Influence of Interest Rates on the Duration of Business Cycles." In *Essays on Interest Rates*, ed. Jack M. Guttentag and Phillip Cagan, vol. 1, pp. 3–28. New York: NBER, 1969.

Central Statistical Office. "Cyclical Indicators for the U.K. Economy." *Economic Trends* 257 (March 1975): 95–109.

Lempert, Leonard H. *Statistical Indicator Associates*, September 16, 1964.

Merriam, John H. "New Economic Indicators." *Western Economic Journal*, June 1968, pp. 195–204.

Mitchell, Wesley C., and Arthur F. Burns. "Statistical Indicators of Cyclical Revivals." New York: NBER. Bulletin 69, May 28, 1938, Reprinted in *Business Cycle Indicators*, ed. Geoffrey H. Moore, pp. 162–83. New York: NBER, 1961.

Moore, Geoffrey H. "Statistical Indicators of Cyclical Revivals and Recessions." Occasional Paper 31. New York: NBER, 1950. Reprinted in *Business Cycle Indicators*, ed. Geoffrey H. Moore, pp. 184–260. New York: NBER, 1951.

_____. "Generating Leading Indicators from Lagging Indicators." *Western Economic Journal*, June 1969, pp. 137–44.

Moore, Geoffrey H., and Philip A. Klein. *Monitoring Business Cycles at Home and Abroad.* New York: NBER, forthcoming.

Moore, Kathleen Harriet. "The Comparative Performance of Economic Indicators for the United States, Canada, and Japan." *Western Economic Journal*, December 1971, pp. 419–27.

Vaccara, Beatrice N., and Victor Zarnowitz. "How Good Are the Leading Indicators?" *1977 Proceedings of the Business and Economic Statistics Section.* American Statistical Association, 1978.

Zarnowitz, Victor, and Charlotte Boschan. "New Composite Indexes of Coincident and Lagging Indicators." *Business Conditions Digest.* (U.S. Department of Commerce), November 1975.

_____. "Cyclical Indicators." *Fifty-Seventh Annual Report.* New York: NBER, September 1977.

Chapter 24

The Forty-second Anniversary of the Leading Indicators

SUMMARY

Forty-two years ago Wesley Mitchell and Arthur Burns completed a brief research report that identified types of economic indicators that "have been tolerably consistent in their timing in relation to business cycle revivals and that at the same time are of sufficiently general interest to warrant some attention by students of current economic conditions."[1] This study was the first of a long series of investigations devoted to extending the system of indicators, testing its performance, explaining the interrelationships among the indicators, and putting the system into practicable form for current use. Since the leading indicators receive much public attention nowadays, their reliability is a matter of some importance.

One way to assess reliability is to examine the subsequent performance of an early version of the system. For this purpose we have used the list and classification of indicators established in 1950 and compared their performance before World War II with their performance since 1948. The pre-1938 information was used in developing the 1950 list and classification; the post-1948 information of course was not.

The results demonstrate that taken as a whole the 1950 version of the indicator system lived up to its promise. The leading indicators continued to lead and the laggers to lag at each succeeding turn in the business cycle. The degree of consistency in performance after

Reprinted from *Contemporary Economic Problems, 1979*, William Fellner, ed. (Washington, D.C.: American Enterprise Institute, 1979).

1948 was not very different from what it was before 1938. The relationships exhibited in earlier cycles resembled those that appeared in subsequent cycles.

Nonetheless, changes did occur. Certain indicators that appeared to lag in earlier cycles moved more promptly in later ones. Some indicators, especially those expressed in current prices, failed to conform to recent business cycles. These and other changes, particularly the availability of new statistical information, have produced many modifications in the system of indicators that promise to enhance its usefulness and to reduce its limitations as a guide to the future.

ORIGIN OF THE NBER LEADING INDICATORS

For four years the U.S. economy had been recovering from a depression. Nearly as many people were then employed as had been at the peak prior to the slump, but unemployment was still high, and the price level was rising again. In an effort to keep up with rising government spending social security taxes were raised. Concerned about inflation, the Federal Reserve raised reserve requirements sharply. Interest rates shot up. By May the recovery had stopped dead in its tracks, and one of the steepest recessions in history began, erasing much of the gain of the four year recovery.

Let me hasten to note that the period just described, despite a superficial resemblance, is not 1979. It was 1937. The recovery was from the Great Depression, and it lasted from March 1933 until May 1937. By coincidence, the most recent recovery also began in March—that is, in March 1975, although the recession that preceded it was brief and mild by comparison with the 1929–1933 decline. Whether the recovery stops in 1979, as it did in 1937, we are far better equipped today to detect a recession in its early stages, to measure its extent and consequences, and hence to take steps promptly to deal with it.

This is partly because of what happened in 1937. In the late summer Secretary of the Treasury Henry Morgenthau, Jr., asked the National Bureau of Economic Research (NBER), a private organization devoted to objective studies of business cycles and other economic problems, to draw up a list of statistical series that would best indicate when the recession would come to an end. Wesley C. Mitchell, then the NBER's director of research and a renowned student of business cycles, enlisted the help of Arthur F. Burns, who later headed the NBER and still later became chairman of the Federal Reserve. In six weeks the job was done. The report that was presented to the Secretary set forth a list of the most reliable indicators of cyclical revivals, explained how they were selected, and included a record of their past performance. It was published in May 1938.[2]

Thus was born the first set of leading, coincident, and lagging indicators that are now widely used to forecast, detect, measure, and appraise recessions and recoveries. In the summer of 1938 they were put to their first test. The recovery began in June, and the first signs of its appearance were registered in the leading indicators that Mitchell and Burns had identified.

Mitchell and Burns drew on an encyclopedic knowledge of the history and theory of business cycles as well as on an enormous stock of empirical information that had been assembled since the 1920s at the NBER. It was a resource that could be called upon as needed, as Secretary Morgenthau recognized. During the next four decades the continuing studies of business cycles at the NBER, in the U.S. Department of Commerce, and elsewhere in this country and abroad led to many improvements in the system of indicators. They were subjected to a series of tests of performance as new business cycles came upon the scene and as new techniques for managing the economy were applied.

SUBSEQUENT PERFORMANCE OF THE 1950 LIST OF INDICATORS

The degree of confidence that any method of analysis attains, and deserves, depends upon its performance after it has been developed. It must be subjected to trial with new data, not used at the time the method was devised and preferably not even available at that time. This kind of test of the leading indicators has indeed been made more than once. In 1950 I examined the performance of the Mitchell-Burns list of indicators at the 1937 peak and 1938 trough of the business cycle, since the data they had used in their analysis ended with the 1933 trough. The test broadly supported their results, but many new series had become available, new findings from research suggested additional materials, and the analysis needed to be extended to cover downturns as well as upturns. Hence a new list and classification of indicators, based on records available through 1938, was published in 1950.[3]

Ten years later, in 1960, another review was undertaken, and in 1966 still another, both under the auspices of the NBER.[4] In 1972 the Department of Commerce initiated an extensive review, publishing the results in 1975.[5] Some of the indicators originally selected by Mitchell and Burns have survived all these tests of performance.

The length of the average workweek in manufacturing establishments and the index of common stock prices are examples. Others have been dropped altogether or replaced by similar series, and new series have been added. It is of some interest, however, to take a long look back to see how the initial system behaved in subsequent business cycles up to the present. For this purpose it will be more productive to concentrate on the 1950 list and classification of indicators rather than the 1938 list of Mitchell and Burns. The 1950 study, as already noted, covered both peaks and troughs, and the classification system bears a closer resemblance to the system now used. Furthermore, current data for each of the series in the 1950 list, or close equivalents, are published in the Commerce Department's monthly *Business Conditions Digest* and hence are conveniently available. The data record employed in the 1950 study ended with the 1938 business cycle trough. The test will pertain to the period from 1948 to 1975, during which time six business cycles occurred, with peaks in 1948, 1953, 1957, 1960, 1969, and 1973 and troughs in 1949, 1954, 1958, 1961, 1970, and 1975.

The principal question to be examined is whether, at these twelve turning points in the economy, the indicators selected and classified in 1950 lived up to the performance suggested by their record prior to 1938. Did the leading indicators lead and the lagging indicators lag? Was their behavior as consistent as their previous record would lead one to expect? What deficiencies became evident and why? The answers can tell something about the effectiveness of the method used to develop the information, as well as the degree of historical continuity in the economic processes that give rise to business cycles.

In 1950, when I began this research, business cycles had been puzzling scholars for more than a century, and efforts to prevent panics, crises, and depressions had long engaged the attention of lawmakers and government officials. Mitchell and others had studied a large number of hypotheses, theories, or models of how business cycles came about. No single theory had proved adequate for all time or all countries, and the evidence bearing upon the phenomenon was scattered and lacked uniform treatment. Mitchell had come to believe that the most promising line of attack was to organize systematically and comprehensively the statistical evidence for a long period of time and for several countries and then to use these data to develop an accurate description of business cycle phenomena as well as to test various hypotheses and to suggest new ones.

As a result, the NBER in 1950 had a large collection of economic time series in monthly, quarterly, or annual form extending back in time as far as each series could be compiled and pertaining to the types of economic process that previous investigators believed relevant to the generation of business cycles. The series had been classified into economic groups deemed most useful in explaining differences in cyclical behavior or in accounting for the influence of one economic variable on another. Finally, a standard set of measures of cyclical behavior had been calculated for each series for the period it covered. The measures showed how consistently the series conformed to business cycles, whether they led or lagged and by how much, what rate of change and pattern of movement they exhibited in successive cycles and on the average, and so on. From these measures one could trace the relationships among numerous economic processes during the periods of prosperity and depression that the data covered, examine what changes had occurred in these relationships, and develop a systematic, reasoned account of past business cycles.

By summarizing a portion of this information, I was able to identify, among these relevant types of economic process, those that had shown highly consistent conformity to business cycles and dominant tendencies either to lead, to coincide with, or to lag behind the turns in the economy as a whole. I used statistical significance tests as a way of reducing the likelihood that a certain record had been achieved by chance. It became clear that there were systematic sequences in the movements of different economic variables, such as orders, production, employment, inventories, prices, interest rates, and so on, and that these sequences had persisted over many business cycles during the past half century or more. It was also clear that some changes had occurred in the way the economy worked and that they had affected and doubtless would continue to affect the observed sequences. Many of the sequences and the changes in them could be readily explained or at least rationalized, but many were of a complex nature that defied simple explanation. The riddle of the business cycle had not been solved. As a result, although the persuasiveness of the explanation and the statistical evidence offered grounds for some confidence that the sequences would persist in the future, how much and exactly what would persist and what would disappear, and when, were the great unknowns.

The types of economic process identified and classified in this way and the particular time series selected to represent them are shown in Table 24-1. In virtually every instance, several indicators were available to represent a given type of process. For example, for employment the most comprehensive available series was (and still is) total civilian employment, based upon data from the household survey. But estimates of nonfarm employment are also compiled from reports by establishments. They cover a much larger sample of employees and are documented by payroll records. Hence the latter series is

Table 24-1.   The 1950 List of Leading, Coincident, and Lagging Indicators and their Current Equivalents.

No.	Original Series in 1950 List	BCD No.	Corresponding Series Currently in Business Conditions Digest
	Leading Group		
1.	Liabilities of business failures	14.	Same
2.	Dow-Jones index of industrial common stock prices	19.	Standard and Poor's index of 500 common stock prices
3.	New orders, durable goods, value	6.	Same
4.	Residential building contracts, floor space	29.	New building permits, private housing units, number
5.	Commercial and industrial building contracts, floor space	9.	Same
6.	Average workweek, manufacturing	1.	Same
7.	New incorporations, number	13.	Same
8.	Wholesale price index, twenty-eight basic commodities	23.	Industrial materials price index, thirteen commodities
	Roughly Coincident Group		
9.	Employment in nonagricultural establishments	41.	Same
10.	Unemployment	37.	Same
11.	Corporate profits after taxes	16.	Same
12.	Bank debits outside New York	56.	Manufacturing and trade sales, value
13.	Freight car loadings	49.	Value of goods output in 1972 dollars
14.	Industrial production index	47.	Same
15.	Gross national product, value	200.	Same
16.	Wholesale price index, industrial commodities	335.	Same
	Lagging Group		
17.	Personal income, value	223.	Same
18.	Sales by retail stores, value	54.	Same
19.	Consumer installment debt, value	66.	Same
20.	Bank rates on business loans	67.	Same
21.	Manufacturers' inventories, book value	71.	Manufacturing and trade inventories, book value

Source: Geoffrey H. Moore, *Statistical Indicators of Cyclical Revivals and Recessions*, Occasional Paper 31 (New York: National Bureau of Economic Research, 1950), Table 12.

generally superior in its performance as an economic indicator and was selected to represent the employment process.

Fifteen of the twenty-one series selected as indicators in 1950 are still carried in *Business Conditions Digest*. More or less close relatives of the remaining six series can also be found in *BCD*, as Table 24-1 shows. Because these series represent the same types of process and are readily available in a computer data bank, I have used them in testing the subsequent performance of the 1950 list.

Table 24-2 summarizes the lead-lag performance at each business cycle peak and trough since 1948 for the groups of leading, coincident, and lagging indicators selected in 1950. The twenty-one series were classified in the three groups according to their performance prior to 1938. The leading group (eight series) shows a mean lead at each business cycle turn except the last trough (March 1975). The lagging group (five series) shows a mean lag at each turn except the initial trough (October 1949). The coincident group (eight series) shows some tendency to lead at peaks but is virtually coincident at troughs. Since several of the coincident series were used, along with others, to determine the business cycle peak and trough dates, it is not surprising that they should roughly coincide with these dates. But the sequence of the turns in the three groups is not determined by the business cycle dates, and the sequence is in the expected direction for all but one of the twelve dates, the one exception being the March 1975 trough, where the averages for the leading and the coincident groups coincide.

Table 24-2 also shows that the proportions of timing comparisons that are in the appropriate class in 1948–1975 are not very different from the proportions in the period prior to 1938. At peaks, for example, 89 percent of the timing comparisons in the leading group during 1948–1975 were leads, as compared with 80 percent for the same group prior to 1938. At troughs, the 1948–1975 percentage of leads was seventy-one, compared with 81 percent for the pre-1938 period. For all three groups of series together, at both peaks and troughs, the percentage of timing comparisons that turned out to be in the appropriate class was almost exactly the same after 1948 (75 percent) as before 1938 (77 percent).

Another aspect of the record that is important to the user of indicators is the likelihood that the indicator will not register a turning point in the vicinity of the business cycle turn or that it will register a turning point when no business cycle turn occurs. The record of the 1950 list of indicators with respect to the first of these contingencies is shown in Table 24-3.

Table 24–2. Subsequent Performance of Three Groups of Indicators Selected and Classified in 1950.

| Business Cycle | | Average Lead (−) or Lag (+), in Months | | | | | |
| | | At Peaks | | | At Troughs | | |
Peak (1)	Trough (2)	Leading Group (3)	Roughly Coincident Group (4)	Lagging Group (5)	Leading Group (6)	Roughly Coincident Group (7)	Lagging Group (8)
November 1948	October 1949	−15	−3	+2	−6	−1	0
July 1953	May 1954	−13	−2	+2	−4	+1	+2
August	April	−21	−6	+2	−2	0	+2
April 1960	February 1961	−9	−4	+2	−2	+3	+4
December 1969	November 1970	−8	−5	+2	−1	0	+15
November 1973	March 1975	−6	+6	+11	0	0	+9
Average 1948–1975		−12	−2	+3	−2	+1	+4
Expected value, based on prior record (through 1938)		−6	0	+5	−5	−2	+3
Timing comparisons, 1948–1975 (number)							
Leads		40	28	4	32	13	6
Rough coincidences		6	26	10	28	36	11
Lags		5	6	15	5	13	16
Total[a]		45	43	22	45	43	22

Percentage of timing comparisons in appropriate class, 1948–1975	89	60	68	71	84	73
Expected percentage, based on record to 1938	80	72	88	81	67	72

Note: The indicators were selected and classified into leading, roughly coincident, and lagging groups (eight series, eight series, and five series, respectively) in Geoffrey H. Moore, *Statistical Indicators of Cyclical Revivals and Recessions*, Occasional Paper 31 (New York: National Bureau of Economic Research, 1950). The prior performance of these indicators or substantially equivalent series during business cycles through 1938 is shown ibid., pp. 64–65. The record for 1948–1975 is based on the same or substantially equivalent series, all of which are shown currently in *Business Conditions Digest*, a monthly publication of the U.S. Department of Commerce (see Table 24–1).

aTotal is the sum of the leads, exact coincidences (not shown), and lags. Rough coincidences include leads or lags of three months or less, as well as exact coincidences; hence the sum of the three classes exceeds the total.

Source: National Bureau of Economic Research, January 1979.

Table 24-3. Percentage of Business Cycle Turns Skipped: 1950 List of Indicators.

Business Cycle Peaks and Troughs	Leading Group (8 series)	Coincident Group (8 series)	Lagging Group (5 series)
Number covered			
Before 1938	200	100	39
1948–1975	96	96	60
Percentage skipped			
Before 1938	6	8	13
1948–1975	6	10	27

Source: National Bureau of Economic Research, January 1979.

The record, both before and after 1938, reflects the relative sensitivity of the series, with the leading series being most sensitive and hence skipping few cycles, while the lagging series are the least sensitive and skip more cycles. In the leading and coincident groups there was little change in performance between the two periods, but in the lagging group more than twice as large a percentage of turns were skipped in the recent period. One of the reasons is that business cycles have been milder in the period since 1948 than before. Another is that four of the five lagging series are expressed in current dollars, and inflation has pulled such series upward even during recessions.

For the second contingency, the problem of false signals, a similar record is more difficult to obtain. The term "false signal" is not easy to define, and the 1950 study did not contain this information. Later work has shown, however, that the leading indicators are more subject to extra cycles that do not match the business cycle chronology, while the lagging indicators, again reflecting their relative insensitivity, seldom exhibit extra cycles.[6] This difference continued to prevail after 1948, as the following materials demonstrate.

Figures 24-1 through 24-3 present another form of summary of the performance of the 1950 list of indicators during 1948–1975. Here the three groups of indicators are combined into indexes by the method that the Department of Commerce currently uses to construct its leading, coincident, and lagging indexes.[7] The indexes move down during each recession, up during each expansion. The sequences among their turning points, identified by the use of a computer program, are with rare exceptions in accordance with the patterns expected when the selection of indicators was made in 1950 (see Table 24-4).[8]

Figure 24-1. Composite Leading Index, Eight Series, 1950 List of Indicators.

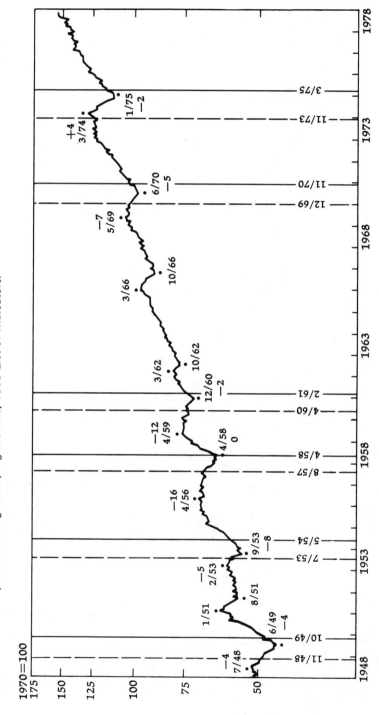

Note: All turning points except March and October 1962 were identified by computer program. The broken vertical lines are business cycle peaks; solid lines are troughs. Leads (−) and lags (+) in months are shown above and below turning point dates.

Figure 24-2. Composite Coincident Index, Eight Series, 1950 List of Indicators.

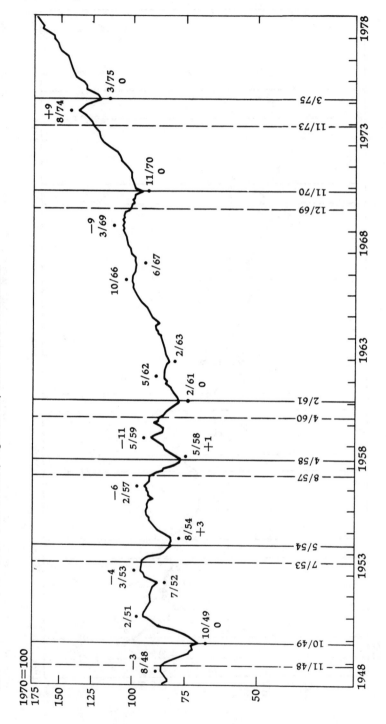

Note: All turning points were identified by computer program. The broken vertical lines are business cycle peaks; solid lines are troughs. Leads (−) and lags (+) in months are shown above and below turning point dates.

Figure 24–3. Composite Lagging Index, Five Series, 1950 List of Indicators.

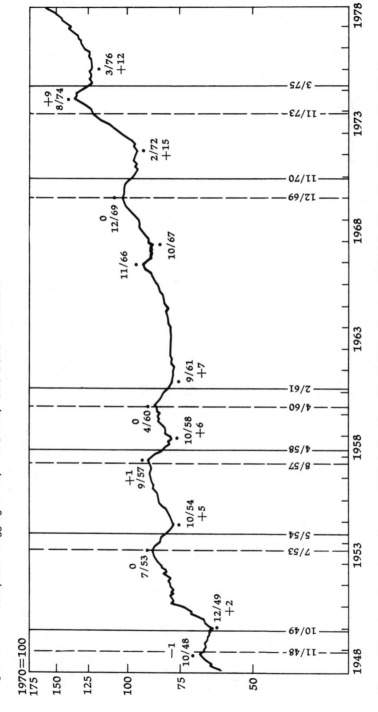

Note: All turning points except February 1972 (shifted from May 1971) and March 1976 (shifted from May 1975) were identified by computer program. The broken vertical lines are business cycle peaks; solid lines are troughs. Leads (−) and lags (+) in months are shown above and below turning point dates.

Table 24-4. Leads and Lags at Business Cycle Peaks and Troughs, Two Sets of Composite Indexes, 1948–1975.

Lead (−) or Lag (+), in Months

Business Cycle		Indexes Based on 1950 List						Indexes Based on 1975 List					
		Leading		Coincident		Lagging		Leading		Coincident		Lagging	
Peak	Trough	P	T	P	T	P	T	P	T	P	T	P	T
(1)	(2)	(3)	(4)	(5)	(6)	(7)	(8)	(9)	(10)	(11)	(12)	(13)	(14)
November 1948	October 1949	−4	−4	−3	0	−1	+2	−10	−4	−1	0	+3	+5
July 1953	May 1954	−5	−8	−4	+3	0	+5	−4	−6	−2	+2	+2	+5
August 1957	April 1958	−16	0	−6	+1	+1	+6	−23	−3	−6	0	+1	+4
April 1960	February 1961	−12	−2	−11	0	0	+7	−11	−2	−3	0	+2	+9
December 1969	November 1970	−7	−5	−9	0	0	+15	−11	−8	−2	0	+2	+15
November 1973	March 1975	+4	−2	+9	0	+9	+12	−5	−1	0	0	+10	+13
Average		−7	−4	−4	+1	+2	+8	−11	−4	−2	0	+3	+8
Standard deviation		7	3	7	1	4	5	7	3	2	1	3	5
Peaks and troughs													
Average		−5		−2		+5		−7		−1		+6	
Standard deviation		5		5		5		6		2		5	
Correlation coefficient[a]		+0.80		+0.69		+0.95							

[a] With the corresponding leads and lags in columns 9 to 14.

Sources: Columns 1 to 8: National Bureau of Economic Research; columns 9 to 14, *Business Conditions Digest*, various issues, p. 10.

In addition to the six recessions identified in the charts, three periods when the indexes declined are not recognized as recessions— namely, 1951–1952, 1962–1963, and 1966–1967. The usual sequences are observed at these turns also (except that the lagging index did not decline in 1951–1952 or 1962–1963). Each of these periods has been identified as a period of slowdown in a chronology of growth cycles, although some of the sensitive leading indicators experienced declines as large as those during the business cycle recessions (see the section following).

During a period as long as 1948–1975, some tendency for the "quality" of the indicators to deteriorate might be expected. Among particular indicators there have been many instances of such deterioration or at least changes in behavior. Railroad freight car loadings, for example, have not kept up with the trend of the economy, partly because of the increasing share of freight hauled by trucks, partly because the production of goods has grown more slowly than services. Inner tube production, one of the indicators in the Mitchell-Burns list, used to be an interesting indicator because of its sensitivity to the new car market and the tire repair business. The advent of the tubeless tire has made the inner tube almost a collector's item, found mostly around swimming holes. There is a possibility, also, of selection bias and regression toward the mean. The top performers selected on the basis of a sample of information covering a certain period are not all likely to remain at the top in a second sample covering a different period. Some were at the top by chance in the first sample and are unlikely to remain there in the next. One can guard against this by making the first sample as large as possible, by applying significance tests in identifying the top performers, and by using other information that explains why they were at the top or that supports the choice indirectly. These safeguards were employed in all the indicator studies, but the possibility of regression bias still remains, as well as deterioration because of economic change.

The lead-lag entries in Table 24-2 give some support to the hypothesis of detorioration. In particular, the average leads of the leading group of indicators have diminished at both peaks and troughs. But this is not decisive, for several reasons. One is that the corresponding entries in Table 24-4, columns 3 and 4, for the composite leading index based on the 1950 list do not show as clear a trend. A stronger test, however, can be made by using the entries for the composite leading index based on the 1975 list, also in Table 24-4. Because the 1975 list was selected toward the end of the period, one would not expect a trend toward deterioration in these observations, and because they are correlated with the entries for the 1950 list (see the correlation coefficients in Table 24-4), they provide a means for allowing for some of the cycle-to-cycle variation in the leads and lags of the 1950 list. A simple way to do this is to subtract the entries in columns 9 and 10 from those in columns 3 and 4, which is equivalent to measuring the leads and lags of the 1950 list against the 1975 list. On this basis the entries in Table 24-4 give some support to the hypothesis of deterioration in the 1950 list, in terms of a trend toward shorter leads or longer lags than in its 1975 counterpart.[9] The entries in Table 24-2, adjusted in a similar manner, give stronger support.[10]

A further consideration with respect to deterioration is that the lags of the lagging group appear to have a tendency to lengthen, especially at troughs. Coupled with the shortening leads of the leading group, this means that the interval between the turns in the leaders and those in the laggers has not diminished. More generally, the sequences among the turns in the three groups of indicators do not reveal strong evidence of deterioration, although at troughs the intervals between the turns in the leading and the coincident groups may have shortened and those between the coincident and the lagging groups may have lengthened.

Table 24-5 summarizes the pre-1938 and post-1948 performance of each of the twenty-one indicators selected in 1950. About two-thirds of the series behaved in substantially the same way in the later period as in the earlier one. That is, the later information supports the earlier classification. Seven of the eight leading indicators are currently classified in *Business Conditions Digest* as leading at both peaks and troughs. The one exception, contracts for commercial and industrial building, is now considered leading at peaks and coincident at troughs. Corporate profits, in the coincident group in 1950, is now classified as a leading indicator. Even in the pre-1938 period, however, profits exhibited some tendency to lead by short intervals (note the average lead of two months at both peaks and troughs). Unemployment is no longer considered a coincident indicator, because of its tendency to lead at peaks and to lag at troughs. Personal income and retail sales, originally classified in the lagging group because they exhibited short lags in the pre-1938 period, have rarely done so since 1948. In addition, inflation has prevented these series from declining in some of the milder recent recessions. For the same reason, the wholesale price index for industrial commodities has not performed as a useful coincident indicator since 1960.

ADDITIONAL TESTS OF THE INDICATOR SYSTEM

Clearly, the 1950 list and classification of indicators has continued to exhibit most of the properties it had when it was established. To users of this system of analysis this result will come as no surprise. As already noted, several reviews of this sort have been made, although none of them tested the 1950 list for the entire 1948–1975 period. Moreover, other kinds of tests have been made. One examines the behavior of the same data in other countries. Investigators in Canada, Japan, Italy, the United Kingdom, Australia, and New Zealand have done this, and within the past few years Philip Klein and I have compiled and analyzed comparable sets of indicators for six countries other than the United States. For this purpose we used the 1966 list rather than the 1950 list of indicators, but many of the same or similar series are in both lists.[11]

Another kind of test uses the same data but in a manner different from that originally contemplated. The use of the leading indicators to forecast the magnitude of change in economic activity is an example, since information on magnitude of change was not used in the 1950 study of indicators. I began carrying out one test of this sort during the recession of 1953–1954 and followed it up again in 1957–1958 and in subsequent recessions. The idea was to compare the severity of the current recession shortly after it began with that of preceding recessions, using the initial changes in the leading and coincident indicators. The leading indicators generally gave earlier indications of the relative severity of the recession than the coincident indicators did.[12] Another test of this sort uses the changes in the leading indicators in a regression model to forecast subsequent changes in the coincident indicators. In these models the leading indicators have exhibited some ability to forecast the magnitude of change in GNP, industrial production, or foreign trade one or two quarters ahead.[13]

Yet another way to test the data is to compare the turning points in the lagging series with the opposite turns in the leading series. The logic of this comparison was recognized in the 1950 study (as well as in the Mitchell-Burns study that preceded it), but the information was not used in selecting the lagging or leading indicators. Briefly, the logic is that many of the lagging indicators represent costs of production (labor costs, interest rates) or factors bearing upon costs (inventories) and that their movements can have an inverse impact upon the leading indicators (new orders, housing starts, construction contracts). This potential inverse effect leads one to expect that up-

Table 24–5. Pre-1938 and Post-1948 Record of Twenty-One Indicators Selected in 1950.

No. Series (1)	Mean Lead (−) or Lag (+), in Months				Percentage of Timing Comparisons in Appropriate Class			
	At Business Cycle Peaks		At Business Cycle Troughs		At Business Cycle Peaks		At Business Cycle Troughs	
	Through 1938 (2)	1948–1975 (3)	Through 1938 (4)	1948–1975 (5)	Through 1938 (6)	1948–1975 (7)	Through 1938 (8)	1948–1975 (9)
Leading Group								
1. Liabilities of business failures	−10	−21	−8	−3	85	100	93	80
2. Common stock price index	−6	−9	−7	−5	80	100	80	100
3. New orders, durable goods	−7	−7	−5	−2	88	83	83	67
4. Residential building contracts	−6	−15	−4	−5	80	100	83	83
5. Commercial and industrial building contracts	−5	−10	−2	+1	80	60	67	20
6. Average workweek, manufacturing	−4	−11	−3	−2	75	100	60	67
7. New incorporations	−2	−14	−4	−5	71	100	79	100
8. Wholesale price index, basic commodities	−3	−10	−3	0	78	67	80	50
Average, eight series	−6	−12	−5	−2	80	89	81	71
Roughly Coincident Group								
9. Employment in nonfarm establishments	0	+1	−3	+1	58	67	58	100
10. Unemployment	n.a.	−7	n.a.	+4	n.a.	33	n.a.	67
11. Corporate profits after taxes	−2	−7	−2	−2	75	17	80	67
12. Bank debits outside New York	+2	−1	−4	−1	69	67	60	83
13. Freight car loadings	0	−1	−1	0	83	83	83	100
14. Industrial production index	+1	−1	−2	0	100	50	83	100
15. Gross national product	n.a.	−1	n.a.	−1	n.a.	100	n.a.	100
16. Wholesale price index, industrial commodities	−4	−1	+4	+9	67	100	60	33
Average, eight series	0	−2	−2	+1	72	60	67	84

Lagging Group

17. Personal income	+4	+1	0	−2	100	33	25	0
18. Sales by retail stores	+4	−2	+2	−2	80	0	60	25
19. Consumer installment debt	+5	+8	+4	+3	100	100	100	100
20. Bank rates on business loans	+6	+3	+5	+10	75	83	100	100
21. Manufacturers' inventories	+6	+5	+8	+4	100	100	100	100
Average, five series	+5	+3	+3	+4	88	68	72	73

n.a.: Not available. For series 10 and 15 no record of timing prior to 1938 is shown in the source; the selection of these series was based on other related series.

Note: See note to Table 20–2. The percentage of timing comparisons in appropriate class (columns 6 to 9) means, for the leading group, the percentage that are leads; for the coincident group, the percentage that are rough coincidences (exact coincidences and leads or lags of three months or less); for the lagging group, the percentage that are lags.

Source: National Bureau of Economic Research, January 1979.

turns in the lagging indicators will precede downturns in the leading indicators and that downturns in the lagging indicators will precede upturns in the leading indicators. Moreover, if the connection is sufficiently close, it should help account for the variation from cycle to cycle in the length of leads of the leading indicators.

Although the twenty-one indicators in the 1950 list were not specifically examined for this property at the time that they were selected, the larger list of indicators studied at that time (seventy-five leading, twenty-nine coincident, and thirty lagging) did exhibit the relationship. Whether the subsequent behavior of the 1950 list conformed to the earlier behavior of this larger list can therefore be determined (see Table 24-6).[14] At all but two of the forty-one turning points since 1885 the upturns in the lagging indicators have preceded the downturns in the leading indicators, and the downturns in the lagging indicators have preceded the upturns in the leading indicators. The two exceptions occurred in 1904 and 1908, when the lagging group reached its peak in the same month that the leading group reached its trough. For nearly seventy years, in other words, there has been no exception to the rule.

Table 24-6 also shows that some of the leads in the inverted lagging series are exceptionally long, and in those instances, a close connection with the leads in the leading series is not plausible. At the December 1969 business cycle peak, for example, the upturn in the lagging group that occurred ninety months before the peak could have little bearing on the downturn in the leading group that occurred nearly seven years later, ten months before the peak. Yet it is fair to say, on the basis of the entire record covering a ninety year span, that these instances are exceptions and that by and large the variability of the intervals between the opposite turns in the leading and lagging groups is not very different from that between the similar turns (see the note to Table 24-6). In this respect the record since 1948 resembles the record prior to 1938.

One factor that helps to account for the variability in the intervals just described is the influence of long-run growth or the occurrence of some extraneous event such as a war on the length of leads and lags. The upward trend in the economy affects both leading and lagging indicators and makes for long expansions and short contractions. When both the leading and lagging series are treated positively, the trend has a similar effect on both, tending to delay peaks and to advance troughs. But when the lagging series are treated invertedly, the trend is inverted also. This tends to increase the intervals between the troughs in the lagging series and the subsequent peaks in the leading series and to reduce the intervals between peaks in the laggers and the subsequent troughs in the leaders. The effect is exaggerated whenever the trend has a dominant effect relative to the cyclical movement of the series.

By adjusting the series for the long-run trend this effect can be eliminated. In recent years this method of cyclical analysis has come to be known, here and abroad, as the growth cycle approach. The 1950 list of indicators can also be analyzed in this manner by trend adjusting the composite indexes constructed from them. The trend-adjusted indexes (Figure 24–4) conform closely to the NBER chronology of growth cycles, and the timing sequences follow the expected pattern (Table 24–7).

The trend-adjusted coincident index based on the 1950 list displays the rare property of coinciding precisely at every one of the nine growth cycle troughs since 1949 (see column 8). It deviates more from the peaks, especially in 1960, where the peak prior to the 1959 steel strike was higher than the peak that followed the strike, and in 1973, where the inclusion of aggregates expressed in current dollars, together with rapid inflation, delayed the peak in the composite index until August 1974. The trend-adjusted leading index led all but three of the growth cycle turns, and the lagging index lagged all but three. When the lagging index is inverted, however, it leads at every turn and by intervals that exceed the leads in the leading index at every turn but one. The variability of the leads in the inverted lagging index, as measured by the standard deviation, is no greater than the variability of the lags in the same index treated positively or of the leads in the leading index. Moreover, the leads in the inverted lagging index are correlated with those in the leading index, supporting the hypothesis that rapid increases in the lagging indicators have deterrent effects on the leading indicators, while slow increases or declines have stimulating effects.

The behavior of the trend-adjusted indexes based on the 1975 list of indicators, which is also recorded in Table 24–7, supports the same inference. Indeed, the correlation just referred to is stronger in the leads based on the 1975 list. Furthermore, there is a high correlation between the timing observations based on the 1975 list and those based on the 1950 list. There is also little evidence of the possible deterioration in the timing behavior of the 1950 list when judged by comparison with the 1975 list, a matter that was explored above in terms of data unadjusted for long-term trends. The growth cycle performance of both sets of indexes is extraordinarily similar.

Table 24-6. Cyclical Timing of Leading and Lagging Indicators, 1885–1975 (number of months).

Business Cycle Peak (1)	Lead (−) or Lag (+) at Business Cycle Peaks — Median Trough, Lagging Group (2)	Median Peak, Leading Group (3)	Median Peak, Lagging Group (4)	Business Cycle Trough (5)	Lead (−) or Lag (+) at Business Cycle Troughs — Median Peak, Lagging Group (6)	Median Trough, Leading Group (7)	Median Trough, Lagging Group (8)	Interval from — Trough, Lagging to Peak, Leading (9)	Peak, Leading to Peak, Lagging (10)	Peak, Lagging to Trough, Leading (11)	Trough, Leading to Trough, Lagging (12)
Mar. 1887	−20	−3	+6	May 1885	n.a.	−6	+2	n.a.	n.a.	n.a.	8
July 1890	−14	−5	+5	Apr. 1888	−7	−2	+13	17	9	5	15
Jan. 1893	−8	−5	+6	May 1891	−5	−4	+12	9	10	1	16
Dec. 1895	−14	−5	+5	June 1894	−11	−4	+4	3	11	7	8
June 1899	−6	−1	+10	June 1897	−13	−9	+18	9	10	4	27
Sept. 1902	−15	−4	+14	Dec. 1900	−8	−5	+6	5	11	3	11
May 1907	−27	−16	+6	Aug. 1904	−9	−9	+6	11	18	0	15
Jan. 1910	−11	−4	+7	June 1908	−6	−6	+8	11	22	0	14
Jan. 1913	−14	−3	+8	Jan. 1912	−17	−13	−2	7	11	4	11
Aug. 1918	−34	−20	+1	Dec. 1914	−14	−1	+10	11	11	13	11
Jan. 1920	−9	−2	+6	Apr. 1919	−7	−3	0	14	21	4	3
May 1923	−13	−4	+4	July 1921	−12	−5	+9	7	8	4	14
Oct. 1926	−24	−11	−1	July 1924	−10	−6	+3	9	8	7	9
June 1929	−15	−5	+2	Nov. 1927	−14	−4	+4	13	10	10	8
May 1937	−50	−2	+3	Mar. 1933	−43	−5	0	10	7	38*	5
Feb. 1945	n.a.	n.a.	n.a.	June 1938	−10	−4	+10	48*	5	6	14
Nov. 1948	n.a.	−11	+2	Oct. 1945	n.a.	n.a.	n.a.	n.a.	n.a.	n.a.	n.a.
July 1953	−45	−8	+3	Oct. 1949	−9	−5	0	37*	13	4	5
Aug. 1957	−38	−20	+2	May 1954	−7	−2	+1	18	11	5	3
Apr. 1960	−23	−11	+2	Apr. 1958	−6	−1	+1	12	22	5	2
Dec. 1969	−90	−10	+2	Feb. 1961	−8	−1	+4	80*	13	6	6
Nov. 1973	−21	−8	+11	Nov. 1970	−9	−2	+15	13	12	7	17
				Mar. 1975	−5	0	+4		19	5	4

Average											
1885–1938	−18	−6	+5		−12	−5	+6		12	11	7	12
1948–1975	−43	−11	+4		−7	−2	+4		32	15	5	6
Standard deviation											
1885–1938	12	5	4		9	3	5		10	5	9	6
1948–1975	28	4	4		2	2	6		29	4	1	5

n.a.: Not available.

Note: If the four extreme items identified by asterisks(*) are excluded, the averages and standard deviations are:

	Column			
	(9)	*(10)*	*(11)*	*(12)*
Average				
1885–1938	10	11	5	12
1948–1975	14	15	5	6
Standard deviation				
1885–1938	4	5	4	6
1948–1975	3	4	1	5

Sources: 1885–1938: Geoffrey H. Moore, *Statistical Indicators of Cyclical Revivals and Recessions*, Occasional Paper 31 (New York: National Bureau of Economic Research, 1950), Table 11, based on seventy-five leading and thirty lagging indicators; 1948–1975: Based on eight leading and five lagging indicators, 1950 list.

Figure 24-4.   Three Trend-adjusted Composite Indexes, 1950 List of Indicators.

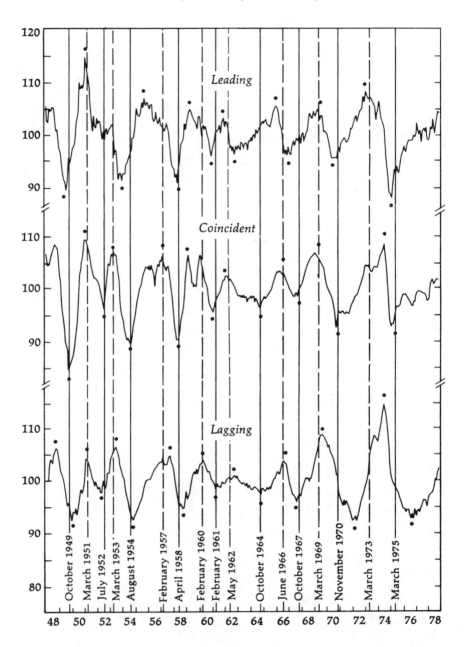

Note: The broken vertical lines are peaks and the solid lines are troughs in NBER growth cycle chronology.

Table 24-7. Leads and Lags at Growth Cycle Peaks and Troughs, Two Sets of Trend-adjusted Composite Indexes, 1948–1975.

Lead (−) or Lag (+), in Months

Growth Cycle		Indexes Based on 1950 List								Indexes Based on 1975 List							
		Lagging Inverted		Leading		Coincident		Lagging		Lagging Inverted		Leading		Coincident		Lagging	
Peak (1)	Trough (2)	P (3)	T (4)	P (5)	T (6)	P (7)	T (8)	P (9)	T (10)	P (11)	T (12)	P (13)	T (14)	P (15)	T (16)	P (17)	T (18)
July 1948	Oct. 1949	_b	−14	−6a	−4	+1	0	+1	+2	_b	−14	−6a	−4	−1	0	+1	+5
Mar. 1951	July 1952	−15	−17	−2	_b	−2	0	−1	−4	−12	_b	−7	−8	−2	0	_b	_b
Mar. 1953	Aug. 1954	−12	−14	_b	−8	+2	0	+3	+2	_b	−11	0	−7	0	0	+6	+8
Feb. 1957	Apr. 1958	−28	−7	−17	0	0	0	+7	+5	−22	−7	−17	−3	−14	+1	+7	+7
Feb. 1960	Feb. 1961	−17	−10	−10	−2	−9	0	+2	+2	−15	−8	−10	−2	−8	0	+4	+10
May 1962	Oct. 1964	−13	−24	−5	−24	−3	0	+5	+2	−5	_b	−3	−28	_b	_b	_b	_b
June 1966	Oct. 1967	−19	−13	−5	−10	0	0	+3	+1	_b	−9	−3	−8	+4	−3	+7	0
Mar. 1969	Nov. 1970	−17	−15	+2	−2	0	0	+5	+19	−17	−13	−2	0	+7	0	+7	+15
Mar. 1973	Mar. 1975	−9	−7	−1	0	+17	0	+17	+20	−13	−6	−1	−1	+8	0	+18	+21
Mean		−16	−13	−6	−6	+1	0	+5	+5	−14	−10	−5	−7	−1	0	+7	+9
Standard Deviation		6	5	6	8	7	0	5	8	6	3	5	8	7	1	5	7

Note: The 1950 list indexes were trend-adjusted by the phase-average method. The 1975 list indexes were trend-adjusted by eliminating the "target trend," 0.282 percent per month.

a Measured from highest value in available data, which begin in January 1948.

b No corresponding cyclical turn.

CHANGES IN THE INDICATOR SYSTEM
SINCE 1950

Strictly speaking, only three of the twenty-one indicators selected by the NBER in 1950 are among the twenty-two indicators selected by the Commerce Department in 1975. They are the average workweek in manufacturing, which is a leading indicator in both lists, and non-farm employment and industrial production, which are coincident indicators in both lists (see Table 24–8). Many of the remaining series in the two lists, however, are substantially equivalent in terms of the concept represented. Indeed, by the criterion of substantial equivalence, all of the leading indicators in the 1950 list are represented in the 1975 list. In the coincident and lagging groups there is more variation between the two lists.

The principal changes in the 1975 list are as follows:

1. Most of the series in the 1975 list are in deflated form. Although there are occasions or purposes for which current dollar value series are important, in times of rapid inflation it is useful to distinguish physical from nominal changes. This was not done systematically when the 1950 list was constructed.

2. The series on new orders and contracts for plant and equipment, constructed initially by Victor Zarnowitz,[15] is an improvement over the two series in the 1950 list that overlap it in content—new orders for durable goods and contracts for commercial and industrial construction. The new series can be better matched conceptually with plant and equipment investment expenditures. The idea for such a series, however, was put forward in the report on indicators by Mitchell and Burns in 1938.

3. The series on net business formation, which takes into account both the formation of new firms and the discontinuance of existing firms, improves upon the two series in the 1950 list that are related to it—new incorporations and liabilities of business failures. The failure series, however, possesses some value in its own right because of its bearing on profits, which are not represented at all in the 1975 list (see below).

4. Personal income and retail sales, both of which were used in current value form in the 1950 list and classified as lagging indicators, are deflated and otherwise modified in the 1975 list and classified as coincident. Transfer payments such as social security and unemployment benefits are omitted from personal income in the 1975 series. Since some types of transfer payments move in a countercyclical manner and the total has been growing rapidly, personal

Table 24-8. Comparison of the 1950 and 1975 Lists of Leading, Coincident, and Lagging Indicators.

BCD No.	Original Series in 1950 List	BCD No.	Corresponding or New Series in 1975 List

Leading Group

BCD No.	Original Series in 1950 List	BCD No.	Corresponding or New Series in 1975 List
1.	Average workweek, manufacturing	1.	Same
	* * *	3.	Layoff rate, manufacturing
6.	New orders, durable goods, value	8.	New orders for consumer goods and materials, in 1972 dollars
	* * *	32.	Vendor performance
13.	New incorporations, number	12.	Net business formation
9.	Commercial and industrial building contracts, floor space	20.	Contracts and orders for plant and equipment, in 1972 dollars
n.a.	Residential building contracts, floor space	29.	New building permits, private housing units, number
	* * *	36.	Net change in inventories on hand and on order, in 1972 dollars
n.a.	Wholesale price index, twenty-eight basic commodities	92.	Change in sensitive prices
n.a.	Dow-Jones index of industrial common stock prices	19.	Standard and Poor's index of 500 common stock prices
14.	Liabilities of business failures		* * *
	* * *	104.	Percent change in liquid assets
	* * *	105.	Money supply (M_1), in 1972 dollars

Roughly Coincident Group

BCD No.	Original Series in 1950 List	BCD No.	Corresponding or New Series in 1975 List
41.	Employment in nonagricultural establishments	41.	Same
37.	Unemployment, number of persons		* * *
16.	Corporate profits after taxes		* * *
n.a.	Bank debits outside New York	57.	Manufacturing and trade sales, in 1972 dollars
47.	Industrial production index	47.	Same
200.	Gross national product		* * *
335.	Wholesale price index, industrial commodities		* * *
	* * *	51.	Personal income less transfer payments, in 1972 dollars

Lagging Group

BCD No.	Original Series in 1950 List	BCD No.	Corresponding or New Series in 1975 List
223.	Personal income, value		* * *
54.	Retail sales, value		* * *
66.	Consumer installment debt, value	95.	Ratio, consumer installment debt to personal income
	* * *	72.	Commercial and industrial loans outstanding
67.	Bank rates on business loans	109.	Prime rate charged by banks
n.a.	Manufacturers' inventories, book value	70.	Manufacturing and trade inventories, in 1972 dollars
	* * *	91.	Average duration of unemployment
	-	62.	Labor cost per unit of output, manufacturing

n.a.: Not available.

Source: See note to Table 24-2.

income exclusive of transfer payments has wider cyclical movements and closer conformity to the business cycle. This treatment, of course, does not mean that the broader concept of income is not useful or indeed more relevant in analyzing income-consumption relationships. Retail sales are combined with manufacturers' and wholesalers' sales in a comprehensive series on the physical volume of trade in the 1975 list. This aggregate had not been constructed in 1950, although the series on bank debits was often used to represent the total volume of trade.

5. The 1975 list contains only monthly series, whereas the 1950 list included three quarterly series—corporate profits, gross national product, and bank rates on business loans (the bank rate series became available monthly only in 1977). The omission of quarterly series is both an advantage and a disadvantage. As a component of a monthly composite index, a quarterly series must be interpolated to be included, and as a rule the figures will not be as up to date as the monthly series. Hence the index will be subject to revision when the quarterly figures become available, and in any case the interpolation is an arbitrary procedure. On the other hand, the exclusion of quarterly series may mean the omission of a significant economic variable. Probably the most serious omission in the 1975 list is profits. GNP is partly represented by other series in the coincident group, and bank rates are reflected in the prime rate, which is the monthly series included in the 1975 list.

6. No series on inventory change was included in the 1950 list of leading indicators, whereas the 1975 list includes the change in inventories on hand and on order. In view of the importance of inventory change as a factor in business cycles, this is clearly a major improvement. Of note, also, is the inclusion of the change in the volume of goods on order, following the work of Ruth Mack and others.[16] From the buyer's point of view, outstanding orders must be considered part of the available inventory and subject to close control through the placement or cancellation of orders. Another series in the 1975 list that adds to the information on ease or tightness of market conditions is vendor performance, an indicator pertinent to the speed with which orders are being filled.

7. The 1975 list contains two series on the volume of means of payment—the money supply expressed in constant prices and the rate of change in liquid assets. Concepts of this sort have long had a place in business cycle theory, and interest in them has broadened since 1950. The deflated money supply (M_1) has fallen victim to obsolescence since 1975, however, as ways of economizing on the use of money have had substantial effects on its behavior. Hence the

inclusion of this indicator in the 1975 list has been a mixed blessing, and in 1979 it was replaced by a broader concept of money, M_2.

In addition to the improvements in the list of indicators available to analysts during the past quarter century, many new devices to aid the analyst have been developed. Seasonal adjustment is now routinely accomplished, thanks largely to the development by Julius Shiskin of a computer program for this purpose. Shiskin was also responsible for the development of the composite index as a method of summarizing the behavior of a group of indicators that are homogeneous with respect to cyclical behavior but heterogeneous with respect to unit of measurement.[17] Charlotte Boschan was largely responsible for devising computer programs that identify cyclical peaks and troughs in time series, that construct patterns of change in time series during successive periods of recession or of recovery, and that measure long-run trends and growth cycles.[18] These aids to analysis have been of enormous value in providing prompt, relevant, comparable, and readily understood measures of economic performance. Without these aids the various publications that present current information on the state of the business cycle, such as *Business Conditions Digest* in the United States, *Japanese Economic Indicators* in Japan, and *Economic Trends* in the United Kingdom, would be far less instructive than they are.

FUTURE DEVELOPMENTS IN INDICATOR ANALYSIS

Public attention to economic indicators and their analysis in the United States as well as in other countries is widespread and growing. Part of the credit for this belongs to the government publications just mentioned, as well as to the news columns, magazine articles, TV coverage, and numerous private reports on the business outlook. Part belongs to the improvements in the quality, relevance, coverage, and timeliness of statistics pertaining to the economy. Credit must also be given to the continuing research effort devoted to the analysis of economic indicators. Without such research, any system of indicators would soon become obsolete and fall into disrepute.

But the fundamental fact that both justifies and sustains the public attention to economic indicator analysis is the continuity in the cyclical behavior and interrelationships of economic variables. We can learn and have learned from the past. The business cycle experience of the United States before World War II has proved a useful guide to business cycles since then. It is this historical continuity that underlies the basic and persistent consistency in the behavior of a set of indicators during the twenty-five years since they were selected. No one could be certain of this behavior in 1950. Only by looking back is it easy to see both the continuity and the significant changes.

Today we can no more foresee the future of economic indicator analysis than we could in 1950. We can, however, confidently predict that it will be useful to keep abreast of changes in economic behavior and to keep devising and testing new methods of analysis. Research along these lines has paid good dividends in the past and probably will do so in the future. As new ideas and new findings are generated by research, they can be applied to the current scene, spurring interest and broadening understanding.

Two relatively recent developments suggest some directions that this research might take. One is the application of indicators on a global scale. Researchers in many countries are pursuing active research programs that apply the techniques of indicator analysis to data for their own country. Application to the analysis of foreign trade flows is in its infancy, but the infant shows promise. Application to the analysis of the external markets of the developing nations, as well as to internal aspects of their economies, is also in its infancy, but the infant is alive and well. Two international agencies— the Organization for Economic Cooperation and Development in Paris and the European Economic Community in Brussels—are starting to develop expertise in indicator analysis, and this may encourage a wider research effort among their member countries and elsewhere.

The second recent development is the application of indicator analysis to the subject of inflation. Swings in the rate of inflation have not attracted the sustained attention of researchers to the same extent that business cycles have. The interest has been more episodic, associated with periods of wartime inflation, hyperinflation, crisis, and panic. Perhaps the present period of inflation is merely another episode, but even if it proves to be such, the application of indicator analysis to the process of inflation will add to public understanding of it.

Chronologies of the rate of inflation, constructed for different countries by methods similar to those used in constructing business cycle chronologies, have much to teach about where and when inflation is subsiding or accelerating. One of the lessons, for example, is that none of the major industrial countries of the West has experienced a decline in its rate of inflation without also undergoing, at about the same time, a slowdown or recession in real economic growth. Studies of the types of prices, costs, or other factors that are most sensitive to or influential in the process of inflation may yield leading indicators of inflation analogous to the leading indicators of business cycles. One of the more obvious bits of evidence attesting to the need for a wider appreciation of such inflation indicators is simply this: the record of economic forecasts of inflation reveals a distinct lag in the forecasts relative to the actual rate of inflation.[19] In part, at least, this lag may be attributable to the fact that forecasters have concentrated too much of their attention upon variables such as capacity utilization rates that do not have a good record in leading or anticipating the rate of inflation. There seems to be no inherent reason why price forecasts should be more susceptible to lags than, say, output forecasts. Yet they have been. The construction of a system of inflation indicators similar to the system that already exists for output may help to improve the record of inflation forecasts.

Extension of the indicator approach on a global scale and its extension to the problem of inflation are but two of the directions requiring research effort. Many other problems, small and large, demand attention. A fully "deflated" set of indicators has not been developed; a satisfactory monthly price-cost ratio is needed; a comprehensive monthly series on credit extensions is not available; measures of the money supply have been suffering from obsolescence; and so on. New methods of seasonal adjustment that require less revision when additional data become available must be tested. "Index models" and "stage of process models" that combine the indicator and econometric approaches may make both more fruitful. If these and other researches prosper, there may be less resemblance between the indicator system forty years hence and the present system than there is between the present system and the one devised when Mitchell and Burns began their work forty-two years ago.

NOTES TO CHAPTER 24

1. Wesley C. Mitchell and Arthur F. Burns, *Statistical Indicators of Cyclical Revivals*, Bulletin 69 (New York: National Bureau of Economic Research, 1938). Reprinted in Moore, *Business Cycle Indicators*, 1961.
2. Ibid.
3. Geoffrey H. Moore, *Statistical Indicators of Cyclical Revivals and Recessions*, Occasional Paper 31 (New York: National Bureau of Economic Research, 1950).
4. Geoffrey H. Moore, ed., *Business Cycle Indicators* (New York: National Bureau of Economic Research, 1961); and Geoffrey H. Moore and Julius Shiskin, *Indicators of Business Expansions and Contractions*, Occasional Paper 103 (New York: National Bureau of Economic Research, 1967).

5. Victor Zarnowitz and Charlotte Boschan, "Cyclical Indicators: An Evaluation and New Leading Indicators," *Business Conditions Digest* (U.S. Department of Commerce), May 1975; and Victor Zarnowitz and Charlotte Boschan, "New Composite Indexes of Coincident and Lagging Indicators," *Business Conditions Digest*, November 1975.

6. Moore, *Business Cycle Indicators*, pp. 52–53.

7. The most nearly comparable set of indexes for the pre-1938 period is in Julius Shiskin, *Signals of Recession and Recovery*, Occasional Paper 77 (New York: National Bureau of Economic Research, 1961), pp. 50, 54. The leading and coincident indexes cover 1919–1940, the lagging index 1929–1949. However, the components do not precisely match the 1950 list of indicators. Another compilation, covering the eight leading and eight roughly coincident series in the 1950 list, 1919–1954, is in the form of diffusion indexes (percent of series rising). See Moore, *Business Cycle Indicators*, pp. 270, 272.

8. The exceptions are at the December 1969 peak, where the coincident index has a longer lead than the leading index, and the November 1973 peak, where the coincident and lagging indexes lag by the same number of months.

9. The correlation coefficient between time and the adjusted leads at peaks (column 3 minus column 9) is +0.28; at troughs (column 4 minus column 10), +0.18; and at peaks and troughs together, +0.13. Hence the trend accounts for a very small, statistically insignificant portion of the variation. Nevertheless, the coefficients have the expected positive sign.

10. The correlation coefficients between time and the adjusted leads at peaks (Table 24-2, column 3 minus Table 24-4, column 9) is +0.73; at troughs, +0.56; at peaks and troughs together, +0.64.

11. See Chapter 6 of this book.

12. Geoffrey H. Moore, "Economic Indicator Analysis during 1969–1972," in *Nations and Households in Economic Growth*, Paul David and Melvin Reder, eds. (New York: Academic Press, 1974); and Geoffrey H. Moore, "Slowdowns, Recessions and Inflation," *Explorations in Economic Research* 2, no. 2 (Spring 1975).

13. Victor Zarnowitz and Beatrice Vaccara, "How Good Are the Leading Indicators?" *1977 Proceedings of the Business and Economic Statistics Section* (American Statistical Association, 1977); and Chapter 5 of the first edition.

14. For additional references, see Chapter 23.

15. Victor Zarnowitz, *Orders, Production, and Investment: A Cyclical and Structural Analysis* (New York: National Bureau of Economic Research, 1973).

16. Ruth P. Mack, *Information, Expectations, and Inventory Fluctuation: A Study of Materials Stock on Hand and on Order* (New York: National Bureau of Economic Research, 1967).

17. Shiskin, *Signals of Recession and Recovery*.

18. Gerhard Bry and Charlotte Boschan, *Cyclical Analysis of Time Series: Selected Procedures and Computer Programs* (New York: National Bureau of Economic Research, 1971).

19. See Chapters 11 and 26 of this book.

Chapter 25

Forecasting Short-Term Economic Change

Economic statisticians do not enjoy an untarnished reputation for accurate forecasting. We have managed, over the years, to come up with some memorable failures. While we have also had our share of successes, they are not as well remembered or as numerous as we should like. Recently, however, we have begun to pay more attention to the record, and a substantial body of evidence on forecasting performance has accumulated. In this chapter I propose to review this record, to try to arrive at a balanced appraisal, and to offer some suggestions for improvement.

To put the economic forecasters among our members in a properly humble mood, let me cite a few of the incidents that have cast doubt on our forecasting abilities. Back in 1929, few economists were pessimistic about the outlook, and fewer still were as pessimistic as would have been appropriate in view of the Depression that left the nation prostrate. One of the statistical casualties was a system of forecasting known as the Harvard *ABC* curves, developed in the 1920s by Warren Persons—a former president of this Association—and others, including a young man who was destined to become our next president, Ross Eckler. The three curves—*A* representing speculative activity—

Presidential address delivered at the 128th Annual Meeting of the American Statistical Association, August 21, 1968, Pittsburgh, Pennsylvania. I am greatly indebted to Arthur F. Burns, Solomon Fabricant, Milton Friedman, Ruth P. Mack, John R. Meyer, and Julius Shiskin for comments on an earlier draft. For statistical assistance I am obliged to Charlotte Boschan, Dorothy O'Brien, and the late Sophie Sakowitz.

Reprinted from the *Journal of the American Statistical Association* 64 (March 1969): 1-22.

that is, stock prices; *B* measuring business activity; and *C* reflecting monetary ease or tightness—were used in formulating periodic reports on the business outlook. Historical studies of the pre–World War I period had shown that series of the *A* type tended to move early in the business cycle, the *B* type next, and the *C* type last, with the lagging upturns in the *C* series preceding downturns in the *A* type. The economic logic of the sequence was that tight money and high interest rates led to a decline in the prospects for business expansion and a drop in stock prices, whereupon businessmen cut back or postponed their commitments for further expansion, causing a recession in business activity. This in turn led to an easing of money and lower interest rates, which eventually improved business prospects, whereupon stock prices turned up, then business activity, and finally interest rates again in a new round.

Such, in brief, was the theory. In the depression of 1920–1921 the Harvard economists had some success in applying it. But in 1929 they maintained an optimistic view and failed to foresee either the downturn or the debacle. This failure dealt a death blow to the *ABC* curves as an influential forecasting scheme—a fate that was not altogether deserved, as I shall note.

A second prominent forecasting failure occurred in 1945, at the end of World War II. The expected curtailment of military spending and the return of soldiers to the civilian labor force led many economists to predict a serious postwar depression and mass unemployment. They failed to anticipate adequately the resilience of the private economy, the power of the pent-up demand for consumer goods, and the wherewithal provided by accumulated liquid assets. Certain econometric models were among the casualties. Based on relationships that fitted the prewar period, they were unable to cope with the transition from a war to a peacetime economy. The reputation of model builders suffered a setback from this failure. Nevertheless, they displayed a resilience that rivaled that of the economy itself and quickly shook off any sense of defeat, while striving to learn from the experience. Model building has since become a flourishing industry.

The next failure on my list is dated 1948–1949. Late in 1948 signs of a recession began to appear, but there were also signs of inflation. President Truman and his Council of Economic Advisers concentrated their attention on the inflationary threat. It failed to materialize, while the recession did. This forecasting failure found the government, during the first half of 1949, fighting the wrong war.

Another significant delay in recognizing the onset of recession occurred in 1957. The Federal Reserve Board failed to foresee the recession that began in midsummer, continued its policy of restraint by raising the discount rate in August, and began to take antirecessionary measures only in November. Again, as in 1949, the forecasters were concerned about inflation when the problem was recession. In 1965, on the other hand, a forecasting error of the opposite kind occurred. Administration economists failed to foresee the powerful inflationary pressures that were developing and urged policies that would continue to stimulate aggregate demand.

These are some of the better known exhibits from the economic forecaster's chamber of horrors—or should I say errors.[2] They reveal fallibility and the need to strive for better results, but they also demonstrate the importance of forecasting in guiding public policy. At the same time, these examples present a one-sided picture. We need a fairer and more systematic review, indeed, a statistical review, of forecasting performance.

Some work recently undertaken at the National Bureau of Economic Research provides a basis for such an appraisal. This is not, of course, the first such effort. The work of Cox [2] in the 1920s and the more recent studies of Okun [9], Stekler [11, 12], Suits [13], Theil [14, 15], and others have contributed to our knowledge of the validity of general economic forecasts. But the National Bureau study has produced a new and more extensive body of data of this sort, reflecting the great proliferation of forecasting activity in recent years.[1]

TURNING POINT FORECASTS

The National Bureau's collection of short-term general economic forecasts pertains largely to the period since World War II. It covers various economic aggregates such as gross national product and its major components, industrial production, employment, unemployment, and price levels, as well as business cycle turning points. The forecasts were made by economists in private business and financial firms, in government agencies, and in universities and research institutions. Some of the forecasts have been regularly published and widely disseminated; others were limited to private use. The record provides materials for analyses of the frequency and magnitude of error, of the factors contributing to error, and of the potential value of techniques for reducing error. It can also be used to analyze the ways in which forecasts or expectations are formed and how the phenomenon of forecasting itself contributes both to the generation of business cycles and to their amelioration.

I shall refer to only a small part of this record, both for lack of time and because studies of it are still under way. First, let us consider what it tells about the forecasting and recognition of business cycle turning points. Suppose the objective of the forecaster is to foresee reversals in the direction of change in the annual level of gross national product—that is, to determine whether GNP will decline between this year and the next if it has been going up or whether it will rise if it has been going down. Such reversals in annual data are not frequent, but when they do occur, it is important to know about them since a downturn may mean the onset of a recession and an upturn the beginning of recovery.[2]

Victor Zarnowitz has assembled the record of 126 such forecasts made toward the end of the calendar year for the year ahead, mostly covering the period 1953 to 1963.[3] If the forecasts had accurately predicted the first official estimates of GNP made immediately after the year being forecast, there would have been forty-three turning point predictions or about one for every three forecasts. In fact, thirty-four turning point predictions were made or about one for every four forecasts. This is better, of course, than assuming that next year will always produce a turning point; it is better than the almost equally naive assumption that gross national product is a series of random numbers (in which case approximately eighty-four turning points would have been forecast); it is better than the slightly more sophisticated assumption that the change in GNP is random (which would have produced about sixty-three turning points); and of course it is better than assuming that no turning point would occur at all.[4] In short, the performance is clearly better than pure guesswork.

The forecasters not only had some success in predicting the total number of turning points, but were also fairly successful in judging when the turns would occur. Of the forty-three turning points that should have been forecast, thirty-two were predicted and only eleven were missed. Of the thirty-four forecasts that turning points would occur, only three were in error. Hence there were only fourteen turning point errors, which is a record of 89 percent accuracy in identifying years that would mark reversals in the movement of GNP. Table 25-1 gives these results in the form of a contingency table, together with some measures of association and a test of significance.[5]

Table 25-1.   Forecasts of Turning Points in Gross National Product, Annual Data, 1947–1965.

1. Forecast Made Near End of Preceding Year

		Forecast		
		No TP	TP	Total
Actual	No TP	80.5 (60.3)	2.5 (22.7)	83
	TP	11 (31.2)	32 (11.8)	43
	Total	91.5	34.5	126

Correct forecasts as percentage of
all forecast turning points (C_1) = 93 (34)
all actual turning points (C_2) = 74 (27)
all years covered (C_3) = 89 (57)
Cross product ration (α) = 93.7
Correlation coefficient (r) = 0.76
x^2 = 72.8
$p < 0.001$

2. Forecast Made Near Middle of Preceding Year

		Forecast		
		No TP	TP	Total
Actual	No TP	6 (5.1)	2 (2.9)	8
	TP	3 (3.9)	3 (2.1)	6
	Total	9	5	14

C_1 = 60 (42)
C_2 = 50 (35)
C_3 = 64 (51)
α = 3.0
r = 0.26
x^2 = 0.95
p = 0.33

Note: Forecasts or actual observations of no change are counted as half turning point and half no turning point. Figures in parentheses are the expected values on the assumption of independence and fixed marginal totals.

Source: Victor Zarnowitz, "The Record of Turning Point Forecasts of GNP and Other Major Aggregate," National Bureau of Economic Research (draft manuscript).

While economists can take heart from this performance, it must be recalled that these are forecasts for the ensuing year made in the late autumn or early winter. The turning point, which in annual data is conventionally dated at midyear, is then actually past. That is to say, if at the end of 1968 a GNP forecast showed 1969 to be lower than 1968, 1968 would be the turning point, but the year would be over. Late autumn is the season of the year when most forecasting is done; records of forecasts made earlier in the year are less abundant. The compilation of fourteen annual forecasts made near the middle of the year for the calendar year ahead presents a very different picture (panel 2 of Table 25-1). Six turning points should have been predicted and five were, but the timing was poor. Of the six turns that should have been forecast, three were not, and of the five predicted turns, two were false signals. The five turning point errors produce an accuracy score of only 64 percent, compared with 89 percent for the forecasts made near the end of the year. This is just barely better than guesswork.

Forecasts made in midyear must, of course, predict the rest of the current year as well as the next. In effect, these forecasts are prepared at about the time of the turn, insofar as it can be dated from annual observations. In terms of the monthly dates of business cycle turns in the postwar period, three occurred before midyear, two were in July, and three after July. The record of annual forecasts, therefore, suggests that those made shortly before or shortly after the monthly turn have not been very successful, while those made a few months later have been quite successful.

Zarnowitz' materials on annual turning point forecasts of other variables yield another interesting conclusion bearing on this point. It is that the accuracy of forecasts is greater for variables that lag in the business cycle than for those that move coincidentally or lead. Turning points in plant and equipment expenditures, which often lag, are forecast more accurately than those in inventory change, which generally lead. Consumer prices, which lag, are forecast more accurately than wholesale prices, which move more promptly. Hence the visibility of a turning point to a forecaster depends partly on how far ahead he looks and partly on whether the variable he is looking at moves earlier or later than others that he can observe and relate to it.

The National Bureau has assembled not only annual forecasts but also quarterly forecasts for several quarters ahead. These provide an additional test of forecasters' ability, since turns can be dated with greater precision from quarterly than from annual data. Quarterly forecasts of turning points depend, in the first instance, on forecasts of direction change. How well, then have forecasters predicted the direction of change in GNP between the current quarter and the next, between that quarter and the one beyond it, and so on? A compilation of nearly fifty forecasts of this type (Table 25-2) suggests that forecasters are well aware that GNP generally increases from one quarter to the next, but possess little ability to predict when declines are coming. For example, out of thirty-eight predicted increases from the current quarter to the next, three-fourths turned out to be correct, while only a third of the nine predicted declines were correct. The combined percentage of correct forecasts—68 percent—is not much better than one would expect if forecasters knew approximately how often declines would occur, but tossed a coin to decide when they would take place. As for quarterly changes still farther in the future, the forecasters seldom predicted declines at all, and when they did, showed no ability to pick the right occasions.

The record for forecasts of semiannual GNP data (from a different group of forecasters) is somewhat better. This is shown in the semiannual Section B of Table 25-2. Ninety percent of the predicted increases and 44 percent of the predicted declines from one half-year to the next proved correct, for a combined percentage accuracy of 73 percent. From the next half-year to the one following that, the accuracy drops to 62 percent, which is not much better than random.

The data as a whole suggest that forecasters have yet to establish their ability to detect turning points in aggregate economic activity well in advance of the event. What they do demonstrate is an ability to recognize turns at about the time or shortly after they occur.[6]

Another type of turning point record has been compiled by Rendigs Fels and C. Elton Hinshaw [4]. Fels developed a system for scoring statements about the business outlook that he applied to the writings of analysts that regularly appear in certain widely read business or financial journals. Hinshaw applied the same system to the statements on the outlook recorded in the minutes of the regular meetings of the Federal Reserve Board's Open Market Committee. Figure 25-1 summarizes part of their results, in terms of the probability, as indicated by the statements, that a turning point soon will be, or has already been reached.

The figure shows, first, that there is a clear improvement in the ability to forecast or recognize a turn as the date of an actual turn approaches and further improvement after it passes. Second, the record is better at troughs than at peaks—perhaps indicating an optimistic bias or maybe that troughs are easier to predict and recognize. Third, the Open Market Committee—the group in whose hands the monetary policy of the nation largely rests—did slightly better than

Table 25-2. Forecasts of Directions of Change in Gross National Product, Quarterly and Semiannual Data, 1947–1964.

A. Forecasts of Quarter-to-Quarter Changes, 1959–1963

| | 0–3 Months | | | 3–6 Months | | | 6–9 Months | | |
| | Forecast | | | Forecast | | | Forecast | | |
	Rise	Fall	Total	Rise	Fall	Total	Rise	Fall	Total
Actual Rise	29 (28.3)	6 (6.7)	35	34 (33.8)	5 (5.2)	39	30.5 (31.0)	2 (1.5)	32.5
Actual Fall	9 (9.7)	3 (2.3)	12	5 (5.2)	1 (0.8)	6	11.5 (11)	0 (0.5)	11.5
Total	38	9	47	39	6	45	42	2	44

0–3 Months:
C_3 = 68 (65)
α = 1.61
r = 0.09
x^2 = 0.38
p = 0.54

3–6 Months:
C_3 = 78 (77)
α = 1.36
r = 0.04
x^2 = 0.07
p = 0.79

6–9 Months:
C_3 = 69 (72)
α = 0
r = −0.13
x^2 = 0.74
p = 0.39

Table 25-2. continued

A. Forecasts of Quarter-to-Quarter Changes, 1959–1963

| | 9–12 Months | | | 12–15 Months | | | 15–18 Months | | |
| | *Forecast* | | | *Forecast* | | | *Forecast* | | |
	Rise	*Fall*	*Total*	*Rise*	*Fall*	*Total*	*Rise*	*Fall*	*Total*
Actual Rise	31 (31.1)	2 (1.7)	33	16.5	0	16.5	14	0	14
Actual Fall	5 (4.7)	0 (0)	5	6.5	0	16.5	2	0	2
Total	36	2	38	23	0	23	16	0	16

9–12 Months:
$C_3 = 82$ (82)
$\alpha = 0$
$r = -0.09$
$x^2 = 0.31$
$p = 0.58$

12–15 Months:
$C_3 = 72$ (72)
$\alpha = 0$
$r = 0$
$x^2 = 0$
$p = 1$

15–18 Months:
$C_3 = 88$ (88)
$\alpha = 0$
$r = 0$
$x^2 = 0$
$p = 1$

Table 25-2. continued

B. Forecasts of Semiannual Changes, 1947–1964

	0–6 Months			6–12 Months		
	Forecast			Forecast		
	Rise	Fall	Total	Rise	Fall	Total
Actual Rise	26 (22.6)	9 (12.4)	35	23 (22)	10 (11)	33
Actual Fall	3 (6.4)	7 (3)	10	7 (8)	5 (4)	12
Total	29	16	45	30	15	45

C_3 = 73 (58) C_3 = 62 (58)
α = 6.74 α = 1.64
r = 0.38 r = 0.11
χ^2 = 6.50 χ^2 = 0.54
p = 0.01 p = 0.46

Note: For definitions and source see Table 22–1. The span 0–3 months refers to the change from the current quarter to the one ending three months hence; 3–6 months refers to the change from the quarter ending three months hence to the one ending six months hence; etc.

Figure 25-1. Recognition Scores at Business Cycle Peaks and Troughs.

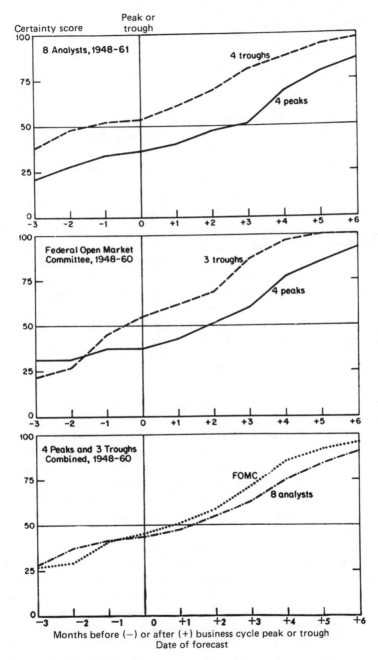

Source: Fels and Hinshaw [4].

the average of the business analysts. The committee's record in avoiding false signals—not shown in the figure—was markedly better than that of the analysts.

Finally, the Fels-Hinshaw study, like Zarnowitz', suggests that there is only a modest ability to anticipate turns. Before the date of the turn, the indicated probability attaching to the occurrence of a turning point averages less than 50 percent. A month or so after the turn it is still only a fifty-fifty proposition. The 75 percent level, or odds of three to one, is reached three or four months after the turn. Not until five or six months after the turn is there virtual certainty (nine to one odds) regarding the event.

In view of the lags in the availability of data and the fact that major economic indicators rarely reach their turns at the same time, this is not necessarily poor performance. Moreover, recognizing a turn in the business cycle a few months after the event does imply some ability to forecast. One must not only be aware of the change in the direction of movement of aggregate economic activity that is taking place, but also judge its likely magnitude and duration. Recognizing business recessions is not the same as recognizing every wiggle on the curve. Major, lasting movements must be distinguished from minor interruptions of the trend. The evidence collected shows that forecasters have achieved some success, if not in anticipating the turn, at least in recognizing it rather promptly.

FORECASTING MAGNITUDES

Most forecasters regard the prediction of turning points as one of the significant challenges in their work. It is easy enough, they say, to anticipate continuing growth. The crucial test comes at the turning point. That is why I began this review by examining turning point forecasts. On the other hand, it is also true that the chief concern of forecasters is not predicting turning points but predicting the magnitude of change.[7] True, predicting a turning point in the business cycle implies something about the magnitude of change. But this is not entirely satisfactory. Missing the turn of a mild recession, say in 1960, is not as serious as missing a 1929. Moreover, between 1961 and 1968 we have enjoyed a period without any business cycle turning points as commonly defined, so the only mark of a forecaster's skill in this respect was his ability to avoid characterizing the minor dips, notably in 1962 and 1966, as recessions. It behooves us, therefore, to look at the record of forecasts of magnitude of change.[8]

One of the most important such series of forecasts covers only the recent period of expansion. These are the forecasts prepared by the

Council of Economic Advisers and published each year beginning with January 1962 in the *Economic Report of the President.* The forecasts pertain to gross national product for the year ahead, in current and in constant prices, and the implicit price deflator, which is one of the broadest measures of the general price level. With respect to GNP in current prices the *Report* has been explicit. The forecast has been stated as the midpoint in a range of plus or minus $5 billion, which since 1962 has been roughly equivalent to plus or minus 0.75 percent of GNP. The *Report* has generally been less explicit with respect to the price level and real GNP, though when the numbers are not stated, the approximate rates of change implied in the forecast can be inferred. One of the conditions implicitly and often explicitly underlying the forecasts is that the President's budget and economic program will be enacted. Hence the forecasts should, strictly speaking, be judged only after taking account of the extent to which these conditions were met. The record in Table 25-3 does not, of course, do this.

During four of the six years when the forecasts can be compared with actual changes, the rate of price increase was underestimated, a tendency particularly marked in 1965-1966, as I noted earlier. On the other hand, the forecasts somewhat overestimated the rate of growth in real GNP. As a result, the average forecast change in current dollar GNP over the period as a whole was almost exactly right.

Nevertheless, the errors in individual years were not inconsequential. For each of the three variables, the errors, on the average, were roughly 20 to 25 percent of the mean rate of change. In five years out of six, the actual value of current dollar GNP fell outside the range within which it was considered likely to fall. A more reasonable range in the light of experience would have been about twice as large—namely, plus or minus one and one-half percentage points, which is plus or minus $12 billion at current levels of GNP. Even this wider margin of error would have been exceeded in two of the six years.

A common way of appraising a set of forecasts is to compare the results with what could have been achieved by some simple method of extrapolation. One such method is to assume that the change in the coming year will be the same as the change last year. The mean errors resulting from this procedure are shown in the table, and they exceed the mean forecast errors for current dollar and real GNP, but not for prices, where the simple extrapolation yields approximately the same results. There is reason to suppose that it should, since the *Report* has often stated its expectation regarding prices in terms of extending the recent trend. In 1965-1966 the forecast explicitly

Table 25-3. Forecasts of Annual Percentage Changes in Gross National Product and in the General Price Level, President's Economic Report, 1961–1968.

	Percentage Change								
	GNP in Current Dollars			GNP in Constant Dollars			GNP Implicit Price Deflator		
Year (1)	Forecast (2)	Actual (3)	Error (4)	Forecast (5)	Actual (6)	Error (7)	Forecast (8)	Actual (9)	Error (10)
1960–1961	—	3.3	—	—	1.8	—	—	1.5	—
1961–1962	9.4	6.7	2.7	8.0[a]	5.3	2.7	1.5[a]	1.4	0.1
1962–1963	4.4	5.4	−1.0	3.5[a]	3.8	−0.3	1.0[a]	1.5	−0.5
1963–1964	6.5	6.6	−0.1	5.0	4.7	0.3	1.5	1.9	−0.4
1964–1965	6.1	7.5	−1.4	4.0[a]	5.4	−1.4	2.0[a]	1.8	0.2
1965–1966	6.9	8.6	−1.7	5.0	5.4	−0.4	1.8	3.0	−1.2
1966–1967	6.4	5.6	+0.8	4.0	2.5	1.5	2.5	3.0	−0.5
1967–1968	7.8			4.3[a]			3.3[a]		
Mean, 1961–1967, disregarding sign	6.6	6.7	1.3	4.9	4.5	1.1	1.7	2.1	0.5
Mean error of extrapolating preceding year's change, 1961–1967			1.8			1.6			0.3
Correlation coefficient, forecast and actual			0.34			0.48			0.72
Correlation coefficient, actual and preceding year's actual			−0.04			−0.44			0.73

Source: Economic Report of The President, January 1962 through February 1968. The actual changes are based on the first official estimates given in the report following the year for which the forecast was made. Changes in constant dollar GNP and in the price deflator are based on estimates in 1954 dollars for 1960–1961 to 1961–1965 and in 1958 dollars thereafter.
[a]Inferred from statements in the report. All other entries are based on figures (dollar levels, dollar changes, or percentage changes) given in the report.

extrapolated the preceding year's change and thereby made its largest error. This extrapolative method applied to annual data will, of course, always be a year late in recognizing an acceleration in the rate of inflation or in anything else.

The GNP forecasts in the President's *Economic Report* achieved a positive correlation with subsequent actual changes, which again is superior to the simple extrapolation of last year's change, since the latter was if anything inversely correlated with the actual change. But the correlation attained by the forecasts is modest. By this measure (that is r^2) the forecasts account for only a small fraction of the variance in actual rates of change—12 percent for GNP in current dollars and 23 percent for GNP in constant dollars. (For a more recent analysis of this record, see Chapter 26.)

I turn next to some other forecasting records. The mean error of forecasting the annual rate of change in gross national product by various groups of economists, according to eight sets of records assembled by Zarnowitz, is set forth in Table 25–4. The records begin generally in 1952 or 1953 and extend through 1963 (more recent figures are available but have not yet been incorporated in summaries). Most of these mean errors range between one and one-half and two and one-half percentage points, and hence are consistently larger than those of the *Economic Report*. However, the period covered is

Table 25–4.   Summary Measures of Error in a Collection of Business Forecasts of Annual Percentage Changes in Gross National Product in Current Dollars.

Forecast Set (1)	Month Forecasts Made (2)	Period Covered (3)	Mean Absolute Error (percent) (4)	Correlation Coefficient, Forecast and Actual Change (5)
B	October	1952–1963	1.9	0.73
D	October	1955–1963	1.7	0.75
E	October	1952–1963	3.0	0.58
A	November–December	1953–1963	2.3[a]	0.79[a]
H	October–January	1953–1963	2.2	0.81
C	November–January	1957–1963	1.9	0.80
F	January	1952–1963	1.4	0.90
G	January	1952–1963	1.6	0.84
Mean, 8 sets			2.0	0.78

Source: Victor Zarnowitz, unpublished tabulations. For descriptions of the samples of forecasts covered and analysis of the results, see Zarnowitz [16].
[a]The figures for the period 1946–49, 1953–1963, for columns 4 and 5, respectively, are 4.0 and 0.19.

different. The records in Table 25-4 encompass three recessions and hence about twice as wide a range of variation in the rates of change to be forecast. Or, to put it somewhat differently, the errors involved in a simple extrapolation of the preceding year's rate of change were about twice as great, on the average, during 1952–1963 as during 1961–1967. Relative to the variation with which the forecasters were faced, therefore, the forecasts in the *Economic Report* do not represent as good a performance as that achieved by most of the forecasting groups in Zarnowitz' sample. This is indicated more directly by the correlation coefficients, which range from 0.6 to 0.9 in Table 25-4 compared with 0.3 in Table 25-3. The collection of forecasts in Table 25-4, therefore, though they made larger errors, captured a substantially larger fraction of the variation in rates of change in GNP than did the forecasts in the *Economic Report*. Unfortunately, we have not yet checked this result by a direct comparison covering the same period, which is necessary if the forecasting hazards are to be matched precisely (See Chapter 26).[9]

Another forecasting record where such a check can be made is shown in Table 25-5. This pertains to forecasts of the annual rate of change in GNP in constant dollars rather than in current dollars and is based on the econometric model originally formulated by Lawrence Klein and Arthur Goldberger and subsequently developed by Daniel Suits.[10] The forecasts have been presented in November of each year at the Conference on the Business Outlook at the University of Michigan.

During the six years, 1961–1967, the errors in the Suits' model forecasts were larger than those in the *Economic Report* in four years and smaller in two, with the mean error exactly the same. The model forecasts and the *Report* forecasts were quite closely correlated with each other, though the correlation between forecast and actual change was somewhat smaller for the model than for the *Economic Report*. However, this difference cannot be given much weight because the sample period is short.

In the earlier period, 1952–1963, as well as in the period 1952–1967 as a whole, the model forecasts were much more highly correlated with the actual changes than during the past six years, though the mean error was somewhat larger. Both the higher correlation and the larger error may be due to the fact that the variability in rates of change in real GNP was substantially larger in the earlier period. In any event, both in the earlier period and more recently the model forecasts have been substantially better than those of a simple extrapolation of preceding year changes. For the fifteen year period as a whole, the model reduced the error of extrapolation by more than

Table 25-5. Forecasts of Annual Percentage Changes in Gross National Product in Constant Dollars, Suits' Econometric Model, 1952–1968.

| Year (1) | Percentage Change, GNP in Constant Dollars | | |
	Forecast (2)	Actual (3)	Error (4)
1951–1952	—	2.1	—
1952–1953	4.8	3.7	1.1
1953–1954	−2.6	−3.1	0.5
1954–1955	0.4 (−0.3, +0.1, +1.4)	6.2	−5.8
1955–1956	2.5	2.5	0
1956–1957	2.3	0.8	1.5
1957–1958	0.1 (−0.6, 0.4, 0.5)	−3.1	3.2
1958–1959	5.3	6.7	−1.4
1959–1960	0.7 (−0.6, 2.0)	2.7	−2.0
1960–1961	1.9 (1.6, 2.2)	1.8	0.1
1961–1962	5.2	5.3	−0.1
1962–1963	3.0 (3.0, 5.4)	3.8	−0.8
1963–1964	4.9 (2.7, 4.9)	4.7	0.2
1964–1965	3.3	5.4	−2.1
1965–1966	4.0	5.4	−1.4
1966–1967	4.3	2.5	1.8
1967–1968	4.6 (3.4, 5.1, 5.3)		

Summary

	1952–1963	1961–1967	1952–1967
1. Mean, disregarding sign			
a. Forecast percentage change	2.6	4.1	3.0
b. Actual percentage change	3.6	4.5	3.8
c. Error in forecast	1.5	1.1	1.5
d. Error in extrapolating preceding year's change	4.2	1.6	3.4
2. Correlation coefficient			
a. Forecast and actual percentage change	.72	.12	.71
b. Actual and preceding year's actual percentage change	−.37	−.44	−.20

Source: Forecast percentage changes are computed from published reports of the Michigan Conference on the Economic Outlook and data supplied by the University of Michigan Research Seminar in Quantitative Economics. Alternative forecasts based upon different data or policy assumptions are given in parentheses. For 1962–1963 and 1963–1964 we use the alternative corresponding to the policy adopted (the 1964 tax cut); for other years we use a simple average. Actual percentage changes are based on the first official estimates given in the *Economic Report of the President* for the year following the year for which the forecast was made. Forecast and actual changes are based on estimates in 1939 prices for 1951-1956, in 1947 prices for 1956-1957, in 1954 prices for 1959-1965, in 1957 prices for 1957-1958, and in 1958 prices for 1958-1959 and 1965-1968.

50 percent and had a mean error of about one and one-half percentage points and correlation between forecast and actual rates of change in real GNP of 0.7. The record was marred especially by the forecast for 1954–1955, which substantially underestimated the rate of expansion actually experienced. Excluding this one year, the mean error would have been approximately one percentage point and the correlation 0.9. Although a direct comparison with the collection of forecasts in Table 25-4 is not possible, since the latter refer to current dollar GNP, where somewhat larger errors might be expected because of the difficulty of forecasting prices, the model forecasts appear to stand up comparatively well.[11]

I conclude that it is reasonable to expect, on the basis of past performance, that economic forecasts made near the end of the year for the year ahead will predict the percentage rate of change in gross national product with an error averaging about one and one-half percentage points. One can expect, also, that the predicted rates of change will be positively, though far from perfectly, correlated with those that actually occur. In both respects this is a much better result than can be achieved by simply extrapolating last year's change in gross national product.

I cannot undertake to examine the results of forecasting the magnitudes of change in GNP by quarters, to consider how forecasting errors increase with the span of the forecast or with the distance of the forecast interval from the present, or to review the available data for other variables. These are fascinating topics, full of instruction for the practitioner as well as for the user of forecasts, but I pass them by in order to discuss standards of forecasting accuracy and ways to improve performance.

ACCURACY STANDARDS

The availability of a fairly systematic record of past forecasts of turning points and of magnitudes of change make it possible to formulate standards by which to judge future forecasts derived by new methods. The record tells us what it is reasonable to expect and what can be considered superior performance. One of the great merits of such a standard is that it has a realistic, historical basis, not a hypothetical one. Another is that it is not subject to the bias of hindsight.

Nevertheless, it does have several limitations. First, the past period may not be comparable with a future period with respect to ease or difficulty of forecasting. Although adjustments can be made for this, they cannot be entirely adequate. A second limitation is that the past forecasts are frequently conditional and the conditions may or may not have been met. A straightforward comparison with what happened, as in our appraisal above, either may not do justice to the forecasts or may treat them more favorably than they deserve, but in any case does not tell as much as we should like to know about what standards to apply to conditional forecasts in the future. A related point is that as the timeliness, power, and appropriateness of governmental actions based upon forecasts improves, the forecasts themselves may be negated. And as forecasts become more widely publicized and more uniform—witness the common phrase "standard forecast"—the reactions of private firms and individuals may place the forecasts in jeopardy or help to bring them about. A simple historical record of accuracy, then, may no longer provide an appropriate benchmark. Finally, a standard based upon the past record may not provide a proper stimulus to improvement. We must seek to do better, not merely to equal our past achievements.

In this last respect, the standard provided by the past record seems to be an improvement over the so-called naive models or extrapolative methods. As we have seen, the record of most forecasters is superior to at least one of the naive models—the extrapolation of the most recent change. Recent work by Zarnowitz, Mincer, Theil, Cunnyngham, and others shows that this "same change" model is inferior to more sophisticated autoregressive models. But many sets of actual forecasts, at least for short periods ahead, beat even the best autoregressive models. In this sense the past record provides a higher standard, as well as a more realistic one.

Recently I have been experimenting with a standard, based upon leading indicators, that incorporates some elements of the historical and some of the extrapolative, and I should like to describe its properties briefly. First, a composite index of leading indicators—those that have generally reached their peaks and troughs at an earlier date than business activity as a whole—is constructed, using methods developed by Julius Shiskin [10]. It is then assumed, as suggested by past evidence, that this index leads various specific measures of aggregate economic activity—such as gross national product, industrial production, or employment—by six months. This implies that the percentage change between fiscal year averages of the leading index should be closely correlated with the percentage change between the subsequent calendar year averages of the aggregates. That is, the change in the leading index between the fiscal years ending June 30, 1967, and June 30. 1968, is associated with the calendar year change in GNP from 1967 to 1968, and so on. It turns out that on this basis, the percentage changes in the leading index, appropriately adjusted by a simple regression, provide fairly accurate estimates of the turning points and the percentage changes in calendar year data for GNP and other aggregates.

If we could wait until just after the middle of the calendar year to make our forecast for that year, by which time fiscal year averages for the leading index would be available, this method, would, in the postwar period, have provided forecasts correlated with the annual percentage changes in GNP to the extent of about 0.8, with an average error of something less than one and one-half percentage points. Unfortunately, forecasts must be made earlier than this. The simple device that we have resorted to is to use whatever part of the current fiscal year figure for the leading index is available as an estimate for the entire fiscal year. For example, if only the initial quarter (July, August, and September) is available because the forecast is being made, say, in October, the change between that quarter and the preceding fiscal year average is used as an estimate of the change between the full fiscal years. Since this in effect shortens the span over which the change is measured and at the same time increases the assumed lead to something like ten and one-half months instead of six, the regression adjustment needed to forecast calendar year changes in GNP is different than before. The mean error on this basis for the postwar period is approximately two percentage points and the correlation coefficient is 0.6.

As more data for the current fiscal year become available, they can be used to revise the forecast. In late January, for example, data for the first two quarters of the fiscal year could be used. We have calculated the forecasts for the postwar period on the alternative assumptions that one, two, three, or four quarters of data are used (this could also be done for successively larger groups of months instead of quarters, since the leading index is available monthly). The regression equations and summary measures of error are given in Table 25-6, for GNP in current and in constant dollars. The table shows how the correlation improves and the mean error is reduced as more recent data for the leading index are used in the forecast.[12]

Table 25-7 compares the actual forecasts referred to above with these results, making use of data on the leading index for only the initial quarter of the current fiscal year—that is, through September of the year preceding the one being forecast. For the most part, the forecasts of change in GNP based upon the leading index compare favorably in terms of magnitude of error and degree of correlation. The experiment suggests, therefore, that this mechanical use of the leading index can produce a standard of forecast accuracy which is not easy to surpass. I have shown previously a modification of this method and an application of it to foreign trade forecasting.[13]

Table 25-6. Regression Analysis of Annual Percentage Changes in Index
of Leading Indicators and in Gross National Product, 1951–1967.

| | *Dependent Variable* | | | | |
| | *Calendar Year Percentage Change in GNP in Current Dollars* | | | | |
Independent Variable	*r*	*a*	*b*	*t*	*MAE*
Leading index, per cent change[a]					
1. Fiscal year to III Q	0.62	4.19	0.44	2.98	1.84
2. Fiscal year to III + IV Q	0.76	3.95	0.42	4.39	1.47
3. Fiscal year to III + IV + I Q	0.82	3.79	0.37	5.42	1.29
4. Fiscal year to fiscal year	0.83	3.64	0.34	5.57	1.28
	Calendar Year Percentage Change in GNP in Constant Dollars				
Leading index, per cent change[a] from					
5. Fiscal year to III Q	0.58	2.16	0.43	2.70	2.01
6. Fiscal year to III + IV Q	0.73	1.88	0.43	4.05	1.63
7. Fiscal year to III + IV + I Q	0.81	1.67	0.39	5.22	1.38
8. Fiscal year to fiscal year	0.83	1.48	0.36	5.66	1.31

Note: Linear regressions were fitted to percentage changes in the revised GNP data, 1951–1967, as available in May 1968, and in the reverse trend-adjusted index of eighteen leading indicators (see n. 12). r is the correlation coefficient; a and b are the regression coefficients; t is the t-ratio for b; and MAE is the mean absolute error in percentage points. The mean absolute error is adjusted for the loss of two degrees of freedom used in fitting the regression (by dividing the sum of the errors by $N-2$ instead of by N). However, this adjustment probably results in an overstatement of the mean absolute error, since the regression was fitted to minimize the mean square error, not the mean absolute error.

[a]Percentage changes for lines 1 and 5 are calculated from the preceding fiscal year average to the third quarter (July-September) of the year preceding the calendar year being forecast; for lines 2 and 6, from the preceding fiscal year to the average of the third and fourth quarters of the year preceding the calendar year being forecast; and so on.

Such a standard has several points to recommend it, apart from its past record. One is that it depends largely upon economic information from outside the series that is being predicted. The various naive models depend only upon the previous history of the forecast series and usually only its very recent history. The outside information that the leading index contains is of a kind that can be expected, on a variety of theoretical grounds, to bear upon future changes in aggregate economic activity. New orders for equipment and contracts for construction have obvious anticipatory elements. Other leading indicators are connected with future activity by more complicated routes, ranging from those that explain why changes in the average workweek ordinarily precede those in employment or

Table 25-7. Summary Measures of Error in Several Sets of Forecasts of Gross National Product.

	Period Covered	Mean Absolute Error (percent)	Correlation Coefficient, Forecast, and Actual Change
1. Forecasts of Annual Percentage Changes of GNP in Current Dollars			
a. Mean, eight sets of business forecasts	1952–1963	2.0	.78
b. Index of leading indicators[a]	1952–1963	1.8	.74
c. Extrapolation of preceding year's change	1952–1963	4.1	− .43
d. *Economic Report*	1961–1967	1.3	.34
e. Index of leading indicators[a]	1961–1967	0.8	.66
f. Extrapolation of preceding year's change	1961–1967	1.8	− .04
2. Forecasts of Annual Percentage Changes of GNP in Constant Dollars			
a. Suits' econometric model	1952–1967	1.5	.71
b. Index of leading indicators[a]	1952–1967	1.6	.71
c. Extrapolation of preceding year's change	1952–1967	3.4	− .20
d. *Economic Report*	1961–1967	1.1	.48
e. Suits' econometric model	1961–1967	1.1	.12
f. Index of leading indicators[a]	1961–1967	0.4	.94
g. Extrapolation of preceding year's change	1961–1967	1.6	− .44

Note: The mean errors and correlation coefficients are calculated using as the "actual" change the first official GNP estimates published in January or February following the year being forecast. In Table 25-6, the corresponding calculations for the leading index, and the regressions as well, are based on the latest revised GNP estimates.

[a] Using the regression equations in Table 25-6, lines 1 and 5 (fitted to data for 1951-1967, based upon changes in the leading index from the preceding fiscal year to the third quarter). An alternative set of forecasts for 1961-1967, based upon regression equations fitted to data for the prior period 1949-1961, yields the following results for 1961-1967:

	Mean Absolute Error (percent)	Correlation Coefficient
GNP in current dollars	0.7	0.64
GNP in constant dollars	0.9	0.95

output to those that explain the delayed reaction of the economy to a change in the rate of growth of the money supply. Moreover, extensive empirical testing, carried out over many years, lies behind the selection of the individual leading indicators. Although no amount of theorizing or empirical testing can insure that past relationships will persist, it is only by these means that we build confidence in particular forecasting procedures.

The empirical evidence examined in selecting the leading indicators pertained primarily to the consistency of their timing in the business cycle. The degree of correlation between the magnitude of their movements and those of GNP or any other aggregate was not considered.[14] This means, then, that the correlations recorded in Tables 25-6 and 25-7 are not just reproducing a relationship used in selecting the leading indicators. To this extent the results do not depend on hindsight. Moreover, although historical evidence with respect to the leads or lags of the indicators at turning points in the business cycle was a vital factor in their selection, much of this evidence goes back to the period before World War II. Indeed, about a third of the eighteen indicators included in the index were originally selected in 1950 on the basis of prewar evidence, and a postwar index constructed from the 1950 list is not unlike the present index (see Chapter 24). Hence, we may have some confidence that the average timing assumed in the method will persist, despite considerable variability at particular turns in the business cycle.

In many respects the method is analogous to the reduced form of a system of econometric equations. In the reduced form, weights or coefficients are applied to the predetermined or exogenous variables in the system to allow for their direct or indirect effects on GNP in order to generate a forecast. In the leading index, weights are applied to various leading indicators to allow for differences in their amplitude of variation and other factors, and as a final step, a regression coefficient is applied to the weighted average change in the indicators to generate a forecast. The choice of variables is different and so is the procedure for deriving weights, but in the end both forms obtain a forecast by applying a reasonable system of weights to a set of variables believed to be related to the future course of GNP.

The procedure I have outlined for generating annual forecasts is easily kept up to date and readily applied to such series as gross national product, industrial production, employment, or unemployment. For states or for countries that are not abundantly endowed with comprehensive economic data and the analytical models that require such data, the method might prove particularly useful. It can be used for shorter time units than a year—say, quarters or half years. By modifying the assumption regarding a six month lead, and perhaps with other modifications in composition or weighting, it might be applied to variables that lag in the business cycle, such as some price indexes or some interest rates. But it must be emphasized that the consistency of forecasts of different variables generated from a single leading index needs to be carefully checked. Forecasts of GNP in current and in constant dollars may or may not imply a reasonable forecast of the price deflator; forecasts of output and of employment may or may not imply a reasonable forecast of productivity; and forecasts of employment and of unemployment may or may not imply a reasonable forecast of the labor force.

In short, a simple and mechanical method cannot be expected to pass all the complex tests one can set for it. It is not a substitute for a carefully reasoned approach to the economic outlook, whether this approach takes the shape of an econometric model or of a less formal apparatus. All that the method does is help to summarize the information contained in a group of leading indicators regarding the near-term future course of GNP or other variables that are systematically related to the business cycle. Hence it can provide the forecaster with some of the information useful in developing his actual forecast, and it can be used as a standard by which to judge his past efforts, perhaps helping him to improve upon them.

IMPROVING PERFORMANCE

Forecasting is the activity of the economic statistician that is most visible to the public. The public is not likely to forget the dramatic failures, like those I mentioned at the outset. But these apparent failures require careful analysis. Sometimes the sequel alters one's view. The demise of the Harvard *ABC* curves after 1929, which I referred to earlier, is a case in point. Did the historical sequence upon which the scheme was based disappear in 1929 never to return? Was it a mere figment of a Harvard professor's imagination? The answer is no. Stock price indexes have continued to lead at business cycle turns as systematically since 1929 as they did before; various types of interest rates, though not all, have continued to lag; and the rise of interest rates and tightening of money during an expansion of business has been one of the factors tending, after a time, to curtail new commitments to invest, shift investor's sentiment from stocks to bonds, cause stock prices to turn down, and bring the business expansion to an end. The Harvard curves oversimplified the situation—it was not as simple as *ABC*—but they did contain a kernel of truth about the way our economic system works.

One lesson I draw from my review is that the development of the science of forecasting depends crucially upon the accumulation and continuing analysis of a record of forecasts. Without a record one cannot evaluate the performance or tell how to improve upon it. All too often forecasts are thrown out and forgotten—or thrown out with the hope that they will be forgotten—as soon as the occasion for them is past. They are often inadequately annotated when they are made. They often fail to specify what the present level of activity is believed to be, what assumptions or conditions are laid down, what probability or range of outcomes is attached to the forecast under these conditions, what is expected to happen if the conditions do not obtain, and what method or information was used to arrive at the results. Sometimes, even, the forecasts are couched in terms that make them unverifiable. Since forecasts are always subject to revision as more information becomes available, a record of the revisions, the reasons for them, and their relation to the final outcome is an important part of the story.

Econometric model forecasts, in principle, meet many if not all of these conditions. But econometric model builders are as human as the rest, as any attempt to resurrect an ex ante record of model forecasts will show. To judge from experience, it is too much to expect the individual forecaster to develop a scientific record of his work on his own initiative. The benefits that may accrue to him are uncertain—the record may even prove to be fatal!—and he always has plenty of other things to do. The benefits really accrue to the profession and sooner or later to society as a whole. In view of this, I believe that the American Statistical Association, and particularly its business and economics statistics section, has a significant role to play.

For a number of years the B&E section has conducted an annual outlook survey among its 5,000 members. Questionnaires are mailed out and the replies tabulated. Last year about 400 members responded, and perhaps half of them indicated that they regularly prepared forecasts. It seems to me that this survey could be developed so that it would become the vehicle for a scientific record of economic forecasts and hence be of far greater service both to the profession and to the public.

If it is to be this, the survey should be conducted quarterly and thereby provide an opportunity to record the frequent revisions that forecasters make. It should provide for the identification, though not the disclosure, of the name of the forecaster, so that a continuing series for each respondent can be accumulated. It should specify, or allow the forecaster to specify, what are the most recent levels or rates of change in relevant series. It should record the assumptions attached to the forecast, allow for probabilistic or alternative forecasts, and call for a description of the methodology.

The questionnaire that was circulated in the July 1968 survey went some way to meet these specifications. Careful consideration must be given, of course, to how far one can go and still retain the cooperation of respondents. Moreover, to be useful the results must be analyzed and compared with subsequent developments, and provision for this on a continuing basis must be made. The analytical work should be closely tied to the survey itself, so that the needs and ideas of the analysts can be reflected in the questions asked.[15]

A systematic, analytical record of forecasts and a continuing review of the results is one step toward better forecasting procedures and results. Other steps must be taken as well. Improvement in the quality of the basic data is fundamental. A study [1] of the revisions in the provisional GNP estimates, upon which all forecasters depend, showed that about 40 percent of the mean error in forecasts was attributable to errors in the current data. Two-fifths is a substantial fraction, and it represents a part of the forecasting error for which forecasters per se cannot be blamed. On the other hand, the agencies constructing the provisional estimates cannot be blamed either, for the fault lies with the inadequacy of the information that they must use to produce estimates promptly. A considerable improvement in the accuracy of forecasts could be brought about by a massive effort to bring the less adequate types of data up to the level of the best. Better coverage of output, wages, and prices in the service industries; greater attention to obtaining transaction prices, both domestic and international, in contrast to list prices or unit values; prompter reporting of information on profits; reduction in erratic elements in anticipatory statistics such as housing starts, new orders, and construction contracts; classification of data on new orders by industry placing the order; and far more comprehensive statistics on job vacancies than are presently available—these are among the items that should be on our statistical agenda. Their development will not only improve analyses of general economic prospects but will also contribute to more enlightened public policy and private decisions at all levels.

Finally, we need to expand the scientific studies that inform us about how our economic system works and what have been the effects of policies and institutions upon its workings. This is not the place to consider systematically the types of analytical studies most needed to support short-term forecasting efforts, but I should like to mention a few relatively neglected types of study. One is a careful review or set of case studies of past forecasting failures to explain what went wrong, how far it was avoidable, and what lessons for future forecasting can be learned from such episodes. A second need is for studies devoted to the forecasting of leading indicators. Their anticipatory value would clearly be enhanced if we could forecast their own movements; yet with few exceptions, little work of this kind has been done. In this connection a promising line of attack is to examine the behavior of various types of lagging indicators. Historically the behavior of many leading indicators, such as new orders or profit margins, appears to have been strongly influenced by the opposite movements of certain lagging indicators such as interest rates or unit labor costs, particularly when the relation of the latter to the level of aggregate activity is taken into account. A third type of study demanding attention concerns the relations between the problems of forecasting short-term fluctuations and those of forecasting intermediate or long-term growth trends. One of the first requirements is the compilation and analysis of a record of longer term forecasts. A great deal of such forecasting is done, it has a considerable influence upon investment and other decisions, and yet we know very little about its accuracy and what contributes to sound results.

All of these paths to progress—better records of forecasting, a sounder statistical base, and a more enlightened economic framework—are costly. But the potential benefits to society are great. The nation is devoting large resources to economic forecasting. Tardiness or failure to identify, measure, and anticipate the forces of inflation or of recession can affect the welfare of millions. Economic forecasters have, in my judgment, demonstrated an ability to forecast. But there is much room for improvement, the limitations need to become better known and more firmly established, and the most dependable techniques must be developed, demonstrated, and adopted. The statistical profession itself should take the leadership in bringing this about.

NOTES TO CHAPTER 25

1. The National Bureau study is under the direction of Victor Zarnowitz of the University of Chicago, and among those responsible for various parts of the project are Rosanne Cole, Jon Cunnyngham, Michael Evans, Rendigs Fels, Yoel Haitovsky, C. Elton Hinshaw, Jacob Mincer, and Julius Shiskin. Results of the project to date have been reported in references 1, 3, 4, 6, 8, 10, and 16. The

study has been supported by grants from Whirlpool Corporation, General Electric Company, Ford Motor Company Foundation, U.S. Steel Corporation, and the Relm Foundation, as well as by other funds of the National Bureau.

2. Because a year is a crude time unit for this purpose, the beginning or end or even the occurrence of a recession is not accurately identified by year-to-year changes in GNP. Indeed, although it is generally agreed that four recessions have taken place in the United States since 1946, only one decline appears in the revised calendar year data for GNP—namely, in 1948–1949. In the first official estimates published at the time, however, year-to-year declines occurred in 1953–1954 and in 1957–1958 as well (though not in 1960–1961). In comparing forecasts with what "actually happened," Zarnowitz [16] uses the first official estimates as most nearly representing what the forecaster is trying to forecast, and I have followed his practice. This choice avoids the conceptual changes contained in the revised estimates, but otherwise is debatable, since (1) the revised estimates, being based on more information, are more accurate than the first official estimates; (2) the latter are themselves forecasts of what the revised estimates will be and conceivably may be less adequate in this respect than the forecasts that antedate them; (3) the forecasts are usually based upon average relationships derived from revised data rather than first estimates; and (4) the averaging process itself abstracts to some degree from measurement error. See Rosanne Cole [1].

3. The record includes twelve sets of forecasts. Some go back to 1947 and some go as far forward as 1965, but the bulk of the forecasts (115 out of 126) pertain to 1953–1963. Six of the sets are forecasts made by individuals or a team; the other six are averages of separate forecasts made by the members of small or large groups. Hence the total number of forecasts included far exceeds 126. The averaging of group forecasts, it should be noted, tends to reduce the range of error.

4. This last assumption would not be wide of the mark if the revised GNP estimates (as of 1965) were the criterion of what happened rather than the first official estimates. Since the revised annual estimates contain turning points only in 1948 and 1949 (cf. n. 2), and few of the forecast records go back that far, the number of turning point predictions consistent with perfect accuracy in terms of the revised estimates would be three.

5. The test assumes that the observations are statistically independent, which clearly is not the case, partly because the occurrence of a turning point in one year has a bearing on its occurrence in the next, partly because the several sets of forecasts included probably have some influence upon one another and in any case cover the same period. These considerations are likely to mean that the statistical significance is exaggerated by the ordinary test.

6. Just as forecasts of year-to-year changes made at the end of the year identify turning points conventionally dated some six months before the date of forecast, so forecasts for the next half-year made at the end of the half-year identify turning points dated three months before the forecast, while forecasts for the next quarter identify turning points dated a month and a half earlier. The implicit lag is longest in the annual case, and since this lag makes other information available to the forecaster, it probably explains why the annual results in

Table 25-1 (first panel) are better than the semiannual (Table 25-2, semiannual changes, first panel), and the semiannual better than the quarterly (Table 25-2, quarter-to-quarter changes, first panel). In addition, the longer time unit doubtless smooths away some of the unpredictable wrinkles, though it also implies a longer future span to be forecast. The annual analysis in Table 25-1, however, is not strictly comparable with that in Table 25-2, since the latter is based on directions of change and the former on turning points, or sequences (pairs) of directions of change. When the data for Tables 25-1 and 25-2 are put in the same form, the correlation coefficients are:

Annual	*Semiannual*	*Quarterly*	*Quarterly*
Forecasts made (x) months after the turning point	0.59 (6)	0.38 (3)	0.09 (1.5)
Forecasts made (x) months before the turning point	0.25 (0)	0.11 (−3)	−0.13 (−4.5)

7. Curiously, in developing and applying their methods (fitting equations, etc.), many forecasters pay close attention to magnitudes (as in the method of least squares) but pay no particular attention to turning points. This procedure does not seem well suited to producing good forecasts of turning points even though, in the end, this is considered to be one of the crucial tests of good performance. See, for example, the analysis of the Commerce Department's model by Liebenberg, Hirsch, and Popkin [5]. Would the use of lagged (postdated) variables get such heavy emphasis in econometric models if the forecasting of turning points were a desideratum? The lagged series may improve the fit, but it cannot forecast its own turning point, and it may (though it need not) prevent other variables from doing so.

8. The materials presented rely largely upon two summary measures of forecasting quality—the mean absolute error in forecasts of percentage change and the correlation coefficient between forecast and actual percentage change. The use of percentage changes rather than first differences as the form in which to express the forecasts has the advantage of facilitating comparisons among different variables. Also, where the variables experience growth or inflationary trends, it puts the most recent changes more nearly on the same level as earlier changes. Logarithmic differences would in principle be superior to percentages, because increases and decreases would then be symmetrical, but since most of the percentage changes here are small, this is not an important consideration, and percentages have the merit of familiarity. The mean absolute error is arithmetically simpler than the root mean square error and avoids the high weights assigned to extreme errors that squaring implies. In practice, the mean absolute error is highly correlated with the root mean square error and is usually about eight-tenths as large (in a normal distribution the expected ratio is 0.798; in a rectangular distribution, 0.866). The correlation coefficient supplements the mean absolute error, since a correlation between forecast and actual changes that is close to zero or is negative diminishes one's confidence in a series of forecasts even when the mean error is small. On the other hand, a high positive cor-

relation does not in itself represent good forecasting performance if the mean error is large, though it may mean good potential performance (via, say, a linear adjustment of the forecasts). The ratio of mean absolute error to the mean absolute actual percentage change, which simply measures the size of the error relative to the magnitudes that are being forecast, is analogous to the inequality coefficient proposed by Theil [15] —namely, the square root of the ratio of the mean square error to the mean square actual change. In Theil's decomposition of this coefficient, the correlation between forecast and actual changes is one of the factors accounting for the total error.

9. Since the above was written, results during 1961–1967 for two of the groups (A and D) in Table 25-4 have been compared with those of the *Economic Report*. Both groups tended to underestimate the rate of growth in current dollar GNP. The mean absolute errors were 1.9 percent and 2.1 percent for A and D respectively, and the correlation coefficients between actual and forecast changes were 0.29 and 0.23. The poorer performance may be partly attributable to the fact that these forecasts antedate those of the *Economic Report* by two or three months.

10. I am indebted both to Suits and to Jon Cunnyngham for information regarding the forecasts. The forecasts were produced not by a single model but by a system of equations that was altered in some respect almost every year.

11. This conclusion was also reached by Cunnyngham [3] on the basis of a direct comparison of constant dollar and current dollar GNP forecasts.

12. The index of leading indicators used in Tables 25-6 and 25-7 is based upon eighteen leading indicators and is "reverse trend adjusted" (see [10]). Virtually the same results can be obtained without the "reverse trend adjustment." Since these computations were completed the U.S. Department of Commerce has begun to publish a monthly index based upon twelve leading indicators (see the November 1968 issue of *Business Conditions Digest*). Regression analysis based on the latter index yields results similar to those given here. The regression equations based on the index of twelve leading indicators, 1951–1967, are as follows:

Independent Variable: Leading index, percent change from	Dependent Variable: Calendar year percent change in							
	GNP in current dollars				GNP in constant dollars			
	r	a	b	t	r	a	b	t
1. Fiscal year to IIIQ	0.60	4.55	0.41	2.78	0.56	2.51	0.40	2.55
2. Fiscal year to III and IVQ	0.74	4.34	0.40	4.12	0.71	2.27	0.40	3.82
3. Fiscal year to III, IV, and IQ	0.81	4.19	0.36	5.08	0.80	2.08	0.37	4.94
4. Fiscal year to fiscal year	0.81	4.05	0.33	5.26	0.82	1.91	0.35	5.37

Regression analysis is, in fact, not essential to the procedure. The method used in constructing the leading index can be adapted so that the index has the same trend and average cyclical amplitude as the series being forecast. Further adjustment by means of regression is then superfluous and may indeed bias the forecasts.

13. Chapter 6 of this book.

14. Note, however, that it has been known for some years that the magnitude of change in various leading indicators during the early stages of recession is correlated with the severity of the recession itself (cf. [7]).

15. The B&E section promptly took up this suggestion and on November 29, 1968, launched the first of a series of quarterly surveys designed to accomplish the above objectives in cooperation with the National Bureau of Economic Research.

REFERENCES

[1]. Cole, Rosanne. "Data Errors and Forecasting Accuracy." In Mincer [6].

[2]. Cox, Garfield V. *An Appraisal of American Business Forecasts.* rev. ed. Chicago: 1930.

[3]. Cunnyngham, Jon. "Econometric Forecasts." *Forty-fifth Annual Report of the National Bureau of Economic Research*, June 1965, pp. 60–64.

[4]. Fels, Rendigs, and C. Elton Hinshaw. *Forecasting and Recognizing Business Cycle Turning Points.* New York: National Bureau of Economic Research, 1968.

[5]. Liebenberg, M.; A.A. Hirsch; and J. Popkin. "A Quarterly Econometric Model of the United States: A Progress Report." *Survey of Current Business*, May 1966, pp. 23–26.

[6]. Mincer, Jacob, ed. *Economic Forecasts and Expectations: Analyses of Forecasting Behavior and Performance.* New York: National Bureau of Economic Research, 1969.

[7]. Moore, Geoffrey H. *Business Cycle Indicators.* Vol. I, ch. 5. New York: National Bureau of Economic Research, 1961.

[8]. Moore, Geoffrey H., and Julius Shiskin. *Indicators of Business Expansions and Contractions.* New York: National Bureau of Economic Research, 1967.

[9]. Okun, Arthur M. "Review of Some Economic Forecasts for 1955–57," *Journal of Business*, July 1959.

[10]. Shiskin, Julius, and Geoffrey H. Moore. "Composite Indexes of Leading, Coinciding, and Lagging Indicators, 1948–67." Supplement to *National Burea Report 1*, January 1968.

[11]. Stekler, Hermon O. "An Evaluation of Quarterly Judgmental Economic Forecasts." *Journal of Business*, July 1968.

[12]. _____ . "Forecasting with Econometric Models: An Evaluation." *Econometrica*, July–October 1968.

[13]. Suits, Daniel B. "Forecasting and Analysis with an Econometric Model." *American Economic Review*, March 1962.

[14]. Theil, Henri, *Economic Forecasts and Policy.* Amsterdam, 1961.

[15]. _____ . *Applied Economic Forecasting.* Chicago, 1966.

[16]. Zarnowitz, Victor. *An Appraisal of Short-Term Economic Forecasts.* New York: National Bureau of Economic Research, 1967.

Chapter 26

The President's Economic Report: A Forecasting Record

Keeping a scorecard on economists' forecasts is not an occupation calculated to please one's professional colleagues. If the forecasts turn out to be very different from one another, and obviously different from what will occur, some wiseacre is likely to remark that economists get rich by begging—to differ. If the forecasts turn out to be much alike, the same fellow will say if you've seen one economist's forecast you've seen 'em all. Nevertheless, forecasting records should be kept, exposed to public view, and analyzed. Only in this way can we learn to what degree they are dependable and how to improve their reliability.

For this reason in 1963 the National Bureau began to develop systematic records of forecasts and analyze the results. First we obtained a number of historical records and then, in 1968, began a quarterly survey of forecasters, in cooperation with the American Statistical Association. The survey not only provides current information on what some fifty economists who regularly produce forecasts are projecting for each of the next five quarters, but also summarizes the methods being used and the crucial assumptions underlying the forecasts. Hence it is a systematic record that had not been available previously.

One of the most widely scrutinized forecasts—not included in the above survey—is the one published each January in the *Economic Report of the President*. The practice of including explicit numerical forecasts in the *Report* began in 1961. Hence a record covering

Reprinted from the *NBER Reporter*, April 1977.

some fifteen years can be compiled and, since 1968, compared with the ASA—NBER survey of forecasters. How close to the mark did these forecasts come? Is the government's forecast more accurate or less accurate than the private forecasts? Is there evidence of bias? How do forecasts of price change compare with forecasts of real growth? Could one do as well simply by extrapolating last year's experience? Have the forecasts been getting better or worse?[1]

Since the *Economic Report* forecasts have been limited, for the most part, to annual totals for the year ahead of gross national product in current and in constant prices and to the price level implied in current dollar GNP, we restrict our analysis to these three variables (the ASA—NBER survey covers other items too, such as unemployment, industrial production, housing starts, and so on). The most useful way to record and analyze these forecasts, I believe, is in terms of year-to-year percentage changes. Changes are harder to predict than levels, and percent changes are more comparable over time than dollar changes. By using them we also avoid some of the problems of revision in the level of the dollar figures and concentrate attention on what is of most interest—the rate of growth and the rate of inflation.

In measuring accuracy we compare the forecast percent change with the actual percent change recorded the following year (ignoring later revisions in the "actuals") and calculate the mean error without regard to sign and the correlation (r^2) between the forecast and actual changes. The mean error simply tells how big the discrepancy in percentage points was, on the average, between the forecast and the actual change, while the correlation indicates on a scale from 0 to 1 how closely related the forecast and actual changes were. If the correlation is close to 0, there is little evidence of forecasting ability, even if the mean error is quite small. Finally, as another test of forecasting accuracy, we compare the forecasts with those that might have been made by simple extrapolation—assuming that next year's percentage change will be the same as that of the previous year. This provides a standard measure of the relative difficulty of forecasting during one period compared with another or forecasting one variable compared with another and, as we shall see, is not always easy to beat.[2]

Figures 26–1 through 26–3 show the record of the forecasts from the *Economic Report* in comparison with the actual figures reported a year later. Clearly the two correspond to a considerable degree. The mean error for the whole period turns out to be almost the same—one percentage point—for current and constant dollar GNP and for the price deflator (Table 26–1, col. 1). That is to say, the government's economists have forecast the rate of nominal growth, of real

Figure 26-1.   Actual and Forecast Percentage Change in GNP in Current Dollars, Economic Report of the President, 1961–1976.

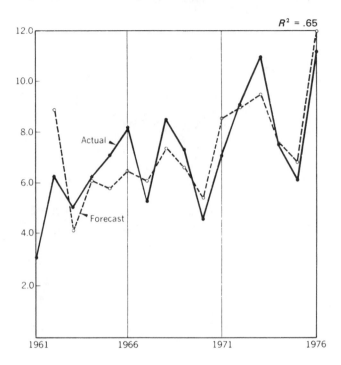

Source: Table 26-3.

growth, and of inflation for the year ahead all with an average margin of one percentage point during the past fifteen years.

Figures 26-1 and 26-2 also clearly show that there has been some improvement during the period in the fidelity with which the forecasts have tracked the actual changes in current and constant dollar GNP. At the same time, the swings in the rates of growth have become wider, which presumably adds to the difficulty of forecasting. The summary measures in Table 26-1, which divide the period roughly in half, show that the mean error in forecasts of GNP in current dollars dropped from 1.3 percent in the first seven years (1962–1968) to 0.8 percent in the last eight (1969–1976).[3] This was more of an accomplishment than it appears at first sight, because between the same two periods the errors made by simple extrapolation of the previous year's change were increasing, reflecting the wider swings in the rates of change. The forecast errors dropped from about two-thirds of the extrapolative errors to about one-third. Also,

Figure 26-2. Actual and Forecast Percentage Change in GNP in Constant Dollars, Economic Report of the President, 1961–1975.

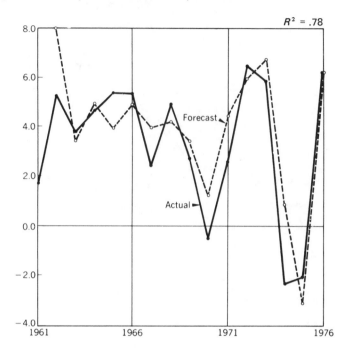

Source: Table 26-3.

the correlation between forecast and actual changes became very much higher.

For real GNP the average size of the forecasting errors did not decline between the two periods, but the errors of simple extrapolation became much larger (the swings in real growth rates increased much more than the swings in nominal growth rates). Hence, relative to the extrapolation standard, the forecasts of real GNP improved just as much as the forecasts of nominal GNP. The correlation of forecast with actual changes also improved substantially.

The government's record for price forecasting is very different, despite the fact that the average error and the correlation for the entire period are virtually the same as for real and nominal GNP. A glance at Figure 26-3 reveals a clear tendency for the forecasts of the inflation rate to lag a year behind the actual rates. As a result, the price forecasts were no better than the extrapolative standard in the first half of the period and only moderately better in the last half. The extrapolation automatically lags a year behind the actual

Figure 26-3. Actual and Forecast Percentage Change, GNP Implicit Price Deflator, Economic Report of the President, 1961–1976.

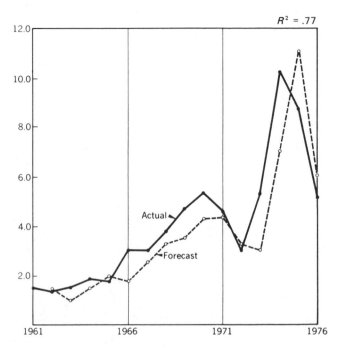

Source: Table 26-3.

changes. Furthermore, the correlation between forecast and actual price changes deteriorated, though not as much as it did for the extrapolation. Of course, the swings in the rate of inflation increased enormously in the 1970s.

It appears, then, that at least in the early part of the period, the rate of inflation had a far greater tendency to persist from year to year than did the rate of change in real GNP. It appears, too, that this tendency has influenced forecasts of the rate of inflation. This influence is demonstrated more directly in Figure 26-4, which compares the errors in the forecasts with the errors in extrapolation. For real and nominal GNP there is little or no relation; the forecast errors simply hew much closer to the zero line than do the extrapolation errors. But for prices there is a close relation—the forecast errors move very much like the extrapolation errors. In price forecasting, forecasters have to a large extent followed the extrapolating route. Indeed, the *Economic Report* has often stated its expectation regarding prices in terms of extending the recent trend.

Table 26-1.   Measures of Error in Forecasts of Year-to-Year Percentage Changes in GNP and Prices.

Period Covered	Mean Absolute Error (percent)				Correlation (r^2), Forecast and Actual Change			
	Economic Report (January)	ASA–NBER Survey (November)	(February)	Simple Extrapolation	Economic Report (January)	ASA–NBER Survey (November)	(February)	Simple Extrapolation
GNP in Current Dollars								
1962–1968	1.3	n.a.	n.a.	2.0	0.19	n.a.	n.a.	0.02[a]
1969–1976	0.8	1.0	0.6	2.6	0.83	0.76	0.89	0
1962–1976	1.0	n.a.	n.a.	2.3	0.65	n.a.	n.a.	0.02
GNP in Constant Dollars								
1962–1968	1.0	n.a.	n.a.	1.7	0.20	n.a.	n.a.	0.22[a]
1969–1976	1.2	1.0	0.8	3.7	0.86	0.94	0.86	0
1962–1976	1.1	n.a.	n.a.	2.8	0.78	n.a.	n.a.	0.01
GNP Implicit Price Deflator								
1962–1968	0.5	n.a.	n.a.	0.4	0.75	n.a.	n.a.	0.71
1969–1976	1.4	1.3	1.2	2.0	0.58	0.53	0.65	0.17
1962–1976	1.0	n.a.	n.a.	1.3	0.77	n.a.	n.a.	0.54
GNP Implicit Price Deflator: Change in Rate								
1963–1969	0.6	n.a.	n.a.	0.5	0.03[a]	n.a.	n.a.	0
1970–1976	1.7	1.6	1.2	2.2	0.39	0.34	0.57	0
1963–1976	1.1	n.a.	n.a.	1.3	0.36	n.a.	n.a.	0

[a] R is negative.
Source: Table 26–3.

Figure 26-4. Forecasting Errors Compared with Simple Extrapolation.

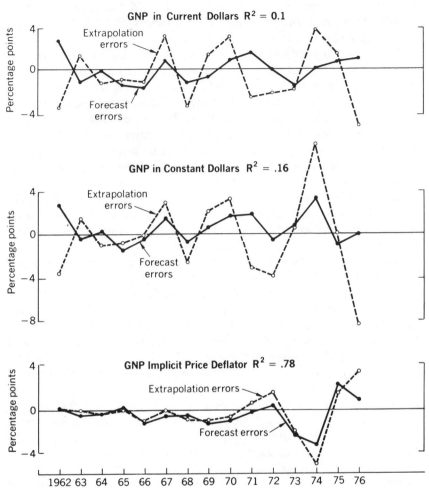

Source: Table 26-3.

Because of the high degree of persistence in the rate of inflation, it is of interest to know how well the *change* in the rate has been forecast. Here of course, simple extrapolation does not do well. It assumes that there is no change in the rate from whatever it was last year. Whenever the rate changes, the simple extrapolation will be wrong by the amount of the change. In recent years, when the changes have been large, the extrapolation errors have been large, too. This is also true of the *Economic Report* forecasts. Nevertheless, in recent years the mean error in the forecasts of the change in the inflation rate has been somewhat smaller than in extrapolations that say that the rate will remain the same, and the forecast changes show a moderate correlation with the actual changes (See the bottom section of Table 26-1). Forecasters have done more than just extrapolate the previous year's rate, but they still have a long way to go.

Figure 26-4 suggests a further observation: the errors in forecasting real GNP and the price deflator have tended to be offsetting, especially in the last half of the period. When the forecasts of real growth were too high, the forecasts of the rate of inflation were too low, and vice versa. The forecasts of GNP in current dollars benefited from these offsetting errors and turned out to be more accurate than one would have expected had the forecasts of real growth and inflation been arrived at independently. The situation resembles one in which the forecasters could forecast the change in nominal GNP quite well, but could not do well at splitting it into the real change and the price change. Most forecasters would, I think, agree that this is the case.

Turning now to the comparison with the private forecasts as represented in the ASA—NBER survey,[4] we use the median forecast from both the survey taken in November or early December, before the President's *Economic Report* is published, and that taken in February, shortly after the *Report* is published. The mean errors in the November survey forecasts are virtually the same as in the *Report* forecasts, and the forecasts themselves are very highly correlated.[5] One could say, therefore, that the November survey gives a very good prediction of what the forecasts in the *Report* are going to be and just as good a prediction for the year ahead as that in the *Report*.

The February survey forecasts, not unexpectedly, are even more closely correlated than the November survey forecasts with the *Report* forecasts (see note 5). But the accuracy record is, on the whole, slightly better than than of the *Report*. In other words, the February survey forecasts come closer to the recently published *Report* forecasts but also a little closer to the final outcome. In general, however, the survey forecasts display many of the same characteristics as the *Report* forecasts and vice versa.[6]

On the matter of bias, two things can be said on the basis of the record. One is that both private and government forecasts have erred on the side of optimism more often than not. Real growth was overestimated by the *Report* in five of the last eight years and underestimated twice; in 1976 the forecast hit the target precisely. The November survey forecasts overestimated six times; underestimated twice. The February survey turned in four overestimates, three underestimates, and one bull's eye. On prices, too, optimism has prevailed. The *Report* underestimated the rate of inflation five times and overestimated it three times; the November survey did likewise. The February survey was similar, underestimating inflation five times, overestimating it twice, and hitting the target once.

The second point is that the government's forecasts have been somewhat more optimistic than the private ones on real growth but to a lesser extent on inflation. The *Report* forecasts of real growth were higher than the November survey in six of the last eight years and higher than the February survey every single year. On the other hand, its forecasts of the inflation rate compared to the November survey were higher five times, lower twice, and the same once and, compared to the February survey, were higher four times, lower twice, and the same twice. As a result of the *Report's* tendency to make higher forecasts of both real output and prices, its forecasts of nominal GNP exceeded both the November and the February surveys for seven out of the eight years.

As a further result of these differences—since both government and private forecasts were too optimistic on real growth and the former more optimistic than the latter—the government overestimated real growth most of the time. But on inflation, since the government's forecasts were higher than the private forecasts, which were too low, the government came closer to the target most of the time. The upshot is that for nominal GNP there is little to choose between the government and private forecasts. The average errors, taking the direction of error into account (unlike Table 26–1, where direction is ignored), are given in Table 26–2 for 1969–1976. Perhaps the most important point is that these differences are all less than one percentage point. Bias is not a dominant feature of the record of either government or private forecasts.

Finally, it should be noted that in all the above comparisons we have used the average (median) forecast from the ASA–NBER survey. In forecasting, as in other games of chance, there is safety in numbers. Over a period of time, the average forecast by a group of forecasters tends to be more accurate than the individual forecasts of

Table 26–2. Average Forecast Errors, 1969–1976.

	Report	*November Survey*	*February Survey*
GNP in Current Dollars	0.2	−0.3	−0.3
GNP in Constant Dollars	0.8	0.7	0.4
Implicit Price Deflator	−0.5	−0.9	−0.7

Source: Table 26–3.

Table 26-3. Prediction and Performance, 1961–1976.

| | Percentage Change from Preceding Year | | | | Error (percent) | | | |
	Forecast, Economic Report (January) (1)	Forecast, ASA-NBER Survey (November) (2)	(February) (3)	Actual (4)	Economic Report (January) (5)	Forecast ASA-NBER Survey (November) (6)	(February) (7)	Simple Extrapolation (8)
				GNP in Current Dollars				
1961	—	—	—	3.3	—	—	—	—
1962	9.4	—	—	6.7	2.7	—	—	−3.4
1963	4.4	—	—	5.4	−1.0	—	—	1.3
1964	6.5	—	—	6.6	−0.1	—	—	−1.2
1965	6.1	—	—	7.5	−1.4	—	—	−0.9
1966	6.9	—	—	8.6	−1.7	—	—	−1.1
1967	6.4	—	—	5.6	0.8	—	—	3.0
1968	7.8	—	—	9.0	−1.2	—	—	−3.4
1969	7.0	6.6	7.0	7.7	−0.7	−1.1	−0.7	1.3
1970	5.7	5.4	5.4	4.9	0.8	0.5	0.5	2.8
1971	9.0	6.8	7.1	7.5	1.5	−0.7	−0.4	−2.6
1972	9.5	8.9	8.9	9.7	−0.2	−0.8	−0.8	−2.2
1973	10.0	9.6	9.8	11.5	−1.5	−1.9	−1.7	−1.8
1974	8.0	7.1	7.7	7.9	0.1	−0.8	−0.2	3.6
1975	7.2	8.1	6.6	6.5	0.7	1.6	0.1	1.4
1976	12.5	12.4	12.4	11.6	0.9	0.8	0.8	−5.1

GNP in Constant Dollars

Year								
1961	—	—	—	1.8	—	—	—	—
1962	8.0[a]	—	—	5.3	2.7	—	—	−3.5
1963	3.5[a]	—	—	3.8	−0.3	—	—	1.5
1964	5.0[a]	—	—	4.7	0.3	—	—	−0.9
1965	4.0[a]	—	—	5.4	−1.4	—	—	−0.7
1966	5.0	—	—	5.4	−0.4	—	—	0
1967	4.0[a]	—	—	2.5	1.5	—	—	2.9
1968	4.3[a]	—	—	5.0	−0.7	—	—	−2.5
1969	3.5	3.3	3.5	2.8	0.7	0.5	0.7	2.2
1970	1.3	1.1	0.7	−0.4	1.7	1.5	1.1	3.2
1971	4.5	2.8	2.7	2.7	1.8	0.1	0	−3.1
1972	6.0	5.5	5.7	6.5	−0.5	−1.0	−0.8	−3.8
1973	6.8	6.1	6.1	5.9	0.8	0.2	0.2	0.6
1974	1.0	1.1	0.6	−2.2	3.2	3.3	2.8	8.1
1975	−3.0	−0.8	−3.8	−2.0	−1.0	1.2	−1.0	−0.2
1976	6.2	5.9	6.1	6.2	0	−0.3	−0.1	−8.2

(Table 26–3. continued overleaf)

Table 26-3. continued

| | Percentage Change from Preceding Year | | | | Error (percent) | | | |
	Forecast, Economic Report (January) (1)	Forecast, ASA–NBER Survey (November) (2)	Forecast, ASA–NBER Survey (February) (3)	Actual (4)	Economic Report (January) (5)	Forecast, ASA–NBER Survey (November) (6)	Forecast, ASA–NBER Survey (February) (7)	Simple Extrapolation (8)
				GNP Implicit Price Deflator				
1961	—	—	—	1.5	—	—	—	—
1962	1.5[a]	—	—	1.4	0.1	—	—	0.1
1963	1.0[a]	—	—	1.5	-0.5	—	—	-0.1
1964	1.5	—	—	1.9	-0.4	—	—	-0.4
1965	2.0[a]	—	—	1.8	0.2	—	—	0.1
1966	1.8	—	—	3.0	-1.2	—	—	-1.2
1967	2.5	—	—	3.0	-0.5	—	—	0
1968	3.3[a]	—	—	3.8	-0.5	—	—	-0.8
1969	3.5	3.3	3.3	4.7	-1.2	-1.4	-1.4	-0.9
1970	4.3	4.7	4.7	5.3	-1.0	-0.6	-0.6	-0.6
1971	4.4	3.9	4.2	4.6	-0.2	-0.7	-0.4	0.7
1972	3.3	3.2	3.0	3.0	0.3	0.2	0	1.6
1973	3.0	3.3	3.4	5.3	-2.3	-2.0	-1.9	-2.3
1974	7.0	5.9	7.0	10.2	-3.2	-4.3	-3.2	-4.9
1975	11.0	9.1	9.9	8.7	2.3	0.4	1.2	1.5
1976	6.0	6.0	6.0	5.1	0.9	0.9	0.9	3.6

Notes to Table 26-3

[a] Inferred from statements in the report. All other entries are based on figures (dollar levels, dollar changes, or percentage changes) given in the report. The inferred entries have been verified as approximately correct, though not in all cases precisely correct, by the Council of Economic Advisers.

Sources: Columns 1 and 4: *Economic Report of the President,* January 1962 through January 1976. The actual changes are based on the first official estimates given in the report following the year for which the forecast was made. Changes in constant dollar GNP and in the price deflator are based on estimates in 1954 dollars for 1960–1961 to 1964–1965, in 1958 dollars for 1965–1966 to 1973–1974, and in 1972 dollars thereafter.

Columns 2 and 3: Quarterly releases by the American Statistical Association and the National Bureau of Economic Research, "Business Outlook Survey." The figures are medians of the forecasts reported by about fifty economists in business, government, and academic institutions.

Columns 5, 6 and 7: Columns 1, 2, and 3 minus column 4.

Column 8: Actual change for preceding year minus actual change for current year (column 4).

the majority in the group. The opportunity for errors to cancel out in the average forecast is lacking in the individual forecasts. Some forecasters will be optimistic, others pessimistic. Consequently, in an extended contest between the average forecast and any individual forecast, the average is likely to win out. The forecasts in the *Economic Report* are like the individual forecasts in such a comparison, though there are some elements of a consensus about them. Thus, the fact that the *Report* forecasts compare closely in accuracy with the average forecasts in the survey is in itself a favorable result. Relatively few forecasters in the survey group would do as well.[7] This, of course, is one of the advantages of conducting the survey and using it as a standard.

A POSTSCRIPT TO UPDATE THE FORECASTING RECORD OF THE PRESIDENT'S ECONOMIC REPORT, 1976-1982

The forecasting record discussed in this chapter ended in 1976. How well have forecasters done since then? The answer, spelled out in Table 26-4 is pretty much the same as before, except in 1982. In that year the error in the forecast of real GNP in the *Economic Report* was larger than in any previous year in the entire twenty-one-year record. The ASA-NBER survey forecasts for 1982 were substantially more accurate than the *Economic Report* forecasts, although they too erred on the optimistic side. The 1981-1982 recession was more severe and lasted longer than the forecasters anticipated.

The errors in the real GNP forecasts for 1982 carried over to GNP in current dollars, producing errors of record size there too. The forecasts of inflation, on the other hand, were close to average in accuracy. Inflation declined more than the forecasters expected, but the error was not unusually large. Nevertheless, since both inflation and real GNP were overestimated, the errors in the current dollar GNP forecasts were spectacular. This is true of both the *Economic Report* and the ASA-NBER survey.

Because of the extreme size of the 1982 errors, and also because final figures for 1982 are not yet available, they are excluded from the averages and correlations in the table. The conclusions reached on the basis of the data through 1976 are broadly supported by the results for the next five years, 1977-1981, namely:

1. The *Report* forecasts are about as accurate as the median forecasts from the ASA-NBER survey in the preceding November. Neither set of forecasts is biased toward optimism.

2. The forecasts of real and nominal GNP are far better than simple extrapolations of last year's rate of growth or decline.

3. The forecasts of the rate of inflation (GNP implicit price deflator) are not much if any better than simple extrapolations of last year's rate. In fact, the errors in the forecasts closely resemble those obtained by simple extrapolation, suggesting that forecasters are heavily influenced by last year's inflation rate in making their predictions.

Table 26–4.   Prediction and Performance, 1977–1982.

	Percentage Change from Preceding Year				Error (%)			
	Forecast, Economic Report (January) (1)	Forecast, ASA–NBER Survey (November) (2)	Forecast, ASA–NBER Survey (February) (3)	Actual (4)	Economic Report (January) (5)	Forecast, ASA–NBER Survey (November) (6)	Forecast, ASA–NBER Survey (February) (7)	Simple Extrapolation (8)
GNP in Current Dollars								
1977	11.0	10.8	10.6	10.8	0.2	0.0	-0.2	-0.8
1978	11.0	10.5	10.7	11.6	-0.6	-1.1	-0.9	-0.8
1979	9.8	10.2	10.8	11.3	-1.5	-1.1	-0.5	0.3
1980	8.0	7.2	9.1	8.8	-0.8	-1.6	0.3	2.5
1981	11.8	11.0	11.6	11.3	0.5	-0.3	0.3	-2.5
1982	10.2	8.7	7.3	4.4[a]	5.8	4.3	2.9	-6.9
Mean absolute error								
1962–1968					1.3	n.a.	n.a.	2.0
1969–1976					0.8	1.0	0.6	2.6
1977–1981					0.7	0.8	0.4	1.4
Correlation (r^2), forecast and actual change								
1962–1968					.19	n.a.	n.a.	.02
1969–1976					.83	.76	.89	.00
1977–1982					.71	.87	.80	.09
GNP in Constant Dollars								
1977	5.2	5.0	4.8	4.9	0.3	0.1	-0.1	1.3
1978	4.8	4.3	4.3	3.9	0.9	0.4	0.4	1.0
1979	2.2	2.4	2.6	2.3	-0.1	0.1	0.3	1.6
1980	-1.0	-1.3	0.0	-0.2	-0.8	-1.1	0.2	2.5
1981	1.4	1.2	1.5	2.0	-0.6	-0.8	-0.5	-2.2
1982	3.0	0.5	-0.4	-1.5[a]	4.5	2.0	1.1	3.5

Mean absolute error

	(1)	(2)	(3)	(4)
1962–1968	1.0	n.a.	n.a.	1.7
1969–1976	1.2	1.0	0.8	3.7
1977–1981	0.5	0.5	0.3	1.7

Correlation (r^2), forecast and actual change

	(1)	(2)	(3)	(4)
1962–1968	.20	n.a.	n.a.	.22
1969–1976	.86	.94	.86	.00
1977–1981	.98	.98	.97	.49

GNP Implicit Price Deflator

Year	(1)	(2)	(3)	(4)	(5)	(6)	(7)	(8)
1977	5.5	5.4	5.4	5.6	-0.1	-0.2	-0.2	-0.5
1978	6.0	5.9	5.9	7.4	-1.4	-1.5	-1.5	-1.8
1979	7.4	7.4	7.9	8.8	-1.4	-1.4	-0.9	-1.4
1980	9.0	8.8	9.1	9.0	0	-0.2	0.1	-0.2
1981	10.2	9.5	9.7	9.1	1.1	0.4	0.6	-0.1
1982	7.2	7.9	7.4	6.0ᵃ	1.2	1.9	1.4	3.1

Mean absolute error

	(5)	(6)	(7)	(8)
1962–1968	0.5	n.a.	n.a.	0.4
1969–1976	1.4	1.3	1.2	2.0
1977–1981	0.8	0.7	0.7	0.8

Correlation (r^2), forecast and actual change

	(5)	(6)	(7)	(8)
1962–1968	.75	n.a.	n.a.	.71
1969–1976	.58	.53	.65	.17
1977–1982	.72	.78	.82	.83

ᵃ Estimates based on average of second and third quarter, 1982, as of October 1982.

Sources: Columns 1 and 4: *Economic Report of the President*, January 1977 through January 1982. The actual changes are based on the first official estimates given in the report following the year for which the forecast was made. Changes in constant dollar GNP and in the price deflator are based on estimates in 1972 dollars. In recent years the forecasts have usually been given in terms of changes from fourth quarter to fourth quarter, and we have converted them to annual changes by linear interpolation. Where forecasts were in terms of ranges, we use the midpoint of the range.

Columns 2 and 3: Quarterly releases by the American Statistical Association and the National Bureau of Economic Research, "Business Outlook Survey." The figures are medians of the forecasts reported by about fifty economists in business, government, and academic institutions.

Columns 5, 6, and 7: Columns 1, 2, and 3 minus column 4.

Column 8: Actual change for preceding year minus actual change for current year (column 4).

NOTES TO CHAPTER 26

1. For some earlier studies on these questions, see the references, below.

2. This method of extrapolation is not necessarily the best. Victor Zarnowitz [7, 8], Jacob Mincer [3], and others have experimented with more effective methods, providing a higher standard against which to measure actual forecasts. One method uses an average rate of growth over a longer period than merely the preceding year. Another uses the most recent quarterly information of GNP available and extrapolates from there.

3. Fellner [1] finds a similar improvement in the forecasting record of the *Economic Report* during approximately the same period.

4. A few government forecasters participate in the survey, but constitute only about 10 percent of the sample.

5. The R^2 for forecasts in the November survey and the *Report* are 0.85, 0.93, and 0.97 for nominal GNP, real GNP, and price deflator, respectively, 1969−1976. For the February survey and the *Report*, the corresponding R^2 are 0.92, 0.97, and 0.98.

6. For an earlier comparison of this kind see Zarnowitz [8]. For 1962−1968 the mean absolute error in the average forecast percent change in current dollar GNP, covering a large number of forecasters, was 1.3 percent. This is exactly the same as for the *Economic Report* (see Table 26-1). Hence, private forecasters have evidently improved their performance since 1968 about as much as the government has. Zarnowitz's record of private forecasts for 1953−1963 shows still larger mean errors, suggesting that a trend toward improving accuracy may have persisted for twenty-five years or so.

7. For a striking illustration of this see Zarnowitz [7]. Using forecasts of GNP in current dollars over spans of four quarters, 1956−1963, he showed that only five forecasters in a group of forty-seven had a smaller average error during the period than that of the average forecast for the group.

REFERENCES

[1]. Fellner, William S. *Towards a Reconstruction of Macroeconomics.* Washington, D.C.: American Enterprise Institute for Public Policy Research, 1976.

[2]. McNees, Stephen K. "An Assessment of the Council of Economic Advisers' Forecast of 1977." *New England Economic Review* (Federal Reserve Bank of Boston), March–April 1977.

[3]. Mincer, Jacob, ed. *Economic Forecasts and Expectations: Analyses of Forecasting Behavior and Performance.* New York: National Bureau of Economic Research, 1969.

[4]. Moore, Geoffrey H. "Forecasting Short-Term Economic Change." *Journal of the American Statistical Association*, March 1969, pp. 1–22 (see Chapter 25).

[5]. _____ . "Economic Forecasting—How Good a Track Record?" *The Morgan Guaranty Survey*, January 1975, pp. 5-8.

[6]. Su, Vincent and Josephine. "An Evaluation of ASA-NBER Business Outlook Survey Forecasts." *Explorations in Economic Research* (National Bureau of Economic Research), Fall 1975, pp. 588-618.

[7]. Zarnowitz, Victor. *An Appraisal of Short-Term Economic Forecasts.* Occasional Paper 104. New York: National Bureau of Economic Research, 1967.

[8]. _____ . "Forecasting Economic Conditions: The Record and the Prospect." In *The Business Cycle Today*, Victor Zarnowitz, ed., pp. 212-14. New York: National Bureau of Economic Research, 1972.

Appendix A

Table A–1. Business Cycle Expansions and Contractions in the United States, 1834–1981.

By Months Trough	By Months Peak	By Quarters Trough	By Quarters Peak	By Calendar Years Trough	By Calendar Years Peak	Contraction (peak to trough)	Expansion (trough to peak)	Cycle Trough to Trough	Cycle Peak to Peak
				1834	1836		24[a]		
				1838	1839	24[a]	12[a]	48[a]	36[a]
				1843	1845	48[a]	24[a]	60[a]	72[a]
				1846	1847	12[a]	12[a]	36[a]	24[a]
				1848	1853	12[a]	60[a]	24[a]	72[a]
Dec. 1854	June 1857	1854:4	1857:2	1855	1856	24[a]	30	84[a]	36[a]
Dec. 1858	Oct. 1860	1858:4	1860:3	1858	1860	18	22	48	40
June 1861	Apr. 1865	1861:3	1865:1	1861	1864	8	46	30	54
Dec. 1867	June 1869	1868:1	1869:2	1867	1869	32	18	78	50
Dec. 1870	Oct. 1873	1870:4	1873:3	1870	1873	18	34	36	52
Mar. 1879	Mar. 1882	1879:1	1882:1	1878	1882	65	36	99	101
May 1885	Mar. 1887	1885:2	1887:2	1885	1887	38	22	74	60
Apr. 1888	July 1890	1888:1	1890:3	1888	1890	13	27	35	40
May 1891	Jan. 1893	1891:2	1893:1	1891	1892	10	20	37	30
June 1894	Dec. 1895	1894:2	1895:4	1894	1895	17	18	37	35
June 1897	June 1899	1897:2	1899:3	1896	1899	18	24	36	42
Dec. 1900	Sept. 1902	1900:4	1902:4	1900	1903	18	21	42	39
Aug. 1904	May 1907	1904:3	1907:2	1904	1907	23	33	44	56
June 1908	Jan. 1910	1908:2	1910:1	1908	1910	13	19	46	32
Jan. 1912	Jan. 1913	1911:4	1913:1	1911	1913	24	12	43	36
Dec. 1914	Aug. 1918	1914:4	1918:3	1914	1918	23	44	35	67
Mar. 1919	Jan. 1920	1919:1	1920:1	1919	1920	7	10	51	17
July 1921	May 1923	1921:3	1923:2	1921	1923	18	22	28	40
July 1924	Oct. 1926	1924:3	1926:3	1924	1926	14	27	36	41
Nov. 1927	Aug. 1929	1927:4	1929:3	1927	1929	13	21	40	34
Mar. 1933	May 1937	1933:1	1937:2	1932	1937	43	50	64	93

June 1938	Feb. 1945	1938: 2	1945: 1	1938	1944	13	80	63	93
Oct. 1945	Nov. 1948	1945: 4	1948: 4	1946	1948	8	37	88	45
Oct. 1949	July 1953	1949: 4	1953: 2	1949	1953	11	45	48	56
May 1954	Aug. 1957	1954: 2	1957: 3	1954	1957	10	39	55	49
Apr. 1958	Apr. 1960	1958: 2	1960: 2	1958	1960	8	24	47	32
Feb. 1961	Dec. 1969	1961: 1	1969: 4	1961	1969	10	106	34	116
Nov. 1970	Nov. 1973	1970: 4	1973: 4	1970	1973	11	36	117	47
Mar. 1975	Jan. 1980	1975: 1	1980: 1	1975	1979	16	58	52	74
July 1980	July 1981	1980: 3	1981: 3	1980	1981	6	12	64	18

Averages

5 cycles,	1834–1855	24[a]	26[a]	50[a]	51[a]
16 cycles,	1854–1919	22	27	48	48
6 cycles,	1919–1945	18	35	53	53
7 cycles,	1945–1981	10	45	60	55
34 cycles,	1834–1981	19	32	52	51

[a] Based upon calendar year dates.

Note: For a basic statement of the method of determining business cycle peaks and troughs, see Arthur F. Burns and Wesley C. Mitchell, *Measuring Business Cycles* (New York: NBER, 1946) ch. 4. Some of the dates shown there (p. 78) have since been revised. For a description of how the method has been applied more recently, see Chapters 1 and 2 above and Victor Zarnowitz and Geoffrey H. Moore, "The 1973–1976 Recession and Recovery," *Explorations in Economic Research*, 4 (Fall 1977). For a related chronology covering the period 1790–1925, see Willard L. Thorp, *Business Annals* (New York: NBER, 1926).

Source: National Bureau of Economic Research.

Table A-2. Selected Measures of Duration, Depth, and Diffusion of Business Cycle Contractions
(from peak [first date] to trough [second date]).

	Jan. 1920 July 1921	May 1923 July 1924	Oct. 1926 Nov. 1927	Aug. 1929 Mar. 1933	May 1937 June 1938	Feb. 1945 Oct. 1945	Nov. 1948 Oct. 1949
Duration (months)							
Business cycle (Table A-1)	18	14	13	43	13	8	11
GNP, current dollars	n.a.	6	12	42	9	6	12
GNP, constant dollars	n.a.	3	3	36	6	n.a.	6
Industrial production	14	14	8	36	12	27	15
Nonfarm employment	n.a.	n.a.	n.a.	43	11	22	13
Depth (percent)[b]							
GNP, current dollars	n.a.	-4.9	-3.0	-49.6	-16.2	-11.9	-3.4
GNP, constant dollars	n.a.	-4.1	-2.0	-32.6	-18.2	n.a.	-1.5
Industrial production	-32.4	-17.9	-7.0	-53.4	-32.4	-38.3	-10.1
Nonfarm employment	n.a.	n.a.	n.a.	-31.6	-10.8	-10.1	-5.2
Unemployment rate							
Maximum	11.9[c]	5.5[c]	4.4[c]	24.9[c]	20.0	4.3	7.9
Increase	+10.3	+2.6[c]	+2.4[c]	+21.7[c]	+9.0	+3.4	+4.5
Diffusion (percent)							
Nonfarm industries, maximum percentage with declining employment, and date when maximum was reached[d]	97 Sept. 1920	94 Apr. 1924	71 Nov. 1927	100 June 1933	97 Dec. 1937	n.a.	90 Feb. 1949

	July 1953 May 1954	Aug. 1957 Apr. 1958	Apr. 1960 Feb. 1961	Dec. 1969 Nov. 1970	Nov. 1973 Mar. 1975	Jan. 1980 July 1980	July 1981 Dec. 1982*
Duration (months)							
Business cycle (Table A-1)	10	8	10	11	16	6	17
GNP, current dollars	12	6	3	a	a	3	3
GNP, constant dollars	12	6	9	6	15	3	6
Industrial production	9	13	13	13	9	16	16
Nonfarm employment	14	14	10	8	6	4	15
Depth (percent)b							
GNP, current dollars	-1.9	-2.8	-0.6	a	a	-0.1	-0.3
GNP, constant dollars	-3.2	-3.3	-1.2	-1.0	-4.9	-2.5	-2.6
Industrial production	-9.4	-13.5	-8.6	-6.8	-15.3	-8.6	-12.3
Nonfarm employment	-3.5	-4.3	-2.2	-1.5	-2.9	-1.4	-3.8
Unemployment rate							
Maximum	6.1	7.5	7.1	6.1	9.0	7.8	10.8
Increase	+3.6	+3.8	+2.1	+2.7	+4.4	+2.1	+3.6
Diffusion (percent)							
Nonfarm industries, maximum percentage with declining employment, and date when maximum was reachedd	87	88	80	80	88	77	79
	Mar. 1954	Sept. 1957	Oct. 1960	May 1970	Jan. 1975	Apr. 1980	Aug. 1982

n.a. = Not available.   *Tentative.

a No decline.

b Percentage change from the peak month or quarter in the series to the trough month or quarter, over the intervals shown. For the unemployment rate the maximum figure is the highest for any month during the contraction, and the increases are from the lowest month to the highest, in percentage points.

c The maximum figures are annual averages for 1921, 1924, 1928, and 1933 (monthly data not available). Increases, in percentage points, are for 1919–1921, 1923–1924, 1926–1928, and 1929–1933.

d Since 1948 based on changes in employment over six month spans, centered on the fourth month of the span in 30 nonagricultural industries, 1948–1959; 172 industries, 1960–1971; 186 industries, 1972–1980. Prior to 1948 based on cyclical changes in employment in forty-one industries.

Sources: U.S. Department of Commerce, U.S. Department of Labor, Board of Governors of the Federal Reserve System, National Bureau of Economic Research. For a fuller version of this table, see Solomon Fabricant, "The Recession of 1969–1970," in The Business Cycle Today, V. Zarnowitz, ed. (New York: National Bureau of Economic Research, 1972), pp. 100–110.

Table A-3.   Recession's Impact on Employment, Past and Future.

	Percentage Change in Number Employed, Average of Seven Recessions, 1948–1980 (1)	Relative Importance: Percentage of Total Employment Accounted for in				
		1959 (2)	1969 (3)	1979 (4)	1985[a] (5)	1990[a] (6)
Industries declining most in recessions						
Durable manufactures	-10.1	14	14	12	12	12
Construction	-4.5	5	5	6	6	6
Mining	-4.2	1	1	1	1	1
Nondurable manufactures	-4.0	11	10	8	8	7
Transportation, communication, public utilities	-3.7	6	5	5	5	5
Agriculture	-3.3	8	4	3	2	2
All of the above	-6.0	44	39	35	34	33
Industries declining least in recessions						
Wholesale and retail trade	-0.6	19	19	21	22	22
Personal and business services	+1.9	17	19	21	22	23
Finance, insurance, and real estate	+2.0	4	4	5	5	6
Government	+2.2	16	19	17	17	16
All of the above	+1.1	56	61	65	66	67
All industries: total employment	-2.4	100	100	100	100	100
Estimated decline in total employment, based upon						
1959 Industry Composition (col. 2)	-2.0					
1969 " " (col. 3)	-1.7					
1979 " " (col. 4)	-1.4					
1985 " " (col. 5)	-1.4					
1990 " " (col. 6)	-1.3					

Notes to Table A-3

Note: For an earlier version of this table see Chapter 10. The data used to compute recession changes (column 1) are from the establishment survey (jobs) except for agriculture, where the household survey (persons) is used. The data used for the distribution of employment (columns 2–6) are based on the jobs concept also, but differ from those used to measure recession changes largely because they include self-employed, unpaid family workers, and paid household employees. The total number of jobs represented in the distributions are: 1959, 70,512,000; 1969, 86,278,000; 1979, 104,120,000; 1985, 113,775,000; 1990, 121,971,000. See Valerie A. Personick, "The Outlook for Industry Output and Employment through 1990," *Monthly Labor Review* (August 1981).

[a] Projected by the U.S. Bureau of Labor Statistics.

Source: Center for International Business Cycle Research, Rutgers University.

Table A–4. Growth Cycles in the United States, 1948–1978.

Peak (P)	Trough (T)	Duration, in Months, of		Interval, in Months, from Growth Cycle to Business Cycle	
		Downswing (P to T)	Upswing (T to P)	Peak	Trough
July 1948	October 1949	15	17	4	0
March 1951	July 1952	16	8	a	a
March 1953	August 1954	17	30	3	3[b]
February 1957	April 1958	14	22	6	0
February 1960	February 1961	12	15	2	0
May 1962	October 1964	29	20	a	a
June 1966	October 1967	16	17	a	a
March 1969	November 1970	20	28	9	0
March 1973	March 1975	24	45	8	0
December 1978				13	0
Average 1948–1978		18	22	6	0

[a] No corresponding business cycle turn.
[b] Growth cycle trough lags business cycle trough.
Source: National Bureau of Economic Research.

Table A–5. A Chronology of Peaks and Troughs in the Rate of Inflation.

Date of		Inflation Rate at (percent)		Change in Rate During (percent)		Duration of (months)	
Peak (1)	Trough (2)	Peak (3)	Trough (4)	Downswing (5)	Upswing (6)	Downswing (7)	Upswing (8)
November 1946	July 1949	23.2	-3.1	-26.3	15.9	32	19
February 1951	March 1953	12.8	0.2	-12.6	1.5	25	7
October 1953	October 1954	1.7	-1.2	-2.9	4.9	12	34
August 1957	March 1959	3.7	0.2	-3.5	1.7	19	7
October 1959	June 1961	1.9	0.6	-1.3	3.4	20	64
October 1966	May 1967	4.0	2.1	-1.9	3.4	7	33
February 1970	June 1972	6.3	2.9	-3.4	4.2	28	27
September 1974	June 1976	12.4	4.9	-7.5	9.5	21	45
March 1980		15.2			10.3		
Average: 1946–1980		9.0	0.8	-7.4	6.4	20	30

Note: The chronology is based on the rate of change in the seasonally adjusted consumer price index for all urban consumers. It is a six-month smoothed rate of change, computed by dividing the current month's index by the average for the preceding twelve months, adjusted to a compound annual rate, and dated in the current month. For some purposes it is useful to center the dates in the middle of the span covered by the rate, in which case the dates would be three months earlier than shown here.

Source: Center for International Business Cycle Research, Rutgers University.

Table A-6.   Relationship between the Growth Cycle and the Inflation Cycle.

Growth Cycle		Inflation Rate (CPI)[b]		Lead (−) or Lag (+) in Months of Inflation Rate at Growth Cycle	
Peak (1)	Trough (2)	Peak (3)	Trough (4)	Peak (5)	Trough (6)
July 1948	October 1949	November 1946	July 1949	−20	−3
March 1951	July 1952	February 1951	March 1953	−1	+8
March 1953	August 1954	October 1953	October 1954	+7	+2
February 1957	April 1958	August 1957	March 1959	+6	+11
February 1960	February 1961	October 1959	June 1961	−4	+4
May 1962	October 1964	a	a	a	a
June 1966	October 1967	October 1966	May 1967	+4	−5
March 1969	November 1970	February 1970	June 1972	+11	+19
March 1973	March 1975	September 1974	June 1976	+18	+15
December 1978		March 1980		+15	
Average lead (−) or lag (+), in months				+4	+6

[a] No corresponding inflation cycle turn.
[b] Change over six-month span, smoothed, seasonally adjusted compound annual rate.
Source: Tables A-4 and A-5.

Appendix B

MEASURING RECESSIONS AND RECOVERIES

The diagrams in Figures 6-5 and 16-5 illustrate a method of comparing a current recession, month-by-month as it develops, with the average pattern of previous recessions. The average serves as a guide to what it is reasonable to expect of different economic variables as a recession develops. One can tell at a glance whether the decline is larger or smaller than average, or what is unusual about the current situation. The diagrams may also be used to evaluate forecasts or to make simple projections based upon past experience.

A computer program for recession-recovery patterns is described in Gerhard Bry and Charlotte Boschan in Chapter 4 of *Cyclical Analysis of Time Series: Selected Procedures and Computer Programs*, Technical Paper 20 (New York: National Bureau of Economic Research, 1971).

Index

About the Author

Geoffrey H. Moore is Director of the Center for International Business Cycle Research, Graduate School of Business, Columbia University, formerly at Rutgers University. He is Director-at-Large of the National Bureau of Economic Research and was on the staff of the National Bureau from 1939 to 1979. He served as Commissioner of Labor Statistics, U.S. Department of Labor, from 1969 to 1973. In addition, he has taught at New York University and Columbia University, was a Senior Research Fellow at Stanford University's Hoover Institution and an Adjunct Scholar at the American Enterprise Institute, and is the author of numerous articles. Dr. Moore received a B.S. and an M.S. from Rutgers University and a Ph.D. from Harvard University.